Contents

Acknowledgements

The author and publisher would like to thank the following:

For providing expert advice and guidance during the preparation of this book: Anne Eaton, Associate Director of Programmes, Skills for Health; Linda Nazarko, NVQ trainer and assessor for the NHS; Tim Thomas and Denise Knight, Leicestershire Care Development Group (Tim Thomas is a member of the TOPSS England Occupational Standards and Qualifications Committee); Neil Moonie, former course manager of Health and Social Care at Havering College, author, adviser and consultant

All at the Fremantle Trust, especially Mark Kingman, Yvonne Peace, Lorraine McGinley and the staff and residents at Farnham Common House and Seabrook Court, for their kindness and invaluable assistance (www.fremantletrust.org)

Mencap for permission to reproduce a page from its website www.mencap.org.uk (page 180)

Crown copyright material is reproduced under Class License No. C01W0000141 with the permission of the Controller of HMSO and the Queen's Printer for Scotland

The author and publisher would like to thank the following for permission to reproduce photographs:
Corbis, pages 14, 22, 152, 187, 251, 377 (top)
Getty Images/Photodisc, pages 197, 223
Harcourt Education/Gareth Boden, page 129
Harcourt Education/Trevor Clifford, page 196
Harcourt Education/Tudor Photography, pages 294, 323, 326, 327
David Hoffman Photo Library, page 185
London Ambulance Service, page 79
Science Photo Library, page 375
All other photographs by Richard Smith

Introduction

This new edition of *Level 2 Health & Social Care* comes at a time of change in the sector. So much has happened, both in terms of new legislation, guidelines and policies and in the way that issues are approached and addressed, that some changes to the National Occupational Standards were absolutely essential. Greater regulation of the care sector has been an important factor in continuing improvement, creating higher quality services and giving better protection to vulnerable people who use the services of the sector.

The new standards reflect the changes in the profession, such as the emphasis on quality services, the focus on tackling exclusion, and the influence of the culture of rights and responsibilities. There has been a huge increase, too, in understanding in all parts of the sector, and a recognition of the satisfaction that comes from working alongside service users as partners and directors of their own care, rather than as passive receivers of services.

However, much of what we do in the care sector remains the same; the basic principles of caring, treating people with dignity and respect, ensuring choice and promoting independence will continue, and the skills of good communication remain as vital as ever.

Very large numbers of candidates have undertaken S/NVQ qualifications over the lifetime of the previous editions of this book; their skills, knowledge and understanding are a wonderful recommendation for the sector and should reassure those who use the services, or have loved ones who are in need of care or likely to become so.

I hope that all of you who are using this book to support your work on your S/NVQ will find it a useful reference point and that some of the content will give you pause for thought and reflection. This new edition provides further, up-to-date guidance and background knowledge to support not only your qualification but your day-to-day work in providing care services. You will find a helpful glossary of terms on page 387 and a grid detailing coverage of the Knowledge Specification points on page 388.

All of us who work in this sector are in the position of providing a service for many of the most vulnerable people. They all deserve the best quality care we can give and it is the responsibility of us all to make sure that we are as highly skilled and knowledgeable as possible. However, it is important to remember that it is ultimately the degree of humanitarian care and concern which defines the difference between someone who simply does the job, and someone who really cares about the service provided.

I wish you every success with your NVQ and your future career.

Yvonne Nolan

References

Akehurst, R. (1991) *The Health of the Nation*, The University of York

Bonomini, J. (2003) *Effective Interventions for Pressure Ulcer Prevention* Nursing Standard 17, 52, 45–50

Clark, M. (1998) *Repositioning to Prevent Pressure Sores: What is the evidence?* Nursing Standard 13, 3, 58–64

Collins, F. (2001) *Sitting: Pressure Ulcer Development* Nursing Standard 15, 22, 54–58

Griffith, R., Stevens, M. (2004) *Manual Handling and the Lawfulness of No-Lift Policies* Nursing Standard 18, 21, 39–43

Hawkins, S., Stone, K., Plummer, L. (1999) *An Holistic Approach to Turning Patients* Nursing Standard 14, 3, 52–56

Mace, N. (1985) *The 36-Hour Day: A family guide to caring at home for people with Alzheimer's disease* Hodder and Stoughton

Moonie, N., Spencer-Perkins, D., Bates, A. (2004) *Diversity and Rights in Care* Heinemann

Richards, J. (1999) *The Complete A–Z Health & Social Care Handbook* Hodder and Stoughton

Scott-Moncrieff, C. (1999) *The Vitamin Alphabet* Collins and Brown

Webster-Gandy, J. (2000) *The British Medical Association Family Guide to Food and Nutrition* Dorling Kindersley

Wills-Brandon, C. (2000) *Natural Mental Health* Hay House

www.RNIB.org.uk (Royal National Institute for the Blind)

www.seeitright.co.uk (See It Right, RNIB)

www.RNID.org.uk (Royal National Institute for the Deaf)

www.dlf.org.uk (Disabled Living Foundation)

www.mencap.org.uk (Mencap)

www.alzheimers.org.uk (Alzheimer's Society)

www.directgov.uk (Directgov – government information)

www.hmso.gov.uk (HMSO – government publications)

www.helptheaged.org.uk (Help the Aged)

www.ageconcern.org.uk (Age Concern)

www.scope.org.uk (Scope)

www.ukconnect.org (Connect)

www.speakability.org.uk (Speakability)

www.afasic.org.uk (Afasic)

www.stjohn.org (St John Health)

www.cyh.com (Children, Youth and Women's Health Service)

www.hse.gov.uk (Health and Safety Executive)

www.carers.gov.uk (Caring about Carers)

www.doh.gov.uk (Department of Health)

www.bettercaring.co.uk (Better Caring)

www.nursingtimes.net (Nursing Times)

www.dataprotection.gov.uk (Information Commissioner's Office)

www.nvqcareuk.com (NVQs in care)

www.cpa.org.uk (Centre for Policy on Ageing)

www.dlcc.org.uk (Disabled Living Centres Council)

www.mstrust.org.uk (Multiple Sclerosis Trust)

www.arc.org.uk (Arthritis Research Campaign)

www.arthritiscare.org.uk (Arthritis Care)

www.osteoarthritis-symptoms.co.uk (Osteoarthritis Symptoms)

www.activemobility.co.uk (Active Mobility)

www.painsociety.org (The British Pain Society)

www.acupuncture.org.uk (British Acupuncture Council)

www.sleep-deprivation.co.uk (Sleep Deprivation Information)

www.sleepcouncil.org.uk (Sleep Council)

www.ec-online.net (Elder Care Online)

www.llmedico.com (LL Medico USA Inc)

www.incontinence.org (Bladder Advisory Council)

www.medinfo.co.uk (Medinfo – medical information and advice)

www.backcare.org.uk (Back Care)

http://spine-health.com (Spine Health)

www.diabetes.org.uk (The Diabetes Organisation)

www.asthma.org.uk (The Asthma Organisation)

Communicate with, and complete records for individuals

Working in care is about communication and relationships. It is simply not possible to provide care services without developing relationships with those you care for, and good communication is an essential part of relationship building whatever the nature of the relationship – a personal or family relationship, or a professional one.

Communication is about much more than just talking. It includes the messages you give out from your body language, and there are also a wide range of methods of communication, ranging from telephones to text messages.

You will also need to think about the different ways in which people communicate and the barriers that some people face. Not everyone communicates in the same way and, as a professional care worker, you will need to be able to respond to a range of different ways of communicating.

Recording information is important and serves many valuable purposes. You need to understand the significance of what you record and how it is recorded, in order to be sure that you are doing the best you possibly can for the individuals you work with.

This unit will help you to understand how all of these aspects of communication can be used in order to build and develop relationships and to improve your practice as a professional care worker.

What you need to learn

- Cultural needs
- What communication needs do people have?
- General effects of communication differences
- How to find out about likely communication problems
- How to record information
- Treating people as individuals
- How to listen
- Avoiding stereotypes
- Knowing yourself and your prejudices
- How to communicate clearly
- Stages of an interaction
- Written communication
- The importance of confidentiality
- Looking after information
- When you need to break confidentiality.

HSC 21a Work with individuals and others to identify the best forms of communication

Not everyone communicates in the same way and it is important that you make sure you are able to communicate with the people you work with in the way that is most suitable for them. The needs that people have in relation to communication are very varied, and depend on many different factors such as sensory ability, cultural background, language, self-confidence, level of learning ability or physical ability. As a care professional it is your responsibility to make sure that your communication skills meet the needs of the individuals with whom you work. You should not expect the individuals to adjust their communication to fit in with you.

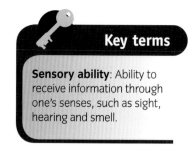

Key terms

Sensory ability: Ability to receive information through one's senses, such as sight, hearing and smell.

People's communication differences can result from differences in culture and background. Culture is about more than the language people speak – it is about the way that they live, think and relate to each other.

For example, some cultures use gestures or touch much more than others. In some cultures it is acceptable to stand very close to someone, whereas in others people would feel extremely uncomfortable if someone stood too close. You need to find out about the person's cultural background when you are thinking about how you can make communication work for him or her. To find out the information you need, you could:

- ask the individual – this is always the best way if possible
- look in the person's records
- speak to a member of the family or a friend, if possible
- ask someone else from the same culture, either a colleague or cultural representatives (contact the appropriate embassy or consulate and ask for the information); alternatively you could try a local multicultural organisation
- use reference books, if necessary.

It is also important that you communicate with people at the correct level of understanding. Make sure that you communicate at a language level the person is likely to understand, but not find patronising. Older people and people who have disabilities have every right to be spoken to as adults and not patronised or talked down to; one of the commonest complaints from people with physical disabilities is that people will talk to their carers about them rather than talk to them directly. This is known as the 'does he take sugar' approach.

How is she today? Is her cold better?

Cultural needs

You will need to be aware of cultural differences between you and the person you are talking to. In some cultures, unless you are related or a very close friend, using first names or touching someone can be viewed as disrespectful. Talking familiarly to someone of a different gender or age group can be unacceptable in some cultures. For example, some young Muslim women do not talk at all to men to whom they are not related.

Many older men and women consider it disrespectful to address people by their first names. You will often find older people with neighbours they have known for 50 years, who still call each other 'Mrs Baker' or 'Mrs Wood'.

In some cultures, children are not allowed to speak in the presence of certain adults. Some people may have been brought up in a background or in a period of time when challenging authority by asking questions was not acceptable. Such people may find it very hard to ask questions of doctors or other health professionals and are unlikely to feel able to raise any queries about how their care or treatment should be carried out.

What words mean

Be aware that the words you use can mean different things to different people and generations – words like 'cool', 'chip' or 'gay'. Be aware of particular local words which are used in your part of the country, which may not mean the same to someone from another area.

Think carefully about the subject under discussion. Some people from particular cultures, or people of particular generations, may find some subjects very sensitive and difficult to discuss. These days, it is not unusual among a younger age group to discuss personal income levels. However, people of older generations may consider such information to be highly personal.

What communication needs do people have?

Language

Where an individual speaks a different language from those who are providing care, it can be an isolating and frustrating experience. The individual may become distressed and frightened as it is very difficult to establish exactly what is happening and he or she is not in a position to ask or to have any questions answered. The person will feel excluded from anything happening in the care setting and will find making relationships with carers extremely difficult. There is the possibility that confusion and misunderstanding will occur.

Check it out

Find out the policy in your workplace for checking on people's cultural preferences. Ask who establishes the information about the cultural background of people who use your service, and what the policies are to ensure their needs are met.

Remember

The golden rule when you are communicating with someone from a different culture is to *find out*. Do not assume that you can approach everyone in the same way. It is your responsibility to find out the way to approach someone.

Remember

Communication differences can result as much from differences in attitude as they can from differences in language.

Overcoming language differences in communication

When you are providing care for someone who speaks a different language from you, it is clear that you will need the services of an interpreter for any serious discussions or communication.

- Your work setting is likely to have a contact list of interpreters.
- Social services departments and the police have lists of interpreters.
- The embassy or consulate for the appropriate country will also have a list of qualified interpreters.

But it is unlikely that you would have a full-time interpreter available throughout someone's period of care, so it is necessary to consider alternatives for encouraging everyday communication.

Be prepared to learn words in the individual's language which will help communication. You could try to give the person some words in your language if he or she is willing and able to learn them.

You could use flash cards or signals, similar to those you would use for a person who has suffered a stroke. This gives the person the opportunity to show a flash card to indicate his or her needs. You can also use them to find out what kind of assistance may be needed.

Some of the flash cards you may use

The most effective way to communicate with a person who speaks a different language is through non-verbal communication. A smile and a friendly face are understood in all languages, as are a concerned facial expression and a warm and welcoming body position.

Hearing loss

A loss or reduction of ability to hear clearly can cause major differences in the ability to communicate.

Communication is a two-way process, and it is very difficult for somebody who does not hear sounds at all or hears them in a blurred and indistinct way to be able to respond and to join in. People can become withdrawn and feel very isolated and excluded from others around them. This can lead to frustration and anger. As a result, people may present some quite challenging behaviour.

Profound deafness is not as common as partial hearing loss. People are most likely to suffer from loss of hearing of certain sounds at certain volumes or at certain pitches, such as high sounds or low sounds. It is also very common for people to find it difficult to hear if there is background noise – many sounds may jumble together, making it very hard to pick out the voice of one person. Hearing loss can also have an effect on speech, particularly for those who are profoundly deaf and are unable to hear their own voices as they speak. This can make communication doubly difficult.

Overcoming hearing difficulties in communication

Check that any means of improving hearing which an individual uses, for example a hearing aid, is working properly and is fitted correctly, that the batteries are fresh and working, that it is clean and that it is doing its job properly in terms of improving the individual's hearing.

Ensure that you are sitting in a good light, not too far away, and that you speak clearly, but do not shout. Shouting simply distorts your face and makes it much more difficult for a person with hearing loss to be able to read what you are saying.

Some people will lip read, while others will use a form of sign language for understanding. This may be BSL (British Sign Language) or MAKATON, which uses signs and symbols. Some people may rely on a combination of lip reading and gestures.

Other services which are extremely helpful to people who have hearing difficulties are telecommunication services, such as using a minicom or typetalk service. These allow a spoken conversation to be translated in written form using a form of typewriter, and the responses can be passed in the same way by an operator who will relay them to the hearing person.

Remember

If you are able to learn even simple signing or the basic rules of straightforward spoken communication with people who have hearing loss, you will significantly improve the way in which they are able to relate to their care environment.

Visual impairment

Visual impairment causes many communication difficulties. An individual may be unable to pick up the visual signals which are being given out by someone who is speaking, and, because he or she is unaware of these signals, the person may also fail to give appropriate signals in communication.

This lack of non-verbal communication can lead to misunderstandings about somebody's attitudes and behaviour. It means that a person's communications can easily be misinterpreted, or it could be thought that he or she is behaving in a way that is not appropriate.

Overcoming visual difficulties in communication

One of the commonest ways of assisting people who have visual impairment is to provide them with glasses or contact lenses. You need to be sure that these are clean and the correct prescription. People should have their eyes tested every two years and have their prescription updated.

For people with a more serious impairment, you will need to take other steps to minimise the differences that will exist in your styles of communication.

Keys to good practice: Communicating with people who have visual impairment

✓ Do not suddenly begin to speak without first of all letting him or her know that you are there by touching and saying hello.

✓ Make sure you introduce yourself when you come into a room. A simple 'Hello John, it's Sue' is all that is needed so that you don't 'arrive' unexpectedly.

✓ You may need to use touch more than you would in speaking to a sighted person, because the concerns that you will be expressing through your face and your general body movements will not be seen.

✓ Ask the individual what system of communication he or she requires – do not impose your ideas of appropriate systems on the person.

✓ Never take the arm of someone who is visually impaired to help him or her to move around. Allow the person to take your arm or shoulder, to ask for guidance and tell you where he or she wishes to go.

Physical disability

Depending on the disability, this can have various effects. People who have suffered strokes, for example, will often have communication difficulties. Not only may there be problems in forming words and speaking, but they often also suffer from aphasia (or dysphasia), which is the inability to understand and to express meaning through words. They lose the ability to find the right words for something they want to say, or to understand the meanings of words said to them. This condition is very distressing for the individual and for those who are trying to communicate. Often this is coupled with a loss of movement and a difficulty in using facial muscles to form words.

In some cases, the communication difficulty is a symptom of a disability. For example, many people with cerebral palsy and motor neurone disease have difficulty in controlling the muscles that affect voice production, and so speaking in a way which can be readily understood becomes very difficult. Other disabilities may have no effect at all upon voice production or the thought processes that produce spoken words, but the lack of other body movements may mean that non-verbal communication may be difficult or not what you would expect.

Overcoming physical disabilities in communication

Physical disability or illness has to be dealt with according to its particular nature. For example, if you were communicating with someone who had had a stroke causing dysphasia, you could best deal with this by:

- using very simple, short sentences, speaking slowly and being prepared to wait while the individual processes what you have said and composes a reply
- using gestures – they are helpful in terms of making it easier for people to understand the idea you are trying to get across
- using simple, closed questions which only need a 'yes' or 'no' answer – avoid long, complicated sentences with interrelated ideas
- drawing sketches or using flash cards to help understanding.

Other illnesses, such as motor neurone disease or cerebral palsy, can also lead to difficulties in speech, although not in comprehension.

- The individual will understand what you are saying to him or her but the difficulty will be in communicating with you.
- There is no need for you to speak slowly, although you will have to be prepared to allow time for a response because of the difficulties the individual will have in producing words.
- You will have to become familiar with the sound of the individual's voice and the way in which he or she communicates. It can be hard to understand people who have illnesses that affect their facial, throat or larynx muscles.

Remember

If you are using gestures to communicate, remember that they can mean different things in different cultures.

Learning disabilities

These may, dependent upon their severity, cause differences in communication in terms of the level of understanding the individual has and his or her ability to respond appropriately to any form of communication. This will vary depending on the degree of learning disability of the individual, but broadly the effect of learning disabilities is to limit the ability of an individual to understand and process information given to him or her. It is also likely that individuals will have a short attention span, so this may mean that communications have to be repeated several times in an appropriate form.

Overcoming learning disabilities in communication

You will need to adjust your methods of communicating to take account of the level of disability the individual experiences. You should have gathered enough information about the person to know the level of understanding that he or she has – and how simply and how often you need to explain things and the kinds of communication which are likely to be most effective.

Many people with a learning disability respond well to physical contact and are able to relate and communicate on a physical level more easily than on a verbal level. This will vary between individuals, but you should be prepared to use a great deal of physical contact and hugs when communicating with people who have a learning disability.

Physical contact can be helpful in communication

Dementia/confusion

This difficult and distressing condition is mostly found in older people and people who suffer from Alzheimer's disease. The confusion can result ultimately in the loss of the ability to communicate, but in the early stages it involves short-term memory loss to the extent of being unable to remember the essential parts of a conversation or a recent exchange. It can mean that you need to constantly repeat any form of communication. This can be frustrating for you as you try to communicate, but it is equally frustrating for the individual. It is important that you do not allow any irritation to show, as this will distress the person even more.

General effects of communication differences

The most common effect of communication differences is for an individual to feel frustrated, frightened and isolated. It is an important part of your job to do everything in your power to reduce the effect of communication differences and to try to lessen the feelings of isolation, fear and frustration that people experience.

You need to remember that any assessment you make about an individual's communication needs is only ever a snapshot of how he or she is at that particular moment. People change and so does their ability to communicate. This could be because of a deterioration or improvement in a physical condition, or it could be due to a change in emotional or personal circumstances, changes in medication or a change in living conditions.

Part of your responsibility is to be aware of changes in people's ability to communicate, and their ability to:

- speak or use their normal means of communication
- hear what is being communicated to them
- understand what is being communicated to them.

When you observe any changes in any of these areas of communication you must record this in the person's plan of care, inform your supervisor and check which other members of the care team will need to be given information about the changes.

Check it out

Try renting a video in a language other than your own, or watch a subtitled film on TV, covering the lower half of the TV screen where the subtitles are. Try to make sense of what is shown in the film.

Note how difficult it is to understand what is happening and how frustrating it is. Notice how quickly you lose interest and decide that you will not bother to watch any more. Imagine how that feels if you are ill or in need of care, and everyone around you is speaking in a language you do not understand.

CASE STUDY: Language barriers

Mrs C is 75 years old. She is Chinese and lives with her son and daughter-in-law in England. She has lived in England for over 30 years, but speaks no English and very rarely goes out apart from shopping within the local Chinese community. Mrs C has now developed a potentially life-threatening, but operable, bowel cancer. She is to have a series of tests which will be followed by surgery, a likely colostomy and radiotherapy. Her son is able to translate during the visits to the hospital, but he will not be able to remain with her during the entire time of her hospital stay.

1 *How do you think Mrs C will be feeling?*

2 *If you were looking after her in hospital, what would be your first step to communicating with her?*

3 *What are the issues for her in having her son translate in these circumstances?*

4 *How could her condition be affected by poor communication?*

How to find out about likely communication problems

You can discover likely communication problems by simply observing an individual. In this way you can find out a great deal about how a person communicates and what the differences are between his or her way of communicating and your own.

By observing, you should be able to find out:
- which language is being used
- whether the service user experiences any hearing difficulties or visual impairment
- whether there is any physical illness or disability
- whether there are any learning difficulties.

Any of these factors could be important in determining how well a person will be able to communicate with you, and what steps you may need to take to make things easier.

Observation will give you some very good clues to start with, but there are other useful sources of information for establishing exactly what a particular individual needs to help with communication.

- Ask the individual, where this is possible – he or she is likely to be your best source of information.
- Discuss with colleagues who have worked with the individual before and who are likely to have some background information and advice.
- Consult other professionals who have worked with the individual and may know about means of communication which have been effective for him or her.
- Read previous case notes or case histories.
- Find out as much as you can about an individual's particular illness or disability, where you have been able to establish this – the most useful sources of information are likely to be the specialist agencies for the particular condition.
- Talk to family or friends. They are likely to have a great deal of information about the differences in communication for the individual. They will have developed ways of dealing with communication, possibly over a long period of time, and are likely to be a very useful source of advice and help.

How to record information

There would be little point in finding out about effective means of communication with someone and then not making an accurate record so that other people can also communicate with that person.

You should find out your employer's policy on where such information is to be recorded – it is likely to be in the service user's case notes.

Be sure that you record:
- the nature of the communication differences
- how they show themselves
- ways which you have found to be effective in overcoming the differences.

Information recorded in notes may look like this:

Mr P has communication difficulties following his stroke. He is aphasic, with left side haemaplaegia. Speech is slurred but possible to understand with care. Most effective approaches are:
a) allow maximum time for communication responses
b) modify delivery if necessary in order to allow understanding
c) speak slowly, with short sentences
d) give only one piece of information at a time
e) physical reassurance (holding and stroking hand) seems to help while waiting for a response
f) can use flash cards on bad days (ensure they are placed on the right-hand side)
g) check Mr P has understood the conversation.

Recording information accurately is important in order to ensure that your colleagues do not have to continually go through a process of establishing the communication needs of each individual.

Keys to good practice: Identifying the best forms of communication

✓ Check what each individual's specific communication needs are.

✓ Confirm with individuals their preferred methods of communication.

✓ Remember that communication needs can be influenced by cultural as well as physical factors.

✓ Examine the effects of communication differences for a particular individual.

✓ Use all possible sources to obtain information and advice.

✓ Make sure you have all the skills necessary to communicate, or look for extra support where necessary.

Test yourself

1   What factors would you take into account when judging the best way to communicate with somebody from a different country?

2   What would you expect to be the effects of partial hearing loss on someone's style of communication?

3   What type of steps could you take to improve communication with someone following a stroke? List three.

4   What would you expect to be the cultural differences between an 80-year-old woman brought up in an industrial town and the 20-year-old son of an Asian consultant cardiac surgeon, who is working as a care assistant in the care home she lives in?

5   What is one of the most important ways of communicating with someone who speaks a different language?

6   An inability to communicate will not affect the rate of recovery or standard of physical care. True or false?

HSC 21b Listen and respond to individuals' questions and concerns

Treating people as individuals

You should always consult the individual before you carry out any procedure, and explain everything you do. Even if the procedure is part of his or her plan of care and has been done many times before, you should never take a person's agreement for granted.

Everyone should be offered choices wherever possible. This may be about when, where or how their care is provided. In cases where a choice is not possible, either because of an individual's circumstances or a lack of resources, this should be explained.

Clearly, the range of choices will vary depending on the circumstances, but the principle remains the same – people should not have care imposed on them without being actively involved in decisions about how and when care is delivered.

Did you know?

One of the fears most frequently expressed by people who need to be cared for, particularly older people whose health has deteriorated or people who have been disabled through an accident or illness, is that they will lose their independence and will no longer be regarded as a person of any value.

More than talking

In order to be an effective care worker, you must learn to be a good communicator. But communication is about much more than talking. People also communicate through:

- facial expression
- body language
- position
- dress
- gestures.

You will have to know how to recognise what is being communicated to you, and be able to communicate with others without always having to use words.

Evidence indicator

Do this with a friend or colleague.

1 Write the names of several emotions (such as anger, joy, sadness, disappointment, fear) on pieces of paper.

2 One of you should pick up a piece of paper. Your task is to communicate the emotion written on the paper to your partner, without saying anything.

3 Your partner then has to decide what the emotion is and say why.

4 Then change places and repeat the exercise. Take it in turns, until all the pieces of paper have been used. Make a list of all the things which made you aware of the emotion being expressed.

5 Discuss with your partner what you have discovered about communication as a result of this exercise.

Keep a record of this activity and your notes.

When you carried out the last exercise, you probably found out that there are many things which tell you what someone is trying to communicate. It is not only the expression on people's faces which tells you about how they feel, but also the way they use the rest of their bodies.

This area of human behaviour is referred to as non-verbal communication. It is very important for developing the ability to understand what people are feeling. If you understand the importance of non-verbal communication, you will be able to use it to improve your own skills when you communicate with someone.

Key terms

Non-verbal communication: A way of communicating without words, through body language, gestures, facial expression and eye contact.

Recognising signals

Look at a person's facial expression. Much of what you will see will be in his or her eyes, but the eyebrows and mouth also contribute.

Notice whether someone is looking at you, or at the floor, or at a point over your shoulder. Lack of eye contact can give a first indication that all may not be well. It may be that the person is not feeling confident. He or she may be unhappy, or feel uneasy about talking to you. You will need to follow this up.

Look at how a person sits. Is he or she relaxed and comfortable, sitting well back in the chair, or tense and perched on the edge of the seat? Is he or she slumped in the chair, head down? Posture can indicate a great deal about how somebody is feeling. People who are feeling well and cheerful tend to hold their heads up, and sit in a relaxed and comfortable way. An individual who is tense and nervous, who feels unsure and worried, is likely to reflect that in the way he or she sits or stands.

Observe hands and gestures carefully. Someone twisting his or her hands, or playing with hair or clothes, is signalling tension and worry. Frequent little shrugs of the shoulders or spreading of the hands may indicate a feeling of helplessness or hopelessness.

People who are happy and relaxed have open body postures and hold their heads up

People who are anxious or unhappy tend to sit hunched, with head down

Case study: Understanding body language

Mrs B is very confused. She has little recognition of time or place and only knows her daughter, who has cared for her for many years. As she became increasingly frail and began to fall regularly, she finally stopped eating or drinking and her daughter had to arrange for her admission to hospital for assessment. She is in a large psycho-geriatric ward. Many of the patients are aggressive and disinhibited in their behaviour. Mrs B is quiet, gentle and confused, and she has no idea where she is. She does not know anyone, and she keeps asking to go home.

1   *What would you expect Mrs B's body language to be?*

2   *What would you look for in her facial expression?*

3   *As her carer, how do you think you might make her feel better?*

4   *How would you communicate with her?*

5   *How might you help her daughter?*

Giving out signals

Being aware of your own body language is just as important as understanding the person you are talking to.

Did you know?

Research shows that people pay far more attention to facial expressions and tone of voice than they do to spoken words. For example, in one study, words contributed only 7 per cent towards the impression of whether or not someone was liked, tone of voice contributed 38 per cent and facial expression 55 per cent. The study also found that if there was a contradiction between facial expression and words, people believed the facial expression.

Keys to good practice: Being a good listener

✓ Make sure that you maintain eye contact with the person you are talking to, although you should avoid staring! Looking away occasionally is normal, but if you find yourself looking around the room, or watching others, then you are failing to give people the attention they deserve.

✓ Be aware of what you are doing and try to think why you are losing attention.

✓ Sit where you can be comfortably seen. Don't sit where someone has to turn in order to look at you.

✓ Sit a comfortable distance away – not so far that any sense of closeness is lost, but not so close that you 'invade their space'.

✓ Make sure that you are showing by your gestures that you are listening and interested in what they are saying – sitting half-turned away gives the message that you are not fully committed to what is being said.

✓ Folded arms or crossed legs can indicate that you are 'closed' rather than 'open' to what someone is expressing.

✓ Nodding your head will indicate that you are receptive and interested – but be careful not to overdo it and look like a nodding dog!

✓ Lean towards someone to show that you are interested in what he or she is saying. You can use leaning forward quite effectively at times when you want to emphasise your interest or support. Then move backwards a little at times when the content is a little lighter.

Continued

Keys to good practice: Being a good listener

✓ Using touch to communicate your caring and concern is often useful and appropriate. Many individuals find it comforting to have their hand held or stroked, or to have an arm around their shoulders.

✓ Be aware of a person's body language, which should tell you if he or she finds touch acceptable or not.

✓ Always be cautious if you are unsure about what is acceptable in another culture. Remember that in some cultures touching may be regarded as disrespectful.

✓ Think about age and gender in relation to touch. An older woman may be happy to have her hand held by a female carer, but may be uncomfortable with such a response from a man.

✓ Ensure that you are touching someone because you think it will comfort him or her, and not because you feel helpless and can't think of anything to say.

Check it out

Do this with at least one other person – two or three is even better.

1 Think of an incident or situation which is quite important and significant to you. Stand still in the middle of a room and begin to tell your partner about your significant incident.

2 Your partner should start at the edge of the room and slowly move closer and closer to you.

3 At the point where you feel comfortable talking to your partner, say 'Stop'. Mark this point and measure the distance from where you are standing.

4 Continue. At the point where you feel that your partner is too close, say 'Stop'. Mark this point and measure the distance from where you are standing.

5 Change places and repeat the exercise.

You may find that you and your partner(s) will have different distances at which you feel comfortable, but it is likely to be in the range of 3–5ft.

Remember

● You can often learn as much by observing as by listening.

● Learn to 'listen with your eyes'.

● Your body sends out as many messages as the person you are talking to.

● Be aware of the messages you give to others.

| Intimate zone | Personal zone | Social zone | Public zone |

How to listen

So far you have looked at some of the factors which assist effective communication, and some of the barriers which can hinder it. Now it is time to look at the key areas of listening and talking. You may think that this comes naturally to most people, but everyone can learn some basic skills which will improve their communication significantly.

Active listening

Active listening is about doing much more than simply hearing the words which an individual is speaking. It includes encouraging someone to talk to you, letting him or her know that you are interested, concerned and supportive, and allowing him or her the space, time and attention to express feelings and concerns.

Evidence indicator

This activity really needs to be done with a friend or colleague. Begin to tell your partner about something simple and straightforward – about your holiday, what you did last Saturday, a planned shopping trip – anything at all. Your partner's job is to look around the room, to look at you but not nod, smile or make any sound, to examine his or her nails – in short to fail to respond to you in any way. You should stop talking when you feel uncomfortable. Then change places.

During this exercise you will begin to see how difficult it is to keep talking when you do not get a positive response.

Make a note of your findings.

The way in which you listen to someone can make all the difference to how easy he or she finds it to talk to you. When someone is talking to you, keep encouraging him or her by responding – nodding and saying 'mm' or 'I see' are often all that is needed. There is nothing worse than talking to someone who gives you no response.

Sometimes people find it difficult to express what they want to say and need some encouragement. You can help by repeating back to them what they have been saying, not in parrot fashion, but in an encouraging way, such as in the following example:

Service user: 'My family are very busy, I don't see them much. They all have important jobs …' [silence].

You: 'So your children don't have much time to come here because they all work so hard …'

Paraphrasing what someone has told you can also be a useful way of showing that you have understood what he or she is saying. In paraphrasing you take what someone has been saying and repeat it in a slightly different way.

This can be used effectively to clarify what someone has said. For example, if an individual has just told you about feelings ranging from sadness and anger to relief at coming into residential care, a reply of something like 'so your feelings are very mixed – that's very understandable' demonstrates that you have heard what he or she said and also offers reassurance that this reaction is normal and only to be expected.

Encouraging communication

The best way to ensure that somebody is able to communicate to the best of his or her ability is to make the person feel as comfortable and relaxed as possible. There are several factors to consider when thinking about how to make people feel confident enough to communicate. They are summarised in the table below.

Communication difference	Encouraging actions
Different language	<ul><li>Smile</li><li>Friendly facial expression</li><li>Gestures</li><li>Use pictures</li><li>Warmth and encouragement – repeat their words with a smile to check understanding</li></ul>
Hearing impairment	<ul><li>Do not shout, speak clearly, listen carefully, respond to what is said</li><li>Remove any distractions and other noises</li><li>Make sure any aids to hearing are working</li><li>Use written communication where appropriate</li><li>Use signing where appropriate and understood</li><li>Use properly trained interpreter if high level of skill is required</li></ul>
Visual impairment	<ul><li>Use touch to communicate concern, sympathy and interest</li><li>Use tone of voice rather than facial expressions to communicate mood and response</li><li>Do not rely on non-verbal communication, e.g. facial expression or nodding head</li><li>Ensure that all visual communication is transferred into something which can be heard, either a tape or somebody reading</li></ul>
Confusion or dementia	<ul><li>Repeat information as often as necessary</li><li>Keep re-orientating the conversation if you need to</li><li>Remain patient</li><li>Be very clear and keep the conversation short and simple</li><li>Use simple written communication or pictures where they seem to help</li></ul>

Continued

Communication difference	Encouraging actions
Physical disability	• Ensure that surroundings are appropriate and accessible • Allow for difficulties with voice production if necessary • Do not patronise • Remember that some body language may not be appropriate
Learning disability	• Judge appropriate level of understanding • Make sure that you respond at the right level • Repeat things as often as necessary • Remain patient and be prepared to keep covering the same ground • Be prepared to wait and listen carefully to responses

Check it out

Take some of the ideas from the table above and discuss them with your supervisor. Ask him or her to give you other ideas and methods which have been found to be effective in your workplace.

CASE STUDY: Dealing with communication difficulties

L has motor neurone disease. He cannot speak, swallow or move any part of his body apart from one hand. He is tube fed and communicates by using a writing machine, very slowly and with great effort, with his one useable hand. The carers in his family have become very good at anticipating what he is typing into the machine, and they finish off the words and sentences for him, hoping to make things easier. Sometimes he makes noises that show he is very distressed by this, but his family do not understand why he is becoming so upset.

1   *What do you think the problem is?*
2   *Why is L becoming angry?*
3   *How would you approach the situation with the family?*
4   *What needs to happen?*
5   *What other options could the family try?*

Keys to good practice: Responding to the individual

✓   The single most important thing that you need to remember is that you must tailor your response to the individual, not the condition.

Test yourself

1 Why is body language important?

2 What do you think it would mean if someone sat on the edge of his or her chair?

3 What signals would tell you that someone is relaxed and confident?

4 What do you need to take into account when deciding where to sit?

5 When may physical contact be helpful?

6 What do you need to take into account before using touch?

7 What factors can affect the way people will respond to you?

8 What could you do to show someone that you are interested in what he or she is saying?

HSC 21c Communicate with individuals

The key word in the title of this element is 'individual'. In order for you to work as an effective communicator, you must know how to deal with people in a way which takes account of their individuality. When time is short and demands are high, it is often easier to treat everyone in a group in the same way, to make plans for a whole group of people or to assume that what is good for one person will be good for all. You will learn how to avoid this.

Each person you work with is an individual – completely different and unique. This may sound obvious but it is so important that it is worth repeating.

You will learn how to avoid making judgements about people which are based not on knowledge and understanding of that person, but on generally accepted stereotypes, often with little truth behind them.

The work you have chosen will involve you in relationships with other people all the time. Working in caring is different from other jobs. It is not only about having good working relationships with colleagues, although good teamwork is essential; it is also about the relationships you will make with the individuals you are caring for, and it is about understanding other relationships they have, with their friends and relatives.

Avoiding stereotypes

One of the most effective ways you have of helping people is by recognising them as individuals. Learn never to make assumptions about people in groups.

Think about the number of ways in which people can be identified – they can be described by age, gender, eye colour, place of residence, job, and so on. This will remind you of the number of different aspects there are to any one individual.

The problem with 'labelling' people by placing them in particular groups for particular purposes is that it is very rarely accurate. It may be very convenient when planning care to decide that 'all individuals will want …' or 'this age group will benefit from …', but the number of individuals contained within any group means that any planning that starts with a generalisation is doomed to be unsatisfactory.

Check it out

Think of a way to describe yourself, starting with the most general – 'I am a woman' or 'I am a man'. So are other people, so that does not describe you. 'I have brown hair' – so do a great many others. Continue thinking of ways to describe yourself, getting closer all the time to finding a description which is unique to you (one which describes you, and no one else). Each time you think of another way to describe yourself, it will eliminate more and more people from the group, until finally you may (depending on how well you know yourself) come up with a description which applies to no one else but you.

Each time you are tempted to treat people as one of a group, remember how long this task took and how many descriptions you listed before you found a unique reference to you. Remember that everyone you deal with is unique – an individual.

What are stereotypes?

Stereotypes are an easy way of thinking about the world. Stereotypes would suggest that all people over 65 are frail and walk with a stick, that all black young people who live in inner cities are on drugs, that all fat people are lazy, or that all families have a mother, father and two children. These stereotypes, or ways of looking at the world, are often reinforced by the media or by advertising. Television programmes will often portray violent, criminal characters as young and black.

Check it out

Next time you watch television note down the number of adverts for cars which show trendy, good-looking young business people with a wealthy lifestyle. The advertisers attempt to convince us that buying that particular brand of car will make us good-looking and trendy and give us the kind of lifestyle portrayed.

1 How many people do you know with those particular makes of car who are anything like the people in the adverts?

2 How many do you know who wish they were?

What effect do stereotypes have?

The effect of stereotypes is to make us jump to conclusions about people. How many times have you felt uneasy seeing a young man with a shaved head walking towards you? You know nothing about him, but the way he looks has made you form an opinion about him. If you have a picture in your mind of a social worker or a policeman, think about how much that is influenced by the media – do they really all look like that?

A

B

C

D

1   What do you think each of the people above does for a living?

2   What kind of place does each of them live in?

3   Why have you given the answers you have?

Accents can often bring out prejudice in others. Think about these stereotypes:

People from ...	are known as ...	are thought to be ...
Liverpool	Scousers	work-shy, scroungers, funny
Birmingham	Brummies	slow, not very bright, boring
London	Cockneys	wheeler dealers, not trustworthy, clever
Glasgow	Glaswegians	aggressive, looking for a fight, drinkers
Newcastle	Geordies	warm, friendly, tough, 'salt of the earth'

The next time you find yourself making a judgement about somebody's character based on an accent, stop and think. Try to avoid a stereotype.

Telling jokes at the expense of particular groups of people is another way of displaying prejudices. Stereotypes about people being mean or stupid because of their nationality fail to treat people as individuals and fail to recognise that there are individuals everywhere and that all people are different.

Part of valuing people as individuals is having respect for all of the people you deal with. Respect is usually something which develops as you form relationships. When you provide care for someone, you will get to know and talk to him or her, and a relationship will grow. This is not easy with all individuals you care for. When there appears to be no two-way communication, you may find that forming a relationship is difficult. If you work with people who do not appear to relate to you, perhaps because they are very confused, because they have a very low level of functioning or even because they are not conscious, then it is easy to forget that they are still individuals and need to be treated as such.

Keys to good practice: Respecting individuals

✓ Make sure that any service you provide for someone is with their agreement. People have a right to choose the care they receive and the way in which they receive it.

✓ You must make sure that each person you care for is treated in the same way, regardless of his or her ability to respond to you. This means talking to people who do not seem to understand you, and to people who may appear not to respond. You should explain everything you are doing and go through the details of any procedures you are carrying out.

If only it were that simple! Of course, you cannot suddenly stop doing and thinking things which you have been doing and thinking all your life, but you can develop an awareness of what you are doing and start to ask yourself questions about why you have acted in the way you have.

Once you realise how your own background and beliefs alter the way you think about people, you can begin to recognise the differences and see the value of other cultures and beliefs. It is inevitable that, by thinking carefully about what has influenced you, you will also consider what has influenced others with whom you come into contact.

You need to talk to people, whether they are colleagues or service users, about aspects of their culture or lifestyle you do not understand. As a care professional, it is your responsibility to make sure that you have considered the culture, beliefs and lifestyle of someone for whom you are providing care. It is not acceptable to expect that they will adapt to your set of cultural beliefs and expectations.

The diversity of the human race is what makes living in our society such a rich and varied experience. If you try to welcome this diversity, rather than resist, condemn or belittle the things you do not understand, you will find that your relationships with colleagues and service users will be much more rewarding and the quality of your care practice will be greatly improved.

Check it out

Stop yourself every time you make a generalisation and look at the prejudice behind it. Think about why you think the way you do, and do something about it. The next time you hear yourself saying 'Social workers never understand what is really needed', 'GPs always take ages to visit' or 'Our residents wouldn't be interested in that', stop and think what you are really doing.

Remember

● Everyone has the right to make choices about care.

● All people are different.

If you accept these points, you will never be guilty of making generalisations or making prejudiced judgements about people again.

Case study: Different values

T is in her mid-30s and has a busy job in an international finance company. She is from a Chinese family who have lived in a large city and run a restaurant for the past 40 years. Her parents have now retired from the restaurant and have both suffered from ill-health in the past year. They are too frail to continue caring for themselves without support. T's brothers are busy running the family business and T has decided to stop working in order to care for her parents.

Her English friends and work colleagues are horrified that she is prepared to give up such a good career to do this. The local social services department has offered to provide domiciliary care for T's parents, but the family have refused, explaining that it will not be necessary. T is having difficulty making her non-Chinese friends, colleagues and even social services understand her view that she is willing to do this for her parents and that their welfare is a greater priority than her career.

1 *Can you see where the key differences are between the attitude of T and the attitudes of many families from a different cultural background?*

2 *Would you encourage T to give up her job? If so – why? If not – why not?*

3 *What should the role of social services be in this situation?*

Remember

- Stereotypes can influence how you think about someone.
- Don't rush to make judgements about people.
- Don't make assumptions.
- Everyone is entitled to his or her own beliefs and culture. If you don't know about somebody's way of life – ask.

Knowing yourself and your prejudices

It is vital, if you are to help anyone effectively, that you understand how you affect any situation. Human beings do not react in the same way to everyone. You have doubtless had the experience of meeting someone who makes you feel relaxed and at ease – you find it easy to talk to them and feel as if you had known them for a long time. Equally, there are other people you meet and find it much harder to talk to – in their presence you feel nervous, or unsure; you can't think of anything to say and feel generally uncomfortable. You are still the same person, but you have reacted in a totally different way to different people.

To be a good practitioner in caring, you have to learn to understand how people react to *you* and the way in which your own beliefs, background and prejudices will influence and alter the outcome of an interaction with another person.

It is essential that you understand about interaction between people if you are working in caring. It is not always easy to understand how it works. It may help if you think about dealing with other people as being like looking in a fairground mirror – all of the reflections look different, some are short and fat, some long and thin, some are wavy and curved; it all depends on the mirror. You are still the same, but the mirror makes everything appear different. In the same way, you will interact differently depending on the person you are talking to.

Dealing with different people is like seeing yourself in different fairground mirrors

Evidence indicator

Try this for yourself at work. Pick two different people and tell them both the same piece of information. For example, you could ask to leave early on the next shift, giving your reasons, or explain why a particular person needs a change in the plan of care, or describe where the new delivery of equipment has been stored – in fact, anything at all.

Note down how you carried out the task with each person and how you felt. Make sure you note the differences in your behaviour and feelings. Try to work out how, and why, each of them made you feel different. Keep your notes as evidence.

Learning about yourself is not an easy task. Everyone thinks they know themselves so well – but do they? Often you never take the time to examine your own behaviour in depth. It can be a shock when someone points out something you are doing, or a way you have of behaving, which you had not realised before.

If you intend to be effective as a carer, you will need to spend some time looking at your own behaviour, and try to look in the mirror of other people's reactions.

Keys to good practice: Examining your own behaviour

✓ If you are talking to someone and he or she suddenly seems to close down the conversation, or appear unsure, try to think back to the point at which the atmosphere changed. Be honest with yourself. Did you react to something he or she said? What did you say? Was it a little thoughtless? Did you laugh? Maybe he or she thought you were laughing at him/her? Or did he or she begin to back away when you looked at your watch, or spoke briefly to someone else who wanted your attention?

✓ Do some individuals seem to find it easier to talk to you than others? Do you find it easier to talk to some individuals than others? Of course, there are bound to be some people you like more than others, but when you are working as a professional carer it is not enough just to acknowledge that. You have to know why in order to make sure that it does not result in individuals being treated differently.

Continued

Keys to good practice: Examining your own behaviour

✓ Only you can work at examining your own behaviour. If you have a manager or colleague to work with you, that is a great help, but essentially, no one can do it for you. You will need to be able to ask yourself a series of questions, and be prepared to answer them: Which people do you find it hard to deal with? Can you work better with women than men? Do you find it hard to talk to young people? or to older people? or to people of a particular social class? or to people of particular races? or to anyone with a different accent?

✓ Do you find that you have less patience with some people? Can you identify which people? Is there a pattern? You may not always like the answers you come up with, but until you can work out how you behave towards others and why, you will never be able to make any adjustments to your responses.

✓ You will need to look at your own culture and beliefs. You may, for example, have grown up surrounded by people who believed that it was unthinkable to owe a penny to anyone, so you may find it difficult to offer empathy and support to someone who is desperate because he or she is deeply in debt. If you have lived in a culture which holds older family members in high regard and gives them great respect, you may find it hard to relate to the family of an older person if they hardly ever visit and do not appear interested in his or her welfare. Nevertheless, in your role as a carer you have to be aware of how your own background may influence you and to ensure that you include that factor in the analysis of any situation.

✓ Don't be too hard on yourself. If you acknowledge your own prejudices you will be more than halfway towards overcoming them. Just being able to understand why you behave in the way you do is more than most people achieve in a lifetime! So don't worry if it takes a while before you feel that you are really thinking effectively about what you do and how you affect others. It may seem unlikely, but knowing how people respond to you and making allowances for that will, eventually, become second nature.

Remember

You can change the way you behave by reflecting on your own behaviour, deciding what you need to change and practising new approaches until they become natural to you.

How to communicate clearly

Overcoming barriers

Never assume that you can be heard and understood and that you can be responded to, without first thinking about the individual and his or her situation. Check first to ensure you are giving the communication the best possible chance of success by dealing with as many barriers to communication as possible.

When you need to provide information to service users, make sure it is in an appropriate form. Being given information in an accessible format is far better than having to receive it second hand. For example, for individuals with visual impairments, think about large-print books, braille or audio tapes. If you need any further information, the Royal National Institute for the Blind (RNIB) will be able to advise you about local sources of supplies.

Did you know?

The Benefits Agency produces a catalogue of its leaflets, posters and information. This lists which items are available in other languages, braille, large print, or on audio tape. Many other agencies and organisations do the same.

Asking the right questions

How you talk to someone matters a great deal. You can ask 'open' or 'closed' questions. Which questions you use makes a difference to the response you will get.

- Closed questions are those which allow people to answer 'Yes' or 'No'. For example, 'Are you worried about the tests tomorrow?' This may get only a one-word response. If you then want to find out any more, you have to ask another question. If you are not careful, individuals can then end up feeling as if they are on 'Twenty Questions'.
- Open questions are those which do not allow a one-word response. If you rephrase the question in the previous example it becomes 'How do you feel about tomorrow's tests?' The difference is obvious, and there is a far greater chance that the person you are talking to will feel able to express his or her feelings.

Advice

There will be occasions when you are asked to give advice. Sometimes this is appropriate. If, for example, someone asked whether he or she would be able to carry on claiming a particular benefit while in residential care, it would not be useful to say 'Well, do you think you will continue to need that benefit?' Clearly, there are three possible answers: 'Yes', 'No' or 'I'm not sure, but I'll find out'. These types of request for factual advice are quite different from a situation where someone is dealing with personal or emotional issues. On those issues it is not appropriate for you to give advice – but you will need to use all your listening skills.

What you say

Make sure that you are not the one doing all the talking. Be careful not to tell someone what you think and keep giving your opinions. Telling someone 'If I were you I would ...' is neither good practice nor good communication.

Don't ever tell someone 'That's silly' or 'You shouldn't feel like that'. Such a remark effectively dismisses people's feelings or tells them that they have no right to feel that way.

How you say it

Think about the speed and volume of your speech. We often fail to realise how quickly we speak. It can often be difficult for someone who has some impairment of hearing or poor eyesight to catch what you say, if you speak too quickly.

Think about your accent, and the individual you are talking to. Local accents can be difficult to understand, if they are unfamiliar.

Evidence indicator

You may not know how strong your own accent is. Try making a tape recording and listening to yourself. Or ask a friend or colleague to advise you honestly about the strength of your accent and the speed at which you talk.

Volume is also important. There is no need to shout – it simply distorts what you say and plays havoc with your facial expression! You should, however, make sure that you speak clearly and at a reasonable level. Generally, speaking too softly can make it hard for you to be understood.

There are some occasions when you may have to balance the volume of what you say with the need to maintain someone's privacy. It may be worth having to repeat yourself a few times, if it helps to keep a discussion private.

Keep the tape and your notes as evidence for your portfolio.

Stages of an interaction

As you spend time in communication with someone, the nature of the interaction will go through changes.

- **Stage 1:** The introduction, which may be light and general. At first, communication may have little content of any significance. This is the stage at which both parties decide whether they want to continue the discussion, and how comfortable they feel. Body language and non-verbal communication are very important at this stage.
- **Stage 2:** The main contact and significant information. The middle of any interaction is likely to contain the 'meat', and this is where you will need to use active listening skills to ensure that the interaction is successful.
- **Stage 3:** Time to reflect, wind up, and end positively. People often have the greatest difficulty in knowing how to end an interaction. Ending in a positive way where all participants are left feeling that they have benefited from the interaction is very important. You may find that you have to end an interaction because of time restrictions, or you may feel that enough has been covered – the other person may need a rest, or you may need a break!

At the end of an interaction you should always try to reflect on the areas you have covered, and try to offer a positive and encouraging ending; for example, 'I'm glad you have talked about how unhappy you have been feeling. Now we can try to work at making things better.'

I'm glad you've talked about how unhappy you've been feeling. Now we can try to work at making things better.

Even if the content of an interaction has been fairly negative, you should encourage the individual to see the fact that the interaction has taken place as being positive in itself.

If you get called away before you have had a chance to properly wind up an interaction with an individual, make a point of returning to end things in a positive way. If you say 'I'll be back in a minute', make sure that you do go back.

Written communication

Using written communication may not be something you do very frequently. You may not write many formal letters, but as a care worker you will have to write information in records which could prove to be of vital importance.

The golden rule of good communication is to consider its purpose. If you are completing a care plan or record for an individual, then the information is needed in order to inform the next carer.

Think about the sort of information that person would need to know. What things are important when handing over care?

You need to record accurately any distress or worries you have tried to deal with, any physical signs of illness or accidents. You may need to record fluid balances or calorie intake charts. It may be important to record visitors, or any medical interventions.

Written communication is useless unless it is legible. There is no point in scribbling something unreadable in someone's notes. It is actually worse than not writing anything, because colleagues will waste time trying to decipher what is there, and be concerned by the fact that there was clearly something worth recording, but they have no idea what it was.

You also need to convey the message in a clear and concise way. People do not want to spend time reading a lengthy report when the main points could have been expressed in a paragraph. Equally, you need to make sure that the relevant points are there. Often bullet points can be useful in recording information clearly and concisely. Look at the examples below.

Mrs P had a bad night

Too little information

Mrs P had a bad night. It began when I found her crying about 10 pm. She said she had been thinking about her husband. I thought she seemed a bit hot, so I made her a cup of tea and got her to sit in the lounge for a while before she went to bed. After about half an hour, I managed to get her to go to her room and I went with her ...

Too much irrelevant information

Mrs P had a bad night because:

a) She was distressed about her husband

b) She wandered out of her room about 2 am crying again

c) Unable to settle despite further cocoa

d) Wandered into Mr W's room at 5.30 believing he was her husband

She will need to be closely observed today. Any further confused episodes should be logged.

Clear, helpful notes give a short picture of problems overnight, and suggest action for next day

The importance of confidentiality

The single most important requirement for anyone who works in a care setting is to be trustworthy. Most individuals want that above all else. It is no use having the kindest and most skilful doctor in the world if you discover that she has been chatting to your next door neighbour about how bad your haemorrhoids are!

You will have to make confidentiality part of your life. Confidentiality means not giving any information to anyone unless there is a reason to do so. This sounds very straightforward, and in theory it is, but you need to know what this means in practice.

Did you know?

Everyone has one friend to whom they can talk in absolute confidence. The problem is that often your friend will have another confidential friend – it does not take long for information to travel if everyone tells just one person.

How you can maintain confidentiality

The most common way in which workers breach confidentiality is by chatting about work with friends or family. It is very tempting to discuss the day's events with your family or with friends over a drink or a meal. This is fine, as it is often therapeutic to discuss a stressful day, and helps to get things into perspective. But you must make it a rule never to mention names.

If you always say 'There was this man today …' or 'You won't believe what one of our patients did today …', that is all it takes. Get into the habit of using not names but other characteristics to describe people who appear in your conversation regularly. For example, 'You remember the woman with the very loud voice I told you about last week …'.

When you are out with a group of colleagues, the risks are even greater that you will be tempted to discuss individuals by name. Clearly, your colleagues are already all aware of the individuals, but there is always the likelihood of being overheard in a public place. You have to make sure that you refer to individuals in a way in which they cannot be identified. The easiest way is to use initials.

It will soon become second nature, and you will find yourself glancing around to make sure you cannot be overheard and referring to individuals by their initials in case conferences and planning meetings!

Think before you speak

You also need to be sure that you do not discuss someone you care for with another person you care for. You may not think that you would ever do this, but it is so easy to do, with the best of intentions.

You never know who's listening!

CARELESS TALK COSTS LIVES

Imagine the scene. Someone says 'Ethel doesn't look too good today' and your well-meant response is 'No, she doesn't. She's had a bit of an upset with her son. She'd probably be really glad of some company later, if you've got the time'. This is the type of response which can cause great distress and, above all, distrust. If the lady you have spoken to later says to Ethel, 'Sue said you were a bit down because of the upset with your son', Ethel is not going to know how much you have said. As far as she knows, you could have given her whole life history to the lady who enquired. The most damaging consequence of this breach of confidentiality is the loss of trust. This can have damaging effects on an individual's self-esteem, confidence and general well-being.

Evidence indicator

Think of a time when you have told someone something in confidence and later discovered that they had told other people. Try to recall how you felt about it. You may have felt angry or betrayed. Perhaps you were embarrassed and did not want to face anyone. Note down a few of the ways you felt.

The best way to respond to that comment about Ethel would have been:
'Don't you think so? Well, perhaps she might be glad of some company later, if you've got the time.'

Policies of the organisation

Every health and caring organisation will have a policy on confidentiality and the disclosure of information. You must be sure that you know what both policies are in your workplace.

The basic rule is that all information an individual gives, or that is given on his or her behalf, to an organisation is confidential and cannot be disclosed to anyone without the consent of the individual.

Passing on information with consent

There are, however, circumstances in which it may be necessary to pass on information.

In many cases, the passing of information is routine and related to the care of the individual. For example, medical information may be passed to a hospital, to a residential home or to a private care agency. It must be made clear to the individual that this information will be passed on in order to ensure that he or she receives the best possible care.

The key is that only information which is required for the purpose is passed on. For example, it is not necessary to tell the hearing aid clinic that Mr S's son is currently serving a prison sentence. However, if he became seriously ill and the hospital wanted to contact his next of kin, that information would need to be passed on.

Each organisation should have a policy which states clearly the circumstances in which information can be disclosed. According to government guidelines (Confidentiality of Personal Information 1988) the policy should state:

- who are the members of senior management designated to deal with decisions about disclosing information
- what to do when urgent action is required
- what safeguards are in place to make sure that the information will be used only for the purpose for which it is required
- arrangements for obtaining manual records and computer records
- arrangements for reviewing the procedure.

Check it out

Ask your manager about the confidentiality policy in your workplace. Find the procedure and make sure you know how to follow it.

People who need to know

It can be difficult when people claim to have a right or an interest in seeing an individual's records. Of course, there are always some people who do need to know, either because they are directly involved in providing care for the individual or because they are involved in some other support role. However, not everyone needs to know everything, so it is important that information is given on a 'need to know' basis. In other words, people are told what they need to know in order to carry out their role.

Relatives will often claim that they have a 'right to know'. The most famous example of this was Victoria Gillick, who went to court in order to try to gain access to her daughter's medical records. She claimed that she had the right to know if her daughter had been given the contraceptive pill. Her GP had refused to tell her and she took the case all the way to the House of Lords, but the ruling was not changed and she was not given access to her daughter's records. The rules remain the same. Even for close relatives, the information is not available unless the individual agrees.

It is difficult, however, if you are faced with angry or distressed relatives who believe that you have information they are entitled to. One situation you could encounter is where a daughter, for example, believes that she has the right to be told about medical information in respect of her parent. Another example is where someone is trying to find out a person's whereabouts.

The best response is to be clear and assertive, but to demonstrate that you understand that the situation is difficult for them. Do not try to 'pass the buck' and give people the idea that they can find out from someone else. There is nothing more frustrating than being passed from one person to another without anyone being prepared to tell you anything. It is important to be clear and say something like, 'I'm sorry. I know you must be worried, but I can't discuss any information unless your mother agrees', or 'I'm sorry, I can't give out any information about where J is living now. But if you would like to leave me a name and contact details, I will pass on the message and she can contact you'.

Proof of identity

You should always check that people are who they claim to be. It is not unknown for newspaper reporters, unwanted visitors or even a nosey neighbour to claim that they are relatives or professionals from another agency. If basic precautions are not taken to confirm their identity, then they may be able to find out a great deal of confidential information.

You could use the following checklist to remind yourself of correct procedures.

In person: if you do not know the person who is claiming to have a right to be given information, you should:
- find out whether he or she is known to any of your colleagues
- ask for proof of identity – if the person claims to be from another agency involved in providing care, he or she will have an official ID (identity card); otherwise ask for driving licence, bank cards, etc.

On the telephone: unless you recognise the voice of the person, you should:
- offer to take his or her telephone number and call back after you have checked
- if various members of the family or friends are likely to be telephoning about a particular service user, you could arrange a 'password'.

Case study: Maintaining confidentiality

Mr R is 59 years old. He is a resident in the nursing home where you work, and he is now very ill. He has Huntington's disease, which is a disease causing dementia, loss of mobility, and loss of speech. It is incurable and untreatable, and it is hereditary. Mr R was divorced many years ago when his children were very young and he has had no contact with his family for over 30 years.

A man who says he is Mr R's son comes to the nursing home in great distress. He is aware, through his mother, that his paternal grandfather died 'insane' and he has now heard about his father being in a nursing home. He is terrified that his father has a hereditary disease and that he also may have it. He has young children and is desperate to know whether they are at risk.

1   *What can you tell Mr R's son?*

2   *Does he have a right to know?*

3   *What do you think should happen?*

4   *Whose rights are your concern?*

Test yourself

1   How can your personality affect how you work?

2   People react in the same way, regardless of whom they speak to. True or false?

3   Why is it important to recognise people as individuals?

4   Name some of the effects of treating people as stereotypes in a caring situation.

5   What is the difference between an open question and a closed question? Name situations where you would use each type of question.

6   How should you end an interaction?

7   You receive a telephone call from someone who says she is your service user's niece. She asks for details about her aunt's condition and well-being. You have never heard your service user mention a niece, and to your knowledge she has never visited her aunt. How would you deal with this telephone call? Give reasons for your answer.

HSC 21d Access and update records and reports

Looking after information

Once something is written down or entered on a computer, it becomes a permanent record. For this reason, you must be very careful what you do with any files, charts, notes or other written records. They must always be stored somewhere locked and safe. People should be very careful with files which leave the workplace. There are many stories about files being stolen from cars or left on buses!

Records must be kept safe and protected. Your workplace will have policies relating to records on computers, which will include access being restricted by a password, and the computer system being protected against the possibility of people 'hacking' into it.

Data Protection Act 1998

The Data Protection Act relates to information held about an individual. This includes medical records or social services files – anything which is personal data (facts and opinions about an individual).

All information, however it is stored, is subject to the rules laid down in the Act. Anyone processing personal data must comply with the eight principles of good practice. These say that data must be:
- fairly and lawfully processed
- processed for limited purposes
- adequate, relevant and not excessive
- accurate
- not kept longer than necessary
- processed in accordance with the data subject's rights
- kept secure
- not transferred to countries without adequate protection.

Individuals are entitled to see information about themselves, but they cannot see any part of their record which relates to someone else. People are entitled to be told if any personal information is held about them and, if so:
- to be given a description of the data/information
- to be told why the record is held
- to be told who information contained in the record may have been given to
- to be given a copy of the record with any technical terms explained
- to be given any information available to the holder of the record about the source of the information
- to be given an explanation as to how any decision taken about them has been made.

Information which may be withheld

In principle individuals have a right to be given a copy of all the information contained in their social work files. There are times, however, when the Data Protection Act allows the social services department to withhold some information. The main situations are as follows.

- If the information on a file identifies other people, it will often be right to remove that information unless those people have agreed to the disclosure. This is less likely to apply to information identifying social workers or other social work professionals, unless to disclose it would cause them serious harm.

- Information may be withheld if disclosure would prejudice the carrying out of social work by causing serious harm to the physical or mental health of the data subject or any other person.

- In the case of requests made on behalf of the person by someone able to exercise such legal rights, if the person concerned has expressly asked that some or all of the information should not be disclosed or if they have provided the social services department with information on the assumption that it will not be disclosed, then it must not be.

- If to provide information would hinder the prevention and detection of crime or the prosecution or apprehension of offenders, it should not be disclosed.

What you need to write in records

The information which you write in files should be clear and useful. Do not include irrelevant information, and write only about the individual concerned. Sign and date the information. Anything you write should be true and able to be justified, as the two examples below show.

> Name: A. Person
>
> Mr P settling back well after discharge from hosp. Fairly quiet and withdrawn today. Son to visit in am. Report from hosp included in file, prognosis not good. Not able to get him to talk today, for further time tomorrow.

> Name: J. Soap
>
> Joe visited new flat today. Very positive and looking forward to move. No access problems, delighted with purpose-built kitchen and bathroom. Further visit from OT needed to check on any aids required. Confirmed with housing assoc. that Joe wants tenancy. Will send tenancy agreement, should start on 1st.
>
> Need to check: housing benefit, OT visit, notify change of address to Benefits Agency, PACT team, etc., shopping trip with Joe for any household items.

Remember

The purpose of a file is to reflect an accurate and up-to-date picture of an individual's situation, and to provide an historical record which can be referred to at any point in the future. Some of it may be required to be disclosed to other agencies. Always think carefully about what you write. Make sure it is ACES:

- Accurate
- Clear
- Easy to read
- Shareable.

When you need to break confidentiality

Check it out

Ask a senior colleague if he or she has ever has a to break confidentiality. Discuss the reasons why this became necessary, and see what you can learn from your colleague's experience.

In the previous element you were reminded about the importance of confidentiality.

But there are several reasons why decisions about disclosing information without consent may need to be made. In these cases the individual should be informed about what has been disclosed at the earliest possible opportunity. The one exception to the rule abut informing individuals of this is where the confidential information is given in order to assist an investigation into suspected child abuse. In that case, the individual should not be told of any information which has been disclosed until this has been agreed by those carrying out the investigation.

Information may be required by a tribunal, a court or by the ombudsman. Ideally information should be passed on with the service user's consent, but it will have to be provided regardless of whether the consent is given.

Another occasion for breaking confidentiality is where you have to consider the protection of the community, if there is a matter of public health at stake. You may be aware that someone has an infectious illness, or is a carrier of such an illness and is putting people at risk. For example, if someone was infected with salmonella, but still insisted on going to work in a restaurant kitchen, you would have a duty to inform the appropriate authorities.

There are other situations where you may need to give information to the police. If a serious crime is being investigated, the police can ask for information to be given. There is no definition of 'serious', but it is generally accepted as involving:

- serious harm to the security of the state or to public order
- serious interference with a legal case or investigation
- death
- serious injury
- substantial financial gain or financial loss.

Information can only be requested in respect of a serious offence such as these, and it has to be asked for by a senior-ranking officer, of at least the rank of superintendent.

This means that if the local constable asks if you know whether Mr J has a history of mental health problems, this is not information you are free to discuss.

There may also be times when it is helpful to give information to the media. For example, an elderly confused man, who wanders regularly, may have gone missing for far longer than usual. A description given out on the local radio and in the local paper may help to locate him before he comes to any serious harm.

- **Individual's best interests,** for example safety of a missing person
- **Court or tribunal orders**
- **Ombudsman**
- **Protection of another,** for example from child abuse
- **Outside carers,** for example foster carers, agency support workers
- **Public health interests**
- **Individual's health**
- **Police,** but only if a serious crime is being investigated, and only at the request of a superintendent or higher-ranking officer

Centre: **Personal information**

Some reasons why information may be disclosed without consent

There are other occasions when it is necessary to pass on information which has been given to you in confidence, or which an individual might expect you to keep confidential. One of the most difficult situations is where a child discloses to you that he or she is being abused. The best practice is to try not to get yourself in the position of agreeing to keep a secret.

Remember

Disclosure of information without consent is always a difficult choice. Your decision must be taken in consultation with your supervisor and in line with your organisation's policy. Remember the following main reasons why you may need to do this:

- if it is in the service user's interest
- if there is a serious risk to the community
- if there has been a serious crime, or if the risk of one exists
- in the case of an official/ legal investigation.

Speech bubble (left): If I tell you something, will you promise not to tell anyone else?

Speech bubble (right): That depends on what it is. I can promise you that I will only tell people who will help you.

Try not to get yourself in the position of agreeing to keep a secret

Keys to good practice: Breaking confidentiality

✓ If you have been given information by a child concerning abuse, you have to pass on the information to your line manager, or whoever is named in the alerting procedures. This is not a matter of choice; even if the child refuses to agree, you have a duty to override his or her wishes. There are no circumstances in which disclosures of abuse of children must be kept confidential.

✓ The situation with an adult, perhaps an older person, who is being abused is different. You can only try to persuade him or her to allow you to pass on the information.

✓ You may be faced with information which indicates that someone intends to harm himself or herself. In that situation, you would be justified in breaking a confidence to prevent harm.

✓ If an individual is threatening to harm someone else, you should pass on the information immediately to your line manager, who will inform the police. It is not appropriate to contact the threatened person directly.

Remember

Decisions about breaking confidentiality are never easy. The following areas are the ones in which you are likely to have to break confidentiality. This is not an exhaustive list, but it covers most of the situations you are likely to encounter:

● abuse or exploitation
● harm to self
● harm to others.

Case study: Consequences of breaking confidentiality

Mrs E was in labour, and it was decided that she needed an emergency caesarean section to deliver her baby safely. Her husband was present and everything was explained to him. He was worried, but understood the reason for the surgery. Mrs E signed the consent form for surgery and was hurriedly wheeled down to theatre. Mr E walked beside her to theatre and noticed that there was a stamp on the front of the case notes saying 'High Risk'. He tried to ask one of the staff what this meant just as they were going into the theatre. She said, 'Hang on a second love, I'll be with you in a minute. I've just got to put on an extra pair of gloves because of your wife being HIV positive.' Mr E had no idea that his wife was HIV positive.

1 *Who was at fault?*

2 *Should Mr E have been told of his wife's HIV status before this stage?*

3 *How could this have been prevented?*

4 *How do you think both of them will be feeling?*

5 *What lessons can you learn from this?*

Test yourself

1 What is the law that governs computer records?

2 Name three of the principles of data protection.

3 What does ACES stand for?

4 Why do records have to be locked away?

5 What are the circumstances in which you can give information to the police?

6 Name three other occasions where you may give information to others.

7 What are the simple steps you can take to make sure that you do not unintentionally give out confidential information?

HSC 21 UNIT TEST

1 List three ways in which communication needs can vary between individuals.

2 Why is it important to consider how close you are to people you are communicating with?

3 What are the main formats of communication?

4 Body language is not important; it's what you say that counts. True or false?

5 What are the key steps you need to take to provide the best possible environment for communication?

6 M is 33 years old and has a learning disability. What barriers to communication is he likely to face?

7 What legislation covers records of information held about people?

8 What are the key factors to remember about recording information in plans of care?

9 Why is it important to record information in a plan of care?

10 If you had to rank all the skills of a care worker in order of importance from 1 to 10, where would you place communication? Why?

Support the health and safety of yourself and individuals

This unit is about the way you can contribute to making your workplace a safe, secure and healthy place for people who use it to meet their care needs, for those who work alongside you, and for yourself. Your workplace may be a home environment or any other facility which provides a health or care service.

In the first element you will need to learn about what needs to be done to ensure a safe workplace environment. In the second element you will be looking at how you may need to adapt the way you work to become more safety conscious and think about the way in which your work can affect others. The third element in this unit is about how to respond in an emergency.

What you need to learn

- What is safety?
- The legal framework
- Dealing with hazardous waste
- How to promote a safe work environment
- How to contribute to infection control
- How to maintain personal safety
- How to help people to move safely
- How to help maintain security
- Fire safety
- Security issues
- Health emergencies.

HSC 22a Carry out health and safety checks before you begin work activities

What is safety?

It sounds very simple and straightforward: make sure that the place in which you work is safe and secure. However, when you start to think about it – safe for whom or from whom? Safe from tripping over things? Safe from hazardous fumes? Safe from infection? Safe from intruders? Safe from work-related injuries? You can begin to see that this is a wide and complex subject. It may help if you think about safety and security in respect of the areas of responsibility shown in the table below.

Responsibilities for safety and security in the workplace

Employer's responsibilities	Employee's responsibilities	Shared responsibilities
Planning safety and security	Using the systems and procedures correctly	Safety of individuals using the facilities
Providing information about safety and security	Reporting flaws or gaps in the systems, equipment or procedures in use	Safety of the environment
Updating systems and procedures		

Safety in the workplace

You share responsibility with your employer for the safety of all the people who use your service. There are many hazards which can cause injury to people, especially if they are old, ill or disabled. You need to be aware of the following types of hazards.

Environmental hazards
These include:
- wet or slippery floors
- cluttered passageways or corridors
- re-arranged furniture
- worn carpets or rugs
- electrical flexes.

Hazards connected with equipment and materials
Examples of such hazards include:
- faulty brakes on beds
- worn or faulty electrical or gas appliances
- worn or damaged lifting equipment
- worn or damaged mobility aids
- incorrectly labelled substances, such as cleaning fluids
- leaking or damaged containers
- faulty waste-disposal equipment.

Hazards connected with people

This category of hazards includes:

- handling procedures
- visitors to the building
- intruders
- violent and aggressive behaviour.

Your role

Your responsibility to contribute to a safe environment means more than simply being aware of these potential hazards. You must take steps to check and deal with any sources of risk.

You can fulfil your role in two ways: you can deal directly with the hazard, or you can report it to your manager.

Dealing directly with the hazard

This means that you have taken individual responsibility. It will probably apply to obvious hazards such as:

- trailing flexes – you can roll them up and store them safely
- wet floors – you can dry them as far as possible and put out warning signs
- cluttered doorways and corridors – you can remove objects and store them safely or dispose of them appropriately; if items are heavy, use assistance or mechanical aids
- visitors to the building – challenge anyone you do not recognise; asking 'Can I help you?' is usually enough to establish whether a person has a good reason to be there
- fire – follow the correct procedures to raise the alarm and assist with evacuation.

After washing floors dry them as much as possible, and set out warning signs

Informing your manager

When you inform your manager, the hazard becomes an organisational responsibility. You should report hazards which are beyond your role and competence, such as:

- faulty equipment – fires, kettles, computers, etc.
- worn floor coverings
- loose or damaged fittings
- obstructions too heavy for you to move safely
- damaged or faulty aids – hoists, bed brakes, bathing aids, etc.
- people acting suspiciously on the premises
- fire.

The legal framework

The settings in which you provide care are generally covered by the Health and Safety at Work Act 1974 (HASAWA). This Act has been updated and supplemented by many sets of regulations and guidelines, which extend it, support it or explain it. The regulations most likely to affect your workplace are shown in the diagram below.

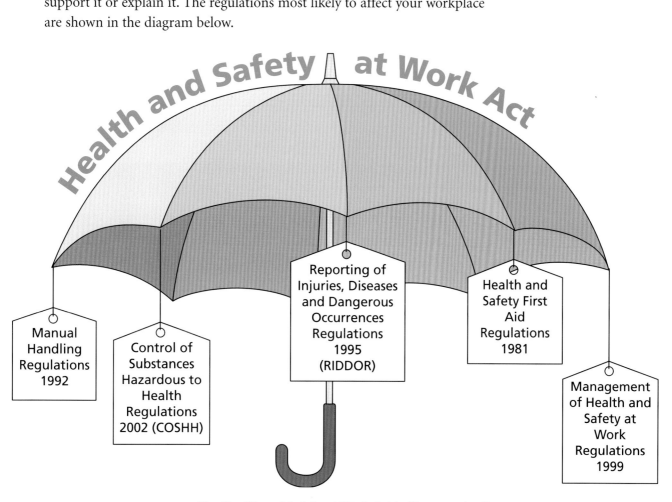

The Health and Safety at Work Act is like an umbrella

You and the law

There are many regulations, laws and guidelines dealing with health and safety. You do not need to know the detail, but you do need to know where your responsibilities begin and end.

The laws place certain responsibilities on both employers and employees. For example, it is up to the employer to provide a safe place in which to work, but the employee also has to show reasonable care for his or her own safety.

Employers have to:
- provide a safe workplace
- ensure that there is safe access to and from the workplace
- provide information on health and safety
- provide health and safety training
- undertake risk assessment for all hazards.

Workers must:

- take reasonable care for their own safety and that of others
- co-operate with the employer in respect of health and safety matters
- not intentionally damage any health and safety equipment or materials provided by the employer.

Both the employee and employer are jointly responsible for safeguarding the health and safety of anyone using the premises.

Each workplace where there are five or more workers must have a written statement of health and safety policy. The policy must include:

- a statement of intention to provide a safe workplace
- the name of the person responsible for implementing the policy
- the names of any other individuals responsible for particular health and safety hazards
- a list of identified health and safety hazards and the procedures to be followed in relation to them
- procedures for recording accidents at work
- details for evacuation of the premises.

Check it out

Find out where the health and safety policy is for your workplace and make sure you read it.

Risk assessment

The Management of Health and Safety at Work Regulations 1999 state that employers have to assess any risks which are associated with the workplace and work activities. This means *all* activities, from walking on wet floors to dealing with violence. Having carried out a risk assessment, the employer must then apply **risk control measures.**
This means that actions must be taken to reduce the risks. For example, alarm buzzers may need to be installed or extra staff employed, as well as steps such as providing extra training for staff or written guidelines on how to deal with a particular hazard.

Risk assessments are vitally important in order to protect the health and safety of both you and the service user. You should always check that a risk assessment has been carried out before you undertake any task, and then follow the steps identified in the assessment in order to reduce the risk.

However, do not forget that you must balance the individual wishes and preferences of each individual who uses your service with your own safety and the safety of others. Some examples of this principle are discussed in the section on manual handling on page 60.

Risks in someone's home

Of course, the situation is somewhat different if you work in an individual's own home. Your employer can still carry out risk assessments and put risk control measures in place, such as a procedure for working in twos in a situation where there is a risk of violence. What cannot be done is to remove environmental hazards such as trailing electrical flexes, rugs with curled up edges, worn patches on stair carpets or old equipment. All you can do is to advise the person whose home it is of the risks, and suggest how things could be improved. You also need to take care!

Control of Substances Hazardous to Health (COSHH)

What are hazardous substances? There are many substances hazardous to health – nicotine, many drugs, even too much alcohol! The COSHH regulations apply to substances which have been identified as toxic, corrosive or irritant. This includes cleaning materials, pesticides, acids, disinfectants and bleaches, and naturally occurring substances such as blood, bacteria, etc. Workplaces may have other hazardous substances which are particular to the nature of the work carried out.

The Health and Safety Executive states that employers must take the following steps to protect employees from hazardous substances.

Step 1 Find out what hazardous substances are used in the workplace and the risks these substances pose to people's health.

Step 2 Decide what precautions are needed before any work starts with hazardous substances.

Step 3 Prevent people being exposed to hazardous substances, but where this is not reasonably practicable, control the exposure.

Step 4 Make sure control measures are used and maintained properly, and that safety procedures are followed.

Step 5 If required, monitor exposure of employees to hazardous substances.

Step 6 Carry out health surveillance where assessment has shown that this is necessary, or COSHH makes specific requirements.

Step 7 If required, prepare plans and procedures to deal with accidents, incidents and emergencies.

Step 8 Make sure employees are properly informed, trained and supervised.

Every workplace must have a COSHH file. This file lists all the hazardous substances used in the workplace. It should detail:
- where they are kept
- how they are labelled

Remember

- It may be your workplace, but it is the person's home. If you work in an individual's home or long-term residential setting, you have to balance the need for safety with the rights of people to have their living space the way they want it.

- Both you and the individuals using the service are entitled to expect a safe place in which to live and work, but remember their rights to choose how they want to live – for example to have a favourite rug in their room, even if it could be a trip hazard.

- their effects
- the maximum amount of time it is safe to be exposed to them
- how to deal with an emergency involving one of them.

Hazardous substances are not just things like poisons and radioactive material – they are also substances like cleaning fluids and bleach.

If you have to work with hazardous substances, make sure that you take the precautions detailed in the COSHH file. This may be wearing gloves or protective goggles, or it may involve limiting the time you are exposed to the substance or only using it in certain circumstances.

The COSHH file should also give you information about how to store hazardous substances. This will involve using the correct containers as supplied by the manufacturers. All containers must have safety lids and caps, and must be correctly labelled.

Never use the container of one substance for storing another, and *never* change the labels.

Check it out

Ask to see the COSHH file in your workplace. Make sure you read it and know which substances you use or come into contact with. Check in the file what the maximum exposure limits are. Your employer must include this information in the COSHH file.

**DANGER
Highly flammable
material**

**DANGEROUS
CHEMICALS**

**DANGER
POISON**

**DANGEROUS
CHEMICALS**

**DANGER
Caustic**

**DANGER
CORROSIVE
SUBSTANCE**

These symbols, which warn you of hazardous substances, are always yellow

The symbols above indicate hazardous substances. They are there for your safety and for the safety of those you care for. Before you use *any* substance, whether it is liquid, powder, spray, cream or aerosol, take the following simple steps:
- check the container for the hazard symbol
- if there is a hazard symbol, go to the COSHH file
- look up the precautions you need to take with the substance
- make sure you follow the procedures, which are intended to protect you.

If you are concerned about a substance being used in your workplace which is not in the COSHH file, or if you notice incorrect containers or labels being used, report this to your supervisor. Once you have informed your supervisor, it becomes his or her responsibility to act to correct the problem.

Reporting of Injuries, Diseases and Dangerous Occurrences (RIDDOR)

Reporting accidents and ill-health at work is a legal requirement. All accidents, diseases and dangerous occurrences should be reported to the Incident Contact Centre. The Centre was established on 1 April 2001 as a single point of contact for all incidents in the UK. The information is important because it means that risks and causes of accidents, incidents and diseases can be identified. All notifications are passed on to either the local authority Environmental Health department, or the Health and Safety Executive, as appropriate.

Your employer needs to report:
- deaths
- major injuries (see below)
- accidents resulting in more than three days off work
- diseases
- dangerous occurrences.

Reportable major injuries and diseases

The following injuries need to be reported:
- fracture other than to fingers, thumbs or toes
- amputation
- dislocation of the shoulder, hip, knee or spine
- loss of sight (temporary or permanent)
- chemical or hot metal burn to the eye or any penetrating injury to the eye
- injury resulting from an electric shock or electrical burn leading to unconsciousness or requiring resuscitation or admittance to hospital for more than 24 hours
- any other injury which leads to hypothermia (getting too cold), heat-induced illness, or unconsciousness; requires resuscitation; or requires admittance to hospital for more than 24 hours
- unconsciousness caused by asphyxia (suffocation) or exposure to a harmful substance or biological agent
- acute illness requiring medical treatment, or leading to loss of consciousness, arising from absorption of any substance by inhalation, ingestion or through the skin
- acute illness requiring medical treatment where there is reason to believe that this resulted from exposure to a biological agent or its toxins or infected material.

Reportable diseases include:
- certain poisonings
- some skin diseases such as occupational dermatitis, skin cancer, chrome ulcer, oil folliculitis acne
- lung diseases including occupational asthma, farmer's lung, pneumoconiosis, asbestosis, mesothelioma
- infections such as leptospirosis, hepatitis, tuberculosis, anthrax, legionellosis (Legionnaires' disease) and tetanus
- other conditions such as occupational cancer, certain musculoskeletal disorders, decompression illness and hand-arm vibration syndrome.

Dangerous occurrences

If something happens which does not result in a reportable injury, but which clearly could have done, then it may be a dangerous occurrence which must be reported immediately.

Accidents at work

If accidents or injuries occur at work, either to you or to an individual you are caring for, then the details must be recorded. For example, someone may have a fall, or slip on a wet floor. You must record the incident regardless of whether there was an injury.

Your employer should have procedures in place for making a record of accidents, either an accident book or an accident report form. This is not only required by the RIDDOR regulations, but also, if you work in a residential or nursing home, by the Commission for Social Care Inspection.

Any accident book or report form must comply with the requirements of the Data Protection Act 1998 by making sure that the personal details of those involved cannot be read by others using the book. This can be

ACCIDENT REPORT FORM

1. Details of person involved in accident

Name……………………………………   Address……………………………………..........................

………

Postcode……………………………...   Occupation……………………………………………………

Department………………………………………………………………………………………………….....

---

2. Details about person filing this report

If you did not have the accident but are filing the report, place your details below.

Name……………………………………..   Address……………………………………………………

………

Postcode……………………………...   Occupation……………………………………………………

Department………………………………………………………………………………………………….....

---

3. Description of incident (use the back of this form if more room is required)

Time and date when accident occurred: Date…………………………..   Time…………………..

Place of accident (room/dept/area)…………………………………………………………………………....

Details of how the accident occurred with cause if known……………………………………………

……

Details of any injury suffered by person involved………………………………………………………....

……

Sign and date this record before handing to nominated record keeper whose name is on the front of book.

Signed…………………………………………………………   Date…………………………………………..

---

4. To be completed by employer only

Only complete this section if you need to report under RIDDOR. After satisfying yourself about the facts, you should decide whether a further risk assessment is necessary and whether the accident should be reported under RIDDOR. How was the report notified to the HSE?

………………………………………….

Date notified……………..   Name (caps)…………………………   Signature………………………..

An example of an accident report form

Make sure you know where the accident report forms or the accident book are kept, and who is responsible for recording accidents. It is likely to be your manager.

You must report any accident in which you are involved, or which you have witnessed, to your manager or supervisor.

Any medical treatment or assessment which is necessary should be arranged without delay. If an individual has been involved in an accident, you should check if there is anyone he or she would like to be contacted, perhaps a relative or friend. If the accident is serious, and you cannot consult the individual – because he or she is unconscious, for example – the next of kin should be informed as soon as possible.

Complete a report, and ensure that all witnesses to the accident also complete reports. You should include the following in any accident report (see the example on the previous page):
- date, time and place of accident
- person/people involved – bearing in mind the Data Protection Act
- circumstances and details of exactly what you saw
- anything that was said by the individuals involved
- the condition of the individual after the accident
- steps taken to summon help, time of summoning help and time when help arrived
- names of any other people who witnessed the accident
- any equipment involved in the accident.

Evidence indicator

Your manager has asked you to design a new incident/accident report form for your workplace. She has asked you to do this because the current form does not provide enough information. The purpose of the new form is to provide sufficient information to:

- ensure the individual receives the proper medical attention
- provide information for treatment at a later date, in case of delayed reactions
- give information to any inspector who may need to see the records
- identify any gaps or need for improvements in safety procedures
- provide information about the circumstances in case of any future legal action.

Think about how you would design the new report form and what headings you would include. Use the list above as a checklist to make sure you have covered everything you need. Make sure that your accident form would comply with the requirements of the Data Protection Act 1998. Keep your notes and your final design as evidence for your portfolio.

Dealing with hazardous waste

As part of providing a safe working environment, employers have to put procedures in place to deal with waste materials and spillages. There are various types of waste, which must be dealt with in particular ways. The types of hazardous waste you are most likely to come across are shown in the table below, alongside a list of the ways in which each is usually dealt with. Waste can be a source of infection, so it is very important that you follow the procedures your employer has put in place to deal with it safely.

Type of waste	Method of disposal
Clinical waste – used dressings	Yellow bags, clearly labelled with contents and location. This waste is incinerated.
Needles, syringes, cannulas ('sharps')	Yellow sharps box. Never put sharps into anything other than a hard plastic box. This is sealed and incinerated.
Body fluids and waste – urine, vomit, blood, sputum, faeces	Cleared and flushed down sluice drain. Area to be cleaned and disinfected.
Soiled linen	Red bags, direct into laundry; bags disintegrate in wash. If handled, gloves must be worn.
Recyclable instruments and equipment	Blue bags, to be returned to the Central Sterilisation Services Department (CSSD) for recycling and sterilising.

Needles and syringes should be put into a hard plastic box, which is sealed and incinerated

Test yourself

1 Look at the picture below. How many possible hazards and risks can you find in the picture?

    a List at least six.

    b Which of these are the responsibility of the employer?

    c Which should you do something about?

2 Name three types of waste and their methods of disposal.

3 How should hazardous substances be stored?

4 What are the employer's responsibilities in respect of hazardous substances?

5 What are the employee's responsibilities for hazardous substances?

6 What should you do if you see someone in your workplace whom you do not recognise?

HSC 22b Ensure your actions support health and safety in the place you work

This element is about what you do when you are working. In the previous element, you looked at the procedures and policies which have to be put in place to protect workers and people who use the service, and the laws which govern health and safety. Now you need to learn about the steps you should be following to ensure that the laws and policies actually work in practice.

How to promote a safe work environment

Care environments are places where accidents can quite often happen, not because staff are careless or fail to check hazards, but because of the vulnerability of the people who use the care facilities.

As people become frail or develop physical conditions which affect mobility such as arthritis or Parkinson's, they become susceptible to falls and trips because they are unsteady, and the slightest change in surface or level can upset their balance. Increasing age can also result in less flexibility of muscles and joints, meaning that people are less able to compensate for a loss of balance or a slip and are more likely to fall than younger people, who may be better able to save themselves by reacting more quickly.

Age is not the only factor to increase risk. Other factors, such as impaired vision, multiply the risk of accidents from trips, falls, touching hot surfaces and knocking into objects. Hearing loss can increase the risk of accidents where people have not heard someone, or perhaps something such as a trolley, approaching around a corner. Dementia can increase risks because people fail to remember to take care when they move about. They can also forget where they have put things down and fail to understand the consequences of actions such as touching hot liquids or pulling on cupboard doors.

It is important that you develop an awareness of health and safety risks and that you are always aware of any risks in any situation you are in. If you get into the habit of making a mental checklist, you will find that it helps. The checklist will vary from one workplace to another, but could look like the one below.

Checklist for a safe work environment

Hazards	Check
Environment	
Floors	Are they dry?
Carpets and rugs	Are they worn or curled at the edges?
Doorways and corridors	Are they clear of obstacles?
Electrical flexes	Are they trailing?
Equipment	
Beds	Are the brakes on? Are they high enough?
Electrical or gas appliances	Are they worn? Have they been safety checked?
Lifting equipment	Is it worn or damaged?
Mobility aids	Are they worn or damaged?
Substances such as cleaning fluids	Are they correctly labelled?

Continued

Hazards	Check
Containers	Are they leaking or damaged?
Waste disposal equipment	Is it faulty?
People	
Visitors to the building	Should they be there?
Handling procedures	Have they been assessed for risk?
Intruders	Have police been called?
Violent and aggressive behaviour	Has it been dealt with?

One of the other factors to consider in your checklist may be what your colleagues do about health and safety issues. It is very difficult if you are the only person following good practice. You may be able to encourage others by trying some of the following options:

- always showing a good example yourself
- explaining why you are following procedures
- getting some health and safety leaflets from your trade union or environmental health office and leaving them in the staffroom for people to see
- bringing in any information you can about courses or safety lectures
- asking your supervisor if he or she can arrange a talk on health and safety.

What you wear

You may not think that what you wear has much bearing on health and safety, but it is important. Even if your employer supplies, or insists on you wearing, a uniform, there are still other aspects to the safety of your work outfit.

There may be restrictions on wearing jewellery or carrying things in your pocket which could cause injury. This can also pose a risk to you – you could be stabbed in the chest by a pair of scissors or ball-point pen!

Many workplaces do not allow the wearing of rings with stones. Not only is this a possible source of infection, but they can also scratch people or tear protective gloves.

High-heeled or poorly supporting shoes are a risk to you in terms of foot injuries and very sore feet! They also present a risk to individuals you are helping, because if you overbalance or stumble, so will they.

Keys to good practice: Reducing risk

 Simple precautions can often be the most effective in reducing the risk. Always look for the risk and take steps to reduce it.

THINK RISK → ASSESS → REDUCE → AVOID

How to contribute to infection control

The very nature of work in a care setting means that great care must be taken to control the spread of infection. You will come into contact with a number of people during your working day – an ideal opportunity for infection to spread. Infection which spreads from one person to another is called 'cross-infection'. If you work in the community, cross-infection is difficult to control. However, if you work in a residential or hospital setting, infection control is essential. There are various steps which you can take in terms of the way you carry out your work (wherever you work) which can help to prevent the spread of infection.

You do not know what viruses or bacteria may be present in any individual, so it is important that you take precautions when dealing with everyone. The precautions are called 'universal precautions' precisely because you need to take them with everyone you deal with.

Wear gloves

When	Any occasion when you will have contact with body fluids (including body waste, blood, mucus, sputum, sweat or vomit), or when you have any contact with anyone with a rash, pressure sore, wound, bleeding or any broken skin. You must also wear gloves when you clear up spills of blood or body fluids or have to deal with soiled linen or dressings.
Why	Because gloves act as a protective barrier against infection.

How

1 Check gloves before putting them on. Never use gloves with holes or tears. Check that they are not cracked or faded.

2 Pull gloves on, making sure that they fit properly. If you are wearing a gown, pull them over the cuffs.

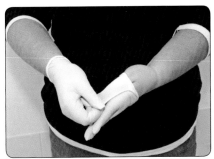

3 Take them off by pulling from the cuff – this turns the glove inside out.

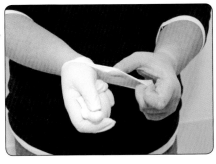

4 Pull off the second glove while still holding the first so that the two gloves are folded together inside out.

5 Dispose of them in the correct waste disposal container and wash your hands.

Wash your hands

When	Before and after carrying out any procedure which has involved contact with an individual, or with any body fluids, soiled linen or clinical waste. You must wash your hands even though you have worn gloves. You must also wash your hands before you start and after you finish your shift, before and after eating, after using the toilet and after coughing, sneezing or blowing your nose.
Why	Because hands are a major route to spreading infection. When tests have been carried out on people's hands, an enormous number of bacteria have been found.
How	Wash hands in running water, in a basin deep enough to hold the splashes and with either foot pedals or elbow bars rather than taps, because you can re-infect your hands from still water in a basin, or from touching taps with your hands once they have been washed. Use the soaps and disinfectants supplied. Make sure that you wash thoroughly, including between your fingers. This should take between 10 and 20 seconds.

How

1 Wet your hands thoroughly under warm running water and squirt liquid soap onto the palm of one hand.

2 Rub your hands together to make a lather.

3 Rub the palm of one hand along the back of the other and along the fingers. Then repeat with the other hand.

4 Rub in between each of your fingers on both hands and round your thumbs.

5 Rinse off the soap with clean water.

6 Dry hands thoroughly on a disposable towel.

Wear protective clothing

When	You should always wear a gown or plastic apron for any procedure which involves bodily contact or is likely to deal with body waste or fluids. An apron is preferable, unless it is likely to be very messy, as gowns can be a little frightening to the individual you are working with.
Why	Because it will reduce the spread of infection by preventing infection getting on your clothes and spreading to the next person you come into contact with.
How	The plastic apron should be disposable and thrown away at the end of each procedure. You should use a new apron for each individual you come into contact with.

Tie up hair

Why	Because if it hangs over your face, it is more likely to come into contact with the individual you are working with and could spread infection. It could also become entangled in equipment and cause a serious injury.

Clean equipment

When	Because infection can spread from one person to another on instruments, linen and equipment just as easily as on hands or hair.
Why	By washing large items like trolleys with antiseptic solution. Small instruments must be sterilised. Do not shake soiled linen or dump it on the floor. Keep it held away from you. Place linen in the proper bags or hampers for laundering.

Deal with waste

Why	Because it can then be processed correctly, and the risk to others working further along the line in the disposal process is reduced as far as possible.
How	By placing it in the proper bags. Make sure that you know the system in your workplace. It is usually: • clinical waste – yellow • soiled linen – red • recyclable instruments and equipment – blue

Take special precautions

When	There may be occasions when you have to deal with an individual who has a particular type of infection that requires special handling. This can involve things like hepatitis, some types of food poisoning or highly infectious diseases.
How	Your workplace will have special procedures to follow. They may include such measures as gowning, double gloving or wearing masks. Follow the procedures strictly. They are there for your benefit and for the benefit of the other individuals you care for.

How to maintain personal safety

There is always an element of risk in working with people. There is little doubt that there is an increase in the level of personal abuse suffered by workers in the health and care services. There is also the element of personal risk encountered by workers who visit people in the community, and have to deal with homes in poor states of repair and an assortment of domestic animals!

However, there are some steps which you can take to assist with your own safety.

Evidence indicator

Make notes of three ways in which infection can be spread. Then note down three effective ways to reduce the possibility of cross-infection. Keep your notes as evidence.

Keys to good practice: Steps to personal safety

✓ If you work alone in the community, always leave details of where you are going and what time you expect to return. This is important in case of accidents or other emergencies, so that you can be found.

✓ Carry a personal alarm, and use it if necessary.

✓ Ask your employer to provide training in techniques to combat aggression and violence. It is foolish and potentially dangerous to go into risky situations without any training.

✓ Try to defuse potentially aggressive situations by being as calm as possible and by talking quietly and reasonably. But if this is not effective, leave.

✓ If you work in a residential or hospital setting, raise the alarm if you find you are in a threatening situation.

✓ Do not tackle aggressors, whoever they are – raise the alarm.

✓ Use an alarm or panic button if you have it – otherwise yell – very loudly.

Case study: Risk in the community

K was a home-care assistant on her first visit to a new service user, Mr W. She had been warned that his house was in a poor condition and that he had a large dog. She also knew that he had a history of psychiatric illness and had, in the past, been admitted to hospital compulsorily under the Mental Health Act.
When K arrived on her first morning, the outside of the house was in a very poor state – the garden was overgrown, and it was full of rubbish and old furniture. The front door was half open and she could see that half the floorboards in the hallway appeared to be missing – there were simply joists and a drop into the cellar below. Mr W's dog was in the hallway growling and barking, and Mr W was at the top of the stairs shouting 'Who are you? You won't get me out of here – I'll kill you first!'

1 **Q** *What should K do?*

   A *Leave! She should leave the house at once and report the situation to her manager.*

2 **Q** *When should she go back?*

   A *Only after a risk assessment has been carried out.*

3 **Q** *What sort of risks need to be assessed?*

   A a *Mr W's mental health and whether any treatment or support is required.*

   b *The safety of the house. Mr W will have to be consulted about whether he is willing for his house to be made safe and the floorboards repaired.*

   c *The dog and whether it is likely to present a risk of attack on a visitor to the house.*

4 **Q** *If Mr W refuses to allow a risk assessment, or his house to be repaired, should K go back in anyway?*

   A *No. K's job is to provide care, but not at the risk of her own safety.*

5 **Q** *Who should carry out the risk assessment?*

   A *K's employer.*

How to help people to move safely

Handling and moving service users is dealt with in detail in Unit HSC 223, but the implications for the safety of both you and the service user are examined in this unit.

The Manual Handling Operations Regulations 1992 require employers to avoid all manual handling where there is a risk of injury 'so far as it is reasonably practical'. Everyone from the European Commission to the Royal College of Nurses has issued policies and directives about avoiding lifting wherever possible. Make sure you check out the policies in use in your workplace and that you understand them.

There is almost no situation in which manual lifting and handling could be considered acceptable.

On the rare occasions when it is still absolutely necessary for manual lifting to be done, the employer has to make a risk assessment and put procedures in place to reduce the risk of injury to the employee. This could involve ensuring that enough staff are available to lift or handle someone safely, which can often mean that four people are needed.

Use the aids which your employer is obliged to provide

Your employer should arrange for you to attend a moving and handling course. You must attend one each year, so that you are up to date with the safest possible practices.

Your employer is required to carry out a risk assessment of any moving and handling which is necessary and to supply the correct equipment, and enough people, to carry out the move.

All moving and handling should be carried out using appropriate aids and sufficient people. Manual lifting is not something to be undertaken in the

Did you know?

Lifting and handling individuals is the single largest cause of injuries at work in health and care settings. One in four workers take time off because of a back injury sustained at work.

Remember

- Always use lifting and handling aids.
- There is no such thing as a safe manual lift.
- Use the aids which your employer is obliged to provide.

Remember

- Many workers in care still lift people manually. It seems quicker and easier than going to all the trouble of using a hoist – it isn't.
- Manual lifting is now actively discouraged throughout the profession.
- Manual lifting presents unnecessary and unacceptable risks to the service user and to you.
- A back injury can end your career. It's not worth the risk.

normal course of events and you should use mechanical lifting aids and hoists wherever possible.

Remember

Your employer has a statutory requirement to install lifting equipment, but it is your responsibility to use the equipment that is there.

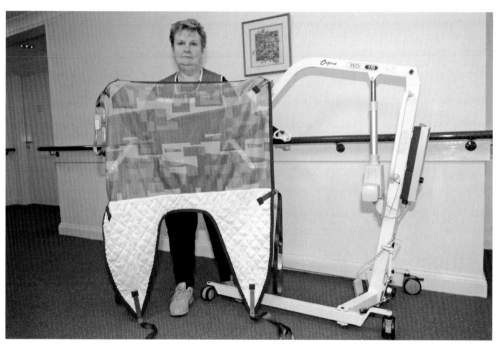

Your employer is required to supply the necessary equipment, such as hoists

If you do have to consider lifting, what should you do?

Encourage all individuals to help themselves – you would be surprised how much 'learned helplessness' exists. This is largely brought about by care workers who find it is quicker and easier to do things themselves rather than allowing a person to do it for himself or herself! Does this sound familiar?

It is also essential that the views of the person being moved are taken into account. While your employer, and you, need to make sure that you are not put at risk by moving or lifting, it is also important that the person needing assistance is not caused pain, distress or humiliation by the policies in place. Groups representing people with disabilities have pointed out that policies which exclude any lifting may infringe the human rights of an individual needing mobility assistance. For example, individuals may in effect be confined to bed unnecessarily and against their will by a lack of lifting assistance.

A High Court judgement (A & B vs East Sussex County Council 2003) found in favour of two women with disabilities who had been denied access to lifting because the local authority had a blanket ban on lifting regardless of the circumstances. Such a ban was deemed unlawful. It is likely that similar cases will be brought under the Human Rights Act, which gives people protection against humiliating or degrading treatment.

There is more detailed information in Unit HSC 223 about maintaining mobility and helping people to move themselves.

How to help maintain security

Most workplaces where care is provided are not under lock and key. This is a necessary part of ensuring that people have choice and that their rights are respected. However, they also have a right to be secure. Security in a care environment is about:

- security against intruders
- people's right to privacy and to make decisions about unwanted visitors
- security of property
- protection against abuse.

Security against intruders

If you work for a large organisation, such as an NHS trust, it may be that all employees are easily identifiable by identity badges with photographs. This makes it easier to identify people who do not have a right to be on the premises. Some of these identity cards even contain a microchip which allows the card to be 'swiped' to gain access to secure parts of the building.

In a smaller workplace, there may be a system of issuing visitors' badges to visitors who have reasons to be there, or the workplace may simply rely on the vigilance of the staff.

 Keys to good practice: Security against intruders

✓ Be aware of everyone you come across. Get into the habit of noticing people and thinking, 'Do I know that person?'

✓ Challenge anyone you do not recognise.

✓ The challenge should be polite. 'Can I help you?' is usually enough to find out if a visitor has a reason to be on the premises.

If a person says that he or she is there to see someone:

✓ Don't give directions – escort him or her.

✓ If the person is a genuine visitor, he or she will be grateful. If not, he or she will disappear pretty quickly!

 Remember

If you find an intruder on the premises, don't tackle him or her – raise the alarm.

The more dependent individuals are, the greater the risk. If you work with babies, high-dependency or unconscious patients, people with a severe learning disability or multiple disabilities, or people who are very confused, you will have to be extremely vigilant in protecting them from criminals.

Protecting people

If very dependent individuals are living in their own homes, the risks are far greater. You must try to impress on them the importance of finding out who people are before letting them in. If they are able to use them, the 'password' schemes from the utilities (water, gas and electricity companies) are helpful. Information record cards like those provided by the 'Safe as Houses' scheme can be invaluable in providing basic information to anyone who is involved in helping in an emergency.

Choosing who to see

People have a right to choose who they see. This can often be a difficult area to deal with. If there are relatives or friends who wish to visit and an individual does not want to see them, you may have to make this clear. It is difficult to do, but you can only be effective if you are clear and assertive. You should not make excuses or invent reasons why visitors cannot see the person concerned. You could say something like: 'I'm sorry, Mr P has told us that he does not want to see you. I understand that this may be upsetting, but it is his choice. If he does change his mind we will contact you. Would you like to leave your phone number?'

Do not allow yourself to be drawn into passing on messages or attempting to persuade – that is not your role. Your job is to respect the wishes and the choices of the person you are caring for. If you are asked to intervene or to pass on a message, you must refuse politely but firmly: 'I'm sorry, that is not something I can do. If your uncle does decide he wants to see you, I will let you know right away. I will tell him you have visited, but I can't do anything else.'

Remember

- Every time you visit, you may have to explain again what the individual should do when someone knocks on the door.
- Give the individual a card with simple instructions.
- Obtain agreement to speak to the local 'homewatch' scheme and ask that a special eye is kept on visitors.
- Speak to the local police and make them aware that a vulnerable individual is living alone in the house.

Check it out

You need to work with a colleague or friend to try this role play. One of you should play the person who has come to visit, and the other the care worker who has to say that a friend or relative will not see him or her. Try using different scenarios – the visitor could be angry, upset, aggressive, and so on. Try at least three different scenarios each. When you have practised a few times, you may feel better equipped to deal with the situation when it happens in reality.

If you cannot find anyone to work with you, it is possible to do a similar exercise by imagining three or four different scenarios and then writing down the words you would say in each of the situations.

Security of property

Property and valuables belonging to individuals in care settings should be safeguarded. It is likely that your employer will have a property book in which records of all valuables and personal possession are entered.

There may be particular policies within your organisation, but as a general rule you are likely to need to:

- make a record of all possessions on admission
- record valuable items separately
- describe items of jewellery by their colour, for example 'yellow metal', not 'gold'
- ensure that individuals sign for any valuables they are keeping, and that they understand that they are liable for their loss

- inform your manager if an individual is keeping valuables or a significant amount of money.

It is always difficult when items go missing in a care setting, particularly if they are valuable. It is important that you check all possibilities before calling the police.

Check it out

Find out where the property book is in your workplace, and how it is filled in. Check who has the responsibility to complete it.

If you are likely to have to use the book at any time, make sure you know exactly what your role is. Do you have to enter the property in the book, then give it to someone else to deal with the valuables? Do you have to make sure the valuables are safe? Do you have to give the individual a copy of the entry in the book? Ask the questions in advance – don't leave it until you have to do it.

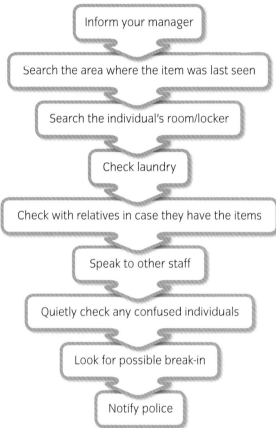

Inform your manager

Search the area where the item was last seen

Search the individual's room/locker

Check laundry

Check with relatives in case they have the items

Speak to other staff

Quietly check any confused individuals

Look for possible break-in

Notify police

Action stages when property goes missing

Protecting people from abuse

Abuse is dealt with in depth in Unit HSC 24, but it can never be repeated often enough that individuals have a right to be protected from abuse, and you must report immediately any abuse you see or suspect.

Test yourself

1 Why are there precautions about the kind of clothing and jewellery you wear?

2 Why do you need to wash your hands?

3 How should you wash them?

4 What are the different ways of disposing of waste?

5 What should you do if you find an intruder on the premises?

6 What type of manual lifting is encouraged?

HSC 22c Take action to deal with emergencies

Fire safety

Your workplace will have procedures which must be followed in the case of an emergency. All workplaces must display information about what action to take in case of fire. The fire procedure is likely to be similar to the one shown below.

Fire Safety Procedure

1 Raise the alarm.

2 Inform the telephonist or dial 999.

3 Ensure that everyone is safe and out of the danger area.

4 If it is safe to do so, attack the fire with the correct extinguisher.

5 Go to the fire assembly point (this will be stated on the fire procedure notice).

6 Do not return to the building for any reason.

Make sure that you know where the fire extinguishers or fire blankets are in your workplace, and also where the fire exits are.

Make sure you know where the fire extinguishers are in your workplace

Remember

Don't be a hero! Never attempt to tackle a fire unless you are confident that you can do so safely, for example:

- you have already raised the alarm
- you have a clear, unobstructed route away from the fire in case it grows larger
- you are confident of your ability to operate the extinguisher
- you have the correct type of extinguisher.

Your employer will have installed fire doors to comply with regulations – never prop them open.

Your employer should provide fire lectures each year. You must attend and make sure that you are up to date with the procedures to be followed.

The Fire Precautions (Workplace) (Amendment) Regulations 1999 require that all workplaces should be inspected by the fire authority to check means of escape, firefighting equipment and warnings, and that a fire certificate must be issued. A breach of fire regulations could lead to a prosecution of the employer, the responsible manager, or other staff members.

Which extinguisher?

There are specific fire extinguishers for fighting different types of fire. It is important that you know this. You do not have to memorise them as each one has clear instructions on it, but you do need to be aware that there are different types and make sure that you read the instructions before use.

Did you know?

All new fire extinguishers are red. Each one has its purpose written on it. Each one also has a patch of the colour previously used for that type of extinguisher.

Extinguisher type and patch colour	Use for	Danger points	How to use	How it works
Red Water	Wood, cloth, paper, plastics, coal, etc. Fires involving solids.	Do **not** use on burning fat or oil, or on electrical appliances.	Point the jet at the base of the flames and keep it moving across the area of the fire. Ensure that all areas of the fire are out.	Mainly by cooling burning material.
Blue Multi-purpose dry powder	Wood, cloth, paper, plastics, coal, etc. Fires involving solids. Liquids such as grease, fats, oil, paint, petrol, etc. but **not** on chip or fat pan fires.	Safe on live electrical equipment, although the fire may re-ignite because this type of extinguisher does not cool the fire very well. Do **not** use on chip or fat pan fires.	Point the jet or discharge horn at the base of the flames and, with a rapid sweeping motion, drive the fire towards the far edge until all the flames are out.	Knocks down flames and, on burning solids, melts to form a skin smothering the fire. Provides some cooling effect.
Blue Standard dry powder	Liquids such as grease, fats, oil, paint, petrol etc. but **not** on chip or fat pan fires.	Safe on live electrical equipment, although does not penetrate the spaces in equipment easily and the fire may re-ignite. This type of extinguisher does not cool the fire very well. Do **not** use on chip or fat pan fires.	Point the jet or discharge horn at the base of the flames and, with a rapid sweeping motion, drive the fire towards the far edge until all the flames are out.	Knocks down flames.

Continued

Extinguisher type and patch colour	Use for	Danger points	How to use	How it works
Cream AFFF (Aqueous film-forming foam) (multi-purpose)	Wood, cloth, paper, plastics, coal, etc. Fires involving solids. Liquids such as grease, fats, oil, paint, petrol, etc. but **not** on chip or fat pan fires.	Do **not** use on chip or fat pan fires.	For fires involving solids, point the jet at the base of the flames and keep it moving across the area of the fire. Ensure that all areas of the fire are out. For fires involving liquids, do not aim the jet straight into the liquid. Where the liquid on fire is in a container, point the jet at the inside edge of the container or on a nearby surface above the burning liquid. Allow the foam to build up and flow across the liquid.	Forms a fire-extinguishing film on the surface of a burning liquid. Has a cooling action with a wider extinguishing application than water on solid combustible materials.
Cream Foam	Limited number of liquid fires.	Do **not** use on chip or fat pan fires. Check manufacturer's instructions for suitability of use on other fires involving liquids.	Do not aim jet straight into the liquid. Where the liquid on fire is in a container, point the jet at the inside edge of the container or on a nearby surface above the burning liquid. Allow the foam to build up and flow across the liquid.	
Black Carbon dioxide CO2	Liquids such as grease, fats, oil, paint, petrol, etc. but **not** on chip or fat pan fires.	Do **not** use on chip or fat pan fires. This type of extinguisher does not cool the fire very well. Fumes from CO2 extinguishers can be harmful if used in confined spaces: ventilate the area as soon as the fire has been controlled.	Direct the discharge horn at the base of the flames and keep the jet moving across the area of the fire.	Vaporising liquid gas smothers the flames by displacing oxygen in the air.
Fire blanket	Fires involving both solids and liquids. Particularly good for small fires in clothing and for chip and fat pan fires, provided the blanket **completely** covers the fire.	If the blanket does not completely cover the fire, it will not be extinguished.	Place carefully over the fire. Keep your hands shielded from the fire. Take care not to waft the fire towards you.	Smothers the fire.

Security issues

As noted in the previous element, you necd to be vigilant about security risks and know who to report any problems to.

Evacuating buildings

In an extreme case it may be necessary to help evacuate buildings if there is a fire, or for other security reasons, such as:

- a bomb scare
- the building has become structurally unsafe
- an explosion
- a leak of dangerous chemicals or fumes.

The evacuation procedure you need to follow will be laid down by your workplace. The information will be the same whatever the emergency is: the same exits will be used and the same assembly point. It is likely to be along the following lines.

- Stay calm, do not shout or run.
- Do not allow others to run.
- Organise people quickly and firmly without panic.
- Direct those who can move themselves and assist those who cannot.
- Use wheelchairs to move people quickly.
- Move a bed with a person in, if necessary.

Health emergencies

Helping in a health emergency is about first aid, and you need to understand the actions you should take if a health emergency arises. **The advice that follows is *not* a substitute for a first aid course, and will only give you an outline of the steps you need to take. Reading this part of the unit will not qualify you to deal with these emergencies. Unless you have been on a first aid course, you should be careful about what you do, because the wrong action can cause more harm to the casualty. It may be better to summon help.**

What you can safely do

Most people have a useful role to play in a health emergency, even if it is not dealing directly with the ill or injured person. It is also vital that someone:

- summons help as quickly as possible
- offers assistance to the competent person who is dealing with the emergency
- clears the immediate environment and makes it safe – for example, if someone has fallen through a glass door, the glass must be removed as soon as possible before there are any more injuries
- offers help and support to other people who have witnessed the illness or injury and may have been upset by it. Clearly this can only be dealt with once the ill or injured person is being helped.

Remember

Only attempt what you know you can safely do. Do not attempt something you are not sure of. You could do further damage to the ill or injured person and you could lay yourself and your employer open to being sued. Do not try to do something outside your responsibility or capability – summon help and wait for it to arrive.

How you can help the casualty in a health emergency

It is important that you are aware of the initial steps to take when dealing with the commonest health emergencies. You may be involved with any of these emergencies when you are at work, whether you work in a residential, hospital or community setting. Clearly, there are major differences between the different work situations.

- If you are working in a hospital where skilled assistance is always immediately available, the likelihood of your having to act in an emergency, other than to summon help, is remote.
- In a residential setting, help is likely to be readily available, although it may not necessarily be the professional medical expertise of a hospital.
- In the community you may have to summon help and take action to support a casualty until the help arrives. It is in this setting that you are most likely to need some knowledge of how to respond to a health emergency.

This section gives a guide to recognising and taking initial action in a number of health emergencies:

- severe bleeding
- cardiac arrest
- shock
- loss of consciousness
- epileptic seizure

- choking and difficulty with breathing
- fractures and suspected fractures
- burns and scalds
- poisoning
- electrical injuries.

Severe bleeding

Severe bleeding can be the result of a fall or injury. The most common causes of severe cuts are glass, as the result of a fall into a window or glass door, or knives from accidents in the kitchen.

Symptoms

There will be apparently large quantities of blood from the wound. In some very serious cases, the blood may be pumping out. Even small amounts of blood can be very frightening, both for you and the casualty. Remember that a small amount of blood goes a long way, and things may look worse than they are. However, severe bleeding requires urgent medical attention in hospital. Although people rarely bleed to death, extensive bleeding can cause shock and loss of consciousness.

Aims

- To bring the bleeding under control
- To limit the possibility of infection
- To arrange urgent medical attention

Action

1   You will need to apply pressure to a wound that is bleeding. If possible, use a sterile dressing. If one is not readily available, use any readily

available absorbent material, or even your hand. Do not forget the precautions (see 'Protect yourself' below). You will need to apply direct pressure over the wound for 10 minutes (this can seem like a very long time) to allow the blood to clot.

2   If there is any object in the wound, such as a piece of glass, *do not* try to remove it. Simply apply pressure to the sides of the wound.

3   Lay the casualty down and raise the affected part if possible.

4   Make the person comfortable and secure.

5   Dial 999 for an ambulance.

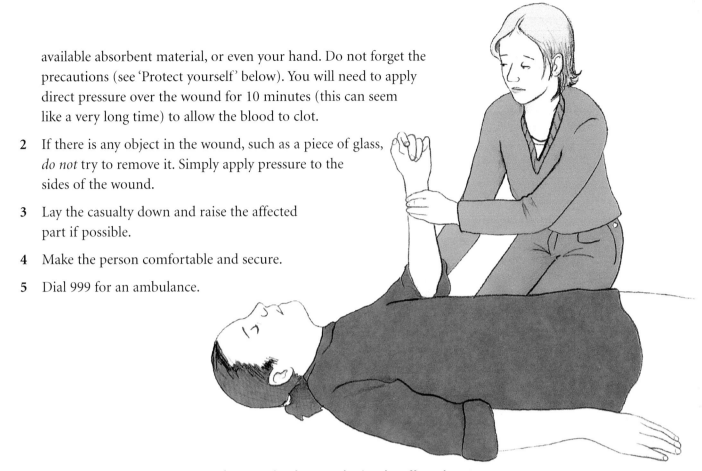

Lay the casualty down and raise the affected part

Protect yourself

You should take steps to protect yourself when you are dealing with casualties who are bleeding. Your skin provides an excellent barrier to infections, but you must take care if you have any broken skin such as a cut, graze or sore. Seek medical advice if blood comes into contact with your mouth, nose or gets into your eyes. Blood-borne viruses (such as HIV or hepatitis) can be passed only if the blood of someone who is already infected comes into contact with broken skin.

● If possible, wear disposable gloves.
● If this is not possible, cover any areas of broken skin with a waterproof dressing.
● If possible, wash your hands thoroughly in soap and water before and after treatment.
● Take care with any needles or broken glass in the area.
● Use a mask for mouth-to-mouth resuscitation if the casualty's nose or mouth is bleeding.

Cardiac arrest

Cardiac arrest occurs when a person's heart stops. Cardiac arrest can happen for various reasons, the most common of which is a heart attack, but a person's heart can also stop as a result of shock, electric shock, a convulsion or other illness or injury.

Symptoms

- No pulse
- No breathing

Aims

- To obtain medical help as a matter of urgency
- It is important to give oxygen, using mouth-to-mouth resuscitation, and to stimulate the heart, using chest compressions. This procedure is called cardio-pulmonary resuscitation – CPR. You will need to attend a first aid course to learn how to resuscitate – you cannot learn how to do this from a book. On the first aid course you will be able to practise on a special dummy.

Action

1 Check whether the person has a pulse and whether he or she is breathing.

2 If not, call for urgent help from the emergency services.

3 Start methods of resuscitation *if* you have been taught how to do it.

4 Keep up resuscitation until help arrives.

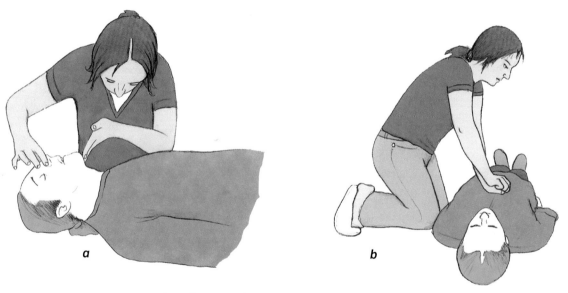

a   *b*

Mouth-to-mouth resuscitation (a) and chest compressions (b)

Shock

Shock occurs because blood is not being pumped around the body efficiently. This can be the result of loss of body fluids through bleeding, burns, severe vomiting or diarrhoea, or a sudden drop in blood pressure or a heart attack.

Symptoms

The signs of shock are easily recognised. The person:
- will look very pale, almost grey
- will be very sweaty, and the skin will be cold and clammy

- will have a very fast pulse
- may feel sick and may vomit
- may be breathing very quickly.

Aims

- To obtain medical help as a matter of urgency
- To improve blood supply to heart, lungs and brain

Action

1   Call for urgent medical assistance.

2   Lay the person down on the floor. Try to raise the feet off the ground to help the blood supply to the important organs.

3   Loosen any tight clothing.

4   Watch the person carefully. Check the pulse and breathing regularly.

5   Keep the person warm and comfortable, but *do not* warm the casualty with direct heat, such as a hot water bottle.

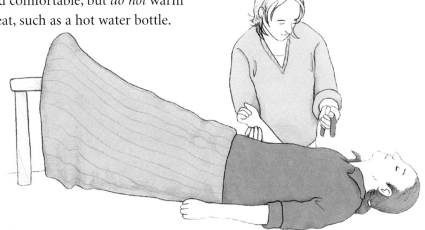

Raise the feet off the ground and keep the casualty warm

Do not:

- allow casualty to eat or drink
- leave the casualty alone, unless it is essential to do so briefly in order to summon help.

Loss of consciousness

Loss of consciousness can happen for many reasons, from a straightforward faint to unconsciousness following a serious injury or illness.

Symptom

A reduced level of response and awareness. This can range from being vague and 'woozy' to total unconsciousness.

Aims

- To summon expert medical help as a matter of urgency
- To keep the airway open
- To note any information which may help to find the cause of the unconsciousness

Action

1 Make sure that the person is breathing and has a clear airway.

2 Maintain the airway by lifting the chin and tilting the head backwards.

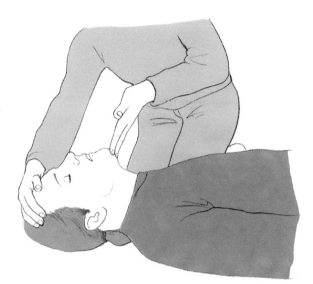

Open the airway

3 Look for any obvious reasons why the person may be unconscious, such as a wound or an ID band telling you of any condition he or she may have. For example, many people who have medical conditions which may cause unconsciousness, such as epilepsy or diabetes, wear special bracelets or necklaces giving information about their condition.

4 Place the casualty in the recovery position (see below), *but not if you suspect a back or neck injury*, until the emergency services arrive.

Do not:

● attempt to give anything by mouth
● attempt to make the casualty sit or stand
● leave the casualty alone, unless it is essential to leave briefly in order to summon help.

The recovery position

Many of the actions you need to take to deal with health emergencies will involve you in placing someone in the recovery position. In this position a casualty has the best chance of keeping a clear airway, not inhaling vomit and remaining as safe as possible until help arrives. This position should not be attempted if you think someone has back or neck injuries, and it may not be possible if there are fractures of limbs.

1 Kneel at one side of the casualty, at about waist level.

2 Tilt back the person's head – this opens the airway. With the casualty on his/her back, make sure that limbs are straight.

3 Bend the casualty's near arm as in a wave (so it is at right angles to the body). Pull the arm on the far side over the chest and place the back of the hand against the opposite cheek (**a** in the diagram opposite).

4 Use your other hand to roll the casualty towards you by pulling on the far leg, just above the knee (**b** in the diagram). The casualty should now be on his or her side.

5 Once the casualty is rolled over, bend the leg at right angles to the body. Make sure the head is tilted well back to keep the airway open (**c** in the diagram).

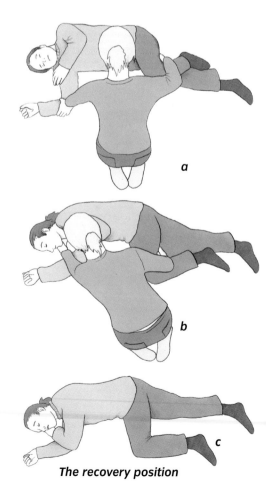

a

b

c

The recovery position

Epileptic seizure

Epilepsy is a medical condition that causes disturbances in the brain which result in sufferers becoming unconscious and having involuntary contractions of their muscles. This contraction of the muscles produces the fit or seizure. People who suffer with epilepsy do not have any control over their seizures, and may do themselves harm by falling when they have a seizure.

Aims

- To ensure that the person is safe and does not injure himself or herself during the fit
- To offer any help needed following the fit

Action

1 Try to make sure that the area in which the person has fallen is safe.

2 Loosen all clothing.

3 Once the seizure has ended, make sure that the person has a clear airway and place in the recovery position.

4 Make sure that the person is comfortable and safe. Particularly try to prevent head injury.

5 If the fit lasts longer than five minutes, or you are unaware that the casualty is a known epileptic, call an ambulance.

Do not:

- attempt to hold the casualty down, or put anything in the mouth
- move the casualty until he or she is fully conscious, unless there is a risk of injury in the place where he or she has fallen.

Choking and difficulty with breathing (in adults and children over 8 years)

This is caused by something (usually a piece of food) stuck at the back of the throat. It is a situation which needs to be dealt with, as people can quickly stop breathing if the obstruction is not removed.

Symptoms

- Red, congested face at first, later turning grey
- Unable to speak or breathe, may gasp and indicate throat or neck

Aims

- To remove obstruction as quickly as possible
- To summon medical assistance as a matter of urgency if the obstruction cannot be removed

Action

1   Try to get the person to cough. If that is not immediately effective, move on to step 2.

2   Bend the person forwards. Slap sharply on the back between the shoulder blades up to five times (**a** in the diagram opposite).

3   If this fails, stand behind the person with your arms around him/her. Join your hands just below the breastbone. One hand should be in a fist and the other holding it (**b** in the diagram).

4   Sharply pull your joined hands upwards and into the person's body at the same time. The force should expel the obstruction.

5   You should alternate backslaps and abdominal thrusts until you clear the obstruction.

This action (the Heimlich manoeuvre) should not be attempted without proper training.

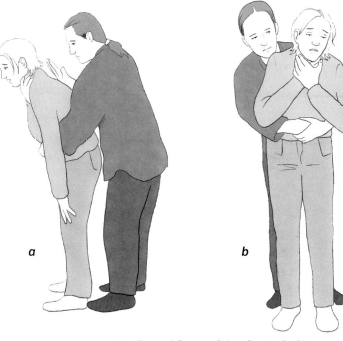

a   *b*

Dealing with an adult who is choking

Fractures and suspected fractures

Fractures are breaks or cracks in bones. They are usually caused by a fall or other type of injury. The casualty will need to go to a hospital as soon as possible to have a fracture diagnosed correctly.

Symptoms

- Acute pain around the site of the injury
- Swelling and discoloration around the affected area
- Limbs or joints may be in odd positions
- Broken bones may protrude through the skin

Action

1   The important thing is to support the affected part. Help the casualty to find the most comfortable position.

2   Support the injured limb in that position with as much padding as necessary – towels, cushions or clothing will do.

3   Take the person to hospital or call an ambulance.

Do not:

- try to bandage or splint the injury
- allow the casualty to have anything to eat or drink.

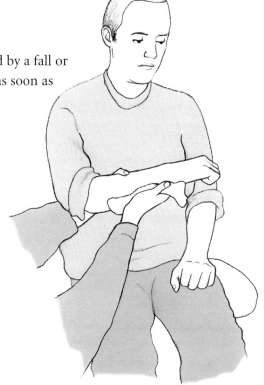

Support the injured limb

Burns and scalds

There are several different types of burn; the most usual are burns caused by heat or flame. Scalds are caused by hot liquids. People can also be burned by chemicals or by electrical currents.

Symptoms

- Depending on the type and severity of the burn, skin may be red, swollen and tender, blistered and raw or charred
- Usually severe pain and possibly shock

Aims

- To obtain immediate medical assistance if the burn is over a large area (as big as the casualty's hand or more) or is deep
- To send for an ambulance if the burn is severe or extensive. If the burn or scald is over a smaller area, the casualty could be transported to hospital by car
- To stop the burning and reduce pain
- To minimise the possibility of infection

Action

1 For major burns, summon immediate medical assistance.

2 Cool down the burn. Keep it flooded with cold water for 10 minutes. If it is a chemical burn, this needs to be done for 20 minutes. Ensure that the contaminated water used to cool a chemical burn is disposed of safely.

3 Remove any jewellery, watches or clothing which are not sticking to the burn.

4 Cover the burn if possible, unless it is a facial burn, with a sterile or at least clean dressing. For a burn on a hand or foot, a clean plastic bag will protect it from infection until it can be treated by an expert.

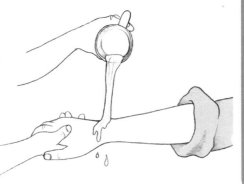

Cool the burn with water

Remember

If a person's clothing is on fire, STOP – DROP – WRAP – ROLL:

- *Stop* him or her from running around.
- Get him/her to *drop* to the ground – push him/her if you have to and can do so safely.
- *Wrap* him/her in something to smother the flames – a blanket or coat, anything to hand. This is better if it is soaked in water.
- *Roll* him/her on the ground to put out the flames.

If clothing is on fire, remember the basics: *stop, drop, wrap* and *roll* the person on the ground.

Do not:

- remove anything which is stuck to a burn
- touch a burn, or use any ointment or cream
- cover facial burns – keep pouring water on until help arrives.

Poisoning

People can be poisoned by many substances, drugs, plants, chemicals, fumes or alcohol.

Symptoms

Symptoms will vary depending on the poison.

- The person could be unconscious
- There may be acute abdominal pain
- There may be blistering of the mouth and lips

Aims

- To remove the casualty to a safe area if he/she is at risk, and it is safe for you to move him/her
- To summon medical assistance as a matter of urgency
- To gather any information which will identify the poison
- To maintain a clear airway and breathing until help arrives

Action

1   If the casualty is unconscious, place him/her in the recovery position to ensure that the airway is clear, and that he/she cannot choke on any vomit.

2   Dial 999 for an ambulance.

3   Try to find out what the poison is and how much has been taken. This information could be vital in saving a life.

4   If a conscious casualty has burned mouth or lips, he or she can be given small frequent sips of water or cold milk.

Do not try to make the casualty vomit.

Electrical injuries

Electrocution occurs when an electrical current passes though the body.

Symptoms

Electrocution can cause cardiac arrest and burns where the electrical current entered and left the body.

Aims

- To remove the casualty from the current when you can safely do so
- To obtain medical assistance as a matter of urgency
- To maintain a clear airway and breathing until help arrives
- To treat any burns

Evidence indicator

Research and write down the steps you would take if you found a person you care for in need of assistance because of an overdose of medication. Keep your notes as evidence.

Action

There are different procedures to follow depending on whether the injury has been caused by a high or low voltage current.

Injury caused by high voltage current

This type of injury may be caused by overhead power cables or rail lines, for example.

1   Contact the emergency services immediately.

2   *Do not* touch the person until all electricity has been cut off.

3   If the person is unconscious, clear the airway.

4   Treat any other injuries present, such as burns.

5   Place in the recovery position until help arrives.

Injury caused by low voltage current

This type of injury may be caused by electric kettles, computers, drills, lawnmowers, etc.

1   Break the contact with the current by switching off the electricity, at the mains if possible.

2   It is vital to break the contact as soon as possible, but if you touch a person who is 'live' (still in contact with the current) you too will be injured. If you are unable to switch off the electricity, then you must stand on something dry which can insulate you, such as a telephone directory, rubber mat or a pile of newspapers, and then move the casualty away from the current as described below.

3   Do not use anything made of metal, or anything wet, to move the casualty from the current. Try to move him/her with a wooden pole or broom-handle, even a chair.

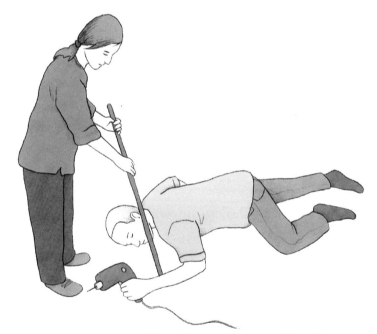

Move the casualty away from the current

4   Alternatively, drag him/her with a rope or cord or, as a last resort, pull by holding any of the person's dry clothing which is *not* in contact with his/her body.

5   Once the person is no longer in contact with the current, you should follow the same steps as with a high voltage injury.

Case Study: Dealing with a health emergency

On the way to lunch one Tuesday, Miss S, who sometimes experiences incontinence, had a little 'accident' in the main hallway. Another resident coming along behind called out, 'Oh look! She's done a puddle!' and stopped to stare. Miss S, feeling embarrassed and distressed, turned quickly to go back to her room and slipped on the wet floor, falling heavily on her hip. The first staff member on the scene was Maria.

1   List the actions that Maria should take, in order.

2   Could this accident have been prevented? If so, how?

Other ways to help

Summon assistance

In the majority of cases this will mean telephoning 999 and requesting an ambulance. It will depend on the setting in which you work and clearly is not required if you work in a hospital! But it may mean calling for a colleague with medical qualifications, who will then be able to make an assessment of the need for further assistance. Similarly, if you work in the residential sector, there should be a medically qualified colleague available. If you are the first on the scene at an emergency in the community, you may need to summon an ambulance for urgent assistance.

If you need to call an ambulance, try to keep calm and give clearly all the details you are asked for. Do not attempt to give details until they are asked for – this wastes time. Emergency service operators are trained to find out the necessary information, so let them ask the questions, then answer calmly and clearly.

Follow the action steps outlined in the previous section while you are waiting for help to arrive.

Assist the person dealing with the emergency

A second pair of hands is invaluable when dealing with an emergency. If you are assisting someone with first aid or medical expertise, follow all his or her instructions, even if you don't understand why. An emergency situation is not the time for a discussion or debate – that can happen later. You may be needed to help to move a casualty, or to fetch water, blankets or dressings, or to reassure and comfort the casualty during treatment.

Make the area safe

An accident or injury may have occurred in an unsafe area – and it was probably for precisely that reason that the accident occurred there! Sometimes, it may be that the accident has made the area unsafe for others. For example, if someone has tripped over an electric flex, there may be exposed wires or a damaged electric socket. Alternatively, a fall against a window or glass door may have left shards of broken glass in the area, or there may be blood or other body fluids on the floor. You may need to make the area safe by turning off the power, clearing broken glass or dealing with a spillage.

It may be necessary to redirect people away from the area of the accident in order to avoid further casualties.

Maintain the privacy of the casualty

You may need to act to provide some privacy for the casualty by asking onlookers to move away or stand back. If you can erect a temporary screen with coats or blankets, this may help to offer some privacy. It may not matter to the casualty at the time, but he or she has a right to privacy if possible.

Make accurate reports

You may be responsible for making a report on an emergency situation you have witnessed, or for filling in records later. Concentrate on the most important aspects of the incident and record the actions of yourself and others in an accurate, legible and complete manner.

How to deal with witnesses' distress – and your own

People who have witnessed accidents can often be very distressed by what they have seen. The distress may be as a result of the nature of the injury, or the blood loss. It could be because the casualty is a friend or relative or simply because seeing accidents or injuries is traumatic. Some people can become upset because they feel helpless and do not know how to assist, or they may have been afraid and then feel guilty later.

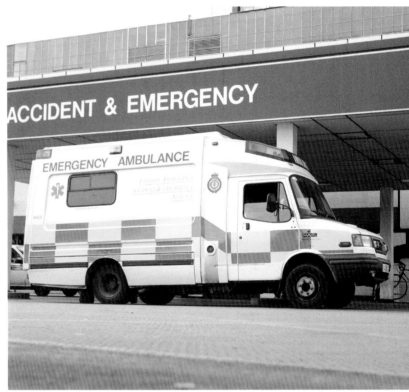

Witnessing accidents is often distressing

You will need to reassure people about the casualty and the fact that he or she is being cared for appropriately. However, do not give false reassurance about things you may not be sure of.

You may need to allow individuals to talk about what they saw. One of the commonest effects of witnessing a trauma is that people need to repeat over and over again what they saw.

What about you?

You may feel very distressed by the experience you have gone through. You may find that you need to talk about what has happened, and that you need to look again at the role you played. You may feel that you could have done more, or you may feel angry with yourself for not having a greater knowledge about what to do.

There is a whole range of emotions which you may experience. Unit HSC 24 covers in detail the different ways to cope with these feelings, but you should be able to discuss them with your supervisor and use any support provided.

If you have followed the basic guidelines in this element, you will have done as much as could be expected of anyone at the scene of an emergency who is not a trained first aider.

Test yourself

1   You should always attempt first aid because it is always better to do something. True or false?

2   What is the single most important thing for an untrained person to do in a health emergency?

3   List three tasks you can carry out at the scene of an emergency which do not necessarily involve first aid.

4   How would you talk to a casualty while you waited for help?

5   What would you say to others who had witnessed the incident?

HSC 22 UNIT TEST

1   Imagine you are just about to start work in a new day-care facility for older people.

   a What kind of substances would you expect to see in the COSHH file?

   b Which tasks would you expect to find in the risk assessment file?

   c Would you expect to see any specialised equipment in the centre? If so, what sort of equipment?

   d What basic precautions would you expect to follow?

   e Do you think there will be an expectation about how you dress? If so, what do you think it will be?

   f What training would you expect to undertake?

   g List at least three security precautions you think the setting might take.

2   Now imagine that you are about to start work in a residential home for teenagers. Answer the same questions, a–g above. Which of your answers are different and which remain the same?

Develop your knowledge and practice

The knowledge and skills addressed in this unit are the key to working effectively in all aspects of your practice. In order to work effectively, it is essential to know how to evaluate your work, how you can improve on what you do, and understand the factors which have influenced your attitudes and beliefs.

The care sector is constantly benefiting from new research, new developments, policies and guidelines. In order to offer the best possible level of service to those you care for, you need to make sure that you are up to date in work practices and knowledge, and aware of current thinking. As a worker in a care setting, you have a responsibility to constantly review and improve your practice. It is the right of service users to expect the best possible quality of care from those who provide it, and high quality care requires all practitioners to regularly reflect on their own practice and look at ways of improving.

Each organisation and each individual owes a **duty of care** to service users; this means that it is your responsibility to make sure that the service provided is the best it can possibly be. This is not an option, but a duty which you accept when you choose to become a professional care worker. The information in this unit will help you to identify the best ways to develop and update your own knowledge and skills.

What you need to learn

- How to explore your own values, interests and beliefs
- How your values, interests and beliefs influence your practice
- Learning from work practice
- How to use feedback and support to improve your practice
- Making good use of training/development opportunities
- Being aware of new developments
- How to ensure your practice is current and up to date.

HSC 23a Evaluate your work

How to explore your own values, interests and beliefs

Everyone has their own values, beliefs and preferences. They are an essential part of who you are. What you believe in, what you see as important and what you see as acceptable or desirable are as much a part of your personality as whether you are shy, outgoing, funny, serious, friendly or reserved.

People whose work involves caring for others need to be more aware than most of how their work can be affected by their beliefs.

Remember

If you worked in a public library, people would continue to borrow and read books that you considered boring, poorly written or distasteful. With the exception of a small number of those who might ask your advice, most of the people for whom you provided a service would remain unaware of your beliefs, interests or values.

However, if you work providing care for others and your work involves forming relationships with vulnerable people and carrying out tasks which affect their health and well-being, your own attitudes, values and beliefs are very important.

The way in which you respond to people is linked to what you believe in, what you consider important and the things that interest you. You may find you react positively to people who share your values and less warmly to people who have different priorities. When you develop friendships it is natural to spend time with people who share your interests and values, those who are 'on your wavelength'.

Choosing your friends and meeting with others who share your interests is one of life's joys and pleasures; however, the professional relationships you develop with people you care for are another matter. As a professional carer you are required to provide the same quality of care for all, not just for those who share your views and beliefs. This may seem obvious, but knowing what you need to do and achieving it successfully are not the same thing.

Professional carers need to provide the same quality of care to all

You may believe that everyone should be treated in the same way, but there can often be differences in approach or attitude you may be unaware of. For example, you may spend more time with someone who is asking your advice about a course of action you think is sensible than you would spend with someone who wanted to do something you considered inadvisable. There are many other ways in which your beliefs, interests and values can affect how you relate to people. Some of these are shown in the table below.

Your beliefs/values/interests	Situation	Possible effect
People have a responsibility to look after their health	You are caring for someone with heart disease who continues to smoke and eats a diet high in fried foods and cream cakes	You find it difficult to be sympathetic when they complain about their condition and you make limited responses
War and violence are wrong and people who fight should not be glorified as heroes	An elderly service user constantly recalls tales of his days as a soldier and wants you to admire his bravery and that of his comrades	You try to avoid spending time chatting with him and limit your contact to providing physical care
Modern chart and disco music	You visit a service user who constantly plays country and western music very loudly	You find it hard not to ask her to turn it down or off. You hurry through your work and your irritation shows in your body language

There is nothing wrong or unusual in behaving differently towards different people – in fact the only way to behave identically towards everyone is to be a robot!

However, it is important that you are aware of it, because it could make a difference to the quality of your work. Being aware of the factors that have influenced the development of your personality is not as easy as it sounds. You may feel you know yourself very well, but knowing *who* you are is not the same as knowing *how* you got to be you.

 Check it out

Step 1
Take a range of items from a newspaper, about six or seven. Make a note of your views on each of them: say what your feelings are on each one – does it shock or disgust you, make you sad, or angry, or grateful that it hasn't happened to you?

Step 2
Try to think about why you reacted in the way you did to each of the items in the newspaper. Think about what may have influenced you to feel that way. The answers are likely to lie in a complex range of factors, including your upbringing and background, experiences you had as a child and as an adult, and relationships you have shared with others.

Unravelling these influences is never easy, and you are not being asked to carry out an in-depth analysis of yourself – simply to begin to realise how your development has been influenced by a series of factors.

Factors which influence our development

Everyone's values and beliefs are affected to different degrees by the same range of factors. These include:

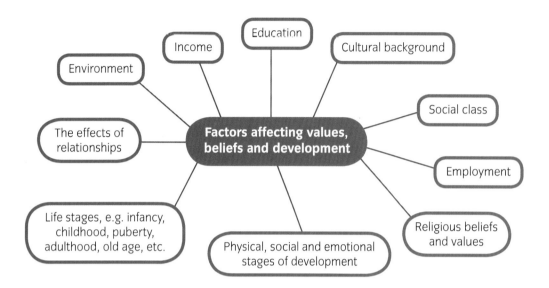

Each of us will be influenced to a greater or lesser degree by some or all of those factors. As each individual is different, the combination of factors and the extent of their influence will be different for each person. It is therefore important that you have considered and reflect on those factors which have influenced your development so that you understand how you became the person you are.

Key influences on development

The following are some of the key influences on your growth and development and on your current values. Some can be classified as belonging to your environment:

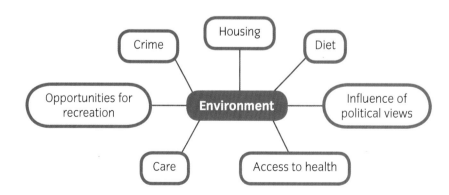

You should be able to begin to see from this how the environment in which you developed may have affected many of your attitudes. You may also have been affected by the social class to which you belonged:

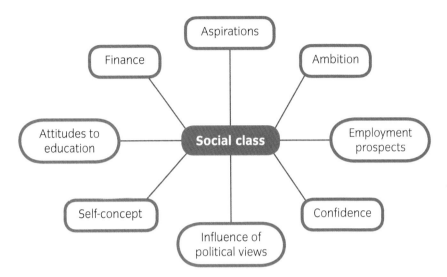

The relationships and emotional bonds you have formed, and the whole of your cultural background, can affect your life in various ways:

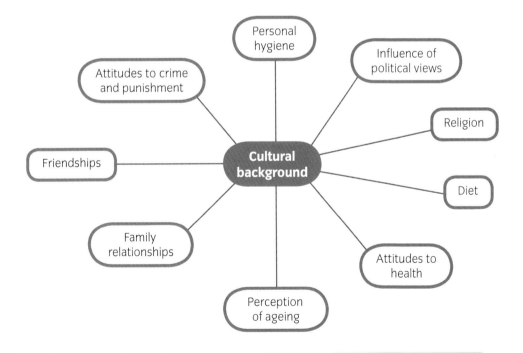

Evidence indicator

Construct spider diagrams for each of the factors which have influenced your development, and from those begin to identify which factors have exercised the greatest influence on you. This exercise should help you to identify what has affected the development of your own personality and abilities, and how this may affect the way in which you work.

Keep your notes as evidence for your portfolio.

How your values, interests and beliefs influence your practice

Once you have begun to identify the major factors which have influenced your development, the next stage is to look at how they have affected the way in which you work and relate both to service users and colleagues. This is the basis of developing into a 'reflective practitioner' – someone who evaluates what he or she does.

Working in care requires that in order to be effective and to provide the best possible service for those you care for, you need to be able to think about and evaluate what you do and the way you work, and to identify your strengths and weaknesses. It is important that you learn to think about your own practice in a constructive way. Reflection and evaluation should not undermine your confidence in your own work; rather you should use them in a constructive way to identify areas which require improvement.

The ability to do this is an indication of excellent practice. Any workers in care who believe that they have no need to improve their practice or to develop and add to their skills and understanding are not demonstrating good and competent practice, but rather an arrogant and potentially dangerous lack of understanding of the nature of work in the care sector.

Becoming a thoughtful practitioner is not about torturing yourself with self-doubts and examining your weaknesses until you reach the point where your self-confidence is at zero! But it is important that you examine the work you have done and identify areas where you know you need to carry out additional development. A useful tool in learning to become a reflective practitioner is to develop a checklist which you can use, either after you have dealt with a difficult situation or at the end of each shift or day's work, to look at your own performance.

Checklist to evaluate practice

1 How did I approach my work?

2 Was my approach positive?

3 How did the way I worked affect the service users?

4 How did the way I worked affect my colleagues?

5 Did I give my work 100 per cent?

6 Which was the best aspect of the work I did?

7 Which was the worst aspect of the work I did?

8 Was this work the best I could do?

9 Are there any areas in which I could improve?

10 What are they, and how will I tackle them?

Learning from work practice

Everything you do at work is part of a process of learning. Even regular tasks are likely to be important for learning because there is always something new each time you do them. A simple task like taking a service user a hot drink may result in a lesson – if, for example, you find that the service user tells you he or she doesn't want tea, but would prefer coffee this morning, thank you! You will have learned a valuable lesson about never making assumptions that everything will be the same.

Learning from working is also about using the huge amount of skills and experience which your colleagues and supervisor will have. Not only will this mean they will be able to pass on knowledge and advice to you, but you have the perfect opportunity to discuss ideas and talk about day-to-day practice in the service you are delivering.

Talking about day-to-day practice with your colleagues is an ideal way to learn

Finding time to discuss work with colleagues is never easy; everyone is busy and you may feel that you should not make demands on their time. But most colleagues and supervisors are happy to talk about good and bad practice and to give guidance and advice whenever they can, so you must develop the skill of timing.

When you have a question, don't choose the moment when your supervisor has a desk overflowing with statistical returns and shift rotas, nor the moment when one of the service users has just tipped a full commode over the bedroom floor! Use supervision time or quiet periods, and take the chance to discuss situations which have arisen, problems you have come across or new approaches you have noticed other colleagues using.

Be sure to choose the right time to ask questions

Check it out

Make notes over the next week about periods of time which seem to be quiet and may offer a good opportunity to talk to a senior colleague. You will also have supervision time with your manager. When you have worked out the good times, take the initiative and raise a question about work you have been doing. It may be something quite straightforward such as 'How do you always manage to keep everything so neat when you do a bedbath?' or more complex such as 'Can you explain why it is OK to let Mr J go out to the shops by himself? It seems such a risk.'

Try this with different experienced colleagues – you will be surprised at how much you will learn.

How to use feedback and support to improve your practice

As already discussed, it is important to regularly examine your own work and consider the ways in which it could have been improved and the strengths and weaknesses of your own practice. However, this is very hard to do without any support from others and without using feedback from colleagues in your workplace. Support networks, whether they are formal or informal, are one of the most effective means of identifying areas of your own practice which need further development.

Case Study: Seeking constructive feedback

L works in a large residential setting for elderly adults where one of the people he cares for is Mrs B, a Pakistani woman who speaks very little English. Mrs B has many relatives who visit her regularly, and has long and animated conversations with them. But when she has no visitors, Mrs B is very quiet. She hardly responds at all when L tries to talk to her and is unwilling to talk to the other residents or to take part in any of the activities on offer. L is concerned that Mrs B may feel isolated; he would like to be able to communicate with her better and to improve his own practice.

1 *What are the barriers to communication between L and Mrs B?*

2 *Who could L speak to about the situation?*

3 *What other actions could he take to improve his practice?*

Formal networks

Formal networks of support are usually put in place by your employer. They are likely to consist of your immediate supervisor and possibly other more senior members of staff on occasions. You are likely to have a regular system of feedback and support meetings, or appraisal sessions, with your supervisor. These could be at differing intervals depending on the system in your particular workplace, but are unlikely to be less frequent than once a month.

These systems are extremely useful in giving you the opportunity to benefit from feedback from your supervisor, who will be fully aware of the work you have been doing, and able to identify areas of practice which you may need to improve and areas in which you have demonstrated strength.

The appraisal or supervision system in your workplace may also be the point at which you identify a programme of development which you need to undertake. Some employers identify this at six-monthly or 12-monthly intervals, and some more frequently. Your supervisor is likely to identify which of the available training and development programmes are appropriate for the areas of your practice which have been identified as needing development.

Making the most of supervision

It is sometimes difficult to take a step back and look at whether your working practices have improved as a result of training, development and increasing experience, so it is very important to seek out and act on feedback from an appropriate person, usually your supervisor.

Asking for feedback on your performance is not always easy – and listening to it can be harder! All of us find it difficult to hear feedback at times, especially if we are being told we could do things better. However, you should learn to welcome feedback – try to think of it as looking in a mirror. You probably never go out without looking in the mirror to check how you look. How will you know how your work performance is looking if you haven't asked anyone who is in a position to tell you?

Your supervisor's role

Your supervisor's role is to support and advise you in your work and to make sure that you know and understand:
- your rights and responsibilities as an employee
- what your job involves and the procedures your employer has in place to help you carry out your job properly
- the philosophy of care where you work – that is, the beliefs, values and attitudes of your employer regarding the way that service users are cared for, and how you can demonstrate values of care in the way you do your work
- your career development needs – the education and training requirements for the job roles you may progress into, as well as for your current job.

Check it out

Ask your supervisor whether there is a policy or plan at work on the supervision of staff.

If there is, read it and note down what it covers, for example how will you be supervised, how often you can expect to be formally supervised and what kinds of things your supervisor will be able to help you with in your work role and career.

If there is no plan for supervision, make a list of the things on which you would like your supervisor's support and agree a time and place to discuss these items with him or her.

Getting the most out of a supervision/appraisal session

Make sure you are well prepared for these sessions with your supervisor so that you can get maximum benefit from them. This will mean bringing together your reflections on your own practice, and using examples and case notes where appropriate. You will need to demonstrate to your supervisor that you have reflected on your own practice and that you have begun identifying areas for development. If you can provide evidence through case notes and records to support this, it will assist your supervisor greatly.

You will also need to be prepared to receive feedback from your supervisor. While feedback is likely to be given in a positive way, this does not mean that it will be uncritical. Many people have considerable difficulty in accepting criticism in any form, even where it is intended to be supportive and constructive. If you are aware that you are likely to have difficulty accepting criticism, try to prepare yourself to view feedback from your supervisor as valuable and useful information which can add to your ability to reflect effectively on the work you are doing.

Check it out

Ask a colleague, or if you don't feel able to do that ask a friend or family member, to offer some constructive criticism on a task you have undertaken – a practical activity such as cooking a meal, work you have done in the garden or in the house, would be suitable.

If you are able to practise receiving feedback on something which is relatively unthreatening, you are more likely to be able to use the same techniques when considering feedback on your working practices.

Your response to negative feedback should not be to defend your actions or to reject the information. You must try to accept and value it. A useful reply would be: 'Thank you, that's very helpful. I can use that next time to improve.' If you are able to achieve this you are likely to make the maximum use of opportunities to improve your practice.

On the other hand, if criticism of any kind undermines your confidence and makes it difficult for you to value your own strengths, you should ask your supervisor to identify areas in which you did well, and use the positive to help you respond more constructively to the negative feedback.

Informal networks

Informal support networks are likely to consist of your work colleagues. These can be major sources of support and assistance. Part of the effectiveness of many teams in many workplaces is their ability to provide useful ideas for improving practice, and support when things go badly.

Informal networks can be major sources of support and assistance

Evidence indicator

Identify any formal and informal support networks in your workplace. Note down the ways in which you use the different types of network and how they support your development. If you identify any gaps or areas where you feel unsupported, discuss this with your supervisor or manager.

Keep your notes as evidence.

Some staff teams provide a completely informal and ad-hoc support system, where people will give you advice, guidance and support as and when necessary. Other teams will organise this on a more regular basis, and they may get together to discuss specific situations or problems which have arisen for members of the team. You need to be sure that you are making maximum use of all opportunities to gain support, advice and feedback on your practice.

Using your mistakes

Everyone makes mistakes – they are one way of learning. It is important not to waste your mistakes, so if something has gone wrong, make sure you learn from it. Discuss problems and mistakes with your supervisor, and work out how to do things differently next time. You will develop as a result of learning from situations which have not worked out the way you planned.

However, it is important that you consider carefully why things turned out the way they did and think about how you will ensure that they go according

to plan next time. Unfortunately, there are real people on the receiving end of our mistakes in care, and learning how not to do it again is vitally important.

Talking to colleagues and supervisors is equally useful when things work out really well. It is just as important to learn why something worked, so that you can repeat it. In order to think about learning from your work, it is helpful to be clear about what you want to achieve and how. Look at the case study below.

 CASE STUDY: Setting aims and objectives

Mr G has been very unhappy since the death of his wife just over a year ago. He has stopped going out and has no interest in meeting other people or becoming involved in any activities. You have to provide domiciliary care to Mr G and decide to support him in re-establishing contact with other people. You make a plan so that you can check how well this has worked.

What needs to be achieved (the aim):

Improve Mr G's social contacts

Goals which help to measure success (objectives):

Mr G to agree to meet local organiser of Age Concern

Mr G to attend St Chad's luncheon club

How to do it (method):

1 Talk to him about meeting the organiser and secure his agreement

2 Arrange the meeting at his home

3 Be there for the meeting

4 Be positive and encouraging

5 Offer to accompany him for his first visit to the luncheon club

6 Arrange transport for his first visit

7 Go with him

This type of plan will help you see if you are achieving your aim at each stage, by checking your progress. You will then know at which point something has not worked and can ask for help if necessary from your colleagues and supervisor. It will also help you to know when something has gone well and your plan has worked. Don't simply pat yourself on the back! Explore why your work went well. Use your supervision time and opportunities to talk with experienced colleagues.

Making good use of training/development opportunities

Personal development is to do with developing the personal qualities and skills that everyone needs in order to live and work with others, such as understanding, empathy, patience, communication and relationship-building. It is also to do with the development of self-confidence, self-esteem and self-respect.

If you look back on the ways in which you have changed over the past five years, you are likely to find that you are different in quite a few ways. Most people change as they mature and gain more life experience. Important experiences such as changing jobs, moving home, illness or bereavement can change people. It is inevitable that your personal development and your professional development are linked – your personality and the way you relate to others are the major tools you use to do your job. Taking advantage of every opportunity to train and develop your working skills will also have an impact on you as a person.

Professional development is to do with developing the qualities and skills that are necessary for the workplace. Examples are teamwork, the ability to communicate with different types of people, time management, organisation, problem solving, decision making and, of course, the skills specific to the job.

Continuous professional development involves regularly updating the skills you need for work. You can achieve this through attending training sessions both on and off the job, and by making the most of the opportunities you have for training by careful planning and preparation.

Key terms

Personal development: Developing the personal qualities and skills needed to live and work with others.

Professional development: Developing the qualities and skills necessary for the workforce.

Legal requirements for training

The Care Standards now lay down the number of trained staff which all residential care establishments must have, and they are periodically inspected by the regulator for each country within the UK. England is regulated by the Commission for Social Care Inspection under the Care Standards Act 2000. The same Act applies in Wales, and facilities are inspected and regulated by the Care Standards Inspectorate for Wales. In Scotland, regulation is by the Care Commission under the Regulation of Care (Scotland) Act 2001. The Social Services Inspectorate inspects social care services in Northern Ireland.

All of the inspectors and regulators apply standards set out in the relevant Acts of Parliament, including clear standards relating to staff training and personal and professional development. All staff are required to undertake induction and foundation training when they first start working in care. There is also a requirement in England and Scotland that at least 50 per cent of staff delivering care must be qualified to NVQ level 2; in Wales, all staff are required to hold or be working towards a level 2 qualification. There are also requirements in the standards that staff receive supervision and are given a personal development plan for ongoing training. Paid training days must be provided. In Wales, there are specific requirements about how many supervision sessions each member of staff must receive during a year.

How to get the best out of training

Your supervisor will work with you to decide on the types of training that will benefit you most. This will depend on the stage you have reached with your skills and experience. There would be little point, for example, in doing a course in advanced micro-surgery techniques if you were at the stage of having just achieved your First Aid certificate! It may be that not all the training you want to do is appropriate for the work you are currently assigned to – you may think that a course in advanced therapeutic activities sounds fascinating, but your supervisor may suggest that a course in basic moving and handling is what you need right now. You will only get the best out of training and development opportunities if they are the right ones for you at the time. There will be opportunities for training throughout your career, and it is important that you work out which training is going to help you to achieve your goals.

Many different types of training opportunities will be open to you

Personal development plans

It is a requirement of many organisations that their staff have personal development plans. A personal development plan is a very important document as it identifies a worker's training and development needs and, because the plan is updated when the worker has taken part in training and development, it also provides a record of participation.

A personal development plan should be worked out with your supervisor, but it is essentially your plan for your career. You need to think about what you want to achieve, and discuss with your supervisor the best ways of achieving your goals.

There is no single right way to prepare a personal development plan, and each organisation is likely to have its own way. However, it should include different development areas, such as practical skills and communication skills, the goals or targets you have set – such as moving and handling, or learning to sign – and a timescale for achieving them. Timescales must be realistic – do not, for example, aim to learn to sign in six weeks, or even six months. But you could aim to complete moving and handling training within six weeks.

When you have set your targets, you need to review how you are progressing towards achieving them – this should happen every six months or so. You need to look at what you have achieved and how your plan needs to be updated.

CASE STUDY: Learning assertiveness

M is a health care support worker in a large hospital, on a busy medical ward. She was very aware of the fact that she lacked assertiveness in the way she dealt with both her colleagues and with many of her service users. M was always the one who agreed to take on additional duties, to run errands and to cover additional tasks which others should have been doing. She knew that she ought to be able to say no, but somehow she couldn't and then became angry and resentful because she felt she was doing far more work than many others on her team.

Her supervisor raised the issue during an appraisal and supervision session and suggested that M should consider attending assertiveness training. Although initially reluctant, M decided to take the opportunity when she saw a local class advertised. After six weeks of attending classes and working with the supportive group she met there, M found that she was able to deal far more effectively with unfair and unreasonable requests from her colleagues and to deal in a firm but pleasant way with her service users. Overall, M's practice improved significantly because of her increase in confidence and her ability to deal with her colleagues and service users more effectively.

1 *Have you ever said 'yes' to extra work or additional responsibility when you wanted to say 'no'?*

2 *How did this make you feel?*

3 *What could you have done about it?*

How to use training and development

Every formal training opportunity you take part in should be in your plan. You should work with your supervisor to prepare for the training and to review it afterwards. You may want to prepare for a training session by:

- reading any materials which have been provided in advance
- talking to your supervisor or a colleague who has attended similar training, about what to expect
- thinking about what you want to achieve as a result of attending the training.

Keys to good practice: Training

Make the most of training by:

✓ preparing well

✓ taking a full part in the training and asking questions about anything you don't understand

✓ collecting any handouts and keeping your own notes of the training.

Think about how to apply what you have learned to your work by discussing the training with your supervisor later. Review the ways in which you have benefited from the training.

Different ways of learning

Formal training and development is not the only way you can expand your knowledge and understanding. There are plenty of other ways to keep up progress towards the goals you have set in your personal development plan. Not everyone learns best from formal training. Other ways people learn include:

- being shown by more experienced colleagues – this is known as 'sitting next to Nellie'
- reading textbooks, journals and articles
- following up information on the Internet
- asking questions and holding professional discussions with colleagues and managers.

One way of learning is to be shown by a more experienced colleague

Check it out

Write down the different ways of learning that you have experienced. Have you, for example, studied a course at college, worked through a distance-learning programme or attended hands-on training sessions? Tick the learning methods which have been the most enjoyable and most successful for you.

How could you use this information about how you best like to learn in order to update your workplace skills?

Here is a checklist of ways of learning that you might find useful:

- watching other people
- asking questions and listening to the answers
- finding things out for yourself
- going to college and attending training courses
- studying a distance-learning course or a course on the Internet.

CASE STUDY: Opportunities for learning

P was a support worker in a young person's unit run by the local authority youth justice team. He was providing support for young people who were involved with the criminal justice system but were still living in the community, who occasionally needed time out in the unit or attended regularly as part of the requirements of the court. P was aware that his knowledge of the legislation relating to young people and to the criminal justice system was not as comprehensive as it ought to be. He often felt unsure when some of his colleagues were referring to Acts of Parliament by short-hand names or by simply quoting dates, and he felt uncertain in answering some of the queries that the young people put to him.

P raised this issue with his line manager, who immediately found that training days were provided by the local authority that would help P to learn about the relevant legislation. Following his training days, P felt far more confident, as not only had he learned a great deal during the course itself, he had also been given some handouts and been informed about useful textbooks. He made sure that he spent some of his own time, in addition to the training days, reading and re-reading the handouts and the textbooks until he felt he had enough knowledge to practise in a way which would be of the greatest benefit to the young people using the centre.

1   *Are you confident about your knowledge of your own work setting?*

2   *If not, what steps are you taking to improve it?*

Evidence indicator

Think about the last training or development session you took part in and write a short report.

- Describe the preparations you made beforehand so that you could benefit fully from it.
- Describe what you did at the session; for example, what and how did you contribute, and what did you learn? Do you have a certificate to show that you participated in the session? Do you have a set of notes?
- How did you follow up the session? Did you review the goals you had set yourself, or discuss the session with your supervisor?
- Describe how you have used what you learned at the session. For example, how has the way you work changed, and how have your service users and colleagues benefited from your learning?

Test yourself

1   List at least three factors which can influence the way you work.

2   Why are personal development plans important?

3   Who would you ask to help you to prepare a personal development plan?

4   Do you agree with the requirements in the Care Standards for training? Give reasons for your answer.

HSC 23b Use new and improved skills and knowledge in your work

The health and social care sector is one which constantly changes and moves on. New standards reflect the changes in the profession, such as the emphasis on quality services, the focus on tackling exclusion, and the influence of the culture of rights and responsibilities. There has been a huge increase in understanding in all parts of the sector, and a recognition of the satisfaction that comes from working alongside service users as partners and directors of their own care, rather than as passive receivers of services.

Developments in technology have brought huge strides towards independence for many service users, thus promoting a changing relationship with carers; at the same time, technological developments have brought different approaches to the way in which work in care is carried out and the administration and recording of service provision.

Legislation and the resulting guidelines are a feature of the work of the sector. Sadly, many of the new guidelines, policies and procedures result from enquiries and investigations which followed tragedies, errors and neglect.

Despite all this, much of what we do in the care sector will remain the same; the basic principles of caring, treating people with dignity and respect, ensuring they have choice and promoting independence will continue, and the skills of good communication remain as vital as ever.

Being aware of new developments

There are many ways in which you can ensure that you keep up to date with new developments in the field of care, and particularly those which affect your own area of work. You should not assume that your workplace will automatically inform you about new developments, changes and updates which affect your work – you must be prepared to actively maintain your own knowledge base and to ensure that your practice is in line with current thinking and new theories. The best way to do this is to incorporate an awareness of the need to constantly update your knowledge into all of your work activities. If you restrict your awareness of new developments to specific times, such as a monthly visit to the library, or a training course every six months, you are likely to miss out on a lot of information.

Sources of information

The media

The area of health and care is always in the news, so it is relatively easy to find out information about new studies and research. You will need to pay attention when watching television and listening to radio news bulletins to find out about new developments, legislation, guidelines and reports related to health and care service users and workers.

T is a support worker, working with a young woman in the community who suffers from multiple sclerosis. T's work enables the young woman to live an independent life.

T spent many years working in a residential setting and is very experienced in dealing with people with disabilities. However, her knowledge of multiple sclerosis was limited. One day she noticed an advertisement for a conference which was describing the outcome of the latest research into multiple sclerosis, so she arranged cover for a day while she went to the conference and found out more about potential new treatments and ways in which symptoms of MS could be eased. She was able to discuss this in detail with the young woman she worked with, and with her agreement she discussed it with her doctor. As a result some new plans for treatment were developed and tried out.

1 *What difference is T's new knowledge likely to make to her service user?*

2 *What difference is T's new knowledge likely to make to herself?*

Articles in newspapers and professional journals are excellent sources of information. When reporting on a recently completed study, they usually give information about where to obtain a copy of it.

Conferences

Professional journals also carry advertisements for conferences and training opportunities. You may also find such information in your workplace. There is often a cost involved in attending these events, so the restrictions of the training budget in your workplace may mean that you cannot attend. However, it may be possible for one person to attend and pass on the information gained to others in the workplace, or to obtain conference papers and handouts without attending.

Check it out

For one week keep a record of every item which relates to health and care services which you hear on a radio bulletin, see in a television programme, or read in a newspaper article. You are likely to be surprised at the very large number of references you manage to find.

The Internet

The development of information technology, and in particular the Internet, has provided a vast resource of information, views and research.

There are clearly some limitations to using the Internet; for example, many people are reluctant to look for information through that route because they are not confident about using computers. However, the use of computers in the health and care sector is becoming increasingly widespread and important. If you have access to a computer, using the Internet is a simple process that you could easily learn.

Another disadvantage is that you need to be wary of the information you obtain on the Internet, unless it is from accredited sources

such as a government department, a reputable university or college, or an established research centre. Make every effort to check the validity of what you are reading. The World Wide Web provides free access to vast amounts of information, but it is an unregulated environment – anyone can publish information on the Internet, and there is no requirement for it to be checked or approved. People can publish their own views and opinions, which may not be based on fact. These views and opinions from a wide range of people are valuable and interesting in themselves, but be careful that you do not assume anything to be factually correct unless it is from a reliable source.

Treated with care, the Internet can prove to be one of the speediest and most useful tools in obtaining up-to-date information.

Your supervisor and colleagues

Never overlook the obvious: one of the sources of information which may be most useful to you is close at hand – your own workplace supervisor and colleagues. They may have many years of experience and accumulated knowledge which they will be happy to share with you. They may also be updating their own practice and ideas, and may have information that they would be willing to share.

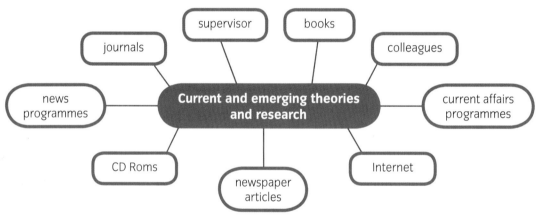

Information can be found from a wide range of sources

How to ensure your practice is current and up to date

There is little point in reading articles, watching TV programmes and attending training days if your work practice is not updated and improved as a result. With the enormous pressures on everybody in the health and care services, it is often difficult to find time to keep up to date and to change the practices you are used to. Any form of change takes time and is always a little uncomfortable or unusual to begin with. So when we are under pressure because of the amount of work we have to do, it is only normal that we tend to rely on practices, methods and ways of working which are comfortable, familiar and can be done swiftly and efficiently.

You will need to make a very conscious effort to incorporate new learning into your practice. Your personal development plan should include time for updating your knowledge, and incorporating it into your practice. You could try the following ways to ensure that you are using the new knowledge you have gained.

Keys to good practice: Applying new skills and knowledge in practice

✓ Plan out how you will adapt your practice on a day-to-day basis, adding one new aspect each day. Do this until you have covered all the aspects of the new information you have learned.

✓ Discuss with your supervisor and colleagues what you have learned and how you intend to change your practice, and ask for feedback on how it is going.

✓ Write a checklist for yourself and check it at the end of each day.

✓ Give yourself a set period of time, for example one month, to alter or improve your practice, and review it at the end of that time.

New knowledge is not only about the most exciting emerging theories. It is also often about mundane and day-to-day aspects of your practice, which are just as important and can make just as much difference to the quality of care you provide for your service users.

CASE STUDY: Skills training

W worked as a home carer in a large team. She was very experienced and an extremely good carer, and was keen to apply for promotion when a team manager's job became available. However, when she received the job description and person specification for the job role, it was obvious that the person appointed would be doing a considerable amount of administration and would have to have a working knowledge of computers and a range of standard software packages. W did not even know how to turn on a computer!

She realised that if she was ever to achieve promotion she would need to understand information technology and overcome her fear of computers and all things technological. W signed up for an 'Introduction to Computers' evening class at her local college and spent a year developing new skills. At the end of the year she was able to achieve her Key Skills in Information Technology and successfully applied for promotion to team manager.

W now uses computer technology as a part of her job every day and can't imagine a time when she didn't know how to use it.

1 *In what other ways could W have responded to the job description information?*

2 *What are the benefits of responding as she did?*

3 *Who gains from W's new skills?*

Evidence indicator

Think about an occasion when you have been able to reflect on an area of your own practice or knowledge which needed improvement, and the steps you took to achieve the improvement. Record what you did and also how you incorporated the new knowledge into your practice. Once you have identified this and recorded it in detail, you should include it in your NVQ portfolio as part of the evidence that you will need to achieve this unit.

Test yourself

1 Name three ways of finding out current and up-to-date information about care practice.

2 Why does it matter that you keep your practice up to date?

3 How could you make sure that you get the most benefit from new knowledge after a training session?

4 Name three ways your practice has changed in the past two years because of new knowledge you have gained.

HSC 23 UNIT TEST

1 What are the factors that can influence the way people work in health and care?

2 What is the key difference between working in health and care and working in most other jobs?

3 What are the most effective ways of reflecting on your own practice?

4 Describe the differences between formal and informal support networks.

5 How would you ensure that you gain the maximum benefit from a supervision session?

6 Name five sources of information where you could find new learning to improve your practice.

Ensure your own actions support the care, protection and well-being of individuals

Caring for individuals is about making sure that you value everyone you work with as an individual, and that you treat them with respect and make sure that they can enjoy life with the dignity that every individual deserves. Well-being is about much more than just health; it is about every part of people's lives including feeling safe, valued and respected. Choice, as much independence as possible and the opportunity to reach your own potential are the key factors in achieving individual well-being.

Feeling safe is also an important part of well-being and everyone has the right to be protected from abuse and harm. You have an important role in making sure that you notice and report signs of abuse.

What you need to learn

- Empowerment
- Relationships
- Active support
- Dealing with conflicts
- Dealing with challenging behaviour
- Treating people as individuals
- How to recognise your own prejudices
- Anti-discriminatory and anti-oppressive practice
- Individuals' rights
- Law, rights and discrimination
- Steps you can take to reduce discrimination
- Forms of abuse
- Signs and symptoms which may indicate abuse
- Who can abuse?
- How to report and record information
- The effects of abuse
- How the law affects what you do.

HSC 24a Relate to and support individuals in a way they choose

Empowerment

One of the vitally important aspects of your job is making sure that people are able to make choices and take control over as much of their lives as possible. This is called **empowerment**, which simply means doing everything you can in your own practice and in your own work setting to make sure people can do this.

Many people who receive care services are often unable to make choices about their lives. This can be because of a range of different circumstances, but it can be because of the way essential services are provided.

In our own daily lives we take many things for granted. You can usually make basic choices in your life without even having to think about them. For example:

you will choose whether to go out or stay in

you will choose the clothes you wear

you will choose what you eat and when you eat it

you will choose the shops and buildings you go into

you will choose the people you see, and those you don't

Most of the time you give little thought to these choices. However, if you consider the individuals in your own setting, you will realise that not all of them have the same options and choices as you do.

Check it out

For a couple of days, keep a list of the choices you make about everyday aspects of your life – use some of the examples above to start you off, but you will soon notice many more.

Now, think about the individuals in your work setting. Write down next to each item on your list the names of individuals who are also able to make the same choice. Do these individuals have all the same choices as you?

In order to understand the importance of the effects of empowerment you must understand what can happen to people who feel that they are powerless in relation to their day-to-day activities. How much we value ourselves – our **self-esteem** – is a result of many factors, but a very important one is the extent of control, or power, we have over our lives.

Of course, many other factors influence our self-esteem, such as:

- the amount of encouragement and praise we have had from important people in our lives, such as parents and teachers
- whether we have positive and happy relationships with other people
- the amount of stimulation and satisfaction we get from our work – paid or unpaid.

Individuals who are unable to exercise choice and control may very soon suffer lower self-esteem and lose confidence in their own abilities. Unfortunately, this means they may become convinced that they are unable to do many tasks for themselves, and that they need help in most areas of their day-to-day lives. It is easy to see how such a chain of events can result in people becoming dependent on others and less able to do things for themselves. Once this downward spiral has begun it can be difficult to stop, so it is far better to avoid the things that make it begin.

Individuals should be given the opportunity to make choices

Self-esteem has a major effect on people's health and well-being. People with a confident, positive view of themselves, who believe that they have value and worth, are far more likely to be happy and healthy than someone whose self-esteem is poor and whose confidence is low.

People who have a positive and confident outlook are far more likely to be interested and active in the world around them, while those lacking confidence and belief in their own abilities are more likely to be withdrawn and reluctant to try anything new. It is easy to see how this can affect someone's quality of life and reduce his or her overall health and well-being.

Empowerment for service users

Empowerment means that people can make choices about the services they receive and the ways in which they receive them. For example, it is often the case that individuals are told the level of support they will receive and the days on which they will receive it. They may even be told the times at which they will receive such help. The reasons for this are obvious: all services have limited budget and staff resources, and these have to be managed in order to provide the best possible service for the largest number of people. However, this leaves a circle to be squared. Organisations that plan and deliver services have to respond on a general scale; they will try to take into account individual needs, but the nature of organisations makes it difficult to do so effectively.

The point at which practices can be adapted to meet needs and empower individuals, their families and carers, is when the care worker delivering the service meets and interacts with the individual. There are many ways in which you can ensure that your own practice empowers individuals as far as possible.

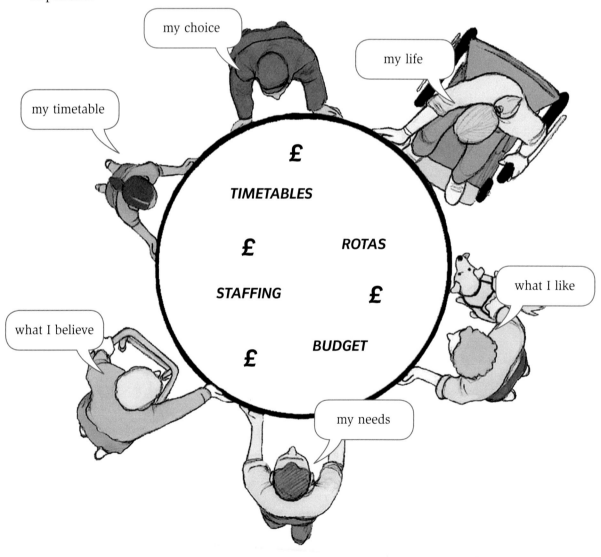

The circle to be squared

Ways in which you can promote choice

Promoting choice and empowerment is about identifying the practical steps you can take in day-to-day activities to give individuals more choice and more opportunities to take decisions. Much of this will depend on your work setting and the particular needs of the individuals, but some aspects of empowerment are common to many settings and most individuals.

If self-esteem is about how we *value* ourselves, **self-concept** (or self-image) is about how we *see* ourselves. These two are different, but both are equally important when you are working. Everyone has a concept of themselves – it can be a positive image overall or a negative one, but a great many factors contribute to an individual sense of identity.

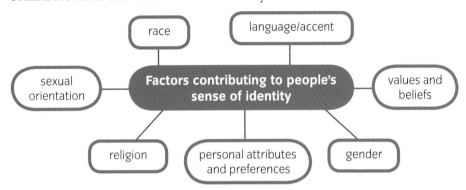

All of these are aspects of our lives which contribute towards our idea of who we are. As a care worker it is essential that you consider how each of the individuals you work with will have developed a self-concept.

As part of empowering individuals, you will need to consider how you can promote their own sense of identity. This is not as difficult as it sounds! It is about making sure that you recognise that the values, beliefs, tastes and preferences which individuals have – the things that make them who they are – must be supported, nurtured and encouraged, and not ignored and discounted because they are inconvenient or don't fit in with the care system.

Showing respect

In your role as a care worker, you will come across situations where a little thought or a small change in practice could give greater opportunities for people to feel valued and respected. For example, you may need to find out how an individual likes to be addressed. Is 'Mr' or 'Mrs' considered more appropriate, or is the person happy for a first name to be used? This, particularly for some older people, can be an important way of indicating respect.

You will need to give thought to the values and beliefs which individuals may have, for example:
- religious or cultural beliefs about eating specific foods
- values about forms of dress which are acceptable
- beliefs or preferences about who should be able to provide personal care.

What you need to do

You need to make sure that people have been asked about religious or cultural preferences and those preferences are recorded so that all care workers and others providing care are able to access them.

There may already be arrangements in your workplace to ask for and record this information. If so, you must ensure that you are familiar with the process and that you know where to find the information for every individual you work with. If your workplace does not have arrangements in place to find out about people's choices and preferences, you should discuss with your line manager ways in which you can help to find this out.

How you need to do it

The prospect of having to ask people questions about their background, values and beliefs can be quite daunting. But it is quite rare for people to be offended by you showing an interest in them! Simple, open questions, asked politely, are always the best way:

Excuse me Mr Khan, the information I have here notes that you are a Muslim. Can you tell me about any particular foods you don't wish to eat?

You can obtain some information by observation – looking at someone can tell you a lot about their preferences in dress, for example. Particular forms of clothing worn for religious or cultural reasons are usually obvious (a turban or a sari, for instance, are easy to spot), but other forms of dress may also give you some clues about the person wearing them. Think about how dress can tell you about the amount of money people are used to spending on clothes, or what kind of background they come from. Clothes also tell you a lot about someone's age and the type of lifestyle they are likely to be used to. Beware, however – any information you think you gain from this type of observation must be confirmed by checking your facts. Otherwise it is easy to be caught out – some people from wealthy backgrounds wear cheap clothes, and some people in their seventies wear the latest fashions and have face lifts!

Look at the form, or other means of recording information, which is used in your workplace to set down the cultural or religious preferences of individuals. Fill it in as if you were a service user. Note down all the factors which make you who you are. Think about:

- gender
- age
- background
- economic and social circumstances
- nationality
- culture
- religion
- sexual orientation
- food preferences
- entertainment preferences
- relaxation preferences
- reading material preferences.

Look at the form you have completed – would it tell care workers enough about you so they could ensure that you were able to be the same person you were before receiving a care service? If not, think about which other questions you would need to ask, and note them down. Make sure that, if appropriate, you ask those questions.

Keep your forms and notes as evidence for your portfolio.

How to give people choice

In the activity on page 104 you looked at the limitations experienced by some people in making choices about their lives. One of the major ways in which you can promote empowerment is to support individuals in being able to make choices. This could be something relatively simple like asking 'what time would you like to eat?', although even this may not be easy to achieve in some residential settings. It could be something far more complex, like making difficult travel and mobility arrangements for someone to get to a particular place for a religious service or a family or social occasion.

Where individuals want to make choices about their lives, you should ensure that you do your best to help them to identify any barriers they may meet and then offer support in overcoming them. If you are working with individuals who are living in their own homes, it is likely to be easier for them to make day-to-day choices about their lives. In some situations they may require help and support in order to achieve the choice, but it is generally less restrictive than a residential or hospital setting, where the needs of many other people also have to be taken into account.

For many disabled individuals living in their own homes, the direct payment scheme has provided a far higher level of choice and empowerment than was possible previously. This system means that payments for the provision of services are made to the disabled individual, who then employs carers directly and determines his or her own levels and types of service. If you think about the implications of this and how it changes the relationship between the disabled individual and the care workers, you can see that this system puts the disabled individual in a position of power – the exact opposite of the position of many other individuals who are not able to exercise that level of control over the service they receive.

You will not be in a position to offer individuals a great deal of choice over the types of services they receive, but you can certainly take steps to ensure that, as far as possible, they are able to make choices about important aspects of their lives. Here are some simple steps to follow.

Keys to good practice: Empowerment: allowing people to make choices

✓ Always ask individuals about their needs, wishes and preferences – whether this is the service they want and if this is the way they want to receive it.

✓ Ask if they prefer other alternatives, either in the service or the way it is delivered.

✓ Look for ways you can actively support individuals in achieving the choice they want – not for reasons why this is impossible.

The process doesn't have to turn into one where you ask a series of demanding questions. It can simply be a matter of checking with the individual as you work, as in the example below.

Mrs Jones, would you like to wear the blue dress today, or is there another one you would prefer?

Well, I did want to wear that grey spotty skirt with the pink blouse today, but I don't think it's back from the laundry, so I can't.

Let me go down to the laundry and find out if it's ready. If there's any way I can get it for you, I will.

Thank you.

The worker in this example has offered Mrs Jones a choice about clothes. Mrs Jones has indicated that she is not happy with the choice offered, and she has also identified the possible barrier to having the clothes she wants. The care worker has looked for a way that the barrier may possibly be overcome. This process can be used in a wide range of situations.

Sometimes individuals are not able, because of the nature of a particular condition or illness, to identify choices or to take part in decision making. In these circumstances, it is important that you make every effort to involve them as far as they are able. For example, if an individual communicates differently from you as the result of a particular condition, or there are language differences, it is important that you ensure the communication differences are reduced as far as possible so that the individual can take part in discussions and decisions. This may involve using specific communication techniques, or arranging to have help from an appropriate specialist. For example:

- if you are communicating with a deaf individual, you may need to arrange for a sign language interpreter
- if you are communicating with someone who has speech difficulties following a stroke, you may need to use visual communication
- if you are communicating with an individual whose first language you do not speak, you will need to use an interpreter.

All of these steps will allow individuals to be involved in decisions.

In other circumstances, you may be dealing with individuals who are not able to fully participate in all decisions about their day-to-day lives because they have a different level of understanding. This could, for example, include individuals with learning difficulties, dementia or brain injury. In this situation, it may be that the individual has an advocate who represents his or her interests and is able to present a point of view to those who are providing services. The advocate may be a professional advocate such as a solicitor, social worker or a rights worker, or it could be relative or friend. It is essential that you include the advocate in discussions as far as possible, to make sure that the individual's point of view is taken into account.

CASE STUDY: Empowerment

E is 78 years old, and she lives alone in her own home. She is mentally alert, but is profoundly deaf. E has difficulty in undertaking day-to-day domestic tasks and some of her personal care as she has severe osteoporosis which has made movement difficult and painful. Presently E receives care three times a week for support with domestic activities and bathing. It is proposed that the timing of her visits be altered, so that the carer will visit in the afternoon instead of the morning as at present.

1 *How will you ensure that E is made aware of the proposed change?*
2 *What steps will you take to allow her to express her views about the change?*
3 *How will you make sure that E's views are treated with value and respect ?*
4 *How will you make sure that E feels valued during the process?*
5 *How can you empower E in this situation?*

Keep up with the changes

As you work with individuals and encourage them to make their own choices, it is likely that you will notice changes in their condition which mean that current services are no longer appropriate. For example, you may have been so successful in encouraging an individual to develop the confidence to go out to the shops that some local transport is now needed. Alternatively, you may have noticed that someone's mobility has deteriorated to the extent that additional support is now needed. Make sure that any such changes are noted in the care plan and reported to your manager.

Check it out

Using the list you made earlier of your own choices, make notes about the differences which could be made to the life of each individual you work with if he or she was able to make the choices you have identified.

Relationships

Being able to develop effective working relationships with individuals is an essential skill for a professional care worker. Making a working relationship with an individual is about using all your communication skills, but it also means establishing a two-way process and making a connection with the other person. We all experience many types of relationships, and you need to understand how they are different and what makes them work, so that you can make useful relationships with the individuals you work with.

Different types of relationships

Everyone has a wide range of relationships with different people, ranging from family to work colleagues. Each of the different types of relationship is important and plays a valuable role in contributing to the overall well-being of each of us. However, the needs and demands of different types of relationships are varied, as are the effects that relationships can have on individuals' views of themselves and the confidence with which they deal with the world.

Types of relationships	Features of relationship
Family relationships	These are relationships with parents, grandparents, siblings and children. Depending on the type of family, they can be close or distant.
Sexual relationships	These relationships can be long or short term. They can be with a spouse or permanent partner, or can be shorter-term non-permanent relationships. The impact of sexual relationships is different from family relationships and more intense than the demands of friendship.
Friendships	Friendships can be long term or can be short term but quite intense. Most people have a few close friends and a much larger circle of friends who are not quite so intimate or close. These may be friends who are part of a wide social circle, but perhaps not close enough to share intimate details. Close friends, on the other hand, are often the ones who are an immediate source of support in times of difficulty, and the first with whom good news is shared.

Continued

Types of relationships	Features of relationship
Working relationships	These can be relationships with employers or with work colleagues. Some may become friendships, but most people relate to work colleagues in a different way from the way they would relate to friends. For example, work colleagues may share very little information about their personal lives even though they may have very close and regular day-to-day contact. It is perfectly possible to spend a great deal more time with work colleagues than with friends, but not to be as close.

We all develop relationships that are important to our lives

Professional caring relationships

As a professional working in a care setting, the relationships you form with service users and work colleagues are essential to providing an effective service.

You will need to make use of all the communication skills you have learned in order to develop relationships which make service users feel valued as individuals, respected and treated with dignity. The caring relationship must provide support and, most importantly, should empower the individual to become as independent as possible.

Working relationships with colleagues should be based on a professional respect for the skills and work of others, and consideration for the demands that work roles place on others. Workloads and responsibility should be shared as appropriate, and so should information and knowledge where this does not conflict with the principles of confidentiality.

Active support

The feeling of having achieved something is a feeling everyone can identify with – regardless of the size of the achievement or its significance when viewed from a wider perspective. Most achievements which give us pleasure are relatively small – passing a driving test, finishing a run, clearing a garden, passing an exam, putting together a set of flat-pack bookshelves …

Key terms

Active support: Support that encourages individuals to maintain their independence and to achieve their potential.

Achievement does not have to mean reaching the North Pole or climbing Everest, or winning the World Cup. Achievements that are much smaller and closer to home are those which provide a sense of fulfilment for most people.

Working with individuals to help them have a sense of achievement is a key part of caring. It is tempting to undertake tasks *for* people you work with because you are keen to care for them and because you believe that you can make their lives easier. Often, however, you need to hold back from directly providing care or carrying out a task, and look for ways you can enable individuals to undertake the task for themselves.

For example, it may be far easier, less painful and quicker for you to put on people's socks or stockings for them. But this would reinforce the fact that they are no longer able to undertake such a simple task for themselves. Time spent in providing a 'helping hand' stocking aid, and showing them how to use it, means that they can put on their own clothing and instead of feeling dependent, have a sense of achievement and independence.

Support individuals to carry out the exercises they can manage; all achievement is relative to people's circumstances

Sometimes you need to realise that achievement is relative to the circumstances of the individual. What may seem an insignificant act can actually be a huge achievement for a particular individual. Someone recovering from a stroke who succeeds in holding a piece of cutlery for the first time may be achieving something that has taken weeks or even months of physiotherapy, painful exercise and huge determination. The first, supported steps taken by someone who has had a hip replacement represent a massive achievement in overcoming pain, fear and anxiety.

What you need to do

Supporting people by encouraging and recognising their achievements is one of the best parts of being a professional carer. Sometimes you may need to spend time guiding individuals and encouraging them in order for them to achieve something.

Check it out

Think about some of the achievements in your life. Note them down in the order of their importance to you. You may be surprised to find that some of the achievements which seem the smallest are actually the most important in your life. If possible, sit down with a colleague or friend and try to explain why the achievements on your list are important. If you are not able to discuss them with anyone else, make notes instead.

- You may need to steady someone's hand while they write a thank-you note, but it is far better that you spend time doing this rather than write it for them.
- You could accompany a service user on many trips round the supermarket, and eventually wait in the car park while he or she goes in alone.
- You could demonstrate to an individual with poor motor control how to create pictures by painting with the fingers.

If you want a real insight into the process of celebrating achievements which may seem small to others but have huge significance, ask the parent of any disabled child!

Make sure you always recognise and celebrate achievements. Think about it – whenever you have achieved something, you usually wanted to share it with someone. Your enthusiasm and recognition are important.

Always recognise and celebrate achievements

Dealing with conflicts

Not all relationships are plain sailing. There are inevitably times when stresses and strains show, and you can find yourself faced with conflict, arguments, angry people or even potential violence. These situations are always difficult, but you can develop skills in dealing with them.

Most care settings, whether residential or providing day-care services, involve living, sharing and working with others. Any situation which involves close and prolonged contact with others has the potential to be difficult. You only have to think about the day-to-day conflicts and difficulties which arise in most families to realise the issues involved when human beings get together in a group.

Disagreements between service users, particularly in residential or day-care settings, are not unusual and you may well find yourself being called on to act as referee. The conflicts can range from disputes over particular chairs or TV channels, to political disagreements or complaints about the behaviour of

others. Conflict resolution is never an easy task, wherever you are and however large or small a scale you are working on. However, there are some basic guidelines to follow:

- remain calm and speak in a firm, quiet voice – do not raise your voice
- make it clear that physical violence is unacceptable
- make it clear that verbal abuse will not be tolerated
- listen in turn to both sides of the argument – don't let people interrupt each other
- look for reasonable compromises which involve both parties in winning some points and losing others
- make it clear to both sides that they will have to compromise – that total victory for one or the other is not an option.

A wide range of difficulties can arise. They can be about behaviour which is unacceptable and causes distress to others, such as playing loud music or shouting. They can also be about matters which seem trivial but can cause major irritation when people live together, such as the way someone eats, or the fact that they mutter out loud as they read the newspaper.

Sometimes conflicts can arise about behaviour which is not anyone's fault, but is the result of someone's illness or condition. For instance, sometimes people experiencing some forms of dementia may shout and moan loudly, which may be distressing and annoying to others. Some people may eat messily or dribble as the result of a physical condition, which may be unpleasant and upsetting for those who share a table with them. These situations require a great deal of tact and explanation. It is simply not possible for the individuals concerned to stop their behaviour, so those around them have to be helped to understand the reasons and to cope with the consequences.

Dealing with challenging behaviour

People's behaviour is as much a means of communication as a facial expression or their words. If people are behaving in an unusual way or present you with a challenge, this tells you something of how they feel about what is going on around them.

You may find yourself dealing with behaviour which is new to you, or behaviour which you have seen before but with individuals you have never met. The type of behaviour which can make relationships difficult can vary in different settings. Each workplace will have policies to deal with challenging behaviour, and you must make sure that you are familiar with them. You should also discuss with your supervisor the types of behaviour you are likely to come across in your workplace.

If you have some knowledge of an individual's background, culture and beliefs, it may be easier to see why he or she is behaving in a particular way. This does not make it acceptable, just easier to understand. For example, an individual who has been in a position of wealth or power may be used to giving people instructions and expecting to have immediate attention, and

Check it out

Find out about your workplace policy for dealiing with challenging behaviour. Talk to your supervisor or senior colleagues about the ways it works in practice.

may be quite rude if it does not happen. This type of attitude is obviously not going to be tolerated, but approaching the situation with some understanding allows people to maintain their dignity while adapting their behaviour.

Many care workers have to deal with verbal abuse or aggression from service users. This may be related to anger and frustration, or it may be caused by the medical condition of the service user. Clearly, reasonable communication is not possible with someone who is being aggressive and abusive, and the situation needs to be calmed before communication can begin.

Communication with people who are violently angry is difficult and, as a general rule, should be undertaken by highly experienced and skilled staff. If you find you are faced with this situation you should speak loudly (without shouting), firmly and clearly. Do not ask questions or enter into a discussion – you should issue short, clear instructions such as 'Stop shouting – now', 'Move way from Jim', 'Go into my office', and so on. This type of short, firm instruction has a chance of defusing the situation and restoring enough calm for problems to be investigated.

Potentially violent situations

There are some situations when verbal abuse and aggressive behaviour turn to violence, and this places you and service users at risk. You should never try to deal with a violent situation alone – you should always get help.

Be alert to the situation you are in and take some common-sense precautions: make sure that you know where the exits are, and move so that the aggressor is not between you and the exit; notice if there is anything which could be used as a weapon, and try to move away from it; make sure that the aggressor has enough personal space, and do not crowd him or her.

If you are faced with a violent situation, you should try to remain calm (even though that is easier said than done!) and not resort to violence or aggression yourself.

It is often the case that a simple technique like holding up a hand in front of you, as if you were directing traffic, and shouting 'Stop' may deflect an attacker, or stop him or her long enough for you to get away. You should remove yourself from the situation as speedily as possible.

If there are other, vulnerable people at risk, you must decide whether you can summon help more effectively from outside or inside the situation.

If you decide to remain, you must summon help at once. You should do one of the following:

- press a panic alarm or buzzer, if one is provided
- shout 'help!' very loudly and continuously
- send someone for help
- call the police, or security, or shout for someone else to do so.

Do not try to be a hero – that is not your job.

Remember

The basic rule is to follow the policies of your workplace in dealing with the particular behaviour, but do not be concerned about trying to communicate effectively until you have dealt with the behaviour and the situation is calm enough for communication to be possible.

HSC 24b Treat individuals with respect and dignity

If you are going to make sure you always respond to individuals in a respectful way which ensures they are treated with dignity, you need to understand the range of ways in which people can fail to be treated with respect or can lose their dignity. It is also important that you are aware of the ways in which the rights of individuals are protected by law, guidelines and charters in addition to the good practice that helps to protect people from discrimination and oppression.

Treating people as individuals

As discussed in Unit HSC 21, you should always consult the individual before you carry out any procedure, and explain everything you do. Everyone should be offered choices wherever possible. Below are examples of the kinds of choices you may be able to offer to people when you provide care.

Care service	Choices
Personal hygiene	Bath, shower or bed bath
	Assistance or no assistance
	Morning, afternoon or evening
	Temperature of water
	Toiletries
Food	Menu
	Dining table or tray
	Timing
	Assistance
	In company or alone

People need to be offered choices because they are all different; don't fall into the trap of stereotyping individuals.

The effects of stereotyping

'All apples are red.' That statement is clearly silly. Of course they're not – some are green, some are yellow. When it comes to people, everyone is different. However, there is a tendency to make sweeping statements (generalisations) which we believe apply to everyone who comes into a particular group. You looked in depth at stereotyping and the effects it has in Unit HSC 21. You need to understand that combating stereotypes is central to ensuring that people get a chance for equality.

The media

One of the major reasons why stereotyping continues is that this type of labelling of groups of people is reinforced by the media, whether it is newspapers, television or films. For example young people, particularly those who are black and live in cities, are often portrayed as violent and involved in crime and drugs. Single mothers and asylum seekers can be portrayed as lazy people abusing the benefits system. Attractive women are all slim and young with perfect hair and make-up. Older people are confused and dependent, with little to offer society.

Not only does labelling and stereotyping affect how you judge people, it also affects how they see themselves (their self-image). A young black man, for example, may feel that he has no choice but to be 'hard' and hang around in a gang, because that is what he has grown to see as his role. He is so used to seeing himself portrayed in that way, that he is not aware of any alternatives.

Similarly, older people may decide that they now have to be 'looked after' because they are over a certain age and have now become dependent. There are so few positive images of older people that it is easy to see how people can come to believe there is no other way to live.

Avoiding stereotyping at work

Take the time and trouble to find out the personal beliefs and values of each individual you work with. Think about all the aspects of their lives: diet, clothing, worship, language, relationships with others, bathing. It is your responsibility to find out – not for the individual to have to tell you. It will be helpful for you, and for other workers, if this type of information is recorded in the individual's personal record.

For example, you may need to know that many Muslims will only accept medical treatment from someone of the same gender, that you will need to enable them to wash in running water, not a bowl, that they do not eat pork, and that any other meat must have been killed and prepared in a particular way – Halal.

Check it out

Complete the following sentences.

Police officers are …

Teenagers are …

Nurses are …

Politicians never …

West Indians are all …

Asians always …

Men all …

Women are …

Americans are …

You can probably think of plenty of statements that you make as generalisations about others. Note some down, then think about how all these generalisations could affect the way you work.

If you are providing care for someone who is an Orthodox Jew, you need to be aware that they will not eat food unless it has been prepared in a specific way – the Kosher way. They do not eat pork. The Jewish Sabbath is a Saturday and Jewish beliefs forbid certain activities on that day.

Although you may hold a different set of values and beliefs from those of the individuals you are caring for, you do not have the right to impose your beliefs upon others. There may, in fact, be occasions when you will have to act as an advocate for their beliefs, even if you do not personally agree with them.

Key terms

Advocate: Person who is responsible for acting and speaking on behalf of an individual when he or she is unable to do so.

CASE STUDY: Acting as an advocate

Mr P is a Jehovah's Witness. He lives alone and has no relations. He has friends in his local religious community, but he is not active in the life of the church any more because of his mobility problems. Mr P is very close to his home-care assistant, who has known him for a long time. She is not a Jehovah's Witness, but she and Mr P have had many discussions over the years and she is well aware of his views. For example, she knows that because of his beliefs he would never agree to receive a blood transfusion.

Mr P suddenly collapsed at home one day and was found by the home-care assistant. He was rushed to hospital and needed emergency surgery. He was unconscious by the time he reached hospital and doctors were of the opinion that he would die if he were not operated on.

1 *Should the home-care assistant advise doctors of Mr P's beliefs?*

2 *Should she act on his behalf to prevent a blood transfusion being given?*

3 *What would you do if you were Mr P's home-care assistant?*

4 *Is it different when someone like Mr P is unconscious and cannot speak for himself?*

Keys to good practice: Valuing diversity

✓ The wide range of different beliefs and values which you are likely to come into contact with, if you work in a care setting, are examples of the rich and diverse cultures of all parts of the world.

✓ Value each person as an individual. The best way to appreciate what others have to offer is to find out about them. Ask questions. People will usually be happy to tell you about themselves and their beliefs.

✓ The other key is to be open to hearing what others have to say – do not be so sure that your values and beliefs and the way you live are the only ways of doing things.

✓ Think about the great assets which have come to the UK from people moving here from other cultures, including music, food and entertainment, and different approaches to work or relaxation or medicine.

Remember

The most terrifying films and the scariest fairground rides are those where you do not know what is going to happen next, or you do not know exactly what you are afraid of. It is always not knowing and feeling unsure that makes you more likely to reject something new and different. Once you have information, it is much easier to welcome and value the variety that others can bring.

How to recognise your own prejudices

One of the hardest things to do is to acknowledge your own prejudices and how they affect what you do. Prejudices are a result of your own beliefs and values, and may often come into conflict with work situations. There is nothing wrong with having your own beliefs and values – everyone has them, and they are a vital part of making you the person you are. But you must be aware of them, and how they may affect what you do at work.

Think about the basic principles which apply in your life. For example, you may have a basic belief that people should always be honest. Then think about what that could mean for the way you work – might you find it hard to be pleasant to someone who was found to have lied extensively? You may believe that abortion is wrong. Could you deal sympathetically with a woman who had had an abortion? You may have been brought up to take great care of people with disabilities and believe that they should be looked after and protected. How would you cope in an environment which encouraged people with disabilities to take risks and promoted their independence?

Exploring your own behaviour is never easy, and you need good support from either your supervisor or close friends to do it. You may be upset by what you find out about some of your attitudes, but knowing about them and acknowledging them is the first step to doing something about them.

As a care worker, it will be easier to make sure that you are practising effectively if you are confident that you have looked at your own practice and the attitudes which underpin it. Don't forget that you can ask for feedback from service users and colleagues too, not only from your supervisor.

Beliefs and values of others

Once you are aware of your own beliefs and values, and have recognised how important they are, you must think about how to accept the beliefs and values of others. The individuals you work with are all different, and so it is important to recognise and accept that diversity.

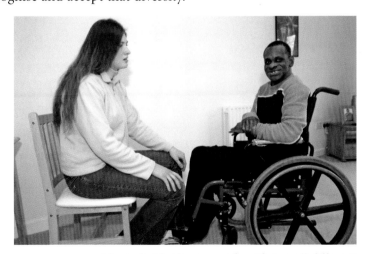

The individuals you work with are all different

Check it out

Make a list of the things you believe in as values, and a second list of how they could affect your work. Then, examine whether they do affect your work – you may need the views of a trusted colleague or your supervisor to help you with this. This exercise is very hard, and it will take a long time to do. It is often better done over a period of time. As you become more aware of your own actions, you will notice how they have the potential to affect your work.

Check it out

This exercise is best done with a group of colleagues, but you can do it on your own – it just takes longer!

1 Think of some ideas for a list of all the cultures and nationalities you know of. Write them down. Next to each one, write something that the culture has given to the world. For example, the Egyptians gave mathematics, the Chinese developed some wonderful medicines, and so on.

2 Next, think about people from the groups you care for. Note down the special angle of understanding each group can bring to society. For instance, someone who is visually impaired will always judge people on how they behave, not on how they look. Older people can often bring a different perspective to a situation based on years of experience and understanding.

Many workplaces now have policies which are about 'managing diversity' rather than 'equal opportunities'. This is because many people have realised that until diversity is recognised and valued, there is no realistic possibility of any policy about equal opportunities being totally effective.

Anti-discriminatory and anti-oppressive practice

Anti-discriminatory practice is what underpins the work in care settings. You, as a care worker, must practise in an anti-discriminatory way in your day-to-day work with service users. In order to be able to practise in a way which opposes discrimination, you must first understand the main concepts involved. You are likely to find that you have come across these ideas before, but perhaps not in these terms or in this context. You will need to understand the terms, because you will hear them used throughout the care and related sectors, and they have important implications for your practice.

Remember

- Stereotypes can influence how you think about someone.
- Don't rush to make judgements about people.
- Everyone is entitled to his or her own beliefs and culture. If you don't know about somebody's way of life – ask.

Stereotyping	Stereotyping leads to whole groups of people being assumed to be the same. It is often present when you hear phrases such as 'these sorts of people all …'. 'Old people love a sing song' or 'black people are good athletes' are stereotyping remarks.
Labelling	Slightly more complex than stereotyping, labelling happens when someone thinks the factor which people have in common is more important than the hundreds of factors which make them different.
	For example, the remark 'We should organise a concert for the elderly' makes an assumption that being older is what is important about the people concerned, and that somehow as you grow older your tastes become the same as all other people your age! It would be much better to say 'We should organise a concert for older people who like music from the shows' or 'We should organise a concert for older people who like opera', etc.
Discrimination	Discrimination means treating people less favourably because they have a feature or characteristic over which they have no control. Some disabled people find it hard to get a job because employers are reluctant to take them on. Research has shown that people with Asian names or from certain areas are told that job vacancies have been filled even though they have not. Disabled people are often unable to go to concerts or eat in the restaurants they want to because there are no suitable facilities for them.

Continued

Anti-discrimination	This means positively working to eliminate discrimination. It is about more than being against discrimination. You must ensure through your practice that you protect individuals from discrimination by identifying it and taking steps to get rid of or reduce it wherever you can.
	For example, when weekly menus are being planned at a day centre, if no account is taken of the religious and cultural needs of individuals, you should raise the issue at a staff meeting and suggest changes.
Oppression	Oppression is the experience people have when they are affected by an abuse of power or discriminated against. People who are oppressed are prevented from exercising their rights. They often lose self-confidence and find it difficult to see a way to change the treatment they are subjected to.
Anti-oppression	This is about the practical steps you can take to counteract oppression. In your work setting you will need to make sure individuals have all the information and support they need to understand the rights they have and how to exercise them. This may mean finding out about what they are entitled to and the ways in which they can be helped, setting up appointments for them and providing written information. It can also mean offering emotional support. It is important to recognise when people are being oppressed and denied their rights, either by another individual or by an organisation. You must work to challenge this, or support individuals to challenge it for themselves.

Your day-to-day practice and attitudes are important in how effective your anti-discriminatory practice will be. There is little point in challenging stereotyping in support of an individual and then returning to your own work setting ready to organise all the 'ladies' for a sewing afternoon!

Individuals' rights

Rights and responsibilities are a huge subject. In order to look at rights in terms of how they affect the people you work with and provide care for, it is helpful to discuss them under the following headings:

- basic human rights
- rights under charters, guidelines and policies
- rights provided by law.

Responsibilities are the other side of the coin to rights – most of our responsibilities are about protecting, improving or not infringing other people's rights. Responsibilities are the balance for rights, and it is impossible to consider one without the other.

Basic human rights

In 1949 the United Nations Universal Declaration of Human Rights identified a set of basic rights which everyone should have. The Declaration sets out to promote and encourage acceptance of personal, civil, political, economic,

> **Evidence indicator**
>
> Find an example of each of the aspects of anti-discriminatory practice. The examples can be from work, or from other parts of your life, or from fiction (a book, film or TV programme). For each example look at what you can learn about working in a way which is anti-discriminatory. Keep your notes as evidence.

social and cultural rights, which are only limited by the need to respect the rights and freedoms of others and the needs of morality, public order and general welfare.

For many people throughout the world, these are rights they can only hope for, and not rights they yet enjoy. The United Nations has a Commission on Human Rights which works to promote the world-wide acceptance of these basic rights and to identify abuses and violations of human rights throughout the world.

Rights under charters, guidelines and policies

These are rights which do not have the force of law, but which are designed to improve the services people receive.

The document called 'Your Guide to the NHS', published in 2000, sets out what people can expect from the National Health Service. It covers issues such as people's rights to receive care from a GP, how long they can reasonably be expected to wait for a hospital appointment, and how long before urgent and non-urgent treatment. However, it is different from the Patient's Charter which it replaced because it also identifies the responsibilities of patients. The guide includes information on how patients can use services and how they can complain if necessary.

Even though this is set out as a guidance document, the government has made it clear that this is the way in which the Health Service is expected to operate. This means that the performance of all NHS trusts is measured against this guidance.

Charters exist for other services, such as the Passenger's Charter, which lays down standards which can be expected for rail travel.

The key role of charters is to make the expected standards public, so there can be no argument that individuals are being unreasonable in their demands, or their expectations are too high. If people know what they have a right to expect, then they can take steps to complain and have things put right if the standards are not met.

Rights provided by law

Most of the provisions of the UK's Human Rights Act came into force on 2 October 2000. This means that residents of the United Kingdom – this Act applies in England, Scotland, Wales and Northern Ireland – will now be entitled to seek help from the courts if they believe that their human rights have been infringed.

Check it out

The organisation you work for is likely to have policies and statements about how it works. Find out what they are, and see how you feel your workplace measures up to its stated aims, mission statements and public charters.

Organisations subject to the Human Rights Act 1998

Residential homes or nursing homes	These perform functions which would otherwise be performed by a local authority
Charities	
Voluntary organisations	
Public services	This could include the privatised utilities, such as gas, electric and water companies

It is likely that anyone who works in health or care will be working within the provisions of the Human Rights Act, which guarantees the following rights.

1 The right to life.

2 The right to freedom from torture and inhuman or degrading treatment or punishment.

3 The right to freedom from slavery, servitude and forced or compulsory labour.

4 The right to liberty and security of person.

5 The right to a fair and public trial within a reasonable time.

6 The right to freedom from retrospective criminal law and no punishment without law.

7 The right to respect for private and family life, home and correspondence.

8 The right to freedom of thought, conscience and religion.

9 The right to freedom of expression.

10 The right to freedom of assembly and association.

11 The right to marry and found a family.

12 The prohibition of discrimination in the enjoyment of convention rights.

13 The right to peaceful enjoyment of possessions and protection of property.

14 The right of access to an education.

15 The right of free elections.

16 The right not to be subjected to the death penalty.

Law, rights and discrimination

Discrimination is a denial of rights. Discrimination can be based on race, gender, disability or sexual orientation. The main Acts of Parliament which are related to rights are:

- the Race Relations Act 1976
- the Equal Pay Act 1970
- the Sex Discrimination Act 1975
- the Disability Discrimination Act 1995.

Race Relations Act 1976 (amended by Race Regulations 2003)

This Act prohibits all forms of racial discrimination, whether in employment, housing or services. It also makes it an offence to incite (encourage) racial hatred. The Act covers all discrimination whether it is about nationality or race, and forbids both direct and indirect discrimination. People's rights to housing and provision of services are also supported by the Act.

Racial discrimination

This can be in a very direct form, such as abuse being shouted in the street, or violence. Large numbers of black and Asian people are subjected to these types of attack. This is clear racial harassment and is a criminal offence under the Race Relations Act.

It can also be less obvious, for example in employment when people with foreign-sounding names, or addresses in a particular part of a town, are not invited for interview. There is now an increasingly common practice among good employers of using a detachable section on job application forms for the personal details of the candidates. This personal information can then remain confidential in the personnel department, and only the part of the application form containing information about the candidate's experience and qualifications is given to the people drawing up shortlists. The results have sometimes been surprising!

Racial discrimination affects not only black and Asian people. Many people who have come to this country seeking refuge from wars and conflicts are subjected to racial abuse and prejudice which affect their day-to-day lives. White people may also experience racial discrimination, for example, when they live in areas populated mainly by people from racial groups different to their own. The Race Relations Act also covers 'positive' racial discrimination, whereby it is unlawful to act favourably towards someone just because they are from a particular racial group. An example of this is an employer trying to balance a predominately white workforce.

Check it out

Find out the percentage of people living in your local area who are from minority ethnic groups. Look at the number of people from these groups who are employed in your workplace. Are the percentages the same? For example, if 5 per cent of the people in your town are from minority ethnic groups, are there 5 per cent in your workplace? Look at the difference, and consider what the reasons for it may be.

CASE STUDY: Tackling prejudice

Woodhey Towers is a block of flats in a large local authority housing estate on the outskirts of a northern city. Families who are seeking asylum from conflicts in other countries have been re-housed in the block, which was scheduled for demolition as no local families wanted to live in it. Many of the newcomers have very little English, and most have been through a terrifying ordeal and have seen their homes destroyed and relatives killed. Among the refugees are three teachers, two doctors, several nurses, a man who used to own a very successful packaging business, two computer analysts and a football coach.

Many people in the local community are very hostile to the idea of having this group of refugees living in the area and have organised protests outside the flats. Abuse has been shouted in the streets and the children have been bullied in school. There is a support worker for the families in the flats and she is trying to develop links between them and the local community. She begins in the local women's centre where two of the nurses who can speak good English offer to help out with a first-aid course. The football coach has been asked to help the local team, which is short of staff, and it is hoped that the people with computer skills will be able to support the cyber session at the youth club.

1 *What feelings do you think the refugees would have about going into the local community in these ways?*

2 *Why do you think the community has been hostile?*

3 *Do you think local people would be surprised at the skills the refugees have? Why?*

4 *What other ways can you think of in which this group of refugees could be helped to become part of the local community?*

The Equal Pay Act 1970

The Equal Pay Act 1970 (amended 1983) is designed to make discrimination on the grounds of gender illegal. It provides a woman with the right to be employed on the same terms and conditions as a man doing an equivalent job, or work of equal value. For example, it has been judged in a court of law that a female canteen cook's work is of equal value to that of a male joiner, painter or sanitation engineer.

This type of legislation is common in many countries now, so the situation for women's pay has improved. However, it is often the kind of work which women do, much of it part-time or low-paid, which causes the difference in average pay. And of course, the work which women do at home is unpaid!

Sex Discrimination Act 1975

This Act is designed to provide equal rights to men and women in respect of employment, goods, services and facilities. It prevents discrimination either directly or indirectly which would prevent women from being employed or receiving a service in the same way as men. Women who, for example, have been repeatedly passed over for promotion at work, even though men who are less qualified have achieved success, can use the Sex Discrimination Act.

Did you know?

Average male wages in the UK are still about 20 per cent higher than women's. In 1965, women's average wage was half that of men.

There have been several well-publicised cases in public services such as the police and fire services.

Women have a right to be admitted to all public places on the same basis as men. This has meant that there are no longer any 'men only' bars – unless they are in private clubs, such as golf clubs.

Men can also use the Act if they have been unfairly discriminated against. For example, the fact that most baby-changing facilities are located in women's public lavatories means that a man who has the care of a baby will have difficulty finding a suitable place to change the baby.

Gender discrimination

Women are generally on the receiving end of gender discrimination, although it can apply to men, particularly those in employment caring for young children.

It is usually in terms of employment that women suffer disadvantages. They may be passed over for promotion, or not considered for some jobs, because they are women. It is also common for some companies to demand such long hours of work that many women with family commitments are unable to meet the requirements of top jobs. It is still true that, although men also have family commitments, it is more likely to be women who take time off work when children are ill, or when appointments connected with health or education have to be made.

Women are also more likely to be subjected to harassment in the workplace, with sexual innuendo or unwelcome advances from male colleagues.

Check it out

Look at the numbers of men and women who work for your employer. Does the proportion of women and men in senior management match the proportion of men and women employed? For example, you may find that 95 per cent of home-care assistants are women, but only 20 per cent of senior manager posts are held by women.

Did you know?

Less than 17 per cent of primary school teachers are men. Over 40 per cent of primary school headteachers are men.

CASE STUDY: Rights and responsibilities

The A family lives in the Midlands. Mr A is a Muslim from Pakistan, and the tradition in the area he comes from is that all young men and women are expected to have their marriages arranged by their families. Mr A's daughter M is 16 years old. She was born in the UK, speaks with a local accent, and has friends, both Muslim and non-Muslim, in the area. Her father has now decided that it is time that she was married. He has arranged for her to be married to a distant relative from the family's home town in Pakistan. M is not happy at the prospect, and wants to meet someone in the UK. She is reluctant to go to Pakistan, where she has never been before.

1   *What are Mr A's rights? What are his responsibilities?*

2   *What are M's rights?*

3   *Does M have responsibilities?*

4   *What decisions could be made?*

5   *Do any laws affect this situation?*

Disability Discrimination Act 1995

This Act is designed to provide rights for people with disabilities in:

- employment
- access to education and transport
- housing
- obtaining goods and services.

The Act defines disability as a condition which makes it difficult for someone to carry out normal day-to-day activities. The disability can be physical, sensory (affecting the senses) or mental but, to be covered by the Act, it must be substantial and have a long-term effect. This means that the disability must last, or be expected to last, for at least 12 months.

Under the Act employers must not treat a disabled person less favourably than an able-bodied person. An employer must examine the changes that need to be made to the workplace, or to how the work is carried out, in order to make it possible for someone with a disability to do the job.

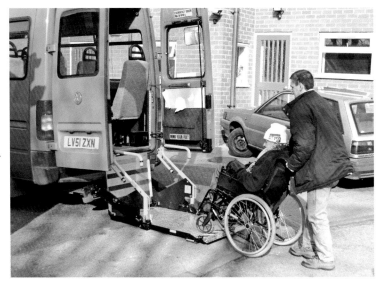

Access rights to education and transport for people with disabilities mean that schools and colleges will have to produce details of how any student will be able to access courses, regardless of disability. All new taxis, buses, trains and coaches have to be accessible for disabled people.

Disabled people need to be able to access vehicles

Landlords are not allowed to discriminate against anyone with a disability when letting a property, or to charge a higher rent than they would for a non-disabled person.

Shops, restaurants and anyone who provides a service have to ensure that disabled people are able to make use of the service and are not charged more than a non-disabled person. They have to make it easier for disabled people to use their services by providing any adaptations needed or by arranging for other ways of using the service, for example by providing a mail-order catalogue.

Discrimination against people with disabilities

In its most obvious forms, discrimination can include abuse and name calling, and even physical attacks. People with a disability can be very vulnerable to abuse, as they may lack the ability to retaliate, or to see what is happening. Unfortunately, there are criminals who are only too willing to take advantage.

At a broader level, there is massive discrimination against all kinds of people because of their disabilities. Historically, local and national governments

Did you know?

There are over 8.6 million disabled people in the UK – and 50 per cent of those of working age are currently employed.

Most disabled people acquire their disability during their working life or later, and fewer than 8 per cent of them use wheelchairs.

Remember

Being disabled is not the same as being ill. Most disabled people are perfectly well. They are no more likely to have time off work for illness than anyone else.

have not allocated the necessary resources to allow people with disabilities to have proper access to public buildings and transport. Current legislation will improve matters, but very slowly.

Employers are concerned about offering employment to people with disabilities, believing that they will be unable to cope, or will often be off sick.

Discrimination against people with mental health problems

There is still a great fear of mental health problems, largely because, in the past, people with such problems were considered to be 'mad' and were shut away in mental hospitals, often for the whole of their lives. The general public, therefore, had little to do with people who suffered from mental health problems, and, as a result, tended to misunderstand and fear them.

It is only in the past 20 years, as the emphasis has changed to caring for people in the community, that many people have had contact with those who suffer mental health problems.

Discrimination against people with a learning disability

Like people with other disabilities, many people with a learning disability are subjected to verbal or physical abuse. They face major problems in finding employment, because of fear and a lack of understanding about how well they can function, if given tasks within their capabilities.

People with learning disabilities simply function at a different level. If they are given tasks which are appropriate for them, they will carry them out very well. You might not function very well if you were asked to take over as managing director of ICI, or as the professor of nuclear physics at Cambridge University!

Older people

Older people are generally undervalued by western society. Most Asian and Chinese cultures recognise that older people are to be respected and valued for their experience and wisdom. They have a role within the family and the community.

Older people in the UK are likely to be dismissed as being 'past it', 'wrinkly' or 'crumbly', and are viewed as having nothing useful to contribute.

It is often difficult for people over 50 to find work, despite being very experienced and skilled. However, there are now some companies, notably supermarket and DIY chains, who are actively employing pensioners. They feel that older people are more conscientious, have more skills to contribute and are more reliable than younger workers.

Sexual orientation

Many people are subjected to both verbal and physical abuse because of their sexual orientation. Gay men, particularly, are likely to be subjected to violence.

Check it out

How many times in a day do you hear, or use, phrases like 'she's a looney', 'you must be mad', 'he's not right in the head'? Having mental health problems is still regarded as something which can be used as an insult.

Did you know?

One woman in nine and one man in 12 will experience mental health problems at some point in their lives. Yet it is still viewed as a secret and shameful thing, which people fear.

In certain professions it is not possible for people openly to express their sexual orientation because, despite statements from employers that they welcome applications from all, many people are unlikely to welcome an openly gay teacher or care worker. Many people working in nursing and midwifery have to be discreet about declaring a lesbian or gay partner because of the likely responses of patients and their relatives.

Steps you can take to reduce discrimination

Think about language. The words and expressions you use are important.

- Do not use words which degrade people with problems or disabilities, such as words that are used as an insult.
- Avoid language which is racist or could cause offence, and think about expressions such as 'play the white man' which suggest that white people are somehow superior.
- Older people should not be referred to as 'grannies' or 'wrinklies'. It is not acceptable to address an older person as 'pop' or 'granddad' unless you are invited to do so.
- Avoid using offensive terms to describe homosexuals. Always try to find out the terms which people find acceptable. These are generally 'gay' and 'lesbian'.
- There are many words and expressions which help to reinforce discrimination against women. Think before using phrases such as 'like a fishwife' or 'he's a right old woman'.

Encourage people you provide care for to achieve their full potential.

- Do not assume that older people are only capable of quiet activities which don't involve too much excitement.
- Avoid the temptation to over-protect people and therefore encourage dependence.
- Support people in challenging the barriers which stand in their way. If you work with people with disabilities, try to think of ways you can show employers what these people are capable of achieving.
- Try to work with the local community. If you work in a facility which is surrounded by neighbours, make sure that they get to know both service users and staff. Knowledge removes the fear which lies behind prejudice.
- Encourage people to behave assertively and to develop confidence in their own abilities.
- Refuse to accept behaviour which you know is discriminatory.
- Do not participate in racist or sexist jokes and explain that you are not amused by 'sick' jokes about people with disabilities or problems.
- If you are uncertain what to do in a particular situation, discuss the problem with your supervisor.

Remember

- Acts of Parliament don't change attitudes.
- Discrimination may be unlawful, but people still have the right to think, write and speak as they wish. *But* does anyone have a right to view another person as inferior because of his or her race? Would it infringe a person's rights to take steps against him/ her because of this view?

HSC 24c Assist in the protection of individuals

In this element you will look at some of the most difficult issues that you will face as a care professional. For many people, starting work in care means coming to terms with the fact that some individuals will be subjected to abuse by those who are supposed to care for them. For others it will not be the first time that they have been close to an abuse situation, either through personal or previous professional involvement.

Regardless of previous experience, coming face to face with situations where abuse is, or has been, taking place is difficult and emotionally demanding. Knowing what you are looking for, and how to recognise it, is an important part of ensuring that you are making the best possible contribution to protecting individuals from abuse. You need to know how society handles abuse, how to recognise it, and what to do about it. It is a tragic fact that almost all disclosures of abuse are true – and you will have to learn to *think the unthinkable*.

The forms of abuse which you will need to be aware of and to understand are abuses which are suffered by individuals at the hands of someone who is providing care for them – abusers can be parents, informal carers, care professionals and/or the policies and practices of the care setting itself. (This element is not about abuse by strangers, which needs to be dealt with in the same way as any other crime.) If you can learn always to consider the possibility of abuse, always to be alert to potentially abusive situations and always to *listen* and *believe* when you are told of abuse, then you will provide the best possible protection for the individuals you care for.

Taking the right steps when faced with an abusive situation is the second part of your key contribution to individuals who are being, or have been, abused.

Forms of abuse

Abuse can take many forms. These are usually classified under five main headings:

- physical
- sexual
- emotional
- financial
- institutional.

Abuse can happen to any individual regardless of his or her age or service needs. Child abuse is the most well-known and well-recognised type of abuse, but all service user groups can suffer abuse. Abuse of the elderly and of those with learning difficulties, sensory impairment or physical disabilities is just as common, but often less well recognised.

Physical abuse

Any abuse involving the use of force is classified as physical abuse. This can mean:

- punching, hitting, slapping, pinching, kicking, in fact any form of physical attack
- burning or scalding
- restraint such as tying up or tying people to beds or furniture
- refusal to allow access to toilet facilities
- deliberate starvation or force feeding
- leaving individuals in wet or soiled clothing or bedding as a deliberate act to demonstrate the power and strength of the abuser
- excessive or inappropriate use of medication
- a carer causing illness or injury to someone he or she cares for in order to gain attention (this is called 'Munchausen's syndrome by proxy').

Sexual abuse

Sexual abuse, whether of adults or children, is also abuse of a position of power. Children can never be considered to give informed consent to any sexual activity of any description. For many adults, informed consent is not possible because of a limited understanding of the issues. In the case of other adults, consent may not be given and the sexual activity is either forced on the individual against his or her will or the individual is tricked or bribed into it.

Sexual activity is abusive when informed consent is not freely given. It is important to recognise the difference between the freely consenting sexual activity of adults who also happen to be service users, and those situations where abuse is taking place because someone who is supposed to be providing care is exploiting his or her position of power.

Sexual abuse can consist of:

- sexual penetration of any part of the body with a penis, finger or any object
- touching inappropriate parts of the body or any other form of sexual contact without the informed agreement of the individual
- exposure to, or involvement in, pornographic or erotic material
- exposure to, or involvement in, sexual rituals
- making sexually related comments or references which provide sexual gratification for the abuser
- making threats about sexual activities.

Emotional abuse

All the other forms of abuse also have an element of emotional abuse. Any situation which means that an individual becomes a victim of abuse at the hands of someone he or she trusted is, inevitably, going to cause emotional distress. However, some abuse is purely emotional – there are no physical, sexual or financial elements involved. This abuse can take the form of:

- humiliation, belittling, putting down
- withdrawing or refusing affection
- bullying
- making threats
- shouting, swearing
- making insulting or abusive remarks
- racial abuse
- constant teasing and poking fun.

Financial abuse

Many service users are very vulnerable to financial abuse, particularly those who may have a limited understanding of money matters. Financial abuse, like all other forms of abuse, can be inflicted by professional or informal carers and can take a range of forms, such as:

- stealing money or property or encouraging others to do so
- tricking or threatening individuals into giving away money or property
- persuading individuals to take financial decisions which are not in their interests
- withholding money, or refusing access to money
- refusing to allow individuals to manage their own financial affairs
- failing to support individuals to manage their own financial affairs.

Institutional abuse

Institutional abuse is not only confined to large-scale physical or sexual abuse scandals of the type which are regularly publicised in the media. Of course this type of systematic and organised abuse goes on in residential and hospital settings, and must be recognised and dealt with appropriately so that service users can be protected. However, individuals can be abused in many

other ways in settings where they could expect to be cared for and protected.
For example:

- individuals in residential settings are not given choice over day-to-day decisions such as mealtimes, bedtimes, etc.
- freedom to go out is limited by the institution
- privacy and dignity are not respected
- personal correspondence is opened by staff
- the setting is run for the convenience of staff, not service users
- excessive or inappropriate doses of sedation/medication are given
- access to advice and advocacy is restricted or not allowed
- complaints procedures are deliberately made unavailable.

You can probably begin to see that the different types of abuse are often interlinked, and individuals can be victims of more than one type of abuse. Abuse is a deliberate act – it is something which someone actively does in order to demonstrate power and authority over another person. It is also done with the motive of providing some sort of gratification or pleasure for the abuser.

Neglect

Neglect is very different from abuse. Whereas abuse involves a deliberate act, neglect happens when care is not given and an individual suffers as a result. The whole area of neglect has many aspects you need to take into account, but there are broadly two different types of neglect:

- self-neglect
- neglect by others.

Self-neglect

Many people neglect themselves; this can be for a range of reasons. People may be ill or depressed and unable to make the effort, or not feel capable of looking after themselves. Sometimes people feel that looking after themselves is unimportant. Others choose to live in a way which does not match up to the expectations of other people. Working out when someone is neglecting himself or herself, given all of these considerations, can be very difficult.

Self-neglect can show itself in a range of ways:

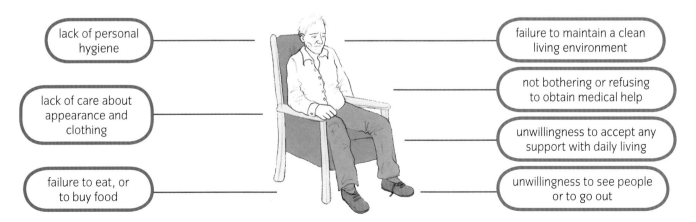

lack of personal hygiene

lack of care about appearance and clothing

failure to eat, or to buy food

failure to maintain a clean living environment

not bothering or refusing to obtain medical help

unwillingness to accept any support with daily living

unwillingness to see people or to go out

However, what may appear to be self-neglect may, in fact, be an informed choice made by someone who does not regard personal and domestic cleanliness or hygiene as priorities. It is always important to make a professional judgement based on talking with the individual and finding out his or her wishes, before making any assumptions about what may be needed.

Remember

Neglect occurs when a person's needs are not being met.

Neglect by others

This occurs when either a professional or informal carer is caring for an individual and the care needs of the person are not met. Neglect can happen because those responsible for providing the care do not realise its importance, or because they cannot be bothered, or choose not, to provide it. As the result of neglect, individuals can become ill, hungry, cold, dirty, injured or deprived of their rights. Neglecting someone you are supposed to be caring for can mean failing to undertake a range of care services, for example:

- not providing adequate food
- not providing assistance with eating food if necessary
- not ensuring that the individual receives personal care
- not ensuring that the individual is adequately clothed
- leaving the individual alone
- failing to maintain a clean and hygienic living environment
- failing to obtain necessary medical/health-care support
- not supporting social contacts
- not taking steps to provide a safe and secure environment for the individual.

In some care situations, carers may fail to provide some aspects of care because they have not been trained, or because they work in a setting where the emphasis is on cost saving rather than care provision. In these circumstances it becomes a form of institutional abuse. Unfortunately, there have been residential care homes and NHS trusts where individuals have been found to be suffering from malnutrition as the result of such neglect. Individual workers who are deliberately neglecting service users in spite of receiving training and working in a quality caring environment are, fortunately, likely to be spotted very quickly by colleagues and supervisors.

However, carers who are supporting individuals in their own homes are in different circumstances, often facing huge pressures and difficulties. Some may be reluctantly caring for a relative because they feel they have no choice; others may be barely coping with their own lives and may find caring for someone else a burden they are unable to bear. Regardless of the many possible reasons for the difficulties which can result in neglect, it is essential that a suspicion of neglect is investigated and that concerns are followed up so that help can be offered and additional support provided if necessary.

As with self-neglect, it is important that lifestyle decisions made by individuals and their carers are respected, and full discussions should take place with individuals and carers where there are concerns about possible neglect.

CASE STUDY: Appropriate ways to care

Julie, aged 43, had been a senior support worker in a residential unit for people with a learning disability for the past five years. Julie loved her job and was very committed to the residents in the unit. She was very concerned for the welfare of the people she supported and did everything she could for them. Many of them had been in the unit for many years and Julie knew them well. The unit was not very large and had only a small staff who were able to work very closely with the resident group.

Julie and the other staff were concerned that the residents could easily be taken advantage of, as some were not able to make effective judgements about other people and potentially risky situations.

Regular mealtimes were arranged so that everyone could share the day's experiences and talk together, and bedtimes and getting-up times were also strictly adhered to. The staff found that this was a good way of keeping the residents organised and motivated. Residents did not go out into the local town in the evenings because of the potential safety risk, but the staff would plan evenings of TV watching, choosing programmes which they thought would interest the residents. Sometimes simple games sessions or walks in the local park were arranged.

A new manager was appointed to the unit and Julie and the other staff were very surprised to find that the new manager was horrified by many of these practices, and wanted to make major changes.

1   *What changes do you think the manager may have suggested?*

2   *Why do you think those changes may be needed?*

3   *Do you consider that Julie and the other staff members were practising in the best way for the residents?*

4   *Think about, or discuss, whether this situation was abusive.*

Signs and symptoms which may indicate abuse

One of the most difficult aspects of dealing with abuse is to admit that it is happening. If you are someone who has never come across deliberate abuse before, it is hard to understand and to believe that it is happening. It is not the first thing you think of when a service user has an injury or displays a change in behaviour. However, you will need to accept that abuse does happen, and is relatively common. Considering abuse should be the first option when an individual has an unexplained injury or a change in behaviour which has no obvious cause.

Abuse happens to children and adults. Victims often fail to report abuse for a range of reasons:

- they are too ill, frail or too young
- they don't have enough understanding of what is happening to them
- they are ashamed and believe it is their own fault
- they have been threatened by the abuser or are afraid
- they don't think they will be believed
- they don't believe that anyone has the power to stop the abuse.

Given the fact that relatively few victims report abuse without support, it is essential that those who are working in care settings are alert to the possibility of abuse and are able to recognise possible signs and symptoms.

Signs and symptoms can be different in adults and children and you need to be aware of both, because regardless of the setting you work in you will come into contact with both adults and children. Your responsibilities do not end with the service user group you work with. If you believe that you have spotted signs of abuse of anyone, you have a duty to take the appropriate action.

Information on signs and symptoms comes with a health warning: none of the signs or symptoms is always the result of abuse, and not all abuse produces these signs and symptoms. They are a general indicator that abuse should be considered as an explanation. You and your colleagues will need to use other skills, such as observation and communication with other professionals, in order to build up a complete picture.

Signs of possible abuse in adults

Abuse can often show as physical effects and symptoms. These are likely to be accompanied by emotional signs and changes in behaviour, but this is not always the case.

Any behaviour changes could indicate that the service user is a victim of some form of abuse, but remember that they are only an indicator and will need to be linked to other factors to arrive at a complete picture.

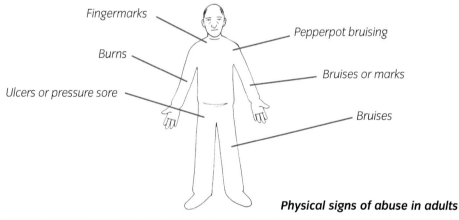

Physical signs of abuse in adults

Type of sign/symptom	Description of sign/symptom	Possible form of abuse indicated
Physical	frequent or regular falls or injuries	physical
Physical	'pepperpot bruising' – small bruises, usually on the chest, caused by poking with a finger or pulling clothes tightly	physical
Physical	fingermarks – often on arms or shoulders	physical
Physical	bruising in areas not normally bruised such as the inside of thighs and arms	physical

Type of sign/symptom	Description of sign/symptom	Possible form of abuse indicated
Physical	unusual sexual behaviour	sexual
Physical	blood or marks on underclothes	sexual
Physical	recurrent genital/urinary infections	sexual
Physical	marks on wrists, upper arms or legs which could be from tying to a bed or furniture	physical/sexual
Physical	burns or scalds in unusual areas such as soles of feet, inside of thighs	physical
Physical	ulcers, sores or rashes caused by wet bedding/clothing	physical
Physical	missing cash or belongings, or bank accounts with unexplained withdrawals	financial
Physical	missing bank account records	financial
Emotional/behavioural	becoming withdrawn or anxious	all forms of abuse
Emotional/behavioural	loss of interest in appearance	sexual/physical/emotional
Emotional/behavioural	loss of confidence	sexual/physical/emotional
Emotional/behavioural	sudden change in attitude to financial matters	financial
Emotional/behavioural	becoming afraid of making decisions	emotional
Emotional/behavioural	sleeping problems	all forms of abuse
Emotional/behavioural	changes in eating habits	all forms of abuse
Emotional/behavioural	no longer laughing or joking	all forms of abuse
Emotional/behavioural	feeling depressed or hopeless	all forms of abuse
Emotional/behavioural	flinching or appearing afraid of close contact	physical
Emotional/behavioural	unusual sexual behaviour	sexual

Signs of possible abuse in children

This is not a comprehensive list of every indicator of abuse. It is not possible to be exhaustive, neither does the existence of one of these signs mean that abuse has definitely taken place. Each is an indicator which needs to used alongside your other skills, such as observation and listening. It is a further piece of evidence – often the conclusive one – in building a complete picture.

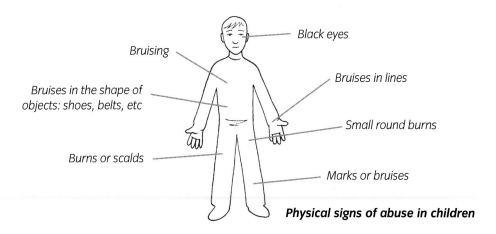

Bruising

Black eyes

Bruises in lines

Bruises in the shape of objects: shoes, belts, etc

Small round burns

Burns or scalds

Marks or bruises

Physical signs of abuse in children

Type of sign/ symptom	Description of sign/symptom	Possible form of abuse indicated
Physical	bruising, or injuries which the child cannot explain	physical
Physical	bruises in the shape of objects – belt buckles, soles of shoes, etc.	physical
Physical	handmarks	physical
Physical	bruises in lines	physical
Physical	injuries to the frenulum (the piece of skin below the tongue), or between the upper and lower lips and the gums	physical
Physical	black eyes	physical
Physical	bruising to ears	physical
Physical	burns, particularly small round burns which could have come from a cigarette	physical
Physical	burns in lines, like the elements of an electric fire	physical
Physical	burns or scalds to buttocks and backs of legs	physical
Physical	complaints of soreness or infections in the genital/anal area	sexual
Physical	frequent complaints of abdominal pain	sexual
Physical	deterioration of personal hygiene	sexual/neglect
Emotional/behavioural	sudden change in behaviour, becoming quiet and withdrawn	sexual/emotional
Emotional/behavioural	change to overtly sexual behaviour, or an obsession with sexual comments	sexual
Emotional/behavioural	problems sleeping or onset of nightmares	sexual/emotional
Emotional/behavioural	a sudden unwillingness to change clothes or participate in sports	sexual/physical
Emotional/behavioural	finding excuses not to go home	physical/sexual/ emotional
Emotional/behavioural	appearing tense or frightened with a particular adult	physical/sexual/ emotional

Carer behaviour which should alert you to possible abuse

Sometimes, it is not the behaviour of the service user which is the first noticeable feature of an abusive situation. It can be that the first behaviour you notice is that of the carer. The following are some indications of behaviour which may give cause for concern, although with the usual warning that each is only a *possible* indicator of problems:

- reluctance to allow visitors to see the individual
- insistence on being present with the individual at all times
- derogatory or angry references to the individual
- excessive interest in financial accounts or assets
- excessive requests for repeat prescriptions.

Who can abuse?

Abuse can take place at home or in a formal care setting. At home, it could be an informal carer who is the abuser, although it could be a neighbour or regular visitor. It can also be a professional care worker who is carrying out the abuse. This situation can mean that abuse goes undetected for some time because of the unsupervised nature of a carer's visits to someone's home.

In a formal care setting, abuse may be more likely to be noticed, although some of the more subtle forms of abuse, such as humiliation, can sometimes be so commonplace that they are not recognised as abusive behaviour.

Abuse is not only carried out by individuals; groups, or even organisations, can also create abusive situations. It has been known that groups of carers in residential settings can abuse individuals in their care. Often people will act in a different way in a group than they would alone. Think about teenage 'gangs', which exist because people are prepared to do things jointly which they would not think to do if they were by themselves.

Abuse in a care setting may not just be at the hands of members of staff. There is also abuse which comes about because of the way in which an establishment is run, where the basis for planning the systems, rules and regulations is not the welfare, rights and dignity of the residents or patients, but the convenience of the staff and management. This is the type of situation where people can be told when to get up and go to bed, given communal clothing, only allowed medical attention at set times and not allowed to go out. This is referred to as 'institutional abuse'.

> No dear, you can't go out now. You nearly slipped last time. You can't go on your own and I don't have anyone to send with you – can't you see how busy we all are?

Up to this point, consideration has been given to abuse by carers, whether parents, informal or professional. But do not forget that in residential or hospital settings, abuse can occur between residents or patients, and it can also happen between visitors and residents or patients. People can also abuse themselves.

Self-harm

The one abuser it is very hard to protect someone from is himself or herself. Individuals who self-harm will be identified in their plan of care, and responses to their behaviour will be recorded. You must ensure that you follow the agreed plan for provision of care to someone who has a history of self-harm. It is usual that an individual who is at risk of harming himself or herself will be closely supported and you may need to contribute towards activities or therapies which have been planned for the individual.

Why does abuse happen?

One of the key contributions you can make towards limiting abuse is to be aware of where abuse may be happening. It is not easy to accept that abuse is going on, and it is often simpler to find other explanations.

Be prepared to *think the unthinkable*. If you know about the circumstances in which abuse has been found to occur most frequently, then you are better able to respond quickly if you suspect a problem.

It is not possible accurately to predict situations where abuse will take place – a great deal of misery could be saved if it were. It is possible, though, to identify some factors which seem to make it more likely that abuse could occur. This does not mean that abuse will definitely happen – neither should you assume that all people in these circumstances are potential abusers. But it does mean that you should be aware of the possibility when you are dealing with these situations.

Situations when vulnerable adults may be abused at home

Adults may be abused at home in situations where:

- carers have had to change their lifestyles unwillingly
- the dependent person has communication problems, has had a personality or behaviour change (such as dementia), rejects help or is aggressive
- there is no support from family or professional carers
- carers are becoming dependent on drugs or alcohol
- carers have no privacy
- the dependent person is difficult and inconsiderate.

 CASE STUDY: Caring at home

S is 48 years old. She has Parkinson's disease, which has recently begun to develop very rapidly. Her mobility has become very limited and she cannot be left alone because she falls frequently. The number of personal care tasks she can carry out has decreased significantly, and she is almost totally dependent on her husband for care.

S has two grown-up sons who live and work considerable distances away. They both visit as often as they can, but are not able to offer any regular caring support. S's husband has given up his career as a ranger in the local country park, a job he loved, in order to look after S. She is very reluctant to go out because she feels people are looking at her. She is very angry about the way Parkinson's has affected her, and has alienated many of the friends who tried to help initially, by being unco-operative and refusing much of the help they offered.

1 *Are there any warning signs in this situation which would make you aware of the possibility of abuse? If so, what are they?*

2 *How would you try to relieve some of the pressures in this situation?*

Situations when child abuse can happen

Child abuse can happen in situations where:

- parents are unable to put a child's needs first
- parents or carers feel a need to show dominance over others
- parents or carers have been poorly parented themselves
- parents or carers were abused themselves as children
- families have financial problems (this does not just mean families on low incomes)
- families have a history of poor relationships or of use of violence.

Situations when abuse can happen in a care setting

Abuse can happen in a care setting when:

- staff are poorly trained or untrained
- there is little or no management supervision or support
- staff work in isolation
- there are inadequate numbers of staff to cope with the workload
- there are inadequate security arrangements
- there is no key worker system and good relationships are not formed between staff and residents.

Your role

If you want to be effective in helping to stop abuse you will need to:

- believe that abuse happens
- recognise abusive behaviour
- be aware of when abuse can happen
- understand who abusers can be
- know the policies and procedures for handling abuse
- follow the individual's plan of care
- recognise likely abusive situations
- report any concerns or suspicions.

Your most important contribution will be to be *alert*. For example, an individual's plan of care or your organisational policy should specify ways in which the individual's whereabouts are constantly monitored – and if you are alert to where a vulnerable person is, and who he or she is with, you can do much to help avoid abusive situations.

Many factors are involved in building protection against abuse

Check it out

Think about individuals you work with. Make a list of how many of them fit into the circumstances outlined. Now resolve to keep a particular eye on those individuals and watch for any signs that abuse may be happening. Be prepared to *think the unthinkable.*

Check it out

Look at your workplace. Do any of the above points apply? If any of these are the case in your workplace, you need to be aware that people can be put under so much stress that they behave abusively. Remember that abuse is not just about physical cruelty.

If none of these things happen in your workplace, then try to imagine what work would be like if they did. Sit down with a colleague, if you can, and discuss what you think the effects of any two of the items in the list would be. If you cannot do this with a colleague, you can do it on your own by making notes.

How to report and record information

Information about abuse you suspect, or situations you are working with which are 'high risk', must be recorded after being reported to your supervisor. Your supervisor will be responsible for passing on the information, if necessary.

Sometimes your information may need to be included in an individual's plan of care or personal records, particularly if you have noticed a change in the way he or she is cared for, or if his/her behaviour could be an 'early warning' that the care team need to be especially observant. Your workplace may have a special report form for recording 'causes for concern'. If not, you should write your report, making sure you include the following:

- what happened to make you concerned
- who you are concerned about
- whether this links to anything you have noticed previously
- what needs to happen next.

Discuss your report and your concerns with your supervisor and colleagues.

You must report anything unusual that you notice, even if you think it is too small to be important. It is the small details which make the whole picture. Sometimes, your observations may add to other small things noticed by members of the team, and a picture may start to emerge. Teamwork and good communication are vitally important.

Teamwork and good communication are vital in preventing problems

The effects of abuse

Abuse devastates those who suffer it. It causes people to lose their self-esteem and their confidence. Many adults and children become withdrawn and difficult to communicate with. Anger is a common emotion among people who have been abused. It may be directed against the abuser, or at those people around them who failed to recognise the abuse and stop it happening.

One of the greatest tragedies is when people who have been abused turn their anger against themselves, and blame themselves for everything that has happened to them. These are situations which require expert help, and this should be available to anyone who has been abused, regardless of the circumstances.

In an earlier section you learned about the signs and symptoms of abuse. Some of the behaviour changes which can be signs of abuse can become permanent, or certainly very long-lasting. There are very few survivors of abuse whose personality remains unchanged, and for those who do conquer the effects of abuse, it is a long, hard fight.

How the law affects what you do

Much of the work in caring is governed by legislation, but the only group where legislation specifically provides for protection from abuse is children. Older people and people with a learning disability, physical disabilities or mental health problems have service provision, rights and many other requirements laid down in law, but no overall legal framework to provide protection from abuse. The laws which cover your work in the field of care are summarised in the table below.

Service user group	Laws which govern their care	Protection from abuse?
Children	Children Act 1989	Yes
People with mental health problems	Mental Health Act 1983 (draft Mental Health Bill 2004)	No
Adults with a learning disability	Mental Health Act 1983	No
Adults with disabilities	Chronically Sick and Disabled Persons Act 1986 Disability Discrimination Act 1995	No
Older people	National Assistance Act 1948 NHS and Community Care Act 1990	No
All service user groups	Care Standards Act 2000	Yes, through raising standards

There are, however, a number of sets of guidelines, policies and procedures in respect of abuse for service user groups other than children, and you will need to ensure that you are familiar with policies for your area of work and particularly with those policies which apply in your own workplace.

Dealing with abuse is difficult and demanding for everyone, and it is essential that you receive professional supervision from your manager. This may be undertaken in a regular supervision or support meeting if you have one; if not, it will be important that you arrange to meet with your supervisor so that you can ensure that you are working in the correct way and in accordance with the procedure in your setting. Your supervisor will also need to be assured that you are coping on a personal and professional level with the effects of having to deal with an abusive situation.

Government policies and guidelines

The most important set of government guidelines which lays down practices for co-operation between agencies is called 'Working Together to Safeguard Children'. It was published in 1999 and forms the basis for child-protection work. This guideline ensures that information is shared between agencies and professionals, and that decisions in respect of children are not taken by just one person.

A similar set of guidelines has been published by the government about adults, called 'No Secrets'. These guidelines state that older people have specific rights, which include being treated with respect, and being able to live in their home and community without fear of physical or emotional violence or harassment.

The guidance gives local authorities the lead responsibility in co-ordinating the procedures. Each local authority area must have a multi-agency management committee for the protection of vulnerable adults, which will develop policies, protocols and practices. The guidance covers:

- identification of those at risk
- setting up an inter-agency framework
- developing inter-agency policy – procedures for responding in individual cases
- recruitment, training and other staff and management issues.

A government White Paper published in 2001, 'Valuing People: A New Strategy for Learning Disability in the 21st Century', sets out the ways in which services for people with a learning disability will be improved. 'Valuing People' sets out four main principles for service provision for people with a learning disability:

- civil rights
- independence
- choice
- inclusion.

The White Paper also makes it clear that people with a learning disability are entitled to the full protection of the law.

Recent policy approaches to protecting children and vulnerable adults in care environments have concentrated on improving and monitoring the quality of the service provided to them. The principle behind this is that if the overall quality of practice in care is constantly improved, then well-trained staff working to high standards are less likely to abuse service users, and are more likely to identify and deal effectively with any abuse they find.

What does the law say about protecting children?

The Children Act 1989 requires that local authority social services departments provide protection from abuse for children in their area. The Act of Parliament gives powers to social services departments, following the procedures laid down by the Area Child Protection Committee, to take legal steps to ensure the safety of children.

What does the law say about protecting vulnerable adults?

The Acts of Parliament which are mainly concerned with provisions for vulnerable adults are the National Assistance Act 1948 and the NHS and Community Care Act 1990. They do not specifically give social services departments a 'duty to protect' but, of course, people are protected by the law. If a vulnerable adult is abused and that abuse is considered to be a criminal offence, then the police will act. It is sometimes thought that because someone is confused, a prosecution will not be brought – this is not so. All vulnerable adults will have the full protection of the law if any criminal offences are committed.

The Mental Health Act 1983 (and the draft Mental Health Bill) forms the framework for service provision for people with mental health problems or a learning disability. There are provisions within this legislation for social services departments to assume responsibility for people who are so 'mentally impaired' that they are not able to be responsible for their own affairs. This is called guardianship. However, like all other vulnerable adults, there is no specific duty to protect people from abuse.

'Valuing People' (see page 146) forms the basis for services to all people with a learning disability and provides rights, but no specific duty of protection.

While the Chronically Sick and Disabled Persons Act and the Disability Discrimination Act provide disabled people with rights, services and protection from discrimination, they do not provide any means of comprehensive protection from abuse.

As with all vulnerable groups, there is a long and tragic history to the physical and emotional abuse suffered by people with physical disabilities or a learning disability. The public humiliation and abuse of those with mental health problems is still visible today, so it is hardly surprising that abuse on an individual level is still all too commonplace.

Did you know

The Protection of Vulnerable Adults - POVA - scheme for England and Wales, published by the Department of Health in 2004, aims to prevent those professionals who have harmed vulnerable adults in their care from taking up employment in the sector. It adds an extra layer of protection to the pre-employment processes, including Criminal Records Bureau checks, which already take place and stop known abusers entering the care workforce.

Information on ways to protect individuals

Safeguarding and protecting vulnerable adults and children is an area of work which has been in the public eye for many years. As a result of this, a great deal of research has been carried out, and plenty of information is available in order to develop and improve your understanding of this difficult subject. You will be able to find training courses available in your local area – all social services departments provide training by their specialists, and many private agencies with specialist knowledge, such as the NSPCC and Action on Elder Abuse, produce very useful training materials and publications.

Your supervisor or manager will be able to advise you about the best way to find out information, and you should choose the way in which you find it easiest to learn – you may prefer to attend a training course, to read a book or to watch a training video. Ask your supervisor to find out what is available in your workplace.

Test yourself

1   What are the signs of financial abuse?

2   What factors may lead you to consider that a carer is abusing an individual?

3   What is the difference between abuse and neglect?

4   Why is it important to record information about suspected or actual abuse?

5   What is your position if an individual asks you not to tell anyone about abuse he or she has experienced?

HSC 24 UNIT TEST

1   Abuse can happen when people are being cared for. Name the circumstances which make this more likely.

2   People are not discriminated against in the UK because there are laws to stop it. True or false?

3   What are the drawbacks to the laws about discrimination?

4   Make a list of the people in your workplace with whom you would need to share information about suspected abuse. Say why each of them is on your list.

5   Make notes about the way you would behave if someone told you he or she had been abused.

6   If you consider an abusive incident to be minor and unimportant, what should you do?

7   What is diversity?

8   What effects might abuse have on an adult?

9   How could you work to encourage a recognition of diversity in your workplace?

10   Are there different factors to consider when dealing with abuse of adults and abuse of children? If so, what are they?

11   What are the two key things to do when someone discloses that he or she has been abused?

Carry out and provide feedback on specific plan of care activities

Services are provided by a wide range of agencies in many different ways. These could be as different as providing a hospital bed for someone who is acutely ill, providing residential accommodation for a homeless young person or providing large-print books for someone who has a visual impairment. One of the most important aspects of the provision of a service is to ensure that it is meeting the needs of the individual.

Individuals' needs are not about what an agency or care worker believes to be needed; they are about what individuals understand their own needs to be. One of the most important roles of a care worker is to find out from individuals about the type of service needed and then to work alongside them and their family, and any other carers, to ensure that the best and most effective level of service is provided and that it meets the needs of all those concerned.

It is also important that a worker understands the limitations of the service that is provided by his or her agency. Sometimes it is necessary to explain these limitations to an individual, even though it may be disappointing not to be able to provide exactly what had been hoped for.

In this unit you will learn about the best ways to ensure that you have the maximum possible information about individuals, about how you can work with them and ensure that they are happy about the service they receive. You will also learn about the importance of continually looking at the service provided to make sure that it continues to meet their needs.

What you need to learn

- Care planning
- A holistic approach
- Following care plans
- Giving people choices
- Obtaining information from other sources
- Why feedback is important
- Ways of monitoring
- The purpose of reviews
- Who is involved in the review process
- How the review process is managed
- How the review process is recorded.

HSC 25a Carry out specific activities to plan of care

Care planning

The process of providing care is something which should be carefully planned and designed to ensure that the service is exactly right for the individual it is meant to be helping. This is of key importance, not just because it is a right to which all people are entitled in a civilised society, but also because health and well-being responds to emotional factors as much as physical. Individuals will benefit if the service they receive is centred around their own needs and the ways in which they wish those needs to be met. Feeling valued and recognised as a person is likely to improve the self-esteem and confidence of individuals and thus contribute to an overall improvement in health and well-being.

Evidence indicator

Think of an occasion when you have felt really special – it may have been a special day, such as a birthday, wedding or anniversary, or a special event such as having a baby, or an achievement like winning an award or passing a test. Note down how you felt and try to recall the reasons why you felt special. Keep your notes as evidence for your portfolio.

When an individual either requests or is referred for a service, the assessment and planning cycle begins. Throughout the consultation and planning which follows, the individual and his or her needs should be at the centre of the process. The worker who is assessing and planning the way in which services will be delivered will need to make sure that the individual has every opportunity to state exactly how he or she wishes those needs to be met. Some individuals will be able to give this information personally. Others will need an advocate who will support them in expressing their views.

The principles of good communication, which were explored in Unit HSC 21, are an important part of making sure that the individual is fully involved in making plans for the service he or she will receive.

All organisations must ensure that the way in which services are provided allows the opportunity for individuals to express their views, and that all those who will play a part in planning and delivering services on an individual level are able to use listening and communication skills in order to allow the individual to participate fully. The consequences of not planning service delivery around the needs of those who receive services can be far reaching. The table on the next page shows some of them.

Need/wish of individual	Ways to meet need	Possible effects of not taking account of need
Food prepared according to religious or cultural beliefs	Ensure that service is provided by people who have been trained to prepare food correctly	Food not eaten so health deteriorates Other services refused Food eaten out of necessity but in extreme distress
To maintain social contacts while in residential care	Provide transport to visit friends and for friends to visit	Individual becomes isolated and depressed
To take control of own arrangements for personal care	Discuss and support the planning of direct payments	Individual loses self-esteem and becomes disempowered

Maintaining the individual's wishes at the core of any plans for care provision can have far-reaching benefits for the individual and his or her family.

A holistic approach

One of the essential aspects of planning care services is to have a holistic approach to planning and provision.

This means recognising that all parts of an individual's life will have an impact on his or her care needs and that you need to look beyond what you see when you meet him or her for the first time.

A wide range of factors will have an impact on the circumstances which have brought an individual to request social care services. All of the following factors will directly affect a service user and they must be taken into account when considering the best way to provide services.

Key terms

Holistic: Looking at the *whole* situation.

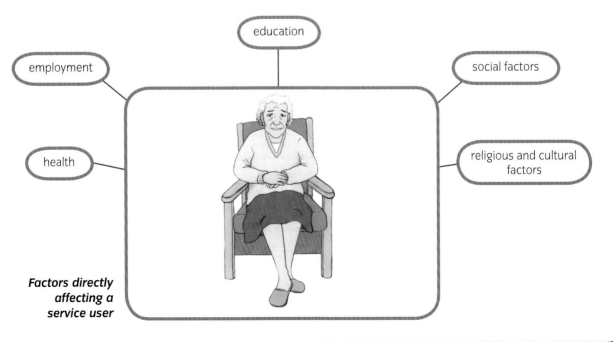

Factors directly affecting a service user

Health

The state of people's health has a massive effect on how they develop and the kind of experiences they have during their lives. Someone who has always been very fit, well and active may find it very difficult and frustrating to find his or her movement suddenly restricted as the result of an illness, such as a stroke. This may lead to difficult behaviour and the expression of anger against those who are delivering services. Alternatively, the individual may become depressed. Someone who has not enjoyed good health over a long period of time, however, may be able to adjust well to a more limited physical level of ability, perhaps having compensated for poor health by developing intellectual interests.

Someone who has always been fit, well and active may find sudden restrictions frustrating

Employment

Health is also likely to have had an impact on a person's employment opportunities, either making employment impossible at times or restricting the types of jobs he or she could do. Whether or not people are able to work has a huge effect on their level of confidence and self-esteem. Employment may also have an effect on the extent to which individuals have mixed with others and formed social contacts. This may be an important factor when considering the possible benefits of residential care as opposed to care provided in a home environment.

Income levels are obviously related to employment, and these will have an effect on standards of living – the quality of housing, the quality of diet and the lifestyle people are able to have. Someone in a well-paid job is likely to have lived in a more pleasant environment with lower levels of pollution, more opportunities for leisure, exercise and relaxation, and a better standard of housing. It is easy to see how all of this can affect an individual's health and well-being.

Education

People's level of education is likely to have affected their employment history and their level of income. It can also have an effect on the extent to which they are able to gain access to information about health and lifestyle. It is important that the educational level of an individual is always considered so that explanations and information are given in a way which is readily understandable. For example, an explanation about an illness taken straight from a textbook used by doctors would not mean much to most of us! However, if the information is explained in everyday terms, we are more likely to understand what is being said.

Some people may have a different level of literacy from you, so do not assume that everyone will be able to make use of written notes. Some people may prefer information to be given verbally, or recorded on tape.

Social factors

The social circumstances in which people have lived will have an immense effect on their way of life and the type of care provision they are likely to need. Traditionally, the social classification of society is based on employment groups, but the social groups in which people live include their family and friends, and people differ in the extent to which they remain close to others. The social circumstances of each individual who is assessed for the provision of care services must be taken into consideration, to ensure that the service provided will be appropriate.

Religious and cultural factors

Religious and cultural beliefs and values are an essential part of everyone's lives. The values and beliefs of the community people belong to and the religious practices which are part of their daily lives are an essential aspect for consideration in the planning of services. Any service provision which has failed to take account of the religious and cultural values of the individual is doomed to fail.

Check it out

Prepare a list of the different types of service provided by the setting in which you work. Remember to include all the aspects of the service you provide – if you work in residential care, you will need to list all parts of your service, such as social activities, providing food, providing entertainment, personal care, etc. If you work in an individual's own home, you may need to list food preparation, cleaning, personal care, and so on.

Make a note about the factors of an individual's life which you would need to take into account in order to provide a holistic assessment of his or her needs.

Record ways in which you may need to adapt the services you provide because of some of the factors you are taking into account.

Following care plans

Every workplace will have its own style of care plan and you will need to be shown how to use the ones in your workplace correctly. But they all follow the same broad principles.

Care plans are important documents that make it possible for individuals to receive appropriate and consistent care

Following a care plan is essential. This makes it possible to ensure that the individual receives the same level of care from all of those involved in providing it. Professional carers do not work 24 hours a day (it just feels that way!) and they do have days off and holidays, so it is important that care services are provided by a team who all work in the same way. The care plan is the document that makes sure this happens, and that the team all work together. If a football team all played to slightly different rules, there would be chaos and a bad result! The same is true of care provision – all the team members should be delivering care to the same standard and in the same way. Following the care plan is the way to make sure this happens.

Every service user will have a plan for his or her care. This will have been developed through discussion and consultation with the individual and those responsible for the care. The care plan will vary according to the work setting, but will include the following details.

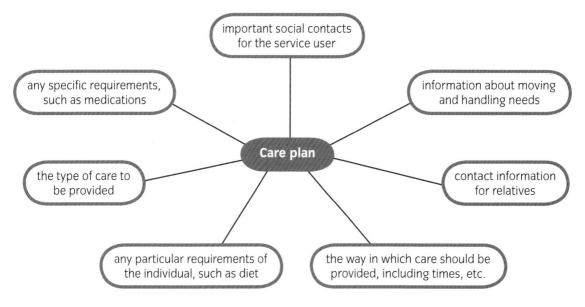

The services you provide must be carried out in accordance with the plan, but it is important that you understand:
- how to access information about the plan
- how the plan has been developed
- how the information is gathered
- who has access to it
- how the individual and carers have contributed to the plan.

Making the plan work

Your role is to ensure that you are carrying out activities in line with what the individual needs and wants, always making sure that every option for maintaining or increasing independence is explored.

Many different care workers undertake the role of obtaining information about individuals and the services they need. Some could be assessing people for domiciliary services, while they remain in their own homes; some could be assessing the needs which people may have once they leave a hospital or a residential care setting; others could be talking to a teenager or a young person about needs for residential or other support services – the possibilities are very broad. However, whatever role you have as a worker and regardless of the kind of services your agency provides, there are some basic principles which apply to the work you do.

One of these is that you must carefully explain to the individual your role in the whole process. Before you can clearly explain your role to someone else in a way that they can understand, you must ensure that you understand it fully yourself.

Your role is to ensure that:
- the needs of the person are met as far as possible by providing the service
- as much information as possible is obtained from the individual
- you provide the individual and his or her carers and family with as much information as you can about the nature of the service that will be provided.

You will also need to explain to an individual exactly which services your agency provides. It can sometimes be helpful to explain how your agency is funded and what the limitations may be on the types of services that can be provided.

Remember

- Give all possible information about your role and the role of your agency.
- You may have to give this information to several people if there are family members or other people involved in the individual's care.
- You may have to repeat the information, write it down or make it available in some other format if the person has hearing or learning difficulties.
- Information is very important and it empowers people. People cannot make informed choices if you fail to give them enough information.

Giving people choices

You need to think carefully about the ways you influence people. It is not only your own personal style of communication that influences them, it is also the way you explain the possibilities of service provision. You will need to beware of pushing individuals and their families into a particular solution, simply because you happen to believe it is the best one.

Individuals will ask for your advice, and perhaps ask: 'What would you do?' You will have to learn to avoid answering that question directly, as it is not your role to give advice about a course of action, nor is it for you to explain what you think you might do if you were in a similar situation. This is not helpful.

What you can usefully do is provide information about services and empower people to make their own decisions. You should simply provide unbiased, accurate and clear information and then support individuals to achieve the best outcome with the decision they have made.

Putting individuals in control

Throughout the process of obtaining information you should make sure you constantly check that individuals are fully aware of what is happening and feel they are in control of the process. One of the problems with the way services are provided, regardless of whether they are services for health, for social care or for children and young people, is that many service users feel they play only a passive role.

It is easy to see how this can happen. Agencies and service providers have well-organised systems which can often involve filling in a great many forms, attending meetings and working through the bureaucracy. If you work for such an organisation these things are a day-to-day part of your life. They do not represent a threat to you. But you need to remind yourself that many of the people you deal with will not be familiar with the workings of your agency and may not feel confident enough to question or challenge what is happening.

There are several steps you can take at each stage of the process to ensure that individuals feel they are in charge of their service.

Step 1   Individuals should make clear who needs to be involved in the process of thinking about and planning their service provision. You may need to prompt them to think about the people they would like to be involved. Sometimes it is helpful to make some suggestions. For example, you could ask 'What about your neighbour, Mrs S, the one who pops in with your dinner? Might it be a good idea to ask her?' Or, 'Your niece Susan might have some ideas about the sort of services you could use.'

Step 2 At each stage of the process you should check with the individual that he or she is in agreement with the steps that have been taken so far. You should do this using the means of communication which the individual prefers. For example, if your normal means of communication is to talk, then you could have a regular chat to ensure that the service provided is what the individual wants and to ask whether there are any specific ways in which he or she wants tasks to be carried out. Alternatively, if the individual has any form of hearing impairment, your means of communication to establish the same information may be by writing or using signs.

Step 3 The use of any additional sources of information, for example previous records from other agencies who may be involved with an individual, must be agreed in advance before you approach the sources for the information.

It is important you do not take this agreement for granted and that you explain exactly what it is you intend to do so it is clear what is being agreed to.

Step 4 Make sure that you record the individual's agreement to other people being approached for information. Some agencies require written confirmation of an individual's agreement before they provide information about him or her. If at any point during your initial assessment and checking of information an individual withdraws consent for you to approach a particular agency or person, you must respect that and not pursue that particular source of information.

CASE STUDY: Consulting the individual

Elizabeth G is 85 years old. She lives alone and has recently become increasingly frail. She has no memory difficulties but finds shopping, cooking and coping with housework increasingly difficult. Elizabeth never married, and in her professional life was head teacher of a large primary school. She has one brother, who emigrated to New Zealand over 50 years ago. After retirement she enjoyed travelling abroad and visited many countries, including New Zealand to see her brother. She usually travelled alone, or occasionally with another teacher from her school. Elizabeth has never been particularly religious and attended her local Anglican church only on formal occasions, such as weddings, baptisms and funerals. She has always enjoyed gardening but recently been unable to do it, so her once lovely garden has now become overgrown.

Elizabeth reluctantly contacted social services to ask for help with the preparation and cooking of meals and some basic housework. She no longer has the money to pay for private provision of any of these services, but she felt uncomfortable asking for help from social services. The assistance provided was in the form of a home help once a week to do some shopping. The person carrying out the assessment of Elizabeth's needs also decided she needed some company. It was decided that the best way for her to get a regular meal and some company would be to attend a local luncheon club. The worker dealing with Elizabeth arranged transport for her to do this, in the hope that Elizabeth would enjoy socialising with the others at the luncheon club.

Some people enjoy socialising at luncheon clubs

Elizabeth attended the luncheon club once. When transport arrived for her the following day she told them that she would not be going again. She then contacted social services to cancel all the other arrangements that had been made for her. She said that she had re-thought her needs and decided that she could manage quite well; there was no need for her to take up services which could be of more use to someone else.

1 *From what you know of Elizabeth's background, would you expect her to be happy with a group of strangers?*

2 *Given her background, what would you expect her interests to be?*

3 *What sort of social situations would you expect Elizabeth to feel comfortable in?*

4 *What do you know of Elizabeth's feelings about asking for help?*

5 *What do you think Elizabeth's reaction would be to any problems in the provision of her service?*

6 *Do you think that the services provided were appropriate for Elizabeth? If not, why not?*

Obtaining information from other sources

Once you have ensured you have an individual's agreement to do so, you may wish to consider accessing a range of other sources to complete the picture of the person and the way in which he or she can most benefit from the services your agency provides. Examples of sources are:

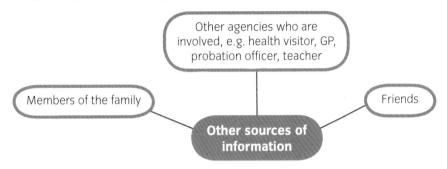

Bear in mind that information you gain, particularly from other professional sources, may be restricted by:

● the rules of confidentiality under which that professional operates
● the legal restrictions as to how information may be passed on.

Most professionals are bound by principles of confidentiality in respect of their clients. You know that there are limits to the information you can share with others about your client, so you must expect that other professionals from whom you are seeking information will be bound by similar rules. Information can be protected under a range of different legislation, as shown below.

Type of information	Relevant legislation
Medical information/hospital records	Data Protection Act 1998
Information relating to children and young people	Children Act 1989
Information relating to people with mental health problems	Mental Health Act 1983
Information relating to people with a disability	Disability Discrimination Act 1995
Any information stored on a computer or in manual records	Data Protection Act 1998

All these Acts work on the basic principle that personal information given or received in what is understood to be a confidential situation and for one particular purpose, may not be used for a different purpose. They also contain the proviso that information may not be passed to anyone else without the agreement of the person who provided the information. The Data Protection Act ensures that individuals have access to their own health or social services records but that these are not available to anyone else without the individual's permission. This applies even after death where an individual has expressly forbidden any information to be passed to anyone else or to a specific individual.

Family and friends

Family and friends can be an invaluable source of information about an individual and his or her needs. However, you must be sure before you discuss anything with family or friends that this is being done with the consent of the person concerned. It is easy to assume that because someone is a relative or close friend there will be no objections over him or her giving information to you. Always confirm with individuals that they have no objection to you discussing their case with family or friends.

Other sources

Sometimes you may find that you have completed all your discussions with individuals and their families, but are still unsure about how best to meet the needs that have been identified. You should discuss this with your supervisor, who will be able to advise you about the alternatives available and the best sources of further information. This could include voluntary or private sector organisations, carers' groups, other carers or individuals already receiving a service.

Evidence indicator

Prepare a record sheet which could be used for someone about whom you have to gather information. This should include the basic factual information required by your agency, but make sure you add to it information you have obtained through your own observation or through your understanding of the individual's values, beliefs and culture.

You could organise this as a checklist so that you can use it whenever you need to gather information. Check your list against any forms which are provided by your agency and see how many additional aspects you have included. This should give you some indication of the importance of obtaining information on all aspects of the needs of individuals, not just the basic factual information which is often all that is required on agency forms.

Test yourself

1 What are the main aspects of the care-planning process?

2 What information do you need before preparing a plan for the care of an individual?

3 What are the main factors which influence the needs and development of individuals?

4 What are the best sources of information about an individual?

5 What can happen to individuals whose needs are not met by the plan of care?

6 How can you help to put individuals in control of their care?

HSC 25b Provide feedback on specific plan of care activities

Why feedback is important

The major and most straightforward reason why feedback is important is that it is essential to ensure that any package of care is continuing to meet the needs that it was designed to meet. However, there are other aspects of monitoring which are also important. A package of care will have originally been assessed, planned and put in place to meet a particular set of circumstances. The original assessment should have:

- involved the individual
- involved the individual's carers and family
- assessed levels of need
- assessed the level of provision which was available
- planned for monitoring and review.

All this does not guarantee that it will still be appropriate six months or a year ahead. Neither does it mean that care packages which were set up, even with the most thorough assessment and careful planning, will necessarily continue to provide services of the quality or at the level originally expected.

Monitoring may seem a complex process but its principles are very simple – and feedback is one of the key components. Most of us monitor many things in our lives on a regular basis without realising it.

Evidence indicator

If you shopped at the same butcher's every week to buy meat, you would soon stop if you found the meat tough, stringy and inedible. In your weekly visit to the butcher you monitor the quality of the meat you are buying, and decide whether to go on buying from this butcher according to the quality of the meat you receive.

Think about other examples of monitoring in your everyday life and make some notes. Then, think about those things you monitor at work, and make notes about how and why you monitor.

According to the Department of Health, over 1.6 million people have services provided for them through care packages. Approximately 1.3 million of those people use community services and 0.3 million have residential services. Almost 600,000 packages of care are reviewed every year, and about half of these result in a new or amended care plan. This shows that people's circumstances and needs change, and therefore the services provided must be able to respond to those changes in needs.

Monitoring of care services needs to pick up changes in the circumstances of those receiving the services, their carers and the service provider. The original care plan will include forms of care and support that reflect the

individual's needs at the time. For example, someone recently discharged from hospital following treatment for mental health problems may receive quite extensive support under the care programme approach, consisting of day care, community psychiatric nurse visits, and access to a support group of carers. However, feedback on that individual's progress may show his or her mental health has improved to the point that day care is no longer needed on the previous level and that an alternative service, such as support in finding employment, is now far more appropriate. A service which is frequently monitored is likely to be one which is responsive to the needs of the individual, and is also an effective use of the resources of the health service or social services department responsible for funding.

Resources

Checking on resources can also be important if changes in the availability of those resources means that a care package will have to be altered in some way. A reduction in available funding or an increase in demand for a particular resource may mean that adjustments in the level of service provision will have to be made. Regular monitoring makes it easier to be aware of where resources are being used and where changes need to be made.

Carers

Regular monitoring and feedback should cover the needs of carers, to make sure the provisions are still meeting their needs. Carers should also be included in providing feedback about the service. Regular feedback from carers, and the knowledge that they will contact you if circumstances change, can be taken into account when monitoring. However, it is not appropriate or reasonable to put all the responsibility on a carer to notify you when changes take place.

Carers cope with tremendous demands on their time and energy, both physical and emotional. Whatever systems you agree in order to keep up to date with feedback from carers, you must make sure you are not placing even more demands on their time.

Ways of monitoring

Whatever approach your agency takes to monitoring, it will be decided at the outset how a particular care package will be monitored and the methods will be agreed with the individual and his or her carers. Your feedback will be an essential part of the process. A monitoring process will involve the following key people:

- the individual receiving the service
- his or her carers or family
- other health care professionals
- the service provider – whose performance will be monitored.

Monitoring by the individual

Obviously the most important person in any monitoring process is the individual receiving the service, so he or she must be clear about how to record and feed back information on the way the care package is working. This can be through:

- completing a checklist on a regular basis (weekly or monthly)
- maintaining regular contact with the care manager/co-ordinator, either by telephone or through a visit
- using an electronic checking and monitoring form which would be e-mailed on a regular basis to the care manager/co-ordinator
- recording and reporting any changes in his or her own circumstances or changes in the provision of the care package.

Opposite is an example of a form that can be used to obtain feedback from an individual in care.

Have there been any changes in your health since the last report? If so, please say what.	Not really - much the same
Have there been any changes in your circumstances since the last report? If so, please say what.	My sister has come to live a few streets away
Are the services you receive still giving the support you need?	Yes, still very good, but don't need day centre on Thursdays now as my sister takes me out every Thursday
How would you like the services to change what you receive?	Cancel Thursday at the day centre, but everything else is fine

A feedback form

Monitoring by carers and families

Carers and families are likely to participate in the monitoring of a care package in similar ways. You will need to make sure that carers are willing to participate in monitoring and they do not feel you are adding yet another burden to their lives.

Monitoring by other health care professionals

Maintaining contact between reviews with other professionals who may be involved with the individual is an essential part of the monitoring process. The most effective method of doing this is to agree the types of changes which will trigger contact. For example:

- the GP may be asked to notify the care manager of any significant health changes or hospital admissions
- the community nurse may be asked to notify any problems in compliance with treatment, or changes in the individual's ability to administer his or her own medication, or changes in home conditions
- the physiotherapist may be asked to notify any significant changes in mobility.

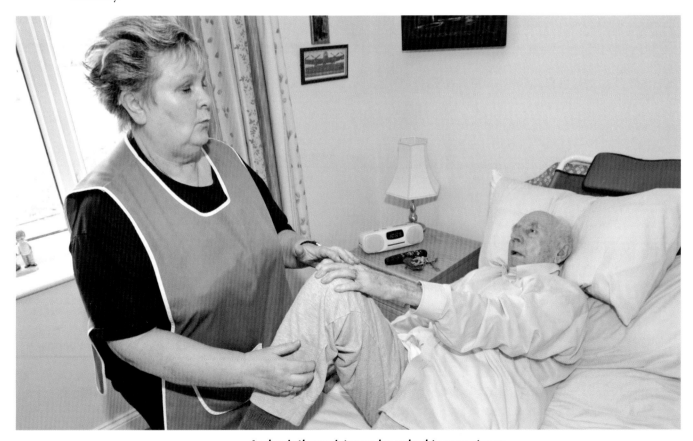

A physiotherapist may be asked to report any significant changes in an individual's mobility

There may be other professionals involved, such as occupational or speech therapists, depending on the circumstances of the individual. The principles of monitoring remain the same.

Feedback from care professionals

Your role in administering the plan of care means that you are in an ideal position to identify changes in an individual's circumstances that may mean a service is no longer appropriate. It may need to be increased, decreased or changed in order to meet a new situation. The changes do not have to be major, but they can have a significant impact on a person's life.

How to identify significant changes which affect the care package

Throughout any monitoring and evaluation process you are looking for and responding to change. It is important you are clear about the difference between types of changes which require action, and those that are simply a part of everyday life and do not involve a major re-think of a care package. For example, an individual who inherits £50,000 will experience significant change, whereas someone who receives a £1.20 per week increase in Income Support will not! Both, however, have experienced a change in their financial circumstances.

Similarly, someone who changes from working two days each week to a full-time job experiences a significant change which will involve alterations in the care package he or she receives. But someone who changes from working two days each week as a telephonist to working the same two days as a receptionist is unlikely to need significant changes in any care package.

CASE STUDY: Acknowledging change

B has a long history of mental health problems which she has experienced since her late teens; she is now in her early 40s. She experiences episodes of elation and disinhibition, and at other times depressive episodes. B has regular medication which controls her mental health most of the time and she has a comprehensive care programme, with her community psychiatric nurse as her care co-ordinator. She lives in a hostel and receives support from hostel-based support workers and the staff at the day centre she attends each day. B's family have lived in a town about 10 miles away from B – her mother, who died last year, was a lone parent, and B has a married sister who has two children. Following the death of her mother, B's sister decided to move nearer to B. They have always been close and her sister has always encouraged B to maintain her treatment regime and to make use of support services. B's sister moved into a new house in the same area as the hostel a few weeks ago.

1 *Is this change significant for B? If so, why? If not, why not?*

2 *What could be the benefits for B?*

3 *Are there any potential disadvantages?*

4 *How could B's care programme be affected?*

Check it out

Look at your own circumstances over the past 10 years and make a list of the ways in which they have changed. For example, you may have more children than you had 10 years ago, or some children may have left home and moved away. Members of your family may have died or been born in the past 10 years, you could be living in a larger or a smaller house, you could have more money or less money, you could be doing the same job or a different job. All these are major changes which have taken place in your life in just the short period of 10 years. Listing them will help you see the types of situations which change and affect people's lives.

Then take a much shorter period, for example the past year, and look at much smaller changes which may have happened to you during that time. They could be changes in your finances and your job role. You could now be undertaking a qualification, you may be driving a different car, you may have acquired digital television – any number of small changes have affected the way you are living your life. Again, make a list of these changes and consider the impact each of them has had. Although the second list may have had a smaller impact than some of the big changes you listed in your first reflection, they will nonetheless have combined to bring about some quite significant changes in your lifestyle.

Consider the results of this exercise when you are thinking about the importance of contributing to the monitoring of care programmes which are in place for people you work with.

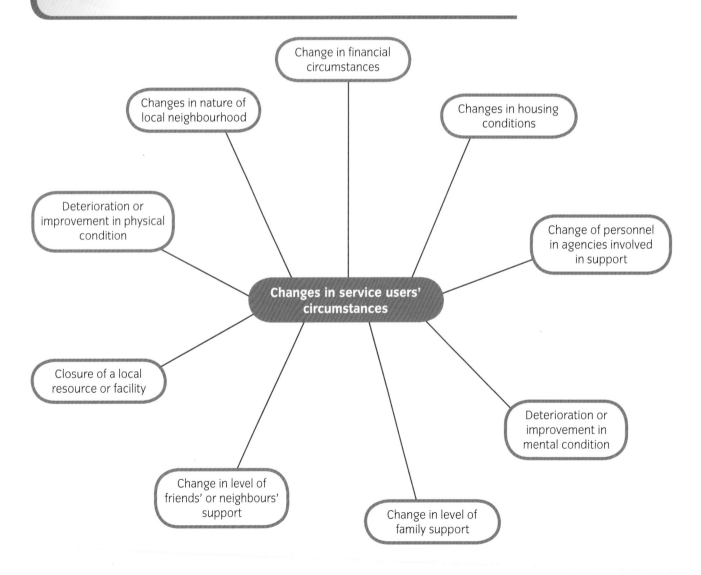

CASE STUDY: Changing levels of support

K is a woman in her early 50s. She has Parkinson's disease, her level of mobility has been decreasing gradually over the past three years, and she has recently begun to fall frequently. She lives with her two sons aged 19 and 25, and her only contact with health and care provision so far has been through her hospital consultant and the primary care team. Her service requirements have been mainly medical with regular support from a physiotherapist.

Her increase in falling has coincided with a major change in her circumstances. Her younger son has been offered a place at an excellent university and her older son has been headhunted for his dream job in the United States on a two-year contract. K does not want either of her sons to miss the opportunities they have been offered – so she now wants to discuss the ways in which she can arrange support which will allow her to remain as independent as possible.

1   *Who should be the first professionals K holds discussions with?*

2   *Who else should be involved in planning?*

3   *How would you help to ensure that K retained control of the process?*

4   *What feelings would you anticipate K would have about her change in circumstances?*

5   *What steps do you think should be taken to make sure that K remains independent?*

Keys to good practice: Plan of care

✓   Always ensure that you have information about all of the individual's circumstances, using observation as well as direct questioning.

✓   Make sure you have the individual's agreement to use any of the information you have acquired.

✓   Ensure that all the relevant information you have about the individual and his or her circumstances is passed on to those who are involved in planning care provision.

✓   Support the individual in making a direct contribution to the process of planning his or her own care programme, and in expressing preferences.

✓   Check that proposals made by professional agencies meet with the agreement of the individual before starting any programme of care.

✓   Make arrangements to regularly feed back on the provision of the service.

✓   Contribute to regular arrangements for reviewing the service and make sure that the individual is involved throughout the process.

HSC 25c Contribute to revisions of specific plan of care activities

The purpose of reviews

Reviews are essential because care situations very rarely remain the same for long periods of time. As circumstances change, the package of care may need to be reviewed in the light of those changes. At agreed intervals, all of the parties involved should come together to reflect on whether or not the package of care is continuing to do the job it was initially set up to do. If there were no reviews, the arrangements would continue for years regardless of whether they were still meeting care needs.

A review will gather together all the information about the circumstances of the individual, the service provided and the service provider. It will give all those concerned with the care of the individual the opportunity to express their opinions and to be involved in a discussion about how effective care provision has been and the changes, if any, that need to be made.

Remember

Nothing stays the same – everything is subject to change. This includes all aspects of people's circumstances. You must make sure that the care people receive changes in line with any changes in their lives.

Who is involved in the review process

Any review should attempt to obtain the views of as many people as possible who are involved in the care of the individual. The most important people at the review are the individual and his or her carers or family. You, as the person (or one of the people) providing services from the plan of care, are a very important contributor. The key worker or care manager/co-ordinator is also central to the review process, as is any organisation providing the care.

It is also important that others with an interest in the care of the individual have the opportunity to participate in a review. For example, a GP, health visitor, community psychiatric nurse, community occupational therapist, physiotherapist, speech therapist, welfare rights support worker, representative of a support group, or anyone else who has been a significant contributor to the life and care of the individual concerned should be involved if at all possible. The status of all the participants should be equal,

in that everyone has the opportunity to give a view and to contribute to the discussion. However, the key person who must agree to any review decision is the individual concerned.

Physiotherapist · **Key worker** · **Relative** · **Service user** · **Occupational therapist** · **GP** · **Support worker** · **Health visitor**

People who might be involved in a review

How the review process is managed

The care manager/co-ordinator or key worker is likely to be the person responsible for organising the review itself and making sure that it takes place at the appropriate time. If the individual receiving care is receiving direct payment, he or she is likely to take responsibility for initiating a review if it is felt to be necessary. Where direct payments are involved your role is very different; it is simply one of being there to provide support and assistance if it is required by the individual – you would only become involved in a review if that was requested by the individual.

The person managing the review is likely to go through a checklist similar to the one below to make sure that the review meets the needs of the individual concerned.

Review checklist

1   Does the individual understand what a review is?

2   Do the individual's carers also understand what a review is and its purpose?

3   Is the review arranged at an appropriate time to check the progress?

4   Is this an annual review or has it been triggered by a change in the individual's circumstances?

---

5   Does the review cover whether the individual continues to need the same level of support and services, whether there have been any changes, what the original care plan intended, and the results of the monitoring?

6   Has the individual been asked when and where would be convenient for the review?

7   Has it been explained to the individual which decisions the review is able to take in respect of his or her continuing care provision and the development of a new care plan?

8   Has the individual been offered an advocate in order to help him or her prepare for the review, to support or to speak for him or her at the review?

9   Does the individual know who is responsible for making sure that the review meeting is managed?

10 Does the individual know all of the people who will be at the review?

11 Can all of the participants contribute either in writing or verbally to the review?

12 Do all the participants in the care plan know that they can request a review?

13 Have carers been consulted about the appropriate time and location for the review?

14 Have crèche facilities been offered for anyone who needs them so that they can attend the review?

During the review everyone should be given a chance to contribute. If the individual receiving care has chosen to use an advocate to present his or her point of view, this person should have every opportunity to contribute on the individual's behalf. If some choose to communicate in writing or by other means, such as e-mail, then those comments must be taken into account. If there have been any changes in organisational policies or access to resources, or changes in the circumstances of the service provider, these are also key matters and should be fed into the review for consideration.

You will have the opportunity to contribute your feedback and observations about the way in which the service meets the present needs of the individual and what changes may be needed.

Don't be intimidated

It can be quite daunting to make a contribution to a review, especially if there is a room full of people. It can help to make notes in advance about what you want to say. Don't forget, your role is essential – no one, apart from the individual and his or her family, has as much information as you do. You are the person undertaking the hands-on care and you have a vitally important view about changes in needs and how the individual is benefiting – or not – from the present provision.

Supporting people to contribute

You may need to support the individual to recognise the impact of significant change and to identify the differences between important and unimportant changes. You may wish to use a prompt such as:

'B, your sister coming to live nearby is something which has happened to you since the last review, isn't it? Do you think things will change much for you?'

'J, have you found that your new job has made much of a difference to you?'

'M, has having an extra afternoon at the centre made the difference you hoped for at the last review?'

Making decisions

Once all the information has been gathered and all contributions have been made, those taking part in the review will need to make a decision about any necessary changes to the care plan and the care package for the next period of time. Decisions should clearly be based on the monitoring of evidence and should particularly take account of contributions from the individual and his or her carers.

A review should not take a decision about changing provision with which the individual fundamentally disagrees. If the proposed changes are because of a change in the level of available resources and result in a reduction in service to the individual, it may be that such a decision is inevitable. However, it is important that the alternative which will be in place is acceptable to the individual.

If the individual is dissatisfied at the end of the review, it is important he or she is informed about the complaints procedure and the process for asking for a further review of the resources available. Full access should be ensured by offering advocacy or any other support services which may be required for individuals to take full advantage of any complaints system or further routes to changing decisions, such as approaching decision makers or accessing pressure groups.

At the end of each review it is essential that the date is set for the next review and that all the participants, particularly the individual and his or her carers, find the date acceptable, both in terms of their own availability and the length of time before the review is due to take place. Reviews must be undertaken at least once a year and if an individual is receiving a care package under the care programme approach system through the mental health services, any admission to hospital must generate a review within a month of discharge.

Check it out

Find out about the arrangements for reviews in your workplace. Check how often they are undertaken, who attends them and who is responsible for arranging them. Ask if you could attend a review as an observer in order to find out what happens.

How the review process is recorded

Keys to good practice: Recording a care package review

All reviews must be recorded in the individual's records and they must include:

✓ written reports from each care service included in the care package

Keys to good practice: Recording a care package review

✓ a record that all relevant staff have been invited to attend the review or to contribute in writing

✓ a record showing how the individual has been prepared for the review and the access he or she has to an advocate if required

✓ evidence that relevant carers and others who offer support have been invited to contribute

✓ a record of all those who attended or who contributed

✓ a careful record of any changes and the revised care plan as a separate document.

All organisations have their own documentation and they are likely to contain most or all of the above points. It is important that all those who have contributed, even if they have not been present at the review, are informed of the outcome and that they know of any changes to the care plan for the individual.

Recorded reviews contribute to the overall quality of the service any organisation offers and they are likely to be included in any file audit undertaken during inspection processes. The review process, if it is well conducted, provides a vital opportunity for individuals to contribute and to make choices about the care package they receive. Reviews which are badly prepared and carelessly undertaken rob individuals of the opportunity to take decisions which affect their lives significantly, and they also result in an ineffective use of scarce and valuable resources.

Test yourself

Mr G is a man aged 79. He has been receiving support at home to assist in basic daily living tasks such as shopping, cooking and maintaining his home. Over the past six months, however, he has become increasingly frail and is now finding it difficult to wash and dress himself. His personal hygiene is deteriorating as a result and he has recently developed a skin rash.

1 What should happen now for Mr G?

2 Who should be involved in considering the next steps?

3 How can you make sure that Mr G is involved in the process?

4 In what ways can changes such as these be monitored?

5 Who is responsible for monitoring changes for Mr G?

HSC 25 UNIT TEST

1 Why is feedback important ?

2 Why is monitoring important in respect of maintaining quality of service provision?

3 Why is monitoring important to promoting the independence of individuals in receipt of care packages?

4 How can individuals contribute to the monitoring process?

5 How can families and carers be involved in monitoring?

6 Who are the people who need to be involved in the review process?

7 What are the types of changes that you may notice in your role providing the service?

8 How can individuals with communication differences be involved in reviews?

9 Why is it important to accurately record reviews?

10 What changes should be documented after a review?

Support individuals to access and use information

In this unit you will have the opportunity to think about how you pass information to individuals and how you help them to gain access to the most useful services and facilities. Regardless of your role and area of work, you will at some point need to provide information to those you work with or their relatives or friends. It is important that you understand how to access and update that information so that it is relevant for people who need to access services.

A wide range of information sources are now available, and many of them involve technology. You will need to be sure that you understand the advice and support individuals may need in order to make the best use of what is available, and you may need to update some of your own skills so that you can offer the most comprehensive support.

What you need to learn

- How to find out what people need
- How to obtain accurate information
- Legislation about information
- Storing information
- The impact of information
- How to make information accessible
- How to support people to use information
- Overcoming barriers
- Enabling people to use services and facilities
- Checking information
- Giving useful feedback.

HSC 26a Support individuals to identify information to meet their needs

How to find out what people need

The key word in the title of this element is 'individuals'. You need to be sure that you establish people's individual needs and wants for information about services and facilities.

This is not about what you think would be best for someone, tempting as it may be to try to persuade people to make use of a facility that you think would benefit them. This is not your role. Your role is to give individuals the information that will help them to reach their own conclusions.

Do not assume that everyone will be in a position to ask directly for the information they need. In order to be able to ask for what you need, you have to know the right questions to ask and you have to know something about the solutions that exist. For example, how could an older person ask about attending a luncheon club unless he or she knew that such a thing exists? How could a carer looking after a parent with Alzheimer's ask about a local carers' support group unless he or she was aware of its existence?

Individuals need to know what is available before they can decide what they would like to do

To establish the type of information or services that an individual needs you may have to ask quite a few questions. You will not be able to rely on individuals being able to identify what it is they want. You will need to use your listening skills in order to pick up what it is that individuals are looking for. It can also help if you ask some prompting questions. This may help to point people in the general direction of a service or facility that they would like to use. The type of questions to use are those beginning: 'Would you like …?', 'Would it help if …?', 'Would you enjoy …?'.

To give people the maximum possible choice in reaching their decisions it may be better to phrase your questions generally. 'Would you enjoy some company for lunch once or twice a week?' may be better than 'Would you like to go to the luncheon club at the community centre once or twice a week?'.

Posing a question in this way allows an individual to gradually get used to a new idea and to think about his or her preferences. It also allows people to stop at the point where they feel they have made enough commitment for the present. It may be sufficient for a first conversation to establish that an individual would like some company; it may take a little more time to decide that he or she would like to join with a group of other people at a luncheon club, rather than arrange for someone to visit once or twice a week. The general question has allowed the individual to make a decision about the idea of company. Later discussion can establish exactly the form and the setting in which company would be welcome. If you had begun the discussion with full details of the luncheon club and the community centre, this may have provoked a negative response from an individual who may not be keen on meeting a lot of strangers in a strange building.

Taking decisions

With careful thought and full information given at the right time, decisions can be taken at a pace which suits the individual. This careful pace will also enable you to be sure that the individual has understood any information you have shared with him or her.

Of course, you may not always be in the position of gradually widening the options for an individual. There may be circumstances where you are faced with the opposite. For example, if you work with a young, enthusiastic person with learning difficulties or a disability, who wants to know about a wide range of opportunities and facilities, you may find that you have to carefully assist him or her to achieve a realistic view of how many things can be undertaken at any one time. The golden rule is not to limit the information you provide, or the ways in which you provide it, because you believe that a particular facility or service is unsuitable for someone. The choice is theirs, and the job of supporting them to access the information is yours.

Support service users to access the information they require and to make choices

If you have worked with an individual for a period of time and have got to know him or her, it will be much easier for you to know about his or her interests and the types of services and facilities that are likely to be useful. It is then easier to raise questions about any new facilities or services that he or she may wish to try.

You will also need to take care that you do not encourage unrealistic expectations about services and facilities available in the local area. When you are asking questions about services and facilities that an individual would like to use, take care that you only provide definite information about those of which you are certain. If you have any doubt whether a particular service or facility is provided in your local area or is restricted because of lack of resources, you should say that you will find out more information and let the individual know.

It may be useful to have a list which you check regularly in respect of all the individuals you work with about the services and facilities which may be of value to them. Facilities vary greatly from area to area and from setting to setting. However, the following table shows a general picture of the services and facilities which individuals may find useful, and which you should be able to provide information about.

Services and facilities checklist

What	Who	Where
Meals	Social services or voluntary organisation	Social services department
Home care	Social services or independent provider	Social services department
Family support	Social services or independent sector	Social services department
Shopping	Local voluntary organisations	Library, Citizens Advice Bureau, social services department, local church
Lunch or social clubs	Social services or local voluntary organisations	Social services department, library, Citizens Advice Bureau, local church
Holidays	Specialist travel companies (e.g. Saga, Winged Fellowship), social services, specialist voluntary organisations (e.g. Royal National Institute for the Blind, Mencap, Scope, Age Concern)	Social services department, library, Citizens Advice Bureau, Internet, travel agent
Pensions/benefits	Benefits Agency, social services, Welfare Rights Centre	Welfare Rights Centre, Claimant's Union, Benefits Agency, Citizens Advice Bureau
Sports and leisure facilities	Leisure services department, National Organisation for Sport for the Disabled, International Paralympic Committee, Riding for the Disabled, etc.	Town hall, Citizens Advice Bureau, library, Internet
Mobile library	Libraries/leisure services department	Town hall
Cinema, theatre and entertainment	Leisure services department, theatres and cinemas	Town hall, library, Internet, What's on Guide

J was a young man in his mid-twenties who used a wheelchair following a spinal injury. J was provided with 24-hour care and had a team of support workers. Recently J had appeared to be somewhat unhappy. He said he was bored and wanted something more exciting to do. His support worker suggested a range of options including visiting the cinema, the theatre, going to a social club or visiting an art gallery – all of which were interests of J's. However, every suggestion was rejected without J giving any clear reason why.

A few days later a different support worker decided to approach matters in a different way, and through questioning she established that J would very much like to take up any of the suggestions made earlier, but had assumed that to do any of them he needed to take a taxi and this was something he felt unable to afford. J had not liked to say that he could not afford the taxi and so had simply refused any of the suggestions. The second support worker was able to explain to J that the local authority operated a dial-a-ride service with a small bus specially adapted for wheelchairs, and that J could book this service and use it for a nominal charge. J was delighted and began to make plans for a range of visits and activities.

1 *What was the mistake made in giving information to J?*

2 *What may have happened if the second support worker had not spoken to J?*

3 *What can you learn from this?*

How to obtain accurate information

No one expects you to have your head full of information to pass on to people! However, you do need to know where to find information and the best and most efficient ways of doing so. You also need to know how to keep information so that you have access to it whenever you need to use or update it.

We now live in an information society – masses of information are available on more subjects than you ever knew existed. It is easy to become confused and end up with information which will not serve a useful purpose for the individuals you work with.

Local sources of information

One of the most useful sources of information is the 'one-stop shop' approach of organisations such as the Citizens Advice Bureau. You may also find that your local Council for Voluntary Service or your local authority may have an information point; these are often located in libraries, town halls, civic centres or other easily accessible places. At these points you can usually obtain leaflets and information, and staff are available to find out more for you and to offer advice on specific areas of need. Most advice centres will find information for you if they do not have it to hand.

You may be looking for specific information in response to an individual's request or you may be generally updating your own information so that you are ready to deal promptly with any information requests. In either case, any of these facilities provide you with a very good starting point.

Many excellent sources of information are available to you locally

Special interest groups

Another excellent source of information is the specific interest groups such as Age Concern, the Alzheimer's Society, Mencap, Scope, and so on.

These are a wonderful source of information about facilities and services, specifically related to those with a particular condition. The contact addresses and telephone numbers for these organisations will be found at your starting point advice centre, such as the Citizens Advice Bureau or your local library or voluntary services. All of these organisations also have websites with a wealth of information and links to other websites of interest. The websites can be found by typing the name of an organisation, or of a condition such as Alzheimer's, into a search engine such as Google.

The Internet

One of the best sources of information is the Internet. To use this you will need access to a computer connected to the Internet and some skill or experience in using the various search engines in order to locate relevant websites.

The information that you can obtain from the Internet is almost unlimited and covers every possible subject. However, you must be aware that this information is not subject to any form of verification or control, and therefore it is not always possible to confirm its accuracy. If you are finding information from the Internet to pass on to individuals, you should obtain it primarily from official websites of relevant organisations for the particular area of interest.

Other useful websites are official government sites and those of universities and research establishments. Using the Internet can be a very quick and easy way of gaining accurate and up-to-date information, often before it has appeared in print or become readily accessible in other ways.

For many individuals, accessing information for themselves over the Internet can be useful and can motivate them to explore the huge potential of the World Wide Web. This can provide many people with a new hobby, as can be seen from the massive interest in 'Silver Surfers' groups being run around the country by Age Concern. The take-up of these classes for older people has been huge, and many people now have the skills to access information for themselves. Beware of assuming that anyone over the age of 60 knows nothing about 'surfing the Net' – you may be surprised to find that they are much more able than you are!

There are increasing opportunities for people to access the Internet even if they do not have their own computers. Cyber cafés and many libraries, local town halls, colleges and universities have facilities for public access to the Internet, usually for a small fee. You might encourage people to do this if appropriate. As always, the best approach to take is to support individuals to be self-managing and to find out information for themselves.

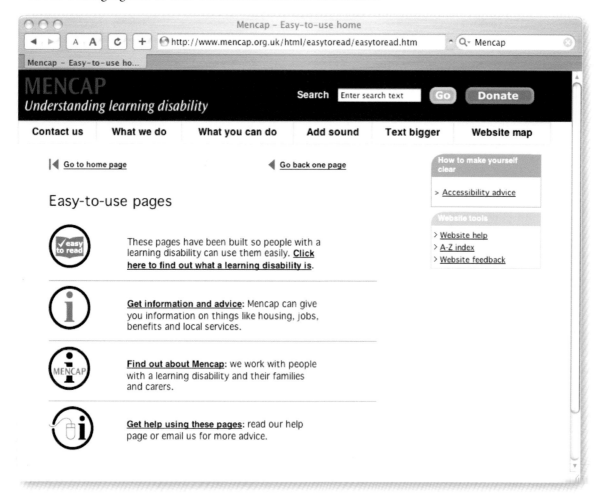

Mencap's website is an excellent source of easy-to-access information

Legislation about information

Access to information is broadly governed by two Acts of Parliament. The first is the **Data Protection Act 1998**, which restricts the way in which personal information can be used and limits those who can access information about individuals. There are basic principles which govern the way information must be handled.

All information, however it is stored, is subject to the rules laid down in the Act; it covers medical records, social service records, credit information, local authority information – in fact, anything which is personal data (facts and opinions about an individual).

Anyone processing personal data must comply with the eight enforceable principles of good practice. As you saw in Unit HSC 21, these say that data must be:

- fairly and lawfully processed
- processed for limited purposes
- adequate, relevant and not excessive
- accurate
- not kept for longer than necessary
- processed in accordance with the data subject's rights
- kept secure
- not transferred to countries without adequate protection.

You will need to be aware of these restrictions in case an individual asks you for help in finding out information about someone else.

The other piece of relevant legislation is the **Freedom of Information Act 2000**. This Act is about accessing information held by public bodies such as local councils, the Health Service and the government. It is concerned with records about the activities and plans of public bodies, not about individuals.

Each public body must set out the details of information it will routinely make available, how the information can be obtained and whether there is any charge for it. Each public authority must comply with requests for the information it holds unless an exemption from disclosure applies. Public authorities normally have a maximum of 20 working days to respond to a request.

This will be useful if you are helping someone find out about the policies and decision-making of a public body.

Storing information

Once you have obtained information for an individual, or to keep your own knowledge up to date and current, you need to be sure that you can store it in an accessible way. You can rely on your memory for many of the main facts, but clearly you need to record individual addresses, telephone numbers, website addresses and detailed information about the services provided.

It is a good idea to create an information store where you can keep leaflets, notes, telephone numbers and cuttings from newspapers or magazines which may be of interest either to people you are currently working with, or to others in the future. A simple filing system, either alphabetical or grouped by subject, in a concertina file or a filing drawer, is probably the easiest way to deal with this.

A small library of information is very useful provided that it is kept up to date. It is important that on a regular basis, perhaps every three months, you go through it, discarding information which has become outdated and replacing it with the most current. If you prefer to store information electronically, create a folder on a computer in which you record the website and e-mail addresses of relevant services. It is also useful to keep important websites in the 'favourites' menu so that they are easily accessible.

Evidence indicator

Collect information and prepare an information store for yourself either in hard copy or on a computer. File the information under clearly distinguishable headings or alphabetically, and ensure you can find any information you require easily and accurately. Make plans to revisit your sources of information or the relevant websites at least once every three months and update information, discarding anything which has become outdated. Make a note of how many times you refer to your information store during the first three months of use.

The impact of information

Sometimes, depending on the information, finding something out may have a significant effect on an individual. Imagine someone who has become convinced that he or she can solve a current financial problem through receiving a particular grant; the individual has heard about the grant and has built up hopes of it. When you support the individual in finding out about the grant, you discover that he or she is not eligible.

In all such cases it is good practice to prepare the ground in advance by encouraging the individual to consider all possibilities and to make contingency plans in case of disappointment. Be ready to suggest alternative approaches to problems, and new areas to explore.

Test yourself

1 List three useful sources of information.

2 What precautions do you need to take when finding information on the Internet?

3 How can information be stored?

4 What are the two main pieces of legislation which cover information?

5 Give two main points from each Act.

HSC 26b Enable individuals to access, select and use information

How to make information accessible

Once you have found out what someone's needs are and referred to your own store of information or made further enquiries, you need to provide the information in a way which is useful to the individual concerned. When you are providing information you will need to give careful thought to:

- the needs of the person receiving the information
- the nature of the information.

The needs of the individual

First, you must be sure that you give the information in a way which can be understood by the individual concerned. You must ensure that any specific communication needs are met. For example, people may require information to be in a particular format such as large print or in braille, or to be communicated using signing. You will need to find out how to change the format of the information, or access it in a suitable format.

You will also need to consider the circumstances when you pass on information about a particular service or facility. You should take into account the situation of the individual at that particular time – remember to look at the bigger picture. An obvious example is that you would not pass on information about social clubs and outings to someone whose partner had just died. That sort of information may be appropriate in a few weeks or months, but it is unlikely to be of any value at the moment. This principle also applies in situations where you are aware that somebody is particularly upset by problems or difficulties. You also need to take into account an individual's state of health and any medical treatment which may affect the relevance or usefulness of the information.

Make sure that information is accessible by:

- presenting it in the most useful format
- making it available at the right time
- taking all the circumstances into account.

There is also a right way and right time for supporting people to access information.

Oh Betty, I did check and there is a painting class on Tuesday afternoons at 2.30, or Thursday mornings at half-past 10, and you can go along to either of them if you just phone the library first ...

Carers must take the time to pass on information clearly, not in a rush

From your work on communication skills, you will remember that it is important you do not rush what you say, and that people are more receptive to information if they are comfortable and at ease. Don't attempt to pass on information as you are rushing out of the door – it is unlikely that someone will remember the details of a hurried remark.

Directly accessed information

If an individual is accessing information independently, he or she may come across other difficulties. Information may not be available in a format the individual can readily use. For example, information about a local theatre production may not be available in large print, or a poster advertising an exhibition may be at the top of a flight of stairs, making it inaccessible for some people. A local information office may not have a loop system, making it difficult for people with impaired hearing to access verbal information. Problems of this type will need to be addressed.

You may come across situations where information clearly discriminates against people on the grounds of race, gender or disability. For example, someone finding out information about a job may be told he need not apply because he has a disability. If you find any instances of discriminatory information, you should offer to support the individual concerned in informing the relevant bodies – see Unit HSC 24, page 126.

Problems with access to information, either because it is in an inappropriate format or location, or because it is inaccurate or out of date, need to be dealt with for two reasons:

- the individual still needs to find out the information
- it needs to be made available for others in the future.

Remember

Throughout this process, your role is to support and encourage people to deal with issues for themselves wherever possible, rather than relying on you to do it for them.

The nature of the information

For many individuals it can be helpful if you write down basic information or give them a relevant leaflet. This may be enough for some people and they may undertake the next stages of research for themselves. Others may want you to do some further research with them.

For most people it is useful to have information in a form they can refer to again while they consider it or commit it to memory. Before meeting someone you should always make sure that you have prepared the information in the most useful form so that passing it on is straightforward.

How to support people to use information

The range of information about services individuals may want to use is large and varied. By no means all the services and facilities which people will want to take advantage of are provided by the health and care services. Many other services and facilities provided by commerce, industry, entertainment and retail organisations will also be useful for people. Once people have the information on what is available, the next stage is to support them to make use of it.

Home services

Depending on individual circumstances, some individuals may wish to take advantage of services which can be supplied to them in their own home rather than having to travel. If you work with someone who is unable or unwilling to travel, you will need to support him or her in finding out whether services can be provided at home. Many organisations provide an off-site service. Examples are:

- mobile shops
- mail-order shopping catalogues
- mobile libraries
- solicitors
- homecare services
- meals services
- doctors and other health services
- pharmacists.

Services such as meals can be provided directly to individuals' own homes

Most banks and building societies provide services on-line and by telephone, as do many large and small retail shopping facilities. Home delivery take-away food is readily available in most areas, as are films via rented videos or through satellite or cable television. Most local councils allow payments on-line, and one social services department is trialling a procedure of carrying out assessments for services on-line. The benefits are enormous for those people who have access to a computer and the skills to use the Internet.

Travelling to services

People have to travel if they want to participate in many forms of entertainment and culture, such as the theatre, concerts, art galleries, or sporting events. They will also have to travel to essential appointments, such as an appearance in court or a visit to the hospital. When you are encouraging individuals to make maximum use of services you may need to discuss travel arrangements with them. Information about travelling and access will be important, and you may need to work with the individual to identify any problems with accessing the services he or she wants to use.

You may need to research information about travel arrangements

Taking a back seat

Many people may need to be encouraged to use services after finding enough information to make a properly considered choice. However, you must be careful not to cross the boundary between encouraging them and pressurising them into using a particular facility or service. Everyone has a right to choose not to take up services and facilities available to them.

You are unlikely to pressurise anyone into reading a particular book or seeing a particular film, simply because you think it is good – you would simply say how enjoyable you found the book or film, and strongly recommend it. However, it is easy to step over the boundary when you believe an individual needs to be encouraged to find out about and use a service that seems to be in his or her interests.

For example, you may feel that receiving additional support services, attending a physiotherapy session or making a claim for additional benefit would be of great advantage to the person concerned. But your role is limited to supporting the individual in finding the information necessary to make an informed choice. You should avoid putting pressure on the individual to take a particular course of action.

Similarly, you should not attempt to prevent someone from following a course of action because you believe it is risky or unsuitable. Professional carers can be faced with difficult situations when people have obtained information about facilities or activities which may expose them to risk of injury or other dangers. There is a fine line between neglecting your responsibilities for the individual's safety and imposing unfair restrictions. Most people working in health and care are likely to be cautious, rather than careless. Although this concern for the safety of individuals is well-intentioned, it can result in restricting people's rights to enjoy the facilities and services available.

CASE STUDY: Encouraging independence

E has lived in a residential facility for people with learning difficulties since she was five years old. She is now 25, and although perfectly able to live in supported group accommodation in the community, she has chosen to remain in the same residential facility in which she has grown up. Because of her unique circumstances of having been there since she was a young child, a decision has been taken that E can remain in the residential facility even though all the present residents require a much higher degree of care than E does. All the former residents who function as well as E does have long since moved on into group homes out in the community.

E helps a great deal at the residential home and carries out simple tasks to support members of staff. She still requires a considerable degree of protection as she has an extremely naïve view of the world and has no understanding of any risk to her personal safety.

E is very sociable and has recently decided that she wishes to make regular visits to a local nightclub. She has become friendly with some local young people and started to visit the local pub with them, and then decided she would like to take up their invitations to join them on nights out further afield.

Staff at the residential home are concerned that E will be at risk in an unsupervised social environment because she has little or no understanding of the personal safety or sexual risks to which she could be exposed. They are therefore considering whether they are able to, or ought to, restrict or refuse permission for E to go on these outings to nightclubs.

1   *Do the staff have any legal right to stop E going to a nightclub?*

2   *Do the staff have any moral right to stop E going to a nightclub?*

3   *How do you think this situation should be handled?*

4   *To what extent should E be allowed to make her own choices?*

5   *Would the circumstances and your views be any different if E were living in group accommodation in the community, rather than in a residential setting?*

6   *Was the decision to allow E to remain in the residential setting the right one?*

Keys to good practice: Encouraging individuals to find out about and use services

✓ Make sure that you support individuals and key people to access a full range of information.

✓ Try to identify difficulties and answer as many questions as possible.

✓ If you do not have information or cannot answer questions, tell the person you will find out, and make sure you do.

✓ Give any information you have about the consequences of using the service or facility, including information about others who may have benefited.

✓ Encourage individuals to find out all the information they need to know about how to access the service or facility, such as whether the service is one they can use at home or have to travel to, and what the travel arrangements need to be.

✓ Offer to assist and support individuals in any way you can, such as offering to introduce them (by previous agreement) to others who may be using the service or facility.

Remember

● If you are using information about other people you should not identify them, in order to maintain their confidentiality.

● If you want to offer to introduce other people, don't forget to respect confidentiality, and never offer this without the express agreement of both parties.

Overcoming barriers

There are many barriers which can restrict access or prevent people from using facilities or services. Information is one of the keys to overcoming barriers. An individual with plenty of accurate and current information, clearly understood and found well in advance, is far more likely to be able to challenge and overcome difficulties than someone who feels uncertain because of a lack of information, and is unprepared for any difficulties.

Barriers to access tend to fall into three categories: environmental, communication, and psychological. Environmental barriers are the most common.

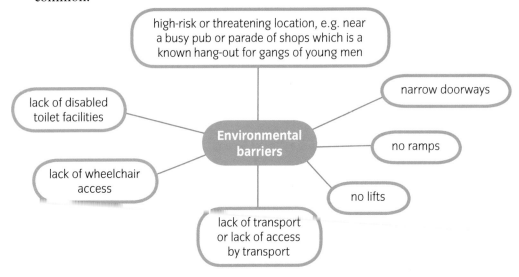

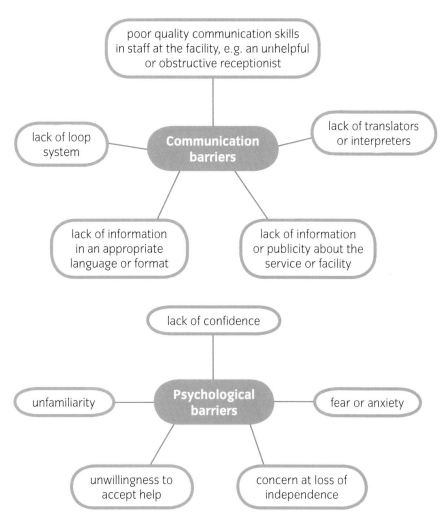

How to challenge and overcome barriers

Start by checking that all possible information is available about the facilities and services, the challenges and the alternatives. Work alongside an individual to help plan ways to challenge and overcome any discrimination and barriers. For example, you may need to support someone to search out alternative facilities if the ones originally found do not have wheelchair access.

If the local theatre does not have wheelchair access, encourage the individual to make arrangements to travel to one that does. Of course, you could also encourage the individual to raise the issue with the local theatre and point out to them that they are in breach of the Disability Discrimination Act.

If there are problems finding suitable transport, it will be necessary to find out about transport with provision for wheelchairs, by checking local taxi or public transport facilities which have the necessary adaptations. Most train companies have support services for people with disabilities, such as ramps and a porter service to enable people to get on and off trains. However, many trains that do provide porterage and ramps do not have readily accessible toilets for disabled people.

Any particular arrangements with a facility to provide access must be agreed with the individual concerned. If a person has to make an important visit to a particular location which cannot be changed and there is no wheelchair access through the main entrance, it may be suggested that the individual use a back entrance or goods entrance and the goods lift. You should always check with the individual before agreeing to this type of arrangement, as not everyone is prepared to access a building through a goods entrance. Many disabled people take the view that they should have the right to access buildings in the same way as everyone else.

In such a case, you may need to support the individual in arranging for the visit to take place at a different location. It is essential you never compromise the right of an individual to choose his or her own means of access and to set boundaries as to what is acceptable in terms of personal space and dignity.

Evidence indicator

Choose three different types of facility which people may wish to access in your locality. They should each be located in a different part of your area. For each, list the potential barriers to access and the ways in which you would begin to tackle the barriers.

An individual has the right to set boundaries as to what is acceptable in terms of dignity

Enabling people to use services and facilities

The level of support which you need to provide to an individual will vary depending on the circumstances. Your support can range from handing someone an information leaflet to making all the arrangements to use a service and accompanying him or her to use it. Between these extremes are a wide range of alternatives. Some people may simply need you to make the initial contact for them. Others may need you to accompany them on a first visit to a new facility or to meet a new group of people, and then to gradually withdraw as they grow in confidence in using the service. On other occasions your role may be to enlist the support of other people who are better qualified, more experienced or who have the resources or time to provide a better service for the individual.

It is important you encourage people to dispense with your support as soon as they feel able to manage independently. You should do this when you notice them becoming more confident in using the facility or service. Do it by gradually and appropriately reducing the level of support.

For example, you may have accompanied someone on a first visit to a Welfare Rights Advice Centre. The individual needed you because he or she was unfamiliar with the service and did not understand the benefit system enough to bc able to explain the information required. However, as the visits continue and the work of the Welfare Rights Advice Centre is under way, you may be able to withdraw from accompanying the individual as he or she becomes more familiar with the workers in the centre. Your involvement may then be limited to driving the individual to the centre, or holding a support session on his or her return.

It may take people a while to adjust with confidence to new social situations. For example, if someone has been supported by you to find out about and then visit a new day centre or social club, it may take a few visits before he or she is confident enough to go alone. As always your role is to do the minimum and to allow individuals the maximum opportunity to make their own lives and to be as independent as possible.

Test yourself

1   What are the main points to consider when providing information?

2   Name three steps you can take to improve accessibility of information.

3   Name three barriers to accessing and using information.

4   How can you help to overcome the barriers?

5   What is the key factor to remember in all the help you provide?

HSC 26c Enable individuals to evaluate the information

Key terms

Evaluate: To decide on the value of something.

Evaluation is often thought to be a difficult and complex process, but in fact it is straightforward. The process of evaluating an event or experience is extremely useful because it allows you to find out:

- what worked well
- what worked badly or didn't work at all
- what was wrong and can be fixed
- what was wrong and can't be fixed
- what you would do/use again
- what you would not do/use again
- what was better than you expected

- what was worse than you expected
- what needs to be changed
- what should stay the same
- what you need to do next time.

The simplest way to find out about any of the items on this list is to ask for feedback. If you are providing something – a service, a product, a facility – you need to know if it is working well. Exactly the same applies to information.

CASE STUDY: Compiling a directory

Students at a local college were studying for a health and social care qualification. For one of their assignments they were asked to produce a directory of information about entertainment and leisure facilities in the local area. When they had completed the project, the students decided to present the finished directory to the supported living unit at 24 The Avenue. This unit provides supported living for eight people with a disability, some of whom have complex needs.

The directory was printed out and stapled to form a booklet. The work had been done very neatly and each facility was identified in bold lettering, followed by a short description of the facilities, like this:

> **Royal Theatre**
> Plays, concerts and shows. Weekly programme of events. Seats 500. Tickets through box office 10.00hrs–20.00hrs 0123 45678. Café available 11.00hrs–18.00hrs. Facilities DT, WA, L, B, H (see key on p. 5)

A few weeks later, staff noticed that the directory was lying in the lounge and no one seemed to have used it.

1 *What do you think may be the reason why the directory was not used?*
2 *How could the directory be improved?*
3 *What sort of information should be in it?*
4 *How should it be presented?*
5 *What should the residents and staff of the unit do now?*

Checking information

The basic requirement for any sort of information is that it should be:
- accurate
- relevant
- up to date
- easy to understand
- accessible to everyone
- within the law.

You need to encourage individuals to check that information is accurate and relevant for their purposes. It also helps if information is interesting!

People who provide information need to know whether it is all of those things, so feedback is essential. You should encourage and support people in providing feedback about information they have accessed or tried to access.

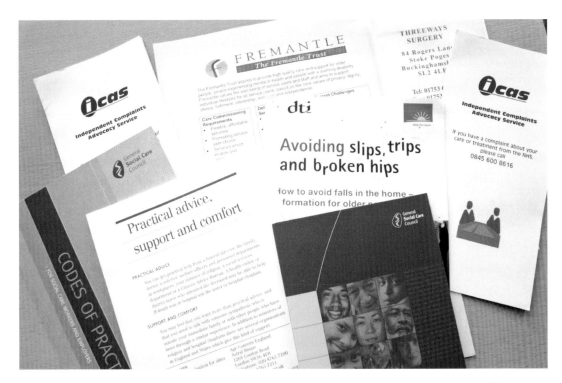

Information needs to be accurate, relevant and accessible

If you have tried to obtain information about welfare rights and it was not available in large print, this fact can be fed back to the co-ordinator of the Welfare Rights Centre. However, it will be important that you encourage the individual concerned to check that information has improved, otherwise the feedback will have been wasted.

In the case of commercial businesses, shops, supermarkets, cinemas, entertainment centres or theatres, feedback should be given to the manager on site. Some businesses may be part of a national or international chain and information may be handled centrally. Where this is the case, you should encourage and support people to seek out those who have responsibility for the information policy of the company and make sure they receive the feedback.

Giving useful feedback

As a care professional you know that receiving feedback is not always easy and that criticism can sometimes make you feel resentful. So you should encourage individuals offering feedback to think about making positive suggestions alongside any complaints they may have. No one likes receiving a long list of complaints and criticism, even if it is well deserved. People are much more receptive to feedback if it is accompanied by useful suggestions about how matters could be improved. This will help them to improve the quality of the information they provide, and should mean that others will not experience the same problems in the future.

Remember

Information is no use if it does not serve the purpose for which it was needed!

Check it out

Find out the process of evaluating information for your workplace. Check who is responsible for evaluating information and how they undertake the task. Ask where the updated information is kept and how its usefulness is checked.

Test yourself

Mrs T is a lady of 65 who was recently diagnosed as having diabetes. She was given information by her GP about how to control her diabetes with diet and exercise, and also given some information leaflets which had been prepared by a nurse practitioner at the surgery.

Mrs T looked on the Internet and visited various websites about diabetes. She read several articles and downloaded more information from a well-known national organisation for diabetes, from a pharmaceutical drug company's website, and from a diabetes chat room where various people with diabetes posted information. She compared the information in the leaflets she had been given and the information she had downloaded, and saw many differences between them. Some seemed to be saying quite different things.

Mrs T took everything along to her next visit to the nurse practitioner at the surgery, who went through it all with her. She was able to help Mrs T to judge which of the information was accurate, which was accurate but did not apply to her, and which was unreliable.

1   Why is it important to check information obtained from the Internet?

2   How can Mrs T find out what information is useful for her?

3   What should Mrs T do when she has found a good source of information?

4   What should she do if she finds that she has been given incorrect or outdated information?

HSC 26 UNIT TEST

1   What are the main sources of information about services and facilities?

2   How would you go about collecting and storing a general information bank?

3   What are the key factors to take into account when providing people with information?

4   What are the potential pitfalls in the way that information is provided?

5   What are the different ways in which you could offer support to people evaluating the information found?

6   What are the effective ways of encouraging people to access and use information?

7   Name four potential barriers to accessing services and facilities.

8   How could these barriers be overcome?

Help individuals to eat and drink

This unit is about helping individuals to choose the food and drink they want and also, if necessary, helping them to eat and drink it. The unit is only about food and drink consumed by mouth, and does not include learning about types of artificial feeding.

You may be working as part of a care team that includes dieticians and occupational therapists, and you may need to know how to use special equipment and keep records of food intake.

To achieve Unit HSC 213 or 214 you will also need to know about basic food hygiene and the processes involved in handling food hygienically – it is likely that you will participate in a food hygiene course and obtain a basic certificate in food hygiene.

If you are undertaking Unit HSC 213, Provide food and drink for individuals, instead of HSC 214, you will find that most of the knowledge you will need will be covered in this unit.

Eating and drinking is vital to life for everyone, but it is also a social activity and one which provides enjoyment and pleasure. Above all, your aim must be to help people to be independent, to eat and drink with dignity and work to make eating and drinking an enjoyable experience.

What you need to learn

- Nutrients
- Giving people choice
- Providing a safe and hygienic environment
- Providing an enjoyable and relaxed environment
- When support may be needed
- Helping people to prepare
- Individual needs
- Checking for a bad reaction
- Clearing away when individuals have finished eating and drinking.

HSC 214a Make preparations to support individuals to eat and drink

Many of the people you work with will have specific dietary needs. These will be identified in the plan of care and you must always be careful to follow the information included in the plan. However, everyone needs a healthy, balanced diet in order to be free from illness and to promote good health and well-being. You will need to check for special requirements such as a diabetic diet, but you also need to know the basic requirements for a healthy, balanced diet and to understand the consequences of a shortage of any of the components.

All human beings require essential nutrients in order to survive. They are classified into five major groups: proteins, carbohydrates, fats, vitamins and minerals. Human beings also need to consume about 2 litres of liquid each day. The liquid can be water, fruit juice, tea, coffee, soda or any kind of non-alcoholic liquid.

It is important that a healthy diet balances the amounts of different nutrients which are taken each day. Clearly the amounts needed will vary depending on the individual. People who are ill may eat very little food, so it may be important that food is presented in small amounts so that people are not put off by a large portion. Some older people will require less food, for example, than an active teenager. The plan of care for each individual will have information about eating and the key facts that are relevant, and it is important that any instructions in the plan of care are followed carefully. Lifestyle, state of health and the amount of exercise an individual takes must be considered when thinking about the amounts of food that people will consume, but it is important to get the balance of nutrients right regardless of quantity.

> ### Key terms
>
> **Nutrients:** The substances in food and drink that provide essential nourishment and promote good health.

Nutrients

Carbohydrates

Carbohydrates are found in starchy foods such as bread, rice, pasta, cereals and potatoes. These should make up about a third of the food eaten. Most people should be eating more starchy foods. Starchy foods are a good source of energy and the main source of a range of nutrients in our diet. As well as starch, these foods contain fibre, calcium, iron and B vitamins.

These foods are rich in carbohydrates

Fibre

Most people don't eat enough fibre. Foods rich in fibre are a very healthy choice, and they include wholegrain bread, brown rice, pasta, oats, beans, peas, lentils, grains, seeds, fruit and vegetables.

Fibre is only found in foods that come from plants. There are two types of fibre: insoluble and soluble.

Insoluble fibre

This is the fibre that the body can't digest and so it passes through the gut, helping other food and waste products move through the gut more easily. Wholegrain bread, brown rice, wholegrain breakfast cereals and fruit and vegetables all contain this type of fibre.

Insoluble fibre helps to keep bowels healthy and prevent constipation. This in turn reduces the risk of some common disorders of the gut. Foods rich in insoluble fibre are bulky and so help make us feel full, which means we are less likely to eat too much.

Soluble fibre

This fibre can be digested fully by the body, and it may help to reduce the amount of cholesterol in the blood. Particularly good sources of soluble fibre include oats and pulses such as beans and lentils.

Fruit and vegetables

Fruit and vegetables should make up about a third of the food eaten each day. They are an essential source of vitamins, minerals and fibre. There is also increasing evidence that people who eat plenty of fruit and vegetables are less likely to develop chronic conditions such as heart disease and some cancers.

It's important to eat a variety. The Food Standards Agency (FSA) recommends that everyone should eat five portions of fruit and vegetables each day. Five-a-day is a good, achievable target, and the FSA identifies the following as portions:

1 apple, banana, pear, orange or other similar-sized fruit	3 heaped tablespoons of fruit salad (fresh or tinned in fruit juice) or stewed fruit
2 plums or similar-sized fruit	1 heaped tablespoon of dried fruit (such as raisins and apricots)
Half a grapefruit or avocado	
1 slice of large fruit, such as melon or pineapple	1 cupful of grapes, cherries or berries
	1 dessert bowl of salad
3 heaped tablespoons of vegetables (raw, cooked, frozen or tinned)	1 glass (150 ml) of fruit juice (however much you drink, fruit juice counts as a maximum of one portion a day)
3 heaped tablespoons of beans and pulses (however much you eat, beans and pulses count as a maximum of one portion a day)	

Protein

Most of the remaining third of the food eaten should be made up of protein, which comes from the following sources.

- Lean meat and poultry. Meat is a good source of iron, zinc, B vitamins (particularly B12) and protein. But meat is also a major source of saturated fat, so try to choose lean cuts of meat and trim off excess fat.
- Fish. Everyone should be eating at least two portions of fish a week, including one of oily fish. But most people aren't eating enough fish. Fish and shellfish are rich in protein and minerals, and oily fish is rich in omega 3 fatty acids.
- Eggs, pulses, nuts and seeds are all good sources of protein and vitamins, and they're easy to prepare. But you need to take care if you're preparing eggs for anyone who is very young or pregnant, or for older people. Eggs must be thoroughly cooked as they are a potential source of food poisoning if they are raw or undercooked.
- Milk and dairy products such as cheese, yoghurt and fromage frais are excellent sources of protein and vitamins A, B12, and D. They are also an important source of calcium, which helps to keep bones strong. The calcium in dairy foods is easy for the body to absorb.

Other nutrients

A small amount of the following nutrients is also needed.

Fats

It's important to have some fat in a diet because fat helps the body absorb some vitamins, is a good source of energy and a source of the essential fatty acids that the body can't make itself. But consuming a lot of fat makes it easy to take in more energy than necessary, which can make people put on weight. For healthy eating, look out for lower-fat alternatives wherever possible and try to include fatty foods only occasionally.

Sugars

Most adults and children in the UK eat too much sugar. A healthy diet should include only a few sugary foods such as sweets, cakes and biscuits, and only occasional sugary soft drinks. Sugars occur naturally in foods such as fruit and milk, but these types of sugars do not need to be restricted. It is food containing added sugars that should be reduced. Sugar is added to many foodstuffs, such as those shown opposite.

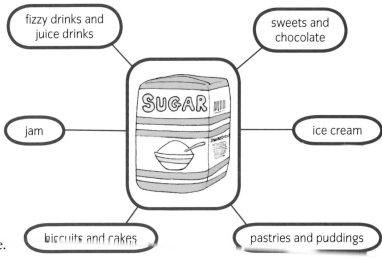

Foodstuffs containing sugar

Salt

Salt is essential in very small amounts for the body to work properly. Adults should have no more than 6 grams of salt a day, which is about a teaspoonful. On average, people are actually consuming about 9.5 grams of salt a day. This means most people are eating nearly 60 per cent more salt than necessary.

Eating too much salt can raise blood pressure, which can make people three times more likely to develop heart disease or have a stroke than people with normal blood pressure.

The salt added during cooking or at the table makes up just a quarter of the salt most people eat. Three-quarters comes from processed food, such as breakfast cereals, soups, sauces, biscuits and ready meals, so be careful to check the salt content in all foods.

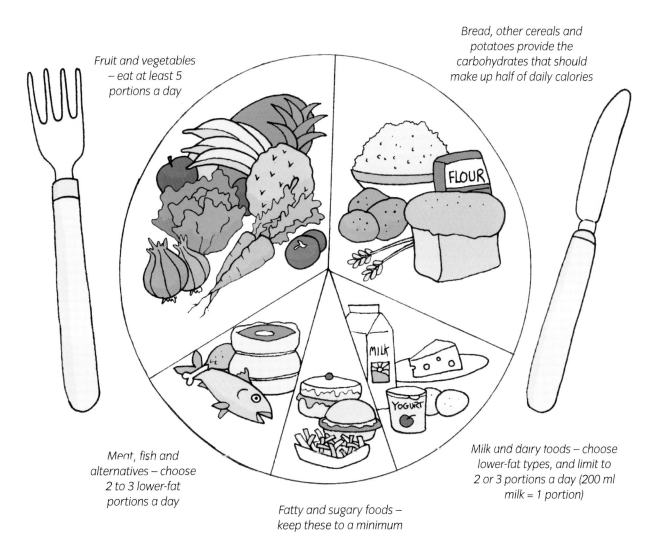

Fruit and vegetables – eat at least 5 portions a day

Bread, other cereals and potatoes provide the carbohydrates that should make up half of daily calories

Meat, fish and alternatives – choose 2 to 3 lower-fat portions a day

Fatty and sugary foods – keep these to a minimum

Milk and dairy foods – choose lower-fat types, and limit to 2 or 3 portions a day (200 ml milk = 1 portion)

A balanced diet

Vitamins and minerals

Vitamins are essential for maintaining good health and maintaining the human body in good condition. Some vitamins are in certain foods in very small quantities, but they are nonetheless essential, as are minerals which similarly may be found in extremely small quantities. All vitamins and minerals have very specific purposes within the body, as the table below shows.

Nutrient	Where found	Purpose
Vitamin A	Found in liver and fish oils, milk, butter, eggs and cheese and can be made by the body from carotene which is found in carrots, tomatoes and green vegetables	Protects from infection and contributes to growth. A lack of vitamin A can cause eye problems
Vitamin B group (there are several)	Found in cereals, liver, yeast and nuts	This is a large group of complex vitamins, all of which are essential for maintaining a good skin. It may be that a lack of vitamin B is responsible for some diseases of the nervous system
Vitamin C	Found in citrus fruits, strawberries, potatoes and some green vegetables	Vitamin C cannot be stored so it must be taken each day. A lack of vitamin C can cause scurvy, a disease which affects the gums and causes bleeding – an extremely serious condition. People who have a lack of vitamin C are also more likely to be affected by viral infections and coughs and colds
Vitamin D	Found in eggs and fish oils, and made by the body when the skin is exposed to sunlight	Vitamin D enables calcium to be absorbed to strengthen and develop bones and teeth. A severe shortage of vitamin D will lead to rickets, a deforming disease seen in children where bones do not develop adequately
Vitamin E	Found in wheat germ, cereals, egg yolks, liver and milk	This helps prevent cell damage and degeneration
Minerals, e.g. iron, calcium, sodium	A wide range of minerals, essential for health, are found in eggs, cocoa, liver, baked beans, cheese and milk	Iron is important for the formation of red blood cells, and a lack of iron can lead to anaemia. Calcium is used for developing firm bones. Sodium is important for maintaining the fluid balance of the body but an excess of sodium can be a contributory cause of oedema (fluid retention)

Giving people choice

It is important to give individuals some choice in the food they eat. This will make meal times more enjoyable. Just imagine being unable to prepare food for yourself and having to sit down day after day to eat boring or unappetising or badly cooked food!

Choice should be offered both in the type of food, the way it is cooked and the quantity of food that is provided. It may also be helpful, if possible, to vary the times at which food is provided, so that individuals can choose the time at which they wish to eat rather than having to fit in with the arrangements of their care setting. Of course, this is not easy as there are always considerations about staffing and running any care facility. You will also need to consider the religious requirements and personal preferences that people have in respect of food. The situations you may come across include the following.

- Vegetarians do not eat meat or meat-based products.
- Vegans are vegetarians who also do not eat dairy products, eggs or any animal-related foods.
- Muslims do not eat pork or meat from carnivorous animals and will only eat meat killed in a particular way (Halal). Alcohol is forbidden.
- Jewish people do not eat pork and do not eat meat and milk together. Meat must have been killed and prepared in a particular way (Kosher).
- Hindus do not eat beef, and many are vegetarian. Alcohol is forbidden.
- Traditionally, Roman Catholics did not eat meat on a Friday, and ate fish on that day. Some older people may still observe this rule.
- Sikhs do not eat beef and do not drink alcohol.
- Rastafarians are mainly vegetarian, although those who do eat meat cannot eat pork.

Keys to good practice: Respecting choices

✓ Ensure that people's religious preferences are discussed with them and support them in choosing suitable food and drink.

✓ Make sure these preferences are recorded in their plan of care and are observed by everybody who is providing care for them.

✓ The personal likes and dislikes of each individual should be discussed with him or her and recorded.

✓ It should be clear to any new member of the care team that there are particular types of food which a person does not eat or does not like.

It is likely that people's preferences will vary according to their life stage. For example, young children are likely to have quite different tastes from those of adults or older people. A meal of burger, chips and ice cream may be very attractive to a ten-year-old, and to a considerable number of adolescents, but may not be welcomed by an older person.

Particular needs

It is absolutely vital that people's dietary needs are noted in the plan of care. This *must* include allergies and special diets, for example a diabetic or gluten-free diet, or a shellfish or nut allergy. Very serious consequences can occur if allergies and medical diets are not recorded in the plan of care, or not followed.

A typical entry on a care plan may read:

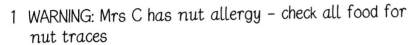

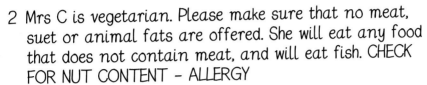

1 WARNING: Mrs C has nut allergy – check all food for nut traces

2 Mrs C is vegetarian. Please make sure that no meat, suet or animal fats are offered. She will eat any food that does not contain meat, and will eat fish. CHECK FOR NUT CONTENT – ALLERGY

3 Likes tea and coffee with hardly any milk

Problems

People may be reluctant, or may even refuse, to eat certain types of food which have been noted in their plan of care as a requirement for their condition – such as a diabetic diet, a weight-reduction diet or a gluten-free diet. This can cause difficulties in terms of being able to offer freedom of choice. You may feel that this places you, and other care staff, in a very difficult position.

If someone is determined to ignore medical advice and to follow a different diet, this should be reported and discussed among the care team and the medical staff responsible for the person's care. Ultimately you have little control over a diabetic who buys and eats Mars bars and sweets. However, you do have a responsibility to provide full information and explanations, and to repeat the explanations regularly to the person and to make every effort to persuade him or her to comply with the dietary requirements. If a person chooses, in full knowledge of the consequences, to ignore medical advice, then that is his or her choice.

The situation is different, however, for children, people who are compulsorily detained under the Mental Health Act or subject to guardianship, and older people who are very confused or severely demented. All of those situations require a high degree of tact, skill and understanding. It is important that you report immediately to your supervisor any difficulties involving a person's consumption of food and drink.

Remember

Your responsibility is to inform, explain and advise. You cannot normally force anyone to follow medical advice about diet.

Did you know?

Despite all the publicity and hype about all the different fast foods such as burgers and pizzas, Britain's favourite fast food is still the sandwich!

Check it out

Find out how your workplace copes with special diets and food preferences. Are the procedures the same with diets followed for medical reasons as with those followed for religious or cultural reasons? Is someone who is a vegetarian by choice given the same treatment as someone who is diabetic? If there appear to be differences, ask your supervisor about the reasons.

Providing a safe and hygienic environment

All establishments where food is prepared and served are governed by the Food Safety (General Food Hygiene) Regulations 1995. These regulations set out the basic hygiene principles that must be followed in relation to staff, premises and food handling.

Under the regulations, all establishments must have effective food safety management measures (or 'controls') in place, to ensure that food is produced safely and that the health of individuals is not put at risk.

When preparing food, safety and hygiene are paramount

Food safety management is all about identifying how and when things could go wrong and introducing checks to stop that happening. Further regulations come into force on 1 January 2006 with the Food Safety Regulations 2005, incorporating the European guidelines on managing food safety.

Hygiene requirements

If you are preparing areas or equipment for people who are about to eat or drink, it is important that you follow basic hygiene procedures. This will also involve you in knowing how to store and prepare food in order that people are able to eat it safely. Study the following questions about food safety.

Q What personal precautions do I need to take to ensure that I am hygienic?

A You must make sure that if you have long hair, it is tied back or covered. You should ensure that your nails are short and clean and that you are not wearing any jewellery in which food could become trapped, such as rings with stones, etc. You must ensure that you wash your hands thoroughly at each stage of food preparation and between handling raw food and cooked food, or raw meat and food which will not be cooked. You must always wash your hands after going to the toilet. Do not touch your nose during food handling or preparation.

Evidence indicator

Think about the daily work of your care setting and how you follow the principles of good hygiene. What checks are you using so you know you are following these principles? Make notes about these for your portfolio.

Q What should I do if I have a cut or sore on my hands?

A You must wear a special blue adhesive plaster dressing. This is because no food is blue, and if the plaster should come off during food preparation it will be easy to locate.

Q How does food become contaminated?

A Food is contaminated by bacteria which infect food directly if it is not heated or chilled properly, or by cross-contamination, which is where bacteria are spread by somebody preparing food with unclean hands or equipment.

Q What are the main bacteria that cause contamination of food?

A Salmonella, campylobacter and e-coli are types of bacteria that can cause serious food poisoning in people who are old, ill or in young children.

Q How can infection and cross-contamination be avoided?

A Raw meat is a source of bacteria and you should be sure to use separate utensils and chopping boards or areas for raw food and for cooked food. For example, do not chop the raw chicken breasts and then chop the lettuce for the accompanying salad on the same chopping board or with the same knife. This could give everybody who eats your salad a nasty dose of salmonella. You should keep separate chopping boards for meat and vegetables, and ensure that you use different knives. Remember to change knives and wash your hands between preparing different types of food.

Q Does it matter whether food is to be cooked or not?

A It is possible to kill bacteria by cooking food. But be careful with foods which are not cooked, such as salads or mayonnaise, that you are not using contaminated utensils to prepare them.

Q How hot does food have to be to kill bacteria?

A A core temperature of 75°C will kill bacteria. Hot food should be heated or re-heated to at least this temperature.

Q How long can you keep food hot?

A Hot food must be kept above 63°C (145°F). When you're serving or displaying hot food, you can keep it below 63°C for a maximum of two hours, and you can only do this once. Then you must throw away the food, or cool it as quickly as possible and keep it chilled until it's used.

Q How cold does food have to be to kill bacteria?

A Food should be stored at below 8°C. A fridge with the door left open rapidly warms up to above 8°C, and food can deteriorate quite quickly and become dangerous. Food in a fridge where the door has been left open or where the power has been cut off should be discarded.

Q What other safety steps should I take with the fridge?

A When you arrange food in a fridge, you should be sure that you put any raw meat on the bottom shelf to stop any moisture or blood dripping from the meat onto any of the foods stored below. Moisture or blood from uncooked meat could be infected with bacteria. Fridges should be kept scrupulously clean and should be regularly washed out with an anti-bacterial solution. Do not allow particles of food to build up on the inside of the fridge. It is also important that the fridge does not become 'iced up' as this will make the motor work harder in order to keep it cold and could result in a warming of the fridge.

Q When do I need to chill food?

A Some foods need to be kept chilled to keep them safe, for example food with a 'Use by' date, food that you have cooked and won't serve immediately, or other ready-to-eat food such as prepared salads. If these foods are not properly chilled, bacteria can grow and make people ill. Check the time between cooking food and chilling it. This should not be longer than one to two hours. Remember, chilled food must be kept below 8°C. When you are serving chilled food you can keep it above 8°C for a maximum of four hours. You can only do this once. Then you must throw away the food or keep it chilled until it's used.

Q What about 'best before' dates?

A These are provided by manufacturers to ensure that food is not kept by retailers beyond a date when it is safe to eat. Many manufacturers now include instructions about how soon the food should be consumed after purchase. These should be followed carefully. As a general rule, unless the manufacturer indicates otherwise, you should consume food by its 'best before' date in order to ensure that it has not begun to deteriorate.

Cross-contamination

Cross-contamination is when bacteria spread between food, surfaces or equipment. It is the commonest way food becomes contaminated, and the Food Standards Agency has issued guidelines to help to avoid it. It is most likely to happen when:
- raw food touches (or drips onto) other food
- raw food touches (or drips onto) equipment or surfaces
- people touch raw food with their hands.

So, if raw meat drips onto a lettuce in the fridge, bacteria will spread from the meat to the lettuce.

If you cut raw meat on a chopping board, bacteria will spread from the meat to the board and knife. If you then use the same board and knife (without washing them thoroughly) to chop a cucumber, the bacteria will spread from the board and knife to the cucumber.

Hands can also spread bacteria. If you touch raw food and don't wash your hands thoroughly you can spread bacteria to other things you touch.

By avoiding cross-contamination, you can stop bacteria spreading.

What you need to do
- Keep raw and ready-to-eat foods separate.
- Clean surfaces and equipment thoroughly before you start to prepare food and after they have been used with raw food.
- Wash your hands thoroughly after touching raw food.

Handwashing
If hands aren't clean they can spread food-poisoning bacteria. A quick rinse won't make sure they're really clean, so it's important for all staff to know how to wash hands properly. Unit HSC 22 has a step-by-step guide to effective handwashing (page 56).

Remember

Everyone who handles food should wash their hands before starting work, after a break, after going to the toilet, after emptying a bin and before starting a new task.

Although the basic rules of hygiene must be followed to avoid the risk of contaminating food and drink, all of us have our own ideas about what is acceptable and hygienic practice in relation to food preparation and eating. For example, some people always wash their hands before starting a meal, whereas others never do. Others will wash in specific ways for religious or cultural reasons. It is important that you are aware of your own values and beliefs about hygienic arrangements for eating and drinking, and recognise that they are your own values and not necessarily those of others. You must never attempt to impose your own values on other people, but at the same time you do need to be aware of any situation where the values of others place people at risk of contamination, and be able to point this out in a tactful and positive way.

CASE STUDY: Cross-contamination

Two of the residents, A and P, of an independent living unit for people with a learning disability were about to prepare their evening meal when the support worker arrived for her evening visit.
The two women were about to prepare a ham salad. They took the salad and ham from the bottom of the fridge and noticed that the chicken which they had taken out of the freezer that morning had dripped onto the ham and onto the lettuce.
'We'll need to wash this lettuce and dry off the ham – look, it's all soggy,' said A.
'Absolutely not – you should not eat the ham or the lettuce,' said the support worker.
'Why not?' P asked.

1 *Why did the support worker not want the women to eat the food?*
2 *What mistakes had they made with storing the food?*
3 *What illness do they risk contracting?*
4 *What should the support worker do now?*

Providing an enjoyable and relaxed environment

As well as storing and preparing food and making sure that people are being given a balanced and healthy diet, you also need to ensure that the environment is safe, hygienic and pleasant for individuals to eat food. The place where food is consumed in your work setting should be clean and attractive. Whether your workplace has an arrangement of people sitting together in small groups or around a large table, it is important that that environment is kept scrupulously clean and that it can be used by everyone with or without assistance.

Mealtimes should be enjoyable occasions in a pleasant environment

If you are dealing with people who are in bed, you will need to prop them up into a comfortable position. Special arrangements will have to be made to provide nutrition for people who are lying flat. If a person needs to be moved in order to eat his or her meal, you should offer any assistance necessary, but otherwise encourage the person to get to the eating area by himself or herself.

Sometimes it is necessary to place protective covers on tables because of the amount of food and drink that can be spilt. These should be as attractive as possible so that eating and drinking can be enjoyed in a pleasant environment.

The consuming of food and drink should be an enjoyable and sociable occasion as well as a necessity for life. You can contribute to this by ensuring that you take note of all your service users' needs and wishes, and offer them pleasant, well-cooked and well-prepared food in an enjoyable and stimulating environment.

Keys to good practice: Preparing food and drink

✓ Ensure hygiene procedures are observed when preparing food.

✓ Follow safe procedures for storing food.

✓ Prepare the environment so that areas for serving food are clean and safe.

✓ Make mealtimes enjoyable.

✓ Treat people with dignity.

✓ Encourage independence as far as possible.

Test yourself

1 Name some ways in which food can be contaminated.

2 What are the basic nutrients that everyone requires?

3 Why are mealtimes an important occasion?

4 How should you arrange a fridge?

5 How would you arrange a dining room in a residential home? Why would you choose this arrangement?

HSC 214b Support individuals to get ready to eat and drink

When support may be needed

People may need support in eating and drinking for many reasons. You will need to consult with them about the kind and level of support they want and make sure that you are not imposing a level of support that suits you rather than the individual. For example, it may be quicker to help some people to eat or drink than for them to do it themselves, but this would be unacceptable practice as it would reduce the level of independence of the individual. It is always vital that the support you provide is the minimum necessary for the activity to be accomplished. People who wish to eat and drink by themselves should be encouraged to do so regardless of how long it takes or how much mess they may make.

Some individuals will experience difficulties in eating and drinking because of their condition, their level of confusion or their level of understanding. There could also be difficulties in eating and drinking properly because of environmental or emotional factors, for example if someone is unhappy or dislikes the care setting. The vast majority of people you deal with will be able to eat and drink by themselves perfectly well, but some may need a level of assistance which can be provided through specially adapted utensils, and others may need considerable assistance to make sure they maintain a healthy intake of food and drink.

You may notice that some individuals are apparently experiencing difficulty in eating by themselves. Their problems could cover a wide range.

- They may be unable to raise their arms and hands to their mouths.
- They may be unable to grip a knife and fork.
- They may be unable to cut up their food.
- A visually impaired person may be unable to see the food and to know what he or she is eating.
- There could be problems where someone is confused and forgets that he or she is in the process of eating and needs to take another mouthful or another drink.
- The problems could be as simple as badly fitting dentures or other dental problems which could be relatively easily resolved.
- Problems could be caused by medication which can lead people to lose their appetites. They may need some assistance and encouragement to make sure they eat an adequate and appropriate diet.
- Sometimes people may have problems with swallowing. This can be because of illness or their condition, and you will need to make special arrangements to ensure that they are able to eat.
- There could be an emotional cause, for example if someone is worried or unhappy and does not feel like eating.
- There could be more serious eating disorders where an individual is having problems in dealing with food.

Any of these, and many other reasons, can result in the need for support.

Evidence indicator

Look at the individuals in your workplace. How many of them need support to eat and drink? List the reasons why, and make notes for your portfolio.

Helping people to prepare

You will need to make sure that people are given the opportunity to wash their hands and go to the toilet before a meal. This can be time consuming if you are working with a group of people who need assistance, so make sure you start in plenty of time so that people are not rushed.

It is also important that people have the opportunity to complete any religious activities which may be important to them at mealtimes, such as saying a prayer, giving thanks, or washing themselves.

People who need to have protective napkins should be provided with them before the start of the meal. You must take care that you do not patronise individuals or treat older people as if they were children by tucking bibs around their necks. Sometimes it is necessary to protect clothing, and for comfort and cleanliness to protect a person's neck and chest if he or she does have some difficulties in eating. It is far better to offer some kind of protection and allow people the dignity and independence of eating by themselves than to assist them to eat simply because they make a mess.

Creating a pleasurable environment

The best way you can assist in making eating and drinking a pleasurable experience is to ensure that both the food and the setting in which it is served are as attractive as possible. Such touches as nice table cloths and attractive crockery, some flowers or pretty napkins, all help to make eating a pleasant occasion. Also the role of the care worker in prompting good conversation and encouraging people to talk to each other during meal times is invaluable.

When serving food, make sure it is presented in an attractive and appetising way

As a care worker you are the person in the best position to assess how well someone is eating and drinking. You will notice if he or she is refusing to eat certain types of food or having any difficulties with foods listed in the care plan as essential. You are in a good position to liaise with other members of the care team who are designing menus and producing meals, so that they are aware of the needs of individuals and can try to accommodate those needs within their general planning. If at any point you are working with someone who refuses to follow a particular diet, you must report it immediately.

There is no reason why people receiving meals in a care setting should not have exactly the same consideration about the presentation, the flavour, content and attractiveness of their food as is given to diners in top restaurants where great trouble is taken with presentation. It is amazing what some careful presentation can achieve with the simplest meal in terms of making it more appetising, more attractive and more likely to be eaten and enjoyed.

Evidence indicator

Make a list of suggestions for making the eating environment in your workplace more attractive. Remember that your ideas can include people as well as physical resources. Keep your notes as evidence for your portfolio.

Test yourself

1   What are the barriers that may mean individuals need support to eat and drink?

2   Describe one way to overcome each barrier you have identified.

3   How can you help to make eating and drinking a pleasant experience?

4   Suggest three different preparations people may need to make before eating or drinking.

HSC 214c Help individuals consume food and drink

Individual needs

The most important thing you need to do is to establish with the individual whether he or she requires your assistance. You should never impose help on a person – it is far better to encourage independence, if necessary through the use of specially adapted utensils, rather than to offer to provide assistance to eat or drink. Some people would be perfectly capable of eating by themselves if they were given a minimal amount of assistance, perhaps in the form of specially designed eating and drinking aids such as those shown below.

(a) *Light, thick-handled cutlery – people with arthritic hands will find these easy to hold*

(b) *An alternative to a feeding cup is to improvise with a glass with an angled straw, or a teapot (not a metal one)*

(c) *A feeding cup – remember that the liquid at the bottom is drunk first, so no tea leaves!*

(d) *A person with the use of only one arm may find a deep bowl or a plate guard useful, especially when they are used with a combined knife and fork or a pusher spoon*

(e) *A person who is frail, or who only has the use of one arm, will find it possible to carry several items at once on a non-slip tray with a handle*

(f) *Specially designed gadgets exist to help with taking the lids off jars*

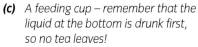

(g) *Someone who only has the use of one hand will be able to butter bread or peel potatoes using a spiked board*

Aids for eating and drinking

All of the aids shown are designed to allow people to maintain independence with only minimal assistance from others.

There are also special ways of helping people who have particular needs. For example, a visually impaired person is often able to manage to eat for himself or herself if you can help to prepare the plate of food in advance. If you arrange the food in separate portions around the plate and then tell the person, using a clockface as a comparison, that potatoes are at 2 o'clock, meat at 6 o'clock, sprouts at 8 o'clock, and so on, then this is often enough to allow the person to work out what he or she is eating and to enjoy the meal.

If you do need, because of additional requirements, to provide direct assistance to a person who has visual impairment, you should try to avoid giving instructions like 'open', which could be patronising, to indicate that you are ready with the next mouthful of food. Perhaps a signal like a tap on the hand or saying 'OK' would be appropriate. You can agree with the person in advance what signal he or she would like you to use.

You may need to observe, record and report an individual's intake of food and drink according to his or her plan of care or your organisation's procedures.

Dentures

One of the commonest causes of eating problems, particularly for older people, is badly fitting dentures. This can often be a source of difficulty for people eating, partly because it is physically difficult to eat and also because they could be embarrassed by the fact that their dentures don't fit properly and could fall out or become clogged with food. This is a problem that can be resolved very simply by making arrangements for the dentures to be properly fitted, perhaps by the use of denture adhesive.

If people have dental problems, a sore mouth or difficulty swallowing, you may need to provide food which has been liquidised or puréed to make it easier to eat.

Reluctance to eat

If someone is reluctant to eat or drink, you will need to talk with him or her and try to find out the reason for the problem. You will need to establish whether it is one of the physical reasons mentioned above, or an emotional problem to do with being unhappy, frightened or worried. In this case, you should use your communication and listening skills to try to find out the nature of the concerns and to establish if there is anything you can do to assist. With reassurance or some greater involvement in settling in to a new care setting, or with some sympathy and understanding, it may be possible gradually to improve the individual's interest and appetite.

Remember

The reasons behind someone's reluctance to eat or drink may be physical or emotional. You will need to treat the issue sensitively.

This unit does not deal with feeding an unconscious person. It is vital that you never attempt to give anyone who is unconscious or semi-conscious a drink or anything to eat as the swallowing reflex is lost when a person lapses into unconsciousness. In this situation, feeding will be through a tube, usually passed through the mouth and into the stomach.

Keys to good practice: Assisting people to eat

When providing active support to people who cannot eat by themselves, remember the following.

✓ Wash your hands.

✓ Check that you have everything you will need: the meal, salt and pepper, feeding utensils, etc.

✓ Ensure that the person is comfortable before you begin the meal. Help him or her to use the toilet or commode if necessary and to wash his or her hands.

✓ If the person is completely unable to eat by himself or herself, you should position him or her comfortably, either propped up or sitting in a chair. The upright position is the easiest to assist digestion of food, so people should be in this position where possible.

✓ Offer the chance to see the meal before you begin and ask what he or she would like to start with. For example, he or she might want the potatoes first or the meat, or may not have a particular preference.

✓ Establish whether he or she likes to eat food piping hot or whether it should be allowed to cool down.

✓ Sit down beside the person, slightly to one side and in front of him or her.

✓ Regardless of whether you feed with a fork or a spoon, you should make sure that you leave enough time for each mouthful to be properly chewed and swallowed.

✓ Bear in mind that if somebody is ill, he or she may take a considerable amount of time to eat. Make sure that you do not rush and find yourself hovering with the next spoonful before the person has finished the last one.

✓ Make sure that the person takes regular drinks before, during or after the meal.

✓ Chat and keep up an interesting conversation throughout the meal, even if the person is unable to respond to you. But beware of the dentist's trick of asking a question that requires an answer just after you have put a spoonful of food into the person's mouth!

✓ Help the individual to wash, if necessary, at the end of the meal, or he or she may be happy with just a wipe of the mouth and to rinse the hands.

✓ Remember that some people may have religious requirements for particular types of washing and cleaning after food.

Checking for a bad reaction

Occasionally, you may find that an individual has an allergic reaction to a particular food.

The commonest signs you may see are:
- flushed or swollen face, neck or mouth
- coughing or choking
- vomiting
- sweating and muscle cramps
- rash or other skin reaction.

There may be other, less immediate allergic reactions to food. Clearly, all of these must be reported immediately to your supervisor and medical help must be summoned at once. Be sure that you:
- tell the doctor or paramedic exactly what food has been eaten and how much
- keep any food left over in case it is needed for analysis
- record clearly in the person's notes or case file that he or she is allergic to the particular food.

Clearing away when individuals have finished eating and drinking

The way in which you clear up is just as important as the way you present and serve food to people. Most of us have had the experience of being in a café or restaurant and having plates cleared away before you are ready to leave, or, even worse, having crumbs swept into your lap and the table wiped with a soggy cloth!

In order to make sure that you do not rush people or make them feel uncomfortable, you should always check with them that they have finished eating and drinking. People may take their time for all sorts of reasons, and, although it can be frustrating if you are busy and need to get on with the next job, you should make sure that people can finish a meal at their own pace. After being sure that people have finished, you should check if they need any support to clean themselves or with handwashing.

Crockery, cutlery and other items from the table should be cleared and removed to the kitchen, or designated area. Depending on the setting in which you work, this may be a trolley rather than an area for cleaning utensils. The cleaning may take place elsewhere and your role may be only to stack utensils in the proper sections of the trolley for removal.

Encouraging individuals to assist

Some individuals may want to clear away for themselves, or want to help you to do this. If it is feasible and safe, you should encourage this as far as possible.

Whether individuals can help with the washing and putting away of dishes and utensils will depend on the setting. If you are working on a hospital ward, clearly it is not possible for individuals to do much about washing up and putting dishes away, but in a supported living environment this is something that should be a normal part of everyday living.

Disposing of waste

Your workplace will have policies about the disposal of food waste; as with all waste disposal you must comply with the set procedures as they are based on safe and hygienic practices to protect both you and the individuals you work with. Policies are likely to include:

- wearing an apron or other protective clothing
- following correct handwashing procedures both before and after clearing away
- placing all leftover food in a marked bin for collection
- never re-using leftover food.

There may be policies about recycling, which will involve separating green waste from cooked food and meat, to be collected separately. Much will depend on the waste collection arrangements in your local area.

CASE STUDY: Flexible mealtimes

M has recently taken up a new job at Marsden Court, a residential care unit for 25 older people. The residents' council, which meets regularly and passes on views about how the home should be run, influences most of the policies and practices at the unit. M previously worked in a very traditionally run unit where meals were provided in a dining room and everyone ate at the same time and sat at the same tables. At Marsden Court, people have a choice of eating with others, or eating alone, having something on a tray, or eating with visitors as a family or group of friends. M notices that everyone moves around at mealtimes and sits with different people; sometimes tables are pushed together if a larger group wants to sit together, or if someone has visitors. People eat at different times, but they all seem to enjoy mealtimes and most people seem to chat and mix with others. M can see the advantages of this, but found it a little difficult to adjust at first.

1   *Why do you think M found it hard to adjust to mealtimes at Marsden Court?*
2   *What are likely to have been the main differences with her previous workplace?*
3   *What advantages do you think M can see with the way things are run at Marsden Court?*
4   *What disadvantages might she think there are?*
5   *How do you think individuals will benefit from this system instead of more traditional mealtimes?*

Test yourself

1   What type of drinking utensil could you use for somebody who is unable to drink without assistance? How is it used?

2   What factors would you take into account when judging how much help to offer a service user?

3   List at least five factors you need to consider when you are assisting an individual to eat.

4   What types of special help may people need?

HSC 214 UNIT TEST

1   Give three reasons why it is important that people are offered choice in the food they eat.

2   Which groups of people are unlikely to eat pork?

3   Which foods contain vitamin C? Why is it important to take some every day?

4   For food safety, at what temperature should a fridge be kept?

5   Apart from physical problems, which other factors could cause a service user to have difficulty with eating?

6   Describe some ways in which you could help a visually impaired person enjoy a meal.

7   Name four possible signs of an allergic reaction to food. What action would you take if you saw any of these signs?

8   Describe what you would do if a person in your care regularly refused to follow a diet recommended in his or her care plan.

Help individuals to keep mobile

Keeping mobile is extremely important for health and for giving a feeling of well-being. The benefits of exercise for any individual, regardless of level of disability or dependency, are both a physical and an emotional improvement in his or her condition. You will need to know about how to maintain people's mobility, despite their age or infirmity or the level of disability or difficulties they may experience. It is important that you are able to offer them encouragement and to help them to exercise to their maximum potential.

Mobility appliances help with walking and getting around, and can make a major difference to someone's life. Being able to be mobile allows people to maintain their independence and allows them to avoid relying on human assistance. There is a world of difference between being able to go where you want, when you want to, even if you go there very slowly, and having to wait while someone else makes special arrangements.

What you need to learn

- Improving mobility through exercise
- How to help individuals to follow a mobility activity plan
- Maintaining individuals' rights
- What mobility appliances to
- How to use mobility appliances
- How to encourage individuals and record progress
- How to monitor and record progress for people using mobility aids.

HSC 215a Support individuals to keep mobile

Improving mobility through exercise

Exercise can be a formal programme, assessed by a physiotherapist, or a specific form of exercise designed to increase mobility or to improve strength, stamina or suppleness. But more importantly, it includes the simple day-to-day activities which everyone carries out involving some form of physical movement.

At its simplest, exercise is the contraction and relaxation of muscles in order to produce movement. These muscle movements use energy and raise the heart rate and breathing rate. These increased heart and breathing rates strengthen the cardiovascular system, while the movement itself tones and strengthens the muscles.

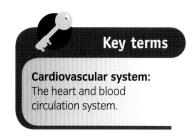

Key terms

Cardiovascular system:
The heart and blood circulation system.

The effects of exercise

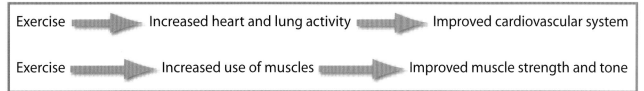

Exercise ➡ Increased heart and lung activity ➡ Improved cardiovascular system

Exercise ➡ Increased use of muscles ➡ Improved muscle strength and tone

All of these outcomes can be achieved through properly designed mobility activities. They are also encouraged by the day-to-day activities which most people carry out, such as getting up from a chair, walking across a room, washing, dressing, going up and down stairs. This is why it is important to encourage service users to be as mobile as possible within the limits of their physical condition.

Why exercise is important

Exercise matters because:
- it strengthens and tones muscles
- it improves the cardiovascular system, which controls breathing and the circulation of blood
- it improves sleep
- it uses up calories and keeps weight balanced
- it promotes a feeling of well-being.

The diagrams on pages 219 and 220 show how the skeletal muscles and cardiovascular system are arranged within the body and how they are all interlinked.

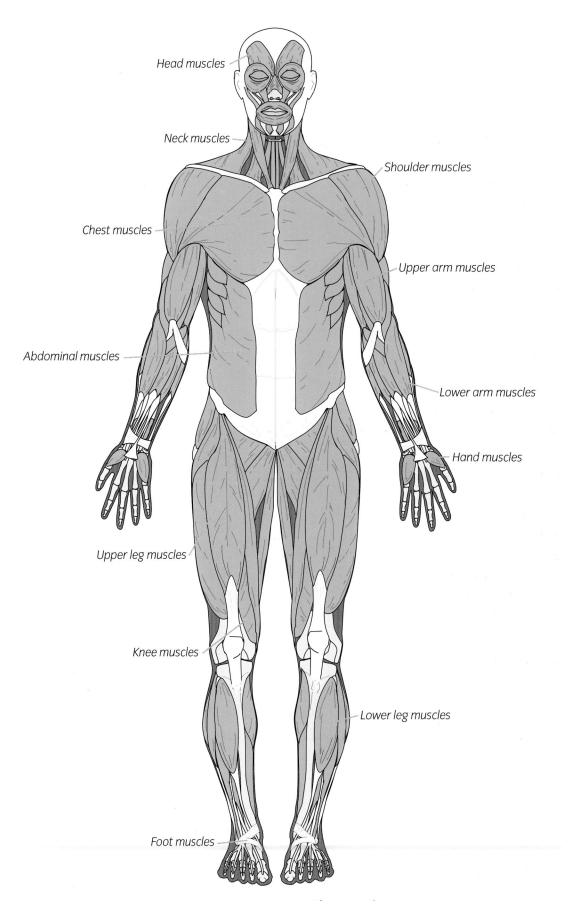

Head muscles

Neck muscles

Shoulder muscles

Chest muscles

Upper arm muscles

Abdominal muscles

Lower arm muscles

Hand muscles

Upper leg muscles

Knee muscles

Lower leg muscles

Foot muscles

The muscular system

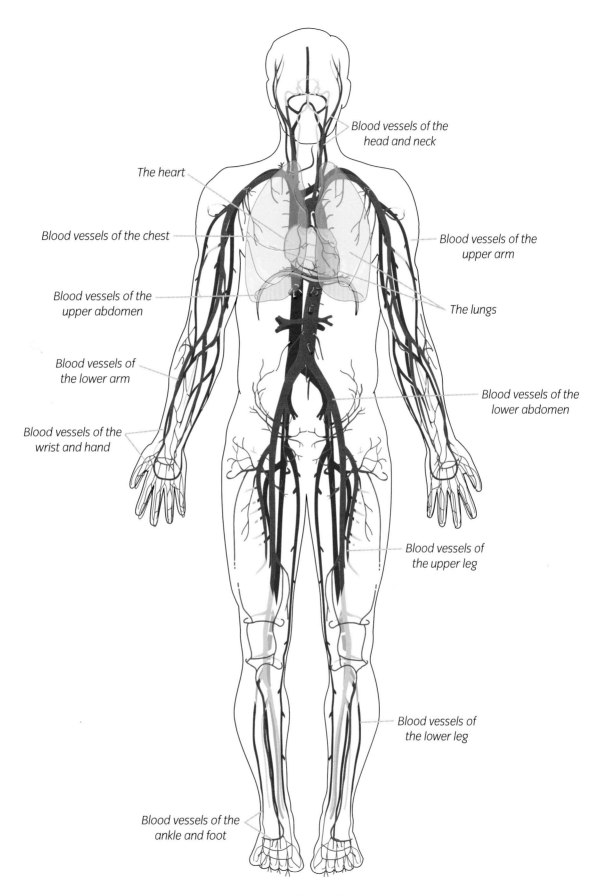

Blood vessels of the
head and neck

The heart

Blood vessels of the chest

Blood vessels of the
upper abdomen

Blood vessels of
the lower arm

Blood vessels of the
wrist and hand

Blood vessels of the
ankle and foot

Blood vessels of the
upper arm

The lungs

Blood vessels of the
lower abdomen

Blood vessels of
the upper leg

Blood vessels of
the lower leg

The cardiovascular system

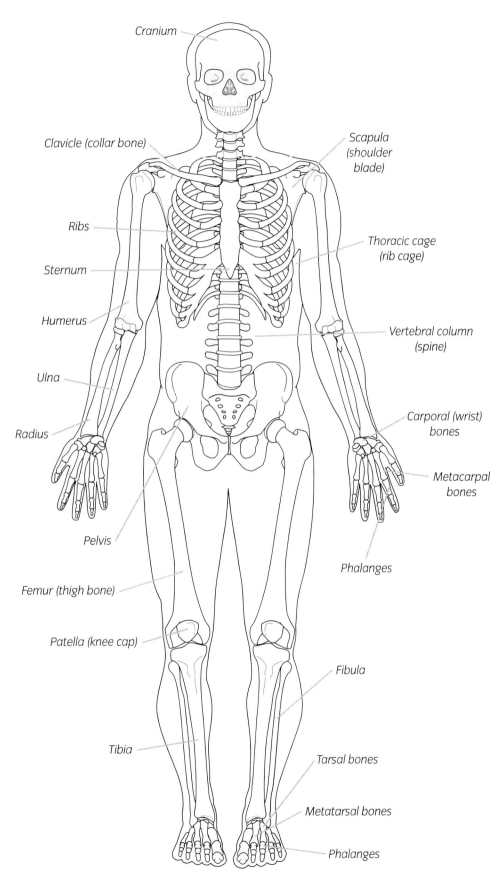

Cranium

Clavicle (collar bone)

Scapula (shoulder blade)

Ribs

Thoracic cage (rib cage)

Sternum

Humerus

Vertebral column (spine)

Ulna

Radius

Carporal (wrist) bones

Metacarpal bones

Pelvis

Phalanges

Femur (thigh bone)

Patella (knee cap)

Fibula

Tibia

Tarsal bones

Metatarsal bones

Phalanges

The skeleton

The diagram of the muscular system illustrates how muscles are attached to the bony skeleton. Muscles work like hinges or levers – they pull and move particular joints. When a muscle contracts (gets shorter), it pulls a joint in the direction that it is designed to move. Muscles can become slack and make movement slower and more difficult, but when muscles are regularly used they are firm and easy to move.

The diagram of the cardiovascular system shows that the heart is made up of muscle and pumps the blood around the body to keep organs and muscles alive. The vessels which carry the blood are called veins and arteries. Together with the heart they comprise the cardiovascular system. The oxygen which the body needs is provided through the lungs, and the efficiency levels of both the lungs and the heart are improved by regular exercise.

Did you know?

During exercise, the heart can pump over 30 times more blood around the body than when at rest. The blood vessels expand to cope with the extra volume of blood.

Exercise can be specifically defined to improve particular conditions. A physiotherapist would make an assessment and design a particular programme for an individual with this in mind. For example:

- following a stroke, a mobility activity will be designed by a physiotherapist to work on strengthening the areas weakened by the stroke
- following surgery to replace a hip joint, the key to recovery and regaining full use of the joint will be the plan devised by the physiotherapist
- many people who use wheelchairs may have special mobility activites to ensure that their muscles remain active as far as possible, and to promote their general fitness levels
- mobility activities are vital for asthmatics and others with chest problems; exercise strengthens and helps to expand airways to make breathing easier.

Did you know?

The latest research has developed a device for asthmatics which actually strengthens the lung muscles. The theory is that this will reduce wheezing. Early trials are showing great success.

If you are working with older people you should never assume that it is 'just old age' when they begin to slow down or become less mobile. There may be a physical condition which is causing the loss of mobility and, if this is noticed at an early stage, it can often be treated or at least alleviated so that many of the mobility problems are reduced.

Remember

Inactivity does not necessarily have to come with growing older. There are a great many fit and active older people who live busy and fulfilled lives.

CASE STUDY: Blaming old age

Mr K is 72. He is a retired schoolteacher who lives with his wife. They are both fit and well and are very involved in the local historical society and interested in art, literature and the theatre. Both are also active members of the local dramatic society and involved in all their productions. Mr K's greatest joy in life is reading, and he has a great interest in the Internet.

Recently he noticed that his eyesight was getting worse. He had had his glasses prescription renewed, so he put the deterioration down to increasing age. He had to stop reading unless he was sitting in bright sunshine, and he could not see the computer screen properly. He stopped attending the dramatic society because he could not read the scripts and he was becoming depressed about his lack of ability to enjoy his interests. Eventually, his wife persuaded him to see the doctor about his eyes, although he still insisted it was 'old age' and nothing could be done. However, the doctor immediately diagnosed cataracts and Mr K was referred for a simple surgical procedure first in one eye and then the second, which completely restored his sight and enabled him to carry on with a full and active life.

1   *How common do you think it is for people to dismiss problems as 'old age'?*

2   *What could have happened if Mr K's wife had not persuaded him to see the doctor?*

3   *Which aspects of Mr K's needs would not be met if he stopped his activities?*

4   *What could be the effects?*

Maintaining mobility is vital as people grow older. It can make the difference between an active old age and one spent sitting in a chair and shuffling around. It does not have to be a specially designed programme, just the fact of remaining active. Walking around the house, preparing a meal and taking a walk are all valid forms of exercise which you must encourage.

Did you know?

In a recent survey, almost 60 per cent of people aged between 70 and 75 had done some gardening in the previous month. Over a third of people over 60 had been for a walk of between 2 and 5 miles in the previous month.

A great many older people remain fit and active

How to help individuals to follow a mobility activity plan

If you are working with an individual who has been given planned mobility activities, it is important to remember that the programme will have been devised by the physiotherapist, or other specialist, for a specific condition or to improve general fitness and mobility. It must, therefore, be carried out exactly as it has been planned.

You must ensure that:

- the mobility activity is detailed in the plan of care
- it is followed accurately
- the individual is given encouragement and support to follow the programme
- progress is carefully recorded, and achievement is recognised and applauded
- any problems are immediately reported to your manager and to the professional who designed the programme.

However, if you are simply trying to encourage someone to be more active, you need to be aware of all the simple activities that can be undertaken. This includes encouraging the person to go and get something for himself or herself, rather than you getting it because it is quicker. It may be much easier for you to go and collect a forgotten cardigan, but it is better to encourage the person to do it himself or herself. You should encourage people to do something active rather than sit and watch TV. If it is possible, within their physical limitations, people should be assisted and encouraged to:

- walk where possible
- climb stairs if they are able
- go swimming or take part in an active game
- do stretching exercises.

Check it out

Find out what the mobility activity plan is for your workplace. Is it formal and organised? Is there a policy of encouraging activity? What is the attitude towards encouraging people to move around and do things for themselves, even if this takes a long time?

Keys to good practice: Agreeing the best ways to keep mobile

✓ Work with individuals to identify and agree the best ways to keep mobile.

✓ Support individuals to communicate their preferences about keeping mobile.

✓ Explain any exercise plan clearly to the individual before you begin and make sure that he or she is in agreement with it and willing to participate.

✓ Never attempt to impose any kind of exercise or activity regime on anyone who is unwilling, because the programme simply will not work unless a person is happy to join in.

✓ Encourage people to do as much as possible for themselves, because part of the benefit of exercise is an increase in independence.

Maintaining individuals' rights

Never forget that any form of mobility activity must take into account people's culture, values and beliefs. It will be important that you consider issues such as:

- the location of the activity – is it taking place in a building or environment that may be inappropriate for some cultures?
- the day on which the activity is taking place – for example if the day is a holy day, then activity may not be appropriate
- the clothing people are wearing for the activity – check that this is acceptable to those taking part.

Environment

You will need to make sure that an individual is able to exercise in a safe environment and that a risk assessment has been carried out in relation to the activity and the individual. This will include checking:

- that the floor surfaces are safe
- that there is nothing that can be tripped over or that could cause injury
- what support, if any, an individual will need
- how many professional carers need to be involved with the activity
- the steps to be taken in an emergency.

If the exercise is being carried out by a person sitting in a wheelchair:

- check that the wheelchair is absolutely stable and steady
- check that the brakes are firmly on.

If the exercise is being carried out by someone in bed:

- make sure that it is stable and steady
- ensure that the bed brakes are firmly on.

If an individual is using any kind of walking aid, you will need to ensure that it is being used properly and has been measured correctly to make sure it is the correct size.

Clothes

The clothes that an individual wears are a part of the exercise environment. You should make sure that they are appropriate for exercise. It is no coincidence that the tracksuits and trainers worn by athletes for many years have now been adopted as regular wear by people relaxing or taking part in leisure exercise, as they are so comfortable and easy to wear.

This type of clothing may be suitable for all kinds of people undertaking exercise. You will need to make sure that shoes are firm and comfortable and offer support, and that any exercise which involves standing or moving the feet is not carried out in loose or ill-fitting shoes or slippers, but in firm, well-fitting, well-supporting shoes with safe, non-slip soles. The correct clothing also helps to maintain people's dignity, as they need not fear that the exercise will involve them in exposing parts of themselves which they would rather keep covered!

Your role

If you are assisting a person to follow a programme designed by a physiotherapist, your role may be quite clearly defined. There may be times when you need to lend physical assistance or you may be required to assist in the case of exercise aids which are used as part of the programme. For example, someone who has had a stroke may be squeezing a rubber ball in his or her hand in order to strengthen the arm and hand muscles on one side of the body. Your job may be to count the number of repetitions of an exercise.

Remember

If you are involved in a policy within your workplace to encourage a higher level of activity among the people you work with, your best contribution may sometimes be not to help! By not helping you can encourage people to be much more active and hence improve their own mobility.

Your role may be to give encouragement and to count the number of repetitions

CASE STUDY: A healthy lifestyle

Strawberry Mill is a hostel for people with mental health problems. The effects of medication and the previous lifestyles of several residents have contributed to the fact that most of the residents (and staff!) are unfit. At a house meeting, it was decided to start a fitness programme. The residents decided to call it 'Best Foot Forward'. It was decided to hold an exercise class every other evening, with a basic exercise video for everyone to follow. They also decided that everyone would walk to the shops instead of getting a lift or using the bus for just two stops, and that there would be a rota for taking the hostel dog for a walk, instead of leaving it to the officer in charge!

Some residents also decided they would try to stop smoking and stop eating so many sweets and chocolates.

They started by weighing everyone, and by asking people to record what they could do before getting out of breath. Most could not even get up the stairs without puffing. After four weeks everyone was weighed again and asked how they felt. Out of the eight who had started, six were still doing the programme. They had lost an average of four pounds each and they all said they felt much better and less lethargic. All the six people felt that they had more energy. One person had stopped smoking and three were eating sweets only on Saturday nights.

1   *What do you think helped to make the programme work?*

2   *What would you have expected the results to be?*

3   *What other activities could the group have tried?*

4   *How can they keep motivated to carry on?*

5   *What other benefits may come from this programme?*

What mobility appliances do

At their simplest, mobility appliances assist a person to become or to continue to be mobile, either by providing support or, like a wheelchair, by providing the actual mobility.

Mobility appliances such as walking sticks, crutches, quadrupeds and walking frames work by providing support for people who have become unsteady or whose joints or muscles are weak or painful. They also provide additional security where someone has had a fall or is recovering from illness. Often, the loss of confidence after an incident such as a fall is as damaging to mobility as any injury sustained.

How to use mobility appliances

Mobility appliances will be recommended by an appropriate professional, either a physiotherapist or occupational therapist. This professional will have explained to the individual how the appliances are to be used, and there will have been an opportunity to try them under supervision. However, you will need to reinforce the advice and continue to support service users until they are confident and are using appliances correctly.

There are particular ways of using the various mobility appliances in order to get the maximum benefit from them. It is important that you ensure that individuals are using them in the correct way, because otherwise they are likely to cause injury or discomfort.

It is also important to explain to individuals how different floor surfaces and floor coverings affect the use and safety of appliances. Make sure that you check the risk assessment which will have been carried out in relation to the individual and the use of the appliance. This will have been recorded in the plan of care, and you should always make sure that the individual is using the appliance in accordance with the risk assessment.

Evidence indicator

One of the most useful things you can do before beginning to teach or encourage anyone in the use of walking aids is to try them out yourself, using the correct methods (see pages 229–231), so that you know how it feels to use the walking aid and the difficulties that you might encounter. Ask your supervisor if you can try the appliances available in your workplace.

Think about how different floor surfaces may affect the use of the appliance you are trying – consider slopes, steps, gravel paths, tiled floors, carpeted floors, etc. Some surfaces, such as steps, may be unsuitable and unsafe. Your supervisor and experienced users can advise you about this.

Write notes about each appliance – how easy or difficult it was to use, how it performs on different surfaces, where it is not safe to use it. Keep the notes for future reference when you are advising individuals, and add to the notes as you gain experience by seeing individuals using the appliances.

Keys to good practice: Mobility appliances

✓   Check the condition of all mobility aids on a regular basis.

✓   It is important that, if you notice any signs of damage or wear, you immediately stop a person from using the aid. Report the fault at once and make arrangements for a replacement or repair.

Remember

A mobility aid which fails during use, when someone is relying on it, is far more dangerous and useless than no mobility aid at all.

Walking sticks

Measuring a walking stick

To measure a stick correctly you need to ask the person to hold it in the hand which is opposite to his or her 'bad side', if he or she has one. If the weakness or pain is not located in a particular side of the body but is more general, for instance spinal problems, the person should use the stick on the side of the body which he or she would normally use most, i.e. the right-hand side for right-handers, the left-hand for left-handed people.

You should ensure that the person's hand is at the same height as the top of his or her thigh when it is resting on the stick handle. The elbow should be slightly bent, but make sure that the shoulders are level and that one side is not pushed higher.

- With an adjustable metal stick, you will be able to measure fairly easily by sliding the inner part of the stick up and down until the correct height is reached. The metal button will then snap into place in the guide holes.
- With a wooden walking stick, you will need to measure the correct height and then the person responsible should saw the stick to the proper length, making sure that the rubber ferrule is firmly attached to the bottom of the stick.
- It is important that you check that the ferrule is in good condition because, if it becomes worn or the suction ridges have become smooth, the stick is likely to slip when leaned on.

Using a walking stick

Depending on how much support a person needs, there are two generally recommended ways of using a walking stick. The method for a person who needs a considerable degree of support is shown in the photographs on the next page.

1 Move the stick forward, slightly to one side.

2 Take a step with the opposite foot, going no further forward than the level of the stick.

3 Take a step with the foot on the same side as the stick. This should go past the position of the stick. Then move the stick again so that it is in front of you, and repeat the sequence.

For a person who needs less support, for example if he or she is just using a stick because of lack of confidence or is just generally a little unsteady, move the stick and the opposite leg forward at the same time. Then move the leg on the stick side forward past the stick. Repeat the sequence.

You may find that there is a natural progression in people who are improving their mobility and that, as they get better, they will automatically begin to move their leg and the stick at the same time. They should be encouraged to do so.

If you need to provide physical support for somebody who is walking with a stick, you should give it from behind and you should support with one hand on each side of the pelvis, just below the person's waist.

Walking correctly with a walking stick

If you find that you need to offer this kind of help on a regular basis, you should consider suggesting an increase in the degree of walking support the person is offered. It is far better for him or her to have a more supportive walking aid than to rely on help from a care worker.

Quadrupeds or tripods

A quadruped should only be used for a person who has considerable difficulty in walking on one particular leg, either because of hip or knee degeneration or a stroke. It is not an appropriate aid for somebody who is generally unsteady.

Measuring a quadruped or tripod is exactly the same procedure as measuring a walking stick. Quadrupeds are made from metal and are adjustable.

You should check that the three or four small ferrules, which are on the suction feet, are safe and not worn.

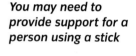

You may need to provide support for a person using a stick

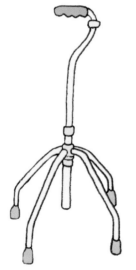
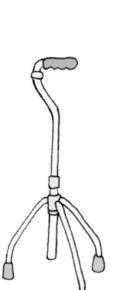

A quadruped and a tripod

Using a quadruped

- The quadruped should be held in the opposite hand to the person's 'bad side'.
- Move the quadruped forward, and then take a step with the opposite foot. Then take a step with the foot on the same side as the quadruped so that it is either at the same level or slightly in front of the quadruped, and then repeat.

If you find that someone's condition is improving and he or she has started to put the quadruped and the opposite leg forward together, rather than after each other, then he or she should be moved on to a walking stick, as the support offered by a quadruped is no longer needed.

Walking frames

An individual should be provided with a walking frame when he or she needs considerable support from one or two care workers and is no longer steady on a walking stick or quadruped.

Measuring a walking frame

Walking frames are measured in the same way as walking sticks. They are usually adjustable in height between 28 and 36 inches (710 and 910 mm), although they do come in different sizes with a range of 3–4 inches (80–100 mm) alteration within each frame.

- To reach the correct height, the person should stand against the frame, holding it and leaning slightly forward. The feet should be level with the back legs of the frame and the arms only slightly bent.
- If a walking frame is too small you will see the individual hunched forward at the frame.
- If the elbows are very bent and the shoulders are hunched up, the frame is too tall.

You will also need to check that the ferrules are in good condition on each leg.

Using a walking frame

It is important that a person follows the proper pattern of walking in order to get the maximum benefit from a walking frame. If there are difficulties, or if the person uses a frame in the wrong way, it can be quite dangerous and may cause a fall or other injuries.

- Put the frame forward so that the person can lean on it with arms almost at full stretch. He or she should then take a step forward – if he or she has a 'bad' side, step first with that leg; if not, then either leg.
- The next step should be taken with the other leg walking past the first leg. Repeat the sequence.
- It is essential that you ensure that the frame has all four feet on the ground at any point when the person is taking a step.

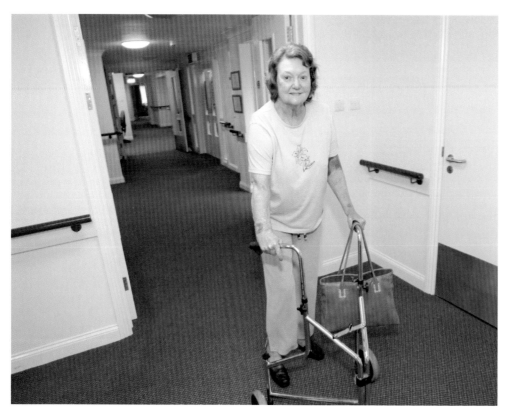

A walking frame with wheels

Offer additional assistance if it is needed. It should be offered from behind the person, as giving assistance under one arm is not possible when a person is using a walking frame.

A walking frame with wheels is also available in various styles. This means that the walking pattern is not interrupted in the way it is with an ordinary walking frame. This is very useful for people who are too confused to be able to cope with learning the walking pattern for an ordinary walking frame, and is also useful for people who have particular arm or shoulder problems, which mean they cannot lift a frame. The assessment of the suitable height for a frame with wheels is carried out in exactly the same way as for an ordinary walking frame.

Wheelchairs

Where an assessment has been made that a person requires a wheelchair, he or she is entitled to have a wheelchair of his or her own which will be correctly measured and assessed by a physiotherapist. Wheelchairs come in a range of sizes and styles. They include chairs which have to be pushed, chairs which people can propel themselves, and electric wheelchairs. Many younger people with disabilities have very decided views about the types of wheelchair they will use, the amount of equipment and additions that they have on their wheelchairs, the colours they are and the speed at which they travel around in them!

Remember

You may need to spend some considerable time supporting individuals so that they can use walking aids properly.

Evidence indicator

Investigate the way walking aids are cleaned and checked for safety in your workplace. Record your findings and any recommendations for improvement.

Mobility scooters

Many people who want to be able to get out and about, but have mobility problems when outdoors, can use powered scooters to get around. Most large shopping centres have a 'shopmobility' centre where powered scooters can be borrowed or rented to make shopping easier. Similarly, many theme parks and large public attractions offer scooter facilities. Scooters can be very useful in supporting individuals in maintaining their independence and their ability to make local journeys without assistance.

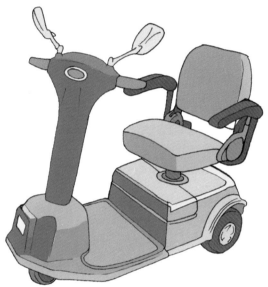

A mobility scooter can make getting out and about much easier

Keys to good practice: Wheelchairs and mobility

✓ All wheelchairs should be fitted with appropriate cushions to minimise the risk of pressure sores for people who are in a wheelchair for long periods of time.

✓ If you work in a residential or hospital setting you may have wheelchairs which you use for pushing people around in. These have small wheels and people cannot self-propel them. They should only be used for people who are ill, or incapable of propelling themselves anywhere.

✓ It is very important that you do not 'take over' a person's right to be in charge of his or her own mobility simply because it is quicker and easier for you to wheel the person to his or her next destination.

The use of wheelchairs should not be seen as negative. Many people with disabilities have described how getting a wheelchair has increased their mobility to such a great extent that their lives have been significantly improved. They progressed from slow, painful movements with walking sticks, where everything was a tremendous effort, to suddenly being able to move themselves around at will.

The biggest problems experienced by wheelchair users are the result of other people's attitudes to them and the limited access available to most buildings. However, the Disability Discrimination Act 1995 does make it a requirement of all public buildings to be accessible to anyone who wants to use them, and this includes people with any type of disability. The Act adds the phrase 'where it is reasonable to do so', and so this will not be universal. But a large number of buildings will become more accessible than they have been, and all new buildings will have to be accessible to all.

Test yourself

1 Why is exercise important?

2 Name three benefits of exercise.

3 What barriers may people face to being able to exercise?

4 List three different types of mobility aid.

5 For each mobility aid you have listed, make notes about how to use it.

HSC 215b Observe any changes in the individual's mobility and provide feedback to the appropriate people

You are in a unique position to monitor changes in the individuals you work with. You will need to watch for changes in the way people are able to get around, and notice if you are having to do more to help them than you used to, or if they are finding walking or climbing stairs more difficult. Your observations are also likely to be an important part of planning for the care of the individual concerned, and so you will be in a key position to note any improvements or deterioration and report it.

Depending on the plan of care, you may need to report to your supervisor, or you may need to liaise directly with the individual's GP, community nurse, physiotherapist or occupational therapist. Regardless of who you report to, you must be sure that you are observing guidelines on confidentiality and data protection (see page 35) in order that the rights of the individual are maintained.

How to encourage individuals and record progress

One of the most significant factors which affects how well people carry out mobility activities is whether they feel confident – and support and encouragement can play a major part in this.

You will need to ensure that any exercise plan is being properly followed – it is important that you do not alter any aspect of an exercise plan. If someone is having problems following the exercises as they have been set, because they are too difficult, too strenuous or are causing discomfort, you must report this immediately to the physiotherapist or to your supervisor.

Never advise anyone to do an exercise in a different way, even though it may seem to you that, if he or she simply moved a little to the left or to the right, or did it a little bit differently, it would be easier and less painful. You should never make such a suggestion, as you could cause injury or further discomfort or pain to the person. Any difficulties should be reported to the professional who prepared the programme.

Keys to good practice: Exercise plans

✓ Follow the exercise plan as it has been designed.

✓ If a person is in pain or discomfort, stop, and report this to your manager.

✓ Do not attempt to adapt the exercise.

Ways of providing support

It may not be necessary for you to assist a person physically in order to give him or her support; it may be sufficient for you simply to be there offering verbal support and encouragement as he or she carries out the mobility activity. Your support and encouragement could range from going along to the local gym to support an individual from your setting who plays in a wheelchair basketball team, to giving words of encouragement to someone following a stroke who is lying in bed trying to raise an arm by two or three inches.

Observing and recording progress for mobility activities

Recording a person's progress on a mobility activity is important. The physiotherapist will want regularly to review the progress that is being made so that he or she can change and update the programme as necessary. You should take careful notes about how many times an exercise has been repeated and whether there is any evidence that flexibility, suppleness or strength is improving as a result. If the aim is for the person to become more active generally, you should regularly note in his or her records the differences that a more active approach is making to his or her general level of fitness, alertness and mobility.

You should observe progress and record any evidence of improved flexibility or strength following exercise programmes

Remember

Mobility aids can make a significant difference to the quality of life that an individual experiences. A mobility aid can often be a way of allowing a person to maintain (or regain) his or her independence and freedom to choose actions and destinations.

How to monitor and record progress for people using mobility aids

It is essential that you regularly check the progress of anyone who is using any type of mobility aid. You should never assume that any condition will remain static – just because somebody was walking well with a frame or a stick when it was given to him or her does not mean that it is now the most appropriate mobility aid for the person to use.

Evidence indicator

Consider the progress of someone you work with who uses a mobility aid. Keep a record of how the person's needs and abilities change over time, and make notes on your role in monitoring and recording this.

✓ Work with individuals to monitor changes in their mobility. The way that progress will be monitored should be included in the plan of care.

✓ Give constructive feedback and encouragement to promote individuals' confidence and dignity.

✓ If someone has begun to regain confidence or had a mobility aid as a temporary measure while recovering from illness or injury, you should encourage him or her to move away from dependence on the aid as soon as possible.

✓ If someone has been using a wheelchair temporarily following illness, he or she should be encouraged with daily exercises to increase his or her own mobility and stop the use of a wheelchair as soon as possible.

✓ If the use of the wheelchair is permanent, you should still record and monitor the progress of its use, simply to ensure that there is no point at which the user is beginning to become too dependent.

✓ It is important that you regularly check all mobility appliances and report any problems to your manager.

✓ You should also be aware of any particular difficulty a person is having in using a mobility aid, and you should report any of those problems immediately. It could be that a reassessment will be needed and a different type or size of aid will need to be provided.

Test yourself

1 Name three different types of mobility aid.

2 Explain why mobility aids are important.

3 Describe how a service user should be measured for a walking stick.

4 Why is it necessary regularly to review a person's progress with a mobility aid?

5 What parts of the body does a mobility aid assist and support?

HSC 215 UNIT TEST

1   You work with an individual who is paraplegic following a motorbike accident. He can move his body from the waist and has full use of his hands and arms. He is young, but feels that his life is over. He spends his days watching TV, and does not think that he can do anything. He is not keen to see his old friends because he thinks they just feel sorry for him.

    a   List at least three ways in which exercise would help him.

    b   Where would you find advice about mobility activities?

    c   What sort of activites would you expect to be included?

    d   What factors would you expect him to take into account when he is choosing and learning to use a wheelchair?

    e   How would you encourage him?

2   You are working in a day centre for older people and a group has come to ask you to arrange a programme of activities they could do to music.

    a   Who would you discuss this request with?

    b   Would you encourage the group to go ahead with this idea? Why?

    c   What are the potential benefits to the group?

    d   What factors would you take into account if you were organising the session?

    e   Write a list of the equipment you would need.

Help address the physical comfort needs of individuals

Dealing with people in pain is never easy. Faced with someone who is suffering, it is natural that you want to do everything in your power to help and to relieve the pain or discomfort. This unit will give you the opportunity to look at the nature of pain and the steps that you can take towards relieving suffering.

You will need to understand how the various approaches to pain can affect the well-being of the individual who is suffering, and how cultural influences affect the way that people experience pain. You will also look at various ways of dealing with pain, ranging from alternative therapy to traditional Western medicine.

Rest and sleep are important for everyone. This is universally recognised – there are well-worn sayings that everybody accepts, such as 'It will all seem better in the morning', 'Sleep on it', and so on. But for many people who are receiving care it is difficult to achieve proper rest and sleep for many reasons. It is important that you, as a care worker, understand the importance of ensuring that the people you care for are adequately rested and are able to sleep.

What you need to learn

- What is pain?
- How to help people to express their pain
- How to respond to individuals who are in pain
- The effect of pain on other people
- Ways of dealing with pain
- Measuring pain
- Why rest and sleep are important
- What happens during sleep
- The barriers to rest and sleep
- How to assist rest and sleep.

HSC 216a Assist in minimising individuals' pain or discomfort

What is pain?

Pain is basically whatever the person who is suffering it feels it to be. Physical pain can be experienced as a result of disease or injury or some other form of bodily distress. Childbirth, for example, is not associated with injury or disease but can nevertheless be an extremely painful experience.

Pain is caused by the transmission of the sensation of pain from the site of the injury, disease or stress along a pain pathway. It is transmitted through sensory nerve endings along nerve fibres to the top of the spinal cord and into the brain. There are thought to be different routes for pain pathways for acute pain, caused by an immediate injury, disease, inflammation or illness, and for chronic pain, which is long-standing and continuous.

The sensations associated with these types of pain are often described very differently. Acute pain may be described as a stabbing or pricking sensation, whereas chronic pain is more likely to be described as a burning sensation and is perhaps quite difficult to locate in one particular spot. Acute pain serves an essential purpose – it is the body's warning system that something is wrong or that there is an injury. But there is often no obvious purpose to chronic pain. It often cannot be cured; it can only be treated so that its effects are reduced as much as possible.

The psychology of pain

Emotions play a considerable part in the experience of pain. If someone is afraid or tense or has no knowledge of what is wrong, he or she is likely to experience more pain than someone who is relaxed, and knows exactly what the cause of his or her pain is. Sometimes the fear of pain can not only make pain worse but can cause additional pain by anticipation. This is commonly seen in a person who has an illness or injury in which movement is extremely painful, and he or she reacts in anticipation of being moved.

There is also compelling evidence that people who have had limbs amputated can continue to feel pain in the limb long after it has been removed. The evidence shows that experiencing pain is a lot more common in a limb which had been painful before removal, and would suggest that the pain pathways somehow still continue to function even after the cause has been removed.

Historically there have been many different interpretations of pain, which to a large extent have affected how we view pain today.

- **Pain as a punishment** In the past, pain or illness was often seen as a kind of judgement on someone who had been wicked. This goes back as far as biblical stories about plagues of boils and the suffering of Job.

- **Pain as a warning** There is a school of thought which believes that pain is an important indication that there is something amiss, that pain has a purpose and that it is designed as a warning. This view still has influence today. Some care and medical practitioners believe that giving pain relief masks the symptoms, and so it is often better to allow people to continue to suffer until a firm diagnosis of their condition has been made. However, most diagnoses today are confirmed by test results or x-rays rather than purely on a patient reporting his or her symptoms.
- **'All in the mind'** As early as the fourth century BC the philosopher Aristotle believed that pain was purely an emotional experience and that it was connected with the heart and not the brain. This view is still influential today – forms of relaxation are found to be extremely beneficial in providing control for pain, both acute and chronic.
- One of the most widely held perceptions of pain today is that it is **an interaction between various factors**, both physical and emotional. It appears logical that both the mind and the body are involved in the experience of pain, and this understanding has given rise to some of the theories of pain control that are used in modern medicine.

Did you know?

A survey carried out by the Pain Research Institute found that 7 per cent of the general population suffered from chronic pain – but 22 per cent of the population over 65. It also found that more than 70 per cent of people who take painkillers for chronic pain are still in pain.

How to help people to express their pain

Because of people's beliefs, values and culture they may not find it easy to say that they are in pain. This can result from a feeling that they do not want to make a fuss, be a nuisance or bother anyone. Many think it is somehow 'wet' or 'babyish' to ask for pain relief and that they should accept pain without complaining.

It is important that you create as many opportunities as possible for people to express their pain and that you contribute towards creating an atmosphere where people know it is acceptable to say that they are in pain and they want something done about it. You can help by:

- noticing when someone seems tense or drawn
- noticing facial expressions, especially if someone is wincing or looking distressed
- observing if someone is fidgeting or trying to move around to get more comfortable
- noticing when someone seems quiet or distracted
- checking when someone is flushed or sweating or seems to be breathing rapidly.

All of these are signals which should prompt you to ask a person whether he or she is in pain and if any help or relief is needed. Even in the absence of any obvious signals, it is important to check regularly and ask if any of the people you work with are in pain or in discomfort or need any assistance.

You will need to be particularly aware of possible pain when you are providing care for people who are not able to communicate directly with you, including:

- people who do not use English as a first language
- people with speech or hearing difficulties
- people with a severe learning disability or multiple disabilities
- people who are extremely confused.

In all of these cases you may need to look for indications of distress and be able to react to those rather than waiting for the individuals to communicate directly in some way. If a person who is very confused is in pain, this can be difficult to detect because he or she may not be able to find appropriate words to communicate with you.

You will need to be especially vigilant if you provide care for anyone who comes into these categories.

You should check regularly whether people you work with are in discomfort or need any assistance

How to respond to individuals who are in pain

Clearly the most natural response you will have to anyone who is in pain is sympathy. This may seem obvious but it is always worth restating that one of the most supportive responses to anyone in pain is to offer sympathy and some 'TLC' – tender loving care.

Remember

Your work is invaluable in reassuring people that expressing pain and discomfort is not only acceptable but preferable to suffering in silence.

Evidence indicator

Find out the guidelines in your workplace for responding to service users' pain. Check the procedure to be followed. Find out the forms of pain relief which can be provided, and those which have to be referred for a medical opinion. Make sure that you know what you can do to help, and what you need to refer to your supervisor. Make notes for your portfolio on what you have learned.

A person's plan of care will include a strategy for dealing with any pain that he or she experiences. This strategy will have been carefully planned by the whole team if the person you are caring for suffers from a condition which is known to involve pain.

Alternatively, someone may be suffering pain as a result of an accident or injury which is a sudden occurrence, and you may need to respond before a plan of care has been drawn up. If this is the case, it is important that you offer sympathy and support, and immediately refer the individual to your team manager or supervisor who can arrange for a medical assessment to take place and appropriate pain relief to be prescribed.

Responses to pain are almost as varied as the individuals involved. Background, culture and beliefs have a great deal of influence on how we respond both to our own pain and to others who are experiencing pain. If you have been brought up with the view that you should 'get on with it' or 'not make a fuss', then you may find it difficult not to become exasperated with someone who constantly complains about the level of pain that he or she is experiencing. There may be a temptation to remind the person that 'there are plenty worse off than you' or that 'if you take your mind off it and think about something else you will feel a lot better'.

That type of response is unlikely to be helpful to someone who is suffering pain. These are not acceptable responses from a care worker.

Remember

Pain is whatever the person experiencing it believes it to be.

CASE STUDY: Ability to communicate about pain

Miss L is 87, and she has very advanced Alzheimer's disease. She has no apparent awareness of her surroundings and no longer speaks. She is cared for on a psycho-geriatric ward in her local hospital. Miss L is very thin and fragile, and spends her days mainly sitting in a chair in the lounge. One day, staff noticed that she was eating even less than usual and seemed to be short of breath and quite agitated. It was decided to x-ray her to see if there were problems with a chest disease. When the x-rays were examined it was clear that Miss L had a broken rib.

The cause of the break was not known, but it was clear that Miss L must have been in pain for several days before it was noticed and any action taken. She calmed down and returned to her usual behaviour once she was given pain relief for her rib.

1 *What steps should have been taken to notice Miss L's behaviour?*

2 *How do you think she must have been feeling?*

3 *What could have happened if no one had noticed?*

Being sympathetic does not mean that you cannot offer suggestions and be constructive in advising an individual about steps he or she can take personally to minimise pain. Sympathy is about more than just patting someone's hand and agreeing that it must be awful; it includes offering practical help and ideas to improve things.

It is also important that you ask the individual what help and support he or she would like you to give. It may be that he or she knows from previous experience that a hot water bottle, a change of position, a cushion or a walk around the garden will help to minimise the pain. Make sure that you ask the individual what he or she would like to do before offering any of your own suggestions.

The effect of pain on other people

One of the most difficult situations to deal with is when an individual is upsetting others with his or her expression of pain. If someone is moaning or crying out, other people can become very distressed. If it is happening at night, it can disturb the sleep of others. In situations where others know that they too may experience similar severe pain at some point in their illness, open expressions of pain may give rise to a great deal of fear and distress.

This is a difficult and delicate situation to handle. The one thing that you must never do is to say to the person who is in pain, 'Be quiet, you are upsetting everyone else'. However, you may need to consider moving the person to a place where he or she will be less disruptive or, if that is not possible, having a quiet word with other people to explain that the person is in pain and that he or she cannot help crying out. If the individual is requesting additional pain relief, it would be appropriate to make an early referral in order to give him or her some rest and relief from the pain.

Keys to good practice: Responding to pain

✓ Report anything that causes you concern to the appropriate people.

✓ Respond to pain at the level the person feels it, not what you think it is.

✓ Be alert for signs of pain, even though people may not complain.

✓ Respond quickly to requests for pain relief.

✓ Reassure people who are frightened and ensure that they are given information by someone who is qualified to do so.

✓ Ask people what methods of pain relief work best for them.

✓ Offer appropriate support to other people who may be disturbed by an individual's pain and discomfort.

Ways of dealing with pain

Before you use any equipment to alleviate pain, or undertake any moving or changing of positions, it is essential that you take note of the risk assessment your employer will have carried out in relation to use of any equipment. You must also carry out a risk assessment for the particular individual before any movements or the use of any equipment. Even simple methods of alleviating discomfort, such as hot water bottles, are not without risks, so it is vital that you protect the individual and yourself by following the correct procedures and taking all necessary precautions.

Gate control theory

One of the most influential theories about pain is the **gate control theory**. Put simply, the theory is that all pain sensations pass through an area at the top of the spinal cord at the base of the brain which is called the substantial gelatinosa. This organ acts as a 'gate' which can be opened or closed to pain depending on external stimulus, such as pain relief or distraction of attention.

Pain messages pass through a set of fibres through the substantial gelatinosa and into the brain. The gate theory says that other fibres can also be stimulated by events such as particular medications, vibration, temperature changes, electrical impulses, massage, and so on. When the other impulses being passed along the fibres are greater than the pain impulses, the 'gate' will stay closed and the pain will not be experienced. Where the pain impulses are greater than the other stimuli, the 'gate' will open and pain will be felt.

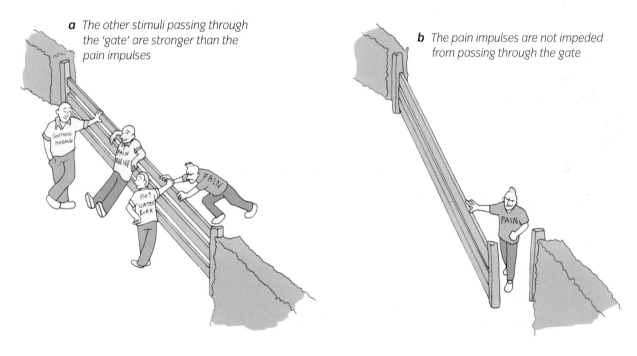

a The other stimuli passing through the 'gate' are stronger than the pain impulses

b The pain impulses are not impeded from passing through the gate

Gate control theory

Gate control theory has created a different approach to dealing with pain in general, and has led to a greater acceptance of methods other than offering straightforward analgesic medication (pain killers). There is now a recognition that pain can be adequately dealt with in other ways. The types of response to pain which are known to be effective are:

- drugs
- physical methods
- self-help methods
- alternative therapies.

Drugs

Drugs used for pain relief are classified as:

- analgesics (aspirin, paracetamol, etc.)
- opiates (morphine, heroin)
- anti-inflammatories (ibuprofen)
- anaesthetic spinal blocks (epidural).

Drugs which are supplied on medical prescription for the relief of pain are likely to be analgesics or, in more extreme cases of severe or prolonged pain, they may be opiates.

Did you know?

Legally, within the UK, drugs can be administered only by a registered general nurse or midwife and prescribed by a medical practitioner, a dentist or a vet!

Check it out

Find out the procedure for the administration of drugs in your workplace. A registered general nurse or midwife must be the person who administers the drugs, and a second person must check the drugs before handing them out.

If additional pain relief is requested, you must refer this to your supervisor and through him or her to a medical practitioner who is able to prescribe additional drugs if necessary.

You should find out the procedure for the administration of drugs in your workplace

Physical methods

Physical methods of pain relief include:

- massage (superficial or pressure)
- vibration
- ice application (with massage)
- superficial heat or cold
- transcutaneous electrical nerve stimulation (TENS)
- transcutaneous spinal electroanalgesia (TSE)
- repositioning.

Self-help methods

Self-help methods of pain relief that have been found to be effective include:

- moving or walking about, if this is possible
- imagining oneself in a pleasant place and in comfort
- taking a warm bath
- taking some recommended exercise
- finding a task to distract from the pain
- having a conversation.

Sometimes even the simplest of methods can be effective in responding to and dealing with pain. It may be sufficient just to alter someone's position or to provide him or her with a hot water bottle or an ice pack. Sometimes a distraction, like getting him or her involved in an activity or talking to him or her, can help.

Many individuals who have long-term problems will have developed their own strategies for dealing with pain and you should make sure that you know what they are and what part you can play in making them effective. Self-management is always the most effective method of dealing with pain and discomfort because it gives the individual the maximum amount of control. People who feel out of control, and who do not have any information, experience a greater degree of pain than people who feel that they are in control and have a strategy that works for them to minimise their pain.

You should note down in the plan of care each individual's preferred way of dealing with discomfort and make sure that you are able to offer him or her the assistance needed. Sometimes it can be a case of simply positioning a limb or feet on a pillow, raising the feet a little or helping the person to get up and move around, and this can make all the difference.

Alternative therapies

Often people get relief from having a massage or from using aromatherapy oils. The practice of reflexology is often a useful way of relieving pain, and many agencies and care settings have experts who visit on a regular basis to offer services like this.

The so called 'alternative therapies' are increasingly being accepted by practitioners of mainstream Western medicine as having an invaluable role to play in the reduction of pain and the improvement of general well-being. Alternative therapies include:

- **aromatherapy** – the use of natural oils
- **homeopathic medicine**, which works by treating the illness or disease with minute quantities of naturally occurring substances which would cause the illness if taken in larger amounts – these may not be used in some care settings
- **reflexology** – specialised foot massage which stimulates particular areas of the feet which are said to be linked to parts of the body

- **acupuncture** – like the other treatments, this must be administered by an expert; it uses ancient Chinese medical knowledge about specific points in the body which respond to being stimulated by very fine needles, and is now being increasingly recognised by Western medicine and becoming available from the National Health Service in many places
- **yoga and meditation** – these work essentially on the emotional component of pain. Meditation works by dealing with the mental response to pain, whereas yoga combines both mind and body in an exercise and relaxation programme. Relaxation can often be a key to relieving discomfort and to helping people cope. Pain is increased by muscles which are tense, so when people are able to relax and to find a relaxation technique that they can practise for themselves when necessary, this can be extremely beneficial.

Alternative therapies should be used only where care professionals are in agreement that they may be used with a particular individual.

Some individuals may prefer to use homely remedies which have been used in their family for many years. This could be something like a 'hot toddy' which will have to be mixed in a particular way. Others may prefer to use alcohol, or they may want to use other drugs, such as cannabis, which is known to provide relief in some conditions, and can be prescribed in specific circumstances. Requests for these forms of pain relief should be referred to your supervisor in the first instance.

Check it out

Your agency is likely to have a policy on the use of alcohol or other drugs, and you must be very clear what this is and make sure that you follow it. If you have concerns about any measures that an individual wants to take to relieve his or her pain, then you should discuss it with your manager or supervisor immediately.

CASE STUDY: Controversial methods of pain relief

G is 37 and has multiple sclerosis. He is currently living in a specialised unit as he is no longer able to care for himself. He hopes to be in the unit for only a short time until his medication and treatment regime is stable, then he plans to employ personal assistants using the direct payment scheme and live in an adapted bungalow. In the meantime he is causing concern among the staff of the unit because he is a regular smoker of cannabis. He finds that cannabis is effective in relieving pain and discomfort, and says he intends to continue to use it. The staff hold a review along with G and his key worker to discuss the situation and how to respond.

1 *What would you do in this situation?*

2 *Is G right to relieve his pain by any means necessary?*

3 *Can the unit support him in this?*

Most methods of pain relief are not curative, that is they are not treatments or cures for any particular illness, disease or injury. They are palliative – they provide relief from the symptoms without curing the illness or disease itself. These palliative treatments may be offered alongside drugs which are designed to cure a particular condition.

For example, an infected wound may be treated with antibiotics to clear the infection and with pain killers to deal with the pain caused by the infection. In other conditions such as arthritis, terminal cancer, osteoporosis or other long-standing, chronic conditions, the cause of the pain may not be curable, but the pain can certainly be relieved and strategies can be developed to help people to cope with it.

Key terms

Curative: Able to cure a disease or condition.

Palliative: Relieving or diminishing pain or discomfort, usually only temporarily.

Recording information

Information about the best ways to manage pain or enable someone to rest and sleep should be entered in the plan of care. You should always check the plan before starting to work with individuals to support them and make them comfortable, and make sure that you enter any new information so that colleagues can take appropriate action.

Do not forget that any information you enter into a plan of care is covered by the Data Protection Act 1998 (see page 35) and you must take all necessary steps to keep information confidential.

Measuring pain

One of the important factors that you need to establish when somebody is experiencing pain is how much pain he or she is feeling. This is difficult because every individual experiences pain at a different level and it is not possible to have an objective measure of pain.

You need to be very clear that pain is about what a particular individual experiences and cannot be measured against pain you suffer or anyone else may suffer. You cannot measure one person's suffering against another's because each is a very individual experience.

Several methods have been developed to try to measure pain, but one of the most effective is to ask the person to describe it to you on a scale of 1–10, with 1 being mild discomfort and 10 being the most excruciating pain he or she has ever felt. This will at least give you some idea of the level of discomfort the person is feeling and the sort of assistance he or she is likely to need.

Remember that this is not about comparing like with like. If two people have arthritis and one only puts his or her pain at 3 while the other puts it at 7, you cannot say that the person who rated his or her pain at 7 is a 'moaning minny' and that the one who put it at 3 is a 'wonderful, brave soul'. It is about individual experience and you need to react to the level at which that individual describes his or her pain.

Check it out

Draw a scale going from 1 to 10. It will probably look like a ruler or a thermometer. Try to remember an occasion when you have experienced pain and rate it on a scale of 1–10. Note it on the scale you have drawn, then think of another occasion in which the pain was less, or more, than the first time. Rate it and note that down too.

Think about the reasons for the difference. Was it just the sensation of pain, or were there other reasons? Did you know more about what was wrong? Were you given pain relief? Were you with people you knew and trusted?

Test yourself

1   Name three factors that influence how people respond to pain.

2   What are the most straightforward ways of relieving someone's pain?

3   Name three types of medication that can be taken for pain.

4   Name two ways of dealing with pain other than medication.

5   Explain gate control theory.

6   Why might two care workers react differently to the same person complaining of the same pain?

7   What factors are likely to make discomfort worse?

8   What factors are likely to help relieve pain and discomfort?

HSC 216b Assist in providing conditions to meet individuals' need for rest

Why rest and sleep are important

A great deal of research has been carried out into sleep, but none of it has yet established exactly what purpose sleep serves. There are many theories, but none have been proven. Some theories suggest that sleep is for the repair and renewal of the body, while other theories say it is for allowing our brains to organise and file all the things which have happened during the day and get the information into some kind of order. Some say that it is about escaping from the world and a chance to recharge our batteries.

Research has been carried out into what happens when people are deprived of sleep and there is a wealth of information available on this subject. One researcher made a famous comment that 'the effect of sleep deprivation is to make the subject fall asleep!'

Researchers have managed to keep volunteers awake for between 100 and 200 hours at a stretch, but after that time they tend to fall asleep anyway, regardless of what steps are taken to keep them awake. So it would seem clear

that sleep is very necessary and that ultimately the body will ensure that it does sleep.

The physical effects of sleep deprivation are quite slight:

- slight changes in temperature
- insignificant changes in heart and breathing rate.

Most people deprived of sleep are still able to carry out physical tasks without any serious change in their ability to do so.

Emotional changes are more noticeable. People tend to become:

- irritable or anti-social
- very depressed
- suspicious almost to the point of paranoia
- very poor at carrying out mental tasks.

Memory also seems to be affected by lack of sleep. People's ability to recall things they learned before being deprived of sleep seems to be quite seriously affected.

How much sleep do we need?

The length of time people sleep varies and is dependent on several factors.

The age of the person involved has a significant effect on the length of time that he or she needs to sleep. For instance, babies sleep for 14–16 hours a day, while older people may need only five or six hours at night, with several short naps during the day. Most people sleep for an average of eight hours.

Did you know?

The Sleep Research Centre has found that people can sleep more than they need to. The research showed that this extra sleep was not beneficial and, like 'over-eating', it is possible to 'over-sleep'.

Babies sleep for 14–16 hours a day

Research has identified two specific groups of sleepers, called long sleepers and short sleepers. Long sleepers sleep for nine hours or more a night, while short sleepers sleep for only five or six hours. There does not seem to be any significant difference between these two groups in their well-being or health.

Remember

Rest, not necessarily sleep, is also important for individuals who are in a care setting. The rest can be relaxation, a period of quiet, the opportunity to relax, read, meditate or simply to have a quiet time on one's own.

What happens during sleep

Sleep has four stages:

- **Stage 1:** This is called non-rapid eye movement or NREM sleep. It happens when you have just dropped off to sleep, when you are easily woken.
- **Stage 2:** This is a relaxed sleep but you can still be woken easily. This is NREM sleep.
- **Stage 3:** This is the stage of complete relaxation, and your pulse rate is beginning to drop. This is rapid eye movement or REM sleep. It is the stage when snoring stops, blood flow to the brain increases and the temperature of the brain rises. This is the stage at which people dream. Their eyes dart underneath their eyelids intermittently, breathing is irregular and people tend to move around.
- **Stage 4:** This is deep sleep when it is difficult to be woken and when sleep walking and bed wetting can occur. This stage is also NREM sleep.

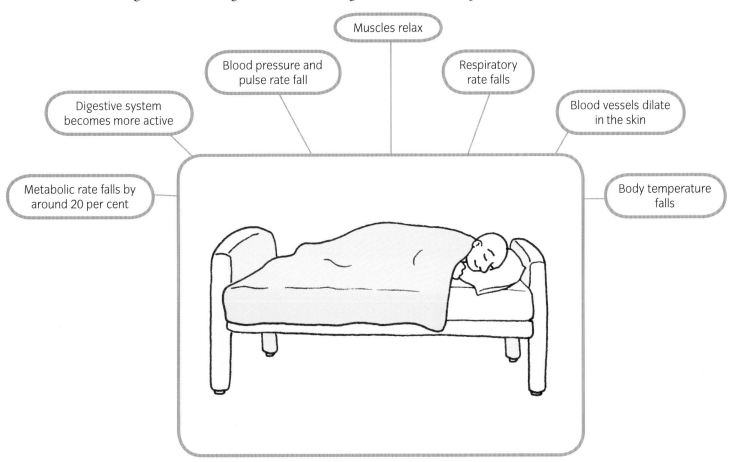

What happens to the body during sleep

Dreams and illness

Research has been carried out into the types of dream people have when they have particular illnesses. Interestingly, dreams appear to be related to types of illness – see the table on the page opposite.

Type of illness	Type of dream
Cardiac	Death/dying (men), separation (women)
Brain injury	Lost resources (money, food, etc.)
Migraine	Terror
Strokes or other neurological damage	Loss of recall, strange dreams in which it is hard to see
Drugs and withdrawal	Loss of recall, vivid or bizarre dreams
Narcolepsy (sleeping sickness)	Vivid or bizarre dreams
Severe organic disease, such as cancer	The ability to dream is lost

Patterns of sleep

The normal pattern of sleep follows natural body rhythms:

- at night people sleep
- during the daytime people work
- evenings are for play.

Shift work disturbs the natural rhythm. Shift workers often find that their health and general feeling of well-being are affected by this changed pattern, which could be:

- night for working
- morning for sleeping
- afternoon for play.

The pattern will vary depending on the timing of shifts.

Other known interruptions to normal sleep patterns are caused by jet lag or by illness when sleep may be disturbed.

Shift work disturbs natural sleep patterns

The barriers to rest and sleep

A range of factors can make it difficult for people to sleep. These broadly fall into three categories:

- physical factors:
  - pain or discomfort
  - lack of exercise
  - disturbed body clock
  - feeling hot or cold
  - illness
  - overeating
  - consuming too many stimulants, such as caffeine, alcohol, etc.
- emotional factors:
  - worry
  - anxiety
  - distress
  - fear of incontinence
  - fear of disturbing dreams
  - fear in a strange place
- environmental factors:
  - noise
  - external temperature
  - uncomfortable bed or bedding
  - light.

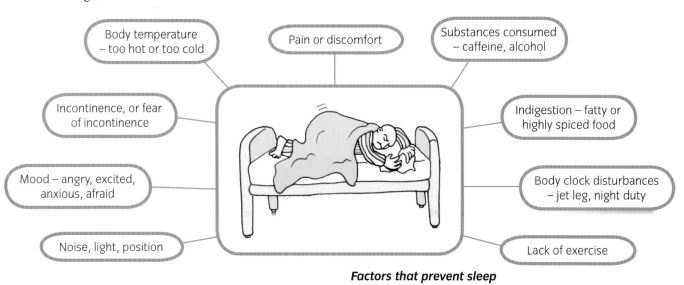

Factors that prevent sleep

How to assist rest and sleep

You have an important role in helping people both to sleep and to rest. You will need to know how best to support people to sleep well at night and to have rest at times during the day.

How to help people to sleep at night

- Reassure the person and make sure that there is nothing that he or she is anxious or worried about.
- Encourage the individual to carry out some relaxation exercises which will put him or her in a better mental and physical state to drift off to sleep gently.
- Offer a warm drink, preferably a milky drink without any caffeine or stimulants.
- Offer a hot water bottle if the person feels cold.
- Ensure that the individual is comfortable.
- Offer to adjust the person's position or the pillows or to make the bed more comfortable, if required.
- Offer to take the individual to the toilet or to provide a bed pan, if necessary. Often a full bladder or bowel will prevent people from going to sleep.

Did you know?

Florence Nightingale wrote: 'Everything you do to a patient after he is "put up" for the night increases tenfold the risk of him having a bad night, but if you rouse him after he has fallen asleep, you do not risk, you secure him a bad night.'

The environment in which the individual is sleeping is just as important as the care of the individual.

- Try to ensure that noise is kept to a minimum and that squeaking trolleys or noisy shoes, loud laughter or talking among the staff are avoided.
- The lights should be dimmed.
- Rooms and sleeping areas should be warm but ventilated.

There is much that can be done during the day which will help to ensure sleep at night. If an individual takes physical exercise, as far as possible coupled with mental stimulation, then he or she is far more likely to achieve satisfactory rest that someone who has been in an environment with nothing to do either physically or mentally during the day.

Pain or discomfort will obviously be a hindrance to sleep, so it is important that you establish that the individual has adequate pain relief to enable him or her to rest. If he or she needs to be turned during the night, ensure that this is done as comfortably and quickly as possible with minimum disturbance.

Positions for resting

While for the many people the most comfortable position for resting and sleeping is to lie down in bed with head supported by a pillow, this may not be the case for everyone. Some medical conditions may mean that people have to rest propped up, or sitting in a chair. You will need to check with the plan of care if there are any reasons for ensuring that someone maintains a particular position; for example a breathing problem, a stoma, a musculo-skeletal condition or a prothesis may mean that someone cannot rest in a particular position. Above all, you will need to check with individuals themselves about positions in which they are comfortable, and positions which are not possible for them.

CASE STUDY: Providing a suitable environment

K works in a 40-bed residential care home. She does not normally work at night, but has recently begun to do some night shifts to earn extra money. On her first night she was horrified to see how the other two care assistants were chatting loudly to each other and laughing. It was clear that some of the residents were disturbed by this behaviour and were having problems sleeping. After a couple of hours, K asked her colleagues to be a little quieter and explained that they seemed to be disturbing some of the residents. The reduction in their noise lasted for a while, but soon began to increase again. Despite asking again for the noise to be reduced, K felt there was little improvement. She was very concerned and felt uncomfortable about the behaviour of her colleagues.

Finally, she decided to notify the second-in-charge, who was on duty that night. The two care assistants were spoken to, the consequences of their behaviour were explained, and the noise levels were reduced.

1   *What would you have done in the same situation?*

2   *What alternatives did K have?*

3   *What were the likely consequences of the behaviour of the care assistants?*

Rest during the day

Rest at other times of the day is also important. When planning care, thought should be given to times in the day when individuals are able to have a period of rest. Rest periods should be, as far as possible, uninterrupted by treatments, procedures, observations or activities, so that individuals can rest and relax. Often this period may fit in best immediately after lunch – an early afternoon nap is often welcome.

Rest may not involve sleeping. Reading, relaxing or just being quiet and undisturbed may be equally useful.

Did you know?

Approximately one third of a person's life is spent sleeping. This means that if you live to be 75, you will have spent 25 years asleep!

Keys to good practice: Rest and sleep

✓ Support individuals to communicate the level and type of support they need to enable them to rest and sleep.

✓ Everyone who is receiving care should have a plan of care drawn up by the care team. It is important that plans for rest and sleep are included in the care plan.

✓ Establish what each individual's normal pattern of sleep and rest is by talking to him or her, and by observation.

✓ Assist individuals to prepare and find a position that is comfortable, and consistent with their plan of care.

✓ Make sure your own behaviour and tone of voice promote conditions suitable for rest.

✓ Any indications of change in an individual's normal sleeping or resting pattern should be recorded and concerns passed on immediately to your supervisor or manager.

✓ Make sure that you talk to the individual concerned about changes in sleep patterns. Try to establish what the cause may be.

Remember

Everyone benefits from rest and sleep. It is an important part of your job that you do everything in your power to ensure that the people in your care get the maximum possible benefit from resting, relaxing and sleeping.

Check it out

Find out if your workplace has a policy on rest and sleep. Is there a specific time of the day for resting? Are there particular procedures to ensure a restful environment? Are the people you care for able to choose how much or how little they rest and sleep, or is your workplace organised around set times?

Test yourself

1 What happens when people sleep?

2 Why is sleep important?

3 Why does working on night duty affect sleep patterns?

4 Name three ways of assisting people to sleep.

5 What kind of things do people find difficult after long periods without sleep?

HSC 216 UNIT TEST

1 Describe some of the ways in which people might express their pain without speaking about it.

2 What are analgesics?

3 What is the aim of palliative care?

4 Describe the possible effects on other people in care if an individual is loudly expressing distress over pain.

5 If you were asked to devise a relaxing afternoon activity for a group of people with painful arthritis, what factors would you consider, and why?

6 List five ways in which you could provide your service users with a restful environment.

7 Describe the different stages of sleep.

8 List some possible physical barriers to achieving proper sleep.

Unit HSC 218

Support individuals with their personal care needs

Being continent – that is, being able to retain body waste until we are in an appropriate place to dispose of it – is an essential part of being acceptable within our society. People who have difficulty in conforming to this accepted way of behaving, because they are unable to access toilet facilities before they become incontinent, are likely to suffer a high degree of humiliation, low self-esteem and embarrassment. There is a very important role to be played in ensuring that people are able to access toilet facilities appropriately when they need them. As a care worker you should be able to encourage them to ask for assistance and to offer it in a way which removes any embarrassment.

Keeping clean and hygienic is something that most people accomplish for themselves on a daily basis. However, when people become ill, disabled or in need of care they often have to rely on others to help with their personal cleanliness. This unit will look at bathing, showering, hair washing, shaving and general personal hygiene.

Most people regard how they look as being very important, and it has an effect on their emotional well-being, self-esteem and general confidence. People who have become ill or who need care are not always able to dress themselves or to keep up their appearance. This unit will give you information on some of the skills and techniques which can help you to provide this type of care.

What you need to learn

- Ensuring the individual is offered choice
- Maintaining the individual's dignity
- Assisting individuals to clean themselves
- Checking for abnormal body waste
- Leaving the area clean after use
- Recording body waste
- Collecting and disposing of body waste
- Encouraging individual choice in hygiene matters
- Why cleanliness is important
- Ensuring cleanliness
- How to deal with problems
- Ensuring choice in grooming and dressing
- How to offer support
- How to deal with problems.

HSC 218a Support individuals to go to the toilet

Ensuring the individual is offered choice

One of the key areas in maintaining independence is to give individuals choice in all areas of their care. This applies no less to toilet facilities than to anything else. It is, of course, a difficult area to discuss and you may find it far from easy to talk to people about their use of toilet facilities and about their body waste. They may well be embarrassed by the discussion, but it will be made worse if you show that you are also embarrassed.

Try to think about toiletting and body waste as a necessary physical process to be undergone in the same way as any other aspect of care. Try not be influenced by any embarrassment about discussing this type of private and personal matter directly with someone. If you are able to treat it in a general, matter-of-fact way, the individual is likely to find it much easier to respond to you.

It is also useful to try to establish whether the person has any preference as to the gender of the worker who will provide any assistance needed. It may become clear that the individual would prefer to hold a discussion on the matter with a worker of the same gender. This is not always possible in every work setting and, if it is not, it will have to be explained to the person. However, if it is possible for a worker of the same gender to talk with an individual at his or her request, that is a choice which should be offered.

To ensure that an individual is provided with the maximum possible choice, certain areas will need to be discussed and established with him or her. You will need to discuss:

- getting to the toilet
- adjusting clothing once he or she has reached the toilet facilities
- being able to get on to the toilet facility
- the type of toilet facility that he or she would prefer to use.

Getting to the toilet

The question of accessing the toilet facilities will need to be looked at in terms of:

- the person's mobility
- the frequency with which he or she needs to use the toilet
- the urgency with which he or she usually needs to use the toilet.

For example, someone who has poor mobility may still be able to reach the toilet independently. But someone who suffers from urgency – an urgent need to empty the bladder – and is not able to 'hold on', may become incontinent as a result of poor mobility, simply because he or she is not able

Did you know?

The capacity of the average bladder is about 1 pint (500 ml). Most people produce about 3 pints (1.5 litres) of urine every day.

to reach toilet facilities in time. Similarly, frequency – a condition where someone often needs to empty his or her bladder – can present difficulties for someone with mobility problems. It is one thing to undertake a painful, slow walk to the toilet every two or three hours, but it is quite another to do it every half hour!

Adjusting clothing

The other area which can present difficulties for people with limited mobility is being able to adjust their clothing once they reach a toilet facility. Being able to undo trouser flies, adjust buttons, or reach to remove underclothes may be extremely difficult for people who have poor or limited use of their arms or who are unsteady and need to be supported with both hands.

Help with accessing the toilet

You may find that you need to offer assistance to an individual who needs help to get on and off the toilet. He or she may have difficulty in sitting or in rising from a seat without help. If a person needs help to get in and out of a chair, then it is possible that he or she will need similar help with a toilet – but may find it much more difficult to ask, or to accept the help.

Toilet facilities may be specially designed to make access easier

Different types of toilet facility

When you are discussing toilet facilities with people, you will need to ask them about the type of facility they prefer to use. This may be dictated by their condition.

● If they cannot get out of bed, they will be limited to using a bed pan and urinal.
● If they can move from bed, they may prefer a commode.

- Those who can reach a toilet with or without assistance may prefer that option.

Don't forget to discuss a person's needs in terms of cleaning himself or herself after using the toilet.

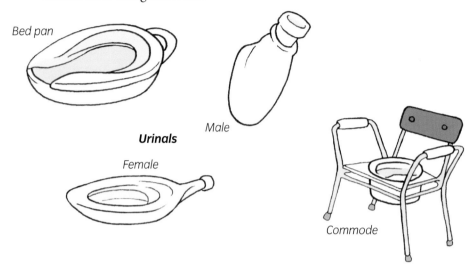

Bed pan

Urinals

Male

Female

Commode

Using the right language

It is important to establish what language and terms an individual uses to refer to all matters connected with the use of toilet facilities and his or her own body waste. There will be many different ones, although there are some widely known and understood terms, such as 'spending a penny', 'having a tinkle', 'going for a wee', and a great many other euphemisms. It is important that you establish exactly what a person means so that you can avoid misunderstandings. A misunderstanding is much more likely to happen with people who are from a different culture, or even from a different part of the same country where different expressions may be used.

People are also likely to have different ways of describing toilet facilities. They may refer to 'a lavatory', 'a loo', 'the bathroom' or 'the john', again depending on the area of the country or their own background or culture. You should ask the individual and be quite clear that you understand exactly what he or she means by particular references. If you are unsure, you should ask the family if the person is unable to make it clear to you. You will also need to establish with an individual directly or by asking his or her family if there are any particular religious or cultural beliefs associated with using toilet facilities.

Check it out

Write down as many different expressions as you can think of for going to the toilet. Think of as many different words as possible to describe the toilet. Note down the ones in use in your workplace. Notice if everyone uses the same words, or whether individuals have their own expressions.

CASE STUDY: Making it easier to ask

Mr J had just arrived in residential care. He had recently had prostate surgery and found that he needed to be able to get to the toilet quickly. He was concerned that he may not know where the toilets were in his new surroundings and was becoming very worried. His key worker, Julie, was very kind and pleasant, but he didn't feel that he could explain his worries to her. When she asked if there was anything else he wanted to ask, Mr J said 'Yes', then 'Er no – it's alright'. Julie guessed that there may be something he was too embarrassed to discuss with her. She offered to ask one of the male care workers to come and talk to him, and Mr J seemed relieved.

Leroy asked Mr J if he had any questions, and he then explained his worries about needing the toilet urgently and not being able to get there. Leroy spent time showing him where the toilets were and promised that he would make sure there was a urine bottle in his room each night until he felt more confident. Mr J was much happier and continued to settle in very well.

1 *What may have happened if Mr J had not been able to speak to Leroy?*

2 *Was Julie right to ask Leroy to step in, or should she have reassured Mr J herself?*

3 *Is there anything else which may have helped Mr J?*

Making choices happen

Once you have established the level of help and assistance that a person is going to need, you must then set about considering how you can adapt the environment as far as possible to increase the level of independence that he or she is able to exercise. You may want to think about:

- providing a mobility aid
- providing a room nearer the toilet facilities
- arranging a regular toiletting visit.

Maintaining the individual's dignity

When you talk to colleagues and individuals about the basic information that you need in respect of using toilets, the discussions should be held in private, and not in full hearing of other residents, visitors or workers. These are generally not matters that people are happy to discuss in front of others and so every effort should be made to maintain privacy. The type of privacy you are able to offer may well be limited by the kind of setting in which you work. If the best level of privacy available is a curtain drawn around a hospital bed, then you should at the very least provide this. If a person has his or her own room or if there is a quiet area where you can go to talk, so much the better. Obviously, if you are discussing these matters in a person's own home, there should be no difficulties in ensuring privacy.

If you do need to provide assistance, after having reached that decision jointly with the person, you should offer it quietly and without any public announcements, whenever it is required. It is not acceptable to walk into a lounge full of residents and say: 'Oh, Mary, you're ready for your trip to the loo, then!' While this may be well meant, it can be humiliating in the extreme.

You will need to establish when you talk to an individual what indication he or she will give you when help is required. He or she may simply call you over, or if help is only needed once he or she is actually in the toilet, it may be a case of pressing a buzzer and getting assistance when it is needed.

If a person is not able to get to toilet facilities, but needs to use a commode or bed pan, again it is important that privacy is maintained. The curtain around the hospital bed is far from ideal, but it is the best that can be provided in some circumstances.

How to help a person to use a bed pan

Check the risk assessment and make sure you follow it.

1   Wash your hands and use gloves.

2   Ensure as much privacy as possible.

3   Ask the person to raise his or her buttocks off the bed by raising the knees with feet flat on the bed and lifting the hips.

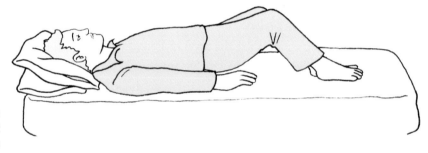

The individual should bend the knees and push up on the feet and hands to raise the hips

4   If the person is unable to raise himself or herself, roll him or her away from you, put the bed pan on the bed and roll the person back onto the pan.

   *Important: If you roll the person, there should be **another worker** at the other side of the bed. If you are alone, you must raise the bed rails on the far side of the bed. If there are no bed rails, do not roll the person alone.*

5   Assist the person to sit up and cover him or her with a sheet.

6   Leave him or her alone to use the bed pan, making sure that the buzzer is within reach for when it is needed.

7   If the person has not buzzed after ten minutes, check that he or she is alright and does not require help.

8   Remove the bed pan and cover it.

9   Wash or clean the person, if required.

10   Provide a bowl of water, soap and flannel to allow the person to wash his or her hands.

11   Dispose of the waste after checking and measuring, if necessary.

12   Wash your hands.

How to help a person to use a commode

Check the risk assessment and make sure you follow it.

1 Wash your hands and use gloves.

2 Make sure there is a clean bed pan in the commode.

3 Assist the person out of bed and onto the commode.

4 Leave the call buzzer within reach.

5 Leave the person alone to use the commode.

6 When he or she has finished, assist with cleaning or washing, if necessary.

7 Dispose of cleaning materials in sluice or toilet.

8 Assist the person back into bed or a chair.

9 Remove the bed pan and cover it.

10 Dispose of the waste after checking and measuring, if necessary.

11 Wash your hands.

Privacy

The toilet door should always be closed so that the individual can be completely private. Toilet doors should have locks in case individuals wish to lock them, but there must be a safety unlocking mechanism on the outside of the door. All toilets must have a means of calling for help in an emergency. Make sure that the individual knows how to use it. This is clearly essential, as a person could remain undiscovered for some time, if he or she was taken ill or had an accident inside a locked toilet cubicle.

A means of calling for help must be accessible and visible – like this red cord

 Keys to good practice: Maintaining dignity

✓ Hold discussions in private.

✓ Agree the level of help needed.

✓ Agree how the person will indicate when he or she needs help.

✓ Ensure privacy for an individual using the toilet – do not interrupt him or her, or allow anyone else to do so.

✓ Offer help quietly and unobtrusively.

Menstruation

It is important to maintain the privacy and dignity of women who are menstruating (having periods) and require assistance to dispose of sanitary towels or tampons. As with toilet facilities, these discussions should be held privately with the individual concerned, and her preferences in respect of disposal should be established.

As long as her wishes in disposing of used sanitary protection are not in conflict with the policies of the care setting, for example wishing to flush away sanitary towels in an ordinary toilet (which is likely to cause major plumbing difficulties), they should be complied with as far as possible. The disposal of sanitary protection and the offer of help should be made discreetly and privately in order to avoid any embarrassment for the woman concerned. It is an area which many women find difficult to deal with publicly, especially in mixed gender care settings.

Keys to good practice: Sanitary protection

If you are talking to a woman about menstruation and sanitary protection, you should observe the same considerations as when talking about using the toilet. You need to find out about:

✓ the type of sanitary protection she prefers

✓ the nature of her periods – heavy, light, sudden, regular, irregular, etc.

✓ how often she likes to change her sanitary protection

✓ what level of assistance she needs

✓ her preferences for disposal.

Check it out

1 Name three factors you should take into account when considering the amount of help a person needs.

2 What steps could you take to increase a person's independence?

3 What sort of help might you need to provide for someone who was mobile, but unsteady?

Assisting individuals to clean themselves

Helping individuals to clean themselves after using the toilet is another area of assistance which will require discussion with the person concerned. If you are providing assistance in terms of accessing the toilet, you may be able to observe just what a person is able to achieve in terms of cleaning appropriately.

Many individuals need help to wipe themselves after using the toilet, particularly if they have limited arm and shoulder movement or spinal problems. The bodily twists and turns involved in effectively cleaning the anal and genital areas after using the toilet are quite difficult to achieve if you have either muscular or joint problems in the upper body. Some people may be able to clean themselves if they are supported while they do so. The questions you will need to ask are:

● Are you able to clean yourself, or do you need help?

- What sort of help do you need – support while you clean yourself? Or someone to clean you?
- Do you clean with toilet paper?
- Do you need a bidet or other facility with running water?
- Do you use wipes?
- Are your requirements different depending on whether you have emptied bowels or bladder?
- Do you need help with cleaning menstrual blood?

Bidets

A bidet is an extremely useful way of cleaning after using the toilet, if it is installed at the right height. Bidets can be difficult for people to use if they are too low. However, a bidet can be helpful for meeting the religious requirements of people who need to clean themselves in running rather than static water. You may need to offer assistance with:

- getting on and off the bidet
- washing the anal and genital areas
- drying.

Bed pans/urinals

A person using a bed pan may find it difficult to clean himself or herself, whether using wipes or ordinary toilet paper, and you will need to discuss with the person whether he or she will need your assistance. A person using a bed pan may need help with:

- getting on and off the bed pan
- cleaning or washing the genital and anal areas
- drying.

Commodes

A person who is able to get out of bed, but cannot manage the walk to the toilet, may be able to use a commode. As with the other options, he or she may need help with:

- getting on and off the commode
- cleaning or washing the genital and anal areas
- drying.

Treatment of catheter bags and stoma care are not covered by this unit, but are dealt with in Unit HSC 225 (see page 362–366).

Keys to good practice: Assisting individuals to clean themselves

✓ Encourage individuals to find the most appropriate methods of cleaning themselves.

Continued

Keys to good practice: Assisting individuals to clean themselves

✓ Establish the level and type of help a person needs.

✓ Wear an apron and gloves.

✓ Wash or wipe the genital and anal areas gently.

✓ If washing, use clear water. Do not use soap.

✓ If using wipes or paper, make sure the area is clean and free from faeces.

✓ Wipe from front to back – never from back to front.

✓ After cleaning, dispose of the cleaning materials in a sluice or toilet.

✓ Wash your hands.

✓ Make sure that you always assist the person to wash his or her hands after using the toilet, regardless of the facility used.

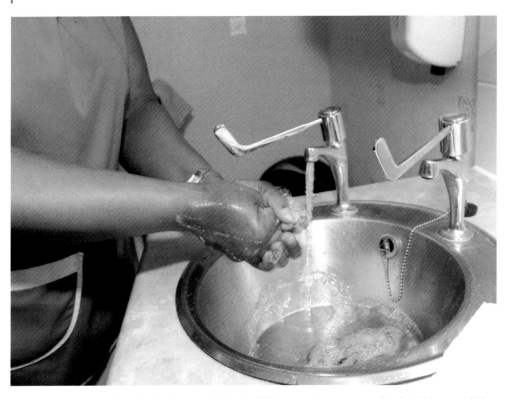

Always wash your hands before and after helping people to use toilet facilities, and if necessary assist them to wash theirs

Checking for abnormal body waste

The waste expelled from our bodies is a good indicator of any health problems which may be developing. It can often be an early indicator of illnesses or potentially serious conditions. Because of this, it is important that you establish with a person his or her normal pattern of body waste, so that you can identify anything which would cause concern. You will need to ask about:

- normal frequency of emptying the bladder
- normal frequency of opening the bowels
- what the normal faeces are like – small and hard, or loose?
- normal quantity and colour of the urine.

Abnormalities can indicate many potential illnesses, and they can range from the common and easily treatable conditions to serious ones. It is important that you always report any changes in a person's normal pattern of waste to your supervisor (see the table below). They should also be recorded in the person's chart.

Changes you may see and should report

Change	Action
Faeces change from soft to small and hard	Constipation – needs to be reported
Faeces change in colour from brown to pale yellow	Could indicate conditions which require urgent medical attention
Loose or liquid faeces	Diarrhoea – should be reported
Dark, concentrated urine	May mean an inadequate fluid intake – should be reported
Cloudy or offensive smelling urine	Could indicate an infection – should be reported
Blood in urine or faeces	May indicate a condition which requires medical attention – should be reported

Checking for changes

It is relatively easy to check for changes in a person's body waste if you provide him or her with assistance to use toilet facilities, or if he or she is using a bed pan or a commode, when you will be disposing of the contents. It is more difficult where a person is fully independent and takes himself or herself to the toilet, flushes and cleans afterwards. In this situation, you will not have the opportunity to monitor any changes and all you can do is to make the person aware that such changes can be significant and that he or she should report any changes.

Did you know?

The flushing toilet that we use today was developed by a man called Thomas Crapper. It was considered a vast improvement on previous water closets, which used static water or earth and became very unpleasant!

Leaving the area clean after use

If you are assisting a person to use toilet facilities, or to use a bed pan or a commode, it is important that you clean and tidy the environment afterwards. If the person is using ordinary toilet facilities, this will involve checking that all of the waste has been flushed away, and that there is no residue left in the toilet pan. You should wipe the seat if there has been any spillage and ensure that the person has washed his or her hands. There are appropriate cleaning fluids that can be used to carry out these procedures and they should all be available in your workplace.

It is important that toilets and commodes are left clean after use so that they will be pleasant for the next person to use. It is also important for the dignity of the individual that he or she knows there is no residue left from the disposing of his or her own waste. The smell created by the disposal of body waste should be dealt with by the use of ventilation and air fresheners where appropriate. However, these should be used with discretion in the presence of the individual, who may feel humiliated by a very obvious use of sprays.

On some occasions, particularly when people are unwell, their body waste may be very offensive in odour. On these occasions, a general cleaning with disinfectants, ventilation and air fresheners may have to be used in combination to combat any remaining odour.

Remember

Throughout the process of assisting individuals in the use of toilet facilities, you should be taking universal precautions, that is wearing gloves and an apron.

CASE STUDY: Maintaining dignity

On a gynaecological ward, a woman was recovering from major surgery and requested to use the commode. She had been severely constipated and had been given an enema which was in the process of working. Just at the point when the commode was brought and the curtains were drawn around her bed, the evening meal was served to the other women in the ward. She heard through the curtains comments being made by the other women. 'This is awful. I can't eat this. I feel sick with the smell.' 'Poor thing, she can't help it, but I can't eat my tea'.

She was left feeling extremely humiliated and spent the rest of the evening crying quietly in her bed.

1 *How could this situation have been avoided?*

2 *What do you think should have happened?*

3 *Should the other women have kept quiet?*

4 *Can you think of a similar situation which could occur in your workplace?*

Check it out

1 What are the main points to remember when helping someone use a bed pan?

2 Name three different changes you may notice in an individual's body waste.

3 How would you check the body waste of someone who was independently accessing toilet facilities?

4 Why is it important to check body waste?

Recording body waste

You may be asked to record four types of body waste:

- urine
- faeces
- vomit
- blood.

Urine

You may be asked to record someone's urine output in order to maintain a fluid balance chart. There are many conditions in which a medical practitioner will need to know how well the body is maintaining its fluid balance, that is passing an appropriate amount of urine in relation to the amount of fluid taken in. Where this type of examination is taking place, you will be asked to keep a record of the drinks an individual is having and the amount of urine he or she is passing.

This information is kept on a fluid balance chart. This will mean that you will have to ask him or her to urinate into a bed pan or other suitable container. This container can be provided in the toilet so that it can be used there, and you will then need to pour the urine into a measuring device and record in millilitres (ml) how much has been passed. This is also a good opportunity to record and examine the nature of the urine – you may be asked to describe its colour and whether its smell is offensive or normal.

Faeces

Many care settings will record how often individuals have their bowels open. This is important to ensure that they are not constipated or that they are not developing an infection which involves frequency or loose stools. Unless there is a particular reason for retaining the faeces, it is normally sufficient to record that bowels have been opened, either by asking an independent individual to inform you or by recording it where you have provided the assistance.

Vomit

Vomits may need to be recorded, depending on the person's circumstances. If the medical practitioner has asked you to record the volume of vomit or nature and contents of the vomit, it should be collected in a bowl and then its description and quantity recorded in the notes.

Blood

In some situations, it may be necessary to record blood loss. For example, on a maternity or gynaecological ward, blood loss may need to be recorded, although the estimating of the amount is likely to be carried out by a qualified health professional, such as a nurse or midwife. The range of blood loss can be from spotting to haemorrhage, and an important role for you is to report immediately any significant change in a person's blood loss. In other situations you may be asked to record the level of blood loss from a wound site, possibly following surgery. Again, it is important to report any significant change immediately.

FLUID CHART
(ADULT)

PLEASE SEE REVERSE SIDE FOR
NOTES ON USE OF THIS CHART

ORAL INTAKE				INTRAVENOUS THERAPY *Before starting this section remember to enter TIME and name of I.V. fluid already in progress and amount brought forward from the previous chart							OUTPUT							
TIME	FLUID	ml	ORAL TOTAL SO FAR ml	STARTED		ENDED		* BROUGHT FORWARD ml		TIME	URINE ml	URINE TOTAL SO FAR ml	ASPIRATE OR VOMIT ml	ASP/VOM TOTAL SO FAR ml	DRAIN ml	DRAIN ml	COMMENTS
				TIME	FLUID	TIME	ml	COMMENTS									
12.00	TEA	250	250	09.00	HARTMANS	12.00	1000	IV DISCONTINUED		12.30	300	300	NIL	NIL	–	–	
13.00	WATER	250	500							16.00	500	800	100	100			
13.45	TEA	250	750							18.30	600	1200		100			

TIME	TOTAL — ORAL ml	TOTAL — I.V. ml	CARRIED FORWARD ml	TOTALS	URINE ml	ASPIRATE/VOMIT ml	DRAIN ml	DRAIN ml

SURNAME ADAMS	OTHER NAMES JULIE	UNIT NUMBER 60671-241	WARD 2A	DATE 28/06/05	CODE CRC 017

An example of a fluid balance chart

Evidence indicator

Make sure you know the procedure for checking and measuring body waste in your workplace. Is it carried out in a particular place? Do you have special equipment? Where do you have to record the measurements? If you cannot find this information in the procedures for your workplace, ask your supervisor. Make notes on what you have learned for your portfolio.

Collecting and disposing of body waste

The commonest way of collecting body waste is in a toilet and the commonest way of disposing of it is simply to flush it away. There may be situations where it is necessary to collect body waste in a bed pan or a commode. This could be because of the needs of the person, that is he or she is unable to reach a toilet, or because of the need to retain the person's body waste for further examination.

- If you are dealing with body waste in a bed pan or a commode and it is for straightforward disposal, it should be covered and taken to the manual sluice or to the toilet in line with the procedures laid down for your workplace.
- If the body waste is required for further medical examination, it should be covered and left in an appropriate place, such as the sluice. The person who has requested this to be carried out should be informed that it has been done, and given the location of the waste.

A similar procedure should be carried out for vomit:

- It should be collected in a bowl and disposed of in the sluice, unless it is needed for medical examination.
- People who feel sick should be given a bowl and, where possible, vomit should be collected in the bowl.

If dressings are blood-soaked, they should be disposed of appropriately in clinical waste containers.

You must be very careful to follow the correct procedures for disposing of clinical waste, such as used dressings. Your workplace will have laid down a very clear set of procedures. The disposal of clinical waste is dealt with in Unit HSC 22, page 51.

Menstrual blood on sanitary towels can be disposed of in a special container designed for disposal of soiled sanitary wear. Alternatively, towels can be disposed of along with other clinical waste.

Soiled linen which has urine, faeces, vomit or blood on it must be dealt with through the special arrangements in your workplace for the disposal of soiled linen. This is likely to consist of a disposal bag in a particular colour, usually red, which goes directly into a washing machine.

Remember

Always wear gloves, and wash your hands after dealing with body waste of any kind.

Maintaining hygiene

Each workplace will have appropriate containers which must be used for clinical waste and you should ensure that you follow the correct practice. It is important always to wear gloves and an apron to reduce to risk of cross-infection whenever you are dealing with body waste and its disposal. You should never leave containers uncovered. If they are awaiting examination, ensure they are removed to an appropriate place. It is never acceptable to leave a container of body waste next to a person's bed or in an environment where people have general access.

If there has been a spillage of body waste, perhaps an accident where somebody has been incontinent or has vomited onto the floor, you must clean it appropriately, ensuring that you use the right types of cleaning fluid – those which contain disinfectant – to deal with the spillage. The utensils which have been used to clean it should either be disposed of or thoroughly washed and disinfected. You should ensure that you wear gloves at all times when dealing with spillages of body waste.

Although the question of dealing with body waste can be embarrassing and not always pleasant, if it is dealt with kindly, professionally and with humour, life can be made much easier for both individuals and care workers.

Test yourself

1   What are the expectations of our society about body waste?

2   How would you discuss normal patterns of body waste with an individual?

3   How might someone feel about being incontinent?

4   What factors do you need to take into account when discussing body waste and individuals' preferences?

5   What kinds of assistance may an individual who has difficulty walking need when using a toilet?

6   What are the ways that you can collect and dispose of body waste?

7   What steps do you need to take to maintain hygiene when cleaning areas used for disposal of body waste?

8   How do you deal with a spillage?

HSC 218b Enable individuals to maintain their personal hygiene

Encouraging individual choice in hygiene matters

Ensure that you always discuss with an individual exactly what he or she would like to achieve, both in terms of his or her personal cleanliness and the way in which personal cleanliness is accomplished. Do not, for example, insist that someone has a shower if he or she prefers a bath, unless of course his or her physical condition makes a bath impossible, or the facilities available in your work setting limit the choices available.

Do not impose your own ideas, and do not take over by doing activities which an individual is perfectly capable of doing for himself or herself, even though this may take a little longer. It is very tempting when you are busy to insist that you will do things because you know it will be quicker. It is important that people feel they are allowed as much independence as possible, according to their condition and levels of ability. This means that you need to consider very carefully the time you allocate to personal washing and cleaning activities, and recognise that it may take longer than just a 'quick rub over' or a 'quick dip' – you may need to allocate a considerable amount of time to the task.

You must also make sure that the choice is real. It is no use discussing with someone what he or she would like to do and then not making it possible to achieve this, because you are rushing the person, or because you are making it clear that you do not approve, or because the things he or she chooses to do are not in line with the policies of the care setting.

You will need to make a judgement for each service user about the time you will need to allocate and the level of assistance you will offer. The table below summarises some of the points you will need to consider.

Service user	Considerations
Older, not confused, quite active	Little support needed, may need a check from time to time. Discuss with individual the level of assistance required
Older, confused	Needs assistance, time needed for individual to carry out process, needs supervision
Individual with a physical disability	Unless recently disabled is likely to have own system of personal hygiene. Discuss help required, be guided by individual
Individual with a learning disability	May need assistance with particular tasks, depending on level of difficulty. Discuss with individual, if possible, the level of help required

Often one of the most difficult problems to tackle in this area is the individual's own values and standards in respect of personal cleanliness. This is not necessarily about religious beliefs but about personal standards which tend to be different for different generations or for people who have been brought up in different circumstances. For example, it is not unusual for many older people to be happy with a pattern of a weekly bath with a daily wash. This kind of hygiene routine is more unusual today, where most people bathe or shower daily, but if a weekly bath is the individual's choice, then it is a very difficult and sensitive area in which to attempt any changes.

You must be careful to ensure that an individual's choice is not inhibited by the prospect of losing his or her privacy or dignity. If people are bathing or showering, then their privacy must be respected. Doors or shower curtains must be closed and there should not be an expectation that they remain unclothed while other people or staff are present.

Keys to good practice: Offering choice

✓ Offer people a choice in their personal hygiene – and make sure it is a real choice.

✓ Do not restrict the time available if someone wants to perform tasks himself or herself.

✓ Respect privacy, even if this is inconvenient for you.

✓ Respect people's rights to decide their own routines for cleansing.

✓ Do not expect people to fit in with a routine which is decided by the care organisation.

Make sure you do not use jargon to describe the assistance you are offering. Refer to the equipment you will use for cleanliness and the parts of the body that you are cleaning in terms the individual understands. It is very intimidating when people use jargon and terms which are not understood. For example:

Do not use	Use instead
Axilla	Armpits
Extremities	Fingers and toes
Genital area	Underneath, down below, private parts, or check with the service user what terms he or she uses
Abdomen	Stomach, tummy
Cleansing agent	Soap

… and so on.

You may find that people have religious beliefs related to maintaining cleanliness. You must establish these carefully and make sure that they are followed and that people have the opportunity to carry out cleaning rituals and bathing in whatever way they wish. For example:

● Muslims and Hindus will need to be provided with running water in which to wash if at all possible. Muslims need to be able to wash their hands, face and feet in running water.

● Hindus will prefer a shower to a bath and will use a bidet rather than paper to clean themselves after using the toilet.

● Sikhs and Rastafarians believe that hair should not be cut.

● Hindus and Muslims will only accept treatment or assistance from a carer of the same gender.

If you are unsure about religious or cultural needs, you must ask the individual and make sure that you provide the assistance which meets his or her needs.

Why cleanliness is important

The skin is the largest organ of the body. It provides a complete covering and protection for the body, and it is the skin which is the main area to be cleaned. The skin consists of two layers: the outer layer (the epidermis) and the inner layer (the dermis).

The epidermis is constantly being renewed, as it sheds its cells and new cells are grown by the body to replace them. You will have noticed how the skin cells are shed when you undress or change bed sheets. The skin also contains glands which produce sweat and others which produce sebum, an oily substance that maintains the water-proofing of the skin.

Skin becomes dirty because of exposure to the environment, but it also collects dried sweat, dead skin cells and oily sebum from the sebaceous glands. All of these factors combine to provide a breeding ground for an assortment of bacteria. These bacteria can cause offensive odours and can lead to infections, so skin needs to be regularly washed and the bacteria removed from the skin.

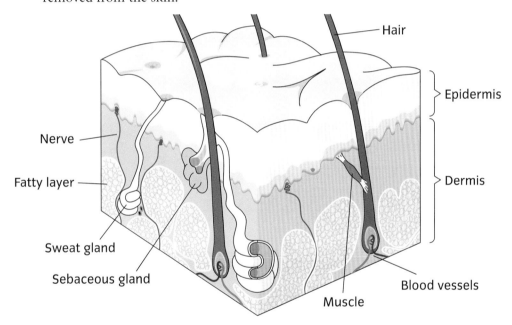

A cross-section through the skin

Some form of cleaning should be undertaken every day. If an individual is not willing to have a daily bath or shower, then at least a daily wash would assist in the removal of accumulated dirt and waste products and will reduce the risk of the service user having an 'odour problem' which may well be remarked upon by others and can produce a difficult situation.

Personal cleanliness is also important because it improves how people feel about themselves. People tend to feel better after having a bath or a shower, so it is good for morale and a feeling of well-being. In fact baths, and how and when they are taken, can become a topic of much discussion and disagreement in many residential situations!

NVQ Level 2 Health and Social Care

 CASE STUDY: Maintaining independence

V has multiple sclerosis and is reasonably mobile, although she can become unsteady at times. She has so far been unwilling to use any mobility aids, and, although she has had several falls, she is happier to manage without any form of support as long as possible. She lives in a flat which she shares with two work colleagues and has a demanding job in a city bank.

V has found it increasingly difficult to manage bathing and showering. As her periods of unsteadiness have increased, she has lost some confidence and so is more inclined to wash rather than have a bath or shower. This has resulted in a skin rash which is very itchy and flaky on many parts of her body.

V checked this with her doctor who provided medication and a bath lotion with instructions to soak in a bath daily. When she told her doctor that she could not get into and out of the bath, he arranged for a visit from the occupational therapist. V is now very concerned about how much of her independence she may lose.

1   *What do you think the occupational therapist will recommend?*
2   *How would you reassure V?*
3   *What do you think should happen now?*
4   *Why is it important for V to bathe or shower each day?*

Ensuring cleanliness

Clearly, the ideal situation is where an individual is able to take care of all his or her own personal cleanliness needs, and all the care setting needs to do is to ensure that the individual is able to access the facilities he or she needs.

If you are providing care for someone in his or her own home:

- check the risk assessment and make sure you follow it
- check that the individual is able to reach the bathing facilities
- if the bathroom is upstairs, it may be necessary to refer the individual for special arrangements to provide access, such as a stairlift or a downstairs shower room
- consider safety aspects and refer the person for the provision of rails and grab handles, if necessary
- make sure you have found out about all the equipment that is available to assist people, and that you have discussed it with the individual.

If an individual wants any type of aid or equipment, you should contact your manager, who will refer the person to the occupational therapist (OT), or another appropriate professional, for an assessment and provision of the necessary equipment.

 Did you know?

Skin is not only the largest organ in the body, it is also the heaviest. If it were possible to remove the skin of an average adult, it would weigh about 20 lb (or 9 kg).

Evidence indicator

What is the procedure for referring people for support in personal hygiene in your workplace? Find out what it is and how it operates. Obtain a catalogue of aids for bathing and cleaning. Think about the people you work with and whether any of them would benefit from additional help. Make notes on what you have learned for your portfolio.

Where you are dealing with an individual in a residential or supported living setting, it is likely that bathrooms and bathing facilities will be designed to ensure the necessary ease of access.

- If it is possible for a person to care for his or her own needs, with perhaps some help in gathering together the equipment needed, then that should be encouraged.
- If help is needed, you should ensure that you offer the minimum amount of help needed to ensure safety for the person.
- You will need to be tactful and discreet when helping people to wash and dress.
- Your workplace may have guidelines about what you should wear when helping people to wash – perhaps an overall or a plastic apron to protect your uniform and reduce the risk of cross-infection, or protective gloves. Make sure you know what the rules are and follow them – they are for everyone's protection.
- Remember to tie your hair back if it is long, and not to wear rings with stones, which can spread infection. See Unit HSC 22 for advice on how to prevent cross-infection and how you should be dressed.
- If you need to wear any particular form of protection, such as gloves, explain this to the individual carefully and using the right communication method – see Unit HSC 21.

Remember

Your personal hygiene and appearance are important too, as is your approach to the tasks you need to undertake.

Bathing and showering

You will need to assess the level of help a person is likely to need. This should be discussed with the care team and detailed in his or her care plan. A risk assessment will have been carried out, and it is important that you follow it. But the most important views to take into account are those of the individual.

Don't forget that sometimes a bathing or showering aid can provide the same sort of help that a care worker could provide, but will enable the individual to maintain his or her own privacy and dignity. This may be considered preferable to having a carer present. Always make sure that you offer a mechanical aid as an alternative, if it is available. The types of aid which can be used include bath and shower seats, non-slip mats, handrails and adapted bath plugs. Baths and showers incorporating lifting mechanisms are also widely used, as illustrated opposite and on the next page.

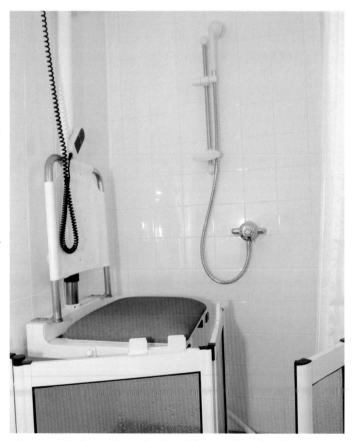

A seat which can be raised and lowered makes the shower more accessible for many people

A bath lift helps a person get into and out of the bath

Bathing

There is a wide range of aids to help people with bathing, ranging from devices to help with removing the bath plug to mechanical hoists and baths which recline. Most care settings are likely to have a selection of these aids, although items like reclining baths are very expensive and are not necessarily available in all care settings.

There will be situations in which it would not be safe to allow someone to bathe alone, or where a person does not feel confident and prefers to have assistance from a care worker. As in all caring situations, manual lifting and assistance should be avoided – mechanical aids, like bath chairs and slings, should be used. They should be available in your workplace and should have been risk assessed as being appropriate for the person you are helping.

1 *Gather together all the items you will require for the bath – towel, flannel, toiletries, etc.*

2 *Start the water running for the bath.*

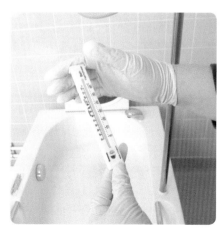

3 *Check that the water temperature is as required by the individual (although water temperature regulations may limit individual preference).*

Keys to good practice: Bathing

✓ The preparations for bathing are just as important as the bathing itself.

✓ Make sure you have gathered together all of the items you will require for a bath – towel, talcum powder, soap, flannel and so on. There is nothing worse for an individual than having to sit undressed while you dash off to find something you have forgotten, like the toenail clippers.

✓ Each person should have his or her own set of equipment for bathing and if everything is kept in one bag, it should be easy to make sure that you have not forgotten anything.

✓ Bathing an individual also gives you a good opportunity to notice any significant changes, either in the skin or in other parts of the body. You will be able to observe any changes in the skin which could be an indication of a developing pressure sore, or a mole or growth which appears to be developing and may require medical attention.

✓ You should immediately report any changes in the skin, including growths, moles, rashes, broken skin or insect bites.

✓ Make sure the service user is thoroughly dried, with assistance if necessary.

✓ Offer assistance with dressing.

✓ Assist the individual to the room he or she wishes to go to and ensure that he or she is comfortable.

✓ Clean the bathroom, and make sure that it is left tidy and hygienic for the next person to use.

Showering

Showering is a very effective way of keeping clean. Standing or sitting in a shower is much easier for some individuals than climbing in and out of a bath. It is also compatible with the religious views of some people and the personal preferences of others who like to clean themselves in running water rather than static water. Some individuals are able to shower themselves with the assistance of a shower seat or a plastic chair placed in the shower. Others are happy to use a shower provided that there are protective grab handles and a non-slip surface to stand on.

✔ Keys to good practice: Showering

✓ Collect together all the equipment needed for the shower, exactly as you would for bathing.

✓ Place a shower seat in the shower, if necessary.

✓ Turn on the water and check that the temperature meets the individual's needs and preferences.

✓ Ensure that the individual is able to sit on the seat in the shower, if necessary.

✓ Check that he or she is able to reach all of the areas that require washing, such as the genitals, the feet, the backs of the legs and the back.

✓ The person may be glad of assistance or may prefer to shower alone, simply calling you when he or she is finished and requires further supervision to leave the shower.

✓ If you are going to leave someone to shower alone, make sure that you explain to him or her how to adjust the water temperature. Ensure that there is a call buzzer within easy reach in case of problems.

✓ After the shower, make sure that the individual is thoroughly dry, providing assistance if requested.

✓ Assist the person to the room he or she requests and ensure that he or she is comfortable.

✓ Tidy the shower room and leave it clean and hygienic.

Washing

If you work with someone who is unable to get out of bed, either permanently or temporarily because of an illness, there may be occasions when bathing or showering is not needed or wanted, but a wash would be welcome and would help to freshen the person up.

✔ Keys to good practice: Washing

✓ Hands and face can be washed with a bowl of warm water, soap and a face flannel. This can be offered several times during the day, particularly after meals.

✓ You should also provide a bowl of water and soap, flannel and towel for an individual to wash his or her hands after using the bed pan or a commode.

Continued

Keys to good practice: Washing

✓ Many individuals may be able to manage a more extensive wash, perhaps of the arms, under arms and upper torso, for themselves, or you could offer to help.

✓ Ensure that a person has sufficient privacy to wash.

✓ Do not leave a bowl with dirty washing water and utensils lying around. Make sure it is cleared away immediately after use.

✓ Some people may prefer to wash at the wash basin, if there is one in the room.

✓ You will need to establish whether the individual needs any assistance, particularly with washing the back and feet.

✓ Some people may need assistance to stand up to have a strip wash, whereas others may be confident that they can manage alone, in which case you should simply return when they have finished.

✓ Tidy up and leave the washbasin clean and hygienic.

Check it out

Make a list of the people you provide care for, and note the procedure each one uses for personal hygiene. Then consider the reasons for each individual.

● Is it because of personal preference?

● Is it because of physical ability?

● Is it because of access problems?

● Is it because of the policies of the organisation or restrictions on staff time?

Bed bathing

Where someone is completely confined to bed, you will need to give a bed bath. This is far more extensive than a simple wash and is not something that an individual can carry out alone.

Keys to good practice: Bed bathing

✓ Collect together all of the items that you require in advance. You cannot leave someone stripped and half-washed while you go to find something you have forgotten.

✓ During a bed bath you should ensure that the person does not become chilled. You may need to close any open windows in the room. You also need to ensure that at no time does the person lie in bed totally uncovered.

Keys to good practice: Bed bathing

✓ You will need a deep bowl for water. You will also need soap, two flannels and two towels – one of each for the face and the body area.

✓ You will need special disposable wipes for washing the genital area. If your workplace does not have these, you will need an additional flannel and towel for the genital area.

✓ Remember to collect together a nail brush, hair brush and nail scissors.

✓ You will also need to have clean linen for the bed and a clean nightdress or pyjamas, as well as sufficient disposal bags for soiled linen and clothing, and disposal bags for the soiled wipes, in appropriate containers.

How to bed bath

- Start by explaining the procedure to the individual and ask if he or she needs to use a commode or bed pan before you begin.
- Make sure that the person consents to being bathed. Do not attempt to bed bath someone against his or her will.
- Ensure that there is privacy before carrying out the bed bath and that the individual feels reassured.
- Ensure that the person is comfortable. For example, lying flat may be the easiest position for many people for bed bathing, but for someone who is breathless or has a chest condition lying flat can be uncomfortable, so he or she might be better propped upright on pillows.
- Ensure you have all the necessary equipment to hand: bowl, two flannels, two towels and soap.
- Fill the bowl three-quarters full with hand-hot water.
- Strip the top bedclothes and undress the service user, leaving him or her covered with a sheet or a blanket.
- Spread the bath towel over the service user's chest. Then follow the procedure outlined below.

1 Wash, rinse and dry the face, ears and neck with one of the flannels. Remember to check whether or not the individual wants soap used on his or her face – some people find it very drying.

2 Change to the body flannel and wash, rinse and dry each hand in turn, and clean the finger nails.

3 Wash, rinse and dry each arm paying particular attention to the underarms, making sure that they are thoroughly dried.

4 Wash the chest and abdomen. Be very careful to dry the area underneath the breasts for women, and any stomach creases where moisture can build up, cause soreness and encourage the development of fungal infections.

5 Change the water and then continue, washing each leg. Place the large bath towel under each leg when you are washing and rinsing.

6 Wash each foot in turn, and then ensure that you have dried everything thoroughly, particularly between the toes where fungal infections develop easily if they are left damp.

7 Roll the person in order to wash his or her back. If you are the only worker present it is important that you roll the person towards you and lean over him or her to wash the back, which reduces the risk of a fall from the bed.

8 When you have finished washing the whole of the body, change to a different flannel or to special wipes, and wash and clean the genital and anal area thoroughly. If you are using disposable wipes, they should be discarded into an appropriate disposal bag.

- Fold the sheet as you wash each part of the body so that only the part you are washing is exposed and the rest of the body is covered by the sheet.
- Make sure that you have taken all the necessary steps to dry the service user thoroughly. This is a good opportunity to check for the development of pressure sores and to ensure that you have taken the necessary preventive measures. If you notice any changes to the skin, you should report them immediately.

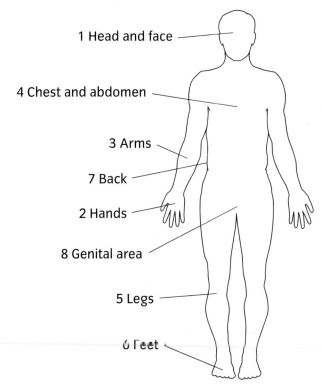

1 Head and face

4 Chest and abdomen

3 Arms

7 Back

2 Hands

8 Genital area

5 Legs

6 Feet

The order in which to give a bed bath

Extra tasks

If the individual is unable to get out of bed, take the opportunity to change the bottom sheet while he or she is rolled onto one side. Then remake the bed with fresh bed linen. If the individual is able to get out of bed, this is a good time to offer a clean nightdress or pyjamas, and assist him or her to sit in the chair while you remake the bed.

Check whether fingernails or toenails need to be clipped. If it is a straightforward job, you should carry this out. If the toenails are particularly hard, they should be left for a chiropodist. You should report this to your supervisor, who will arrange for a chiropodist to visit.

Check it out

Find out the arrangements for chiropody in your workplace. Make sure you know what steps to take to refer a service user to a chiropodist. Find out:

- who you need to speak to
- whether you have to make a written report
- who is responsible for contacting the chiropodist
- how long it takes.

Shaving

Shaving is very important for most men. They usually find it uncomfortable and irritating to have stubble on their faces. If an individual is not able to shave himself, you will have to arrange to carry this out. Ask him what kind of help he needs. He may be able to carry out the shaving himself if you put the soap on his face. Where you need to carry out the whole procedure of shaving, you should remember that it is not straightforward and is not the same for every individual. You will need to establish whether the service user shaves with a safety razor or with an electric razor.

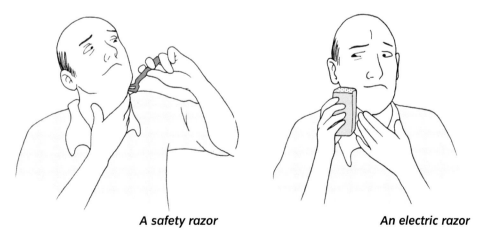

A safety razor   *An electric razor*

If a service user tells you that he shaves with a cut-throat razor, this is probably better left to a visiting barber!

Keys to good practice

Safety razor

✓ Check with the individual which direction he normally shaves in. This makes a difference to how easy it is to shave and to whether or not you are likely to pull any hairs or to make the skin sore.

✓ Make a lather on the chin and cheeks either with a traditional shaving brush or with a hand-rub shaving soap. These are normally available in tubes.

✓ Take long firm strokes with the razor in the direction that he has indicated. Make sure that you rinse the razor frequently as it will become clogged with soap and bristles.

✓ When you have finished shaving, rinse the individual's face and dry it thoroughly.

✓ Ask him if he likes aftershave, and if there is any particular one that he has and uses regularly.

✓ Make sure that you clear away all of the equipment when you have finished.

✓ Ensure that any used blades are disposed of in the sharps box.

Electric razor

✓ First, ensure that it is clean by flipping the top and dusting or blowing out any accumulated stubble.

✓ Shave in the direction that the service user has told you his beard grows.

✓ Do not scrub an electric razor backwards and forwards across the face – just allow the razor to move in the same direction as the stubble growth.

✓ Aftershave lotion should be applied if the individual wishes.

✓ Remove all of the equipment and tidy up afterwards.

Check it out

If you have never shaved anyone before, try shaving a friend or colleague. Even if you shave yourself every day, it is very different shaving someone else! If you cannot find a colleague or friend brave enough to let you try, blow up a balloon, cover it in shaving soap and shave away. If you burst the balloon – you need more practice!

Mouth care

Mouth care (oral hygiene) is extremely important for everyone because bacteria will multiply in a mouth that is not regularly cleaned, and this will lead to infections and diseases of the mouth. Many individuals are able to maintain their own mouth care, perhaps with a little assistance. However, you will need to carry out mouth care for people who are seriously ill or who have special needs.

Much mouth care occurs naturally because, as long as people maintain a sufficient intake of fluids, the saliva in the mouth carries out a great deal of cleaning. However, various illnesses and conditions, as well as the natural ageing process, can change the way in which the mouth works. Saliva production can be reduced and people may suffer from dry and crusted mouths, and infections, such as thrush (a fungal infection), sore tongue or ulcerated gums or cheeks may develop. A reduction in saliva production also increases the incidence of bad breath (halitosis).

Did you know?

The average person produces around 1 litre ($1\frac{3}{4}$ pints) of saliva each day.

Oral hygiene involves:
- cleaning teeth or dentures
- cleaning between teeth to ensure the removal of all food particles
- cleaning of gums and soft parts of the mouth
- checking for problems.

Most people will be able to clean and floss their teeth, clean their dentures, ensure the general cleanliness of their own mouths and deal with minor problems, such as ulcers or cracked and sore lips, without any assistance. However, if you do need to assist you should follow the procedure outlined below.

1   Provide the individual with a bowl of water or assist him or her to a washbasin.

2   Offer to put toothpaste on the toothbrush, if necessary.

3   Assist with brushing only if required. If you do need to assist, you should brush gently but firmly, ensuring that all teeth are brushed on all surfaces. Brushing should be done for at least one minute.

4   Give the individual a glass of water to rinse the toothpaste out of his or her mouth.

5   Offer the individual dental floss to clean between his or her teeth. Be prepared to assist with flossing if required.

6   Note whether any parts of the person's mouth are painful or if there are any sore places.

7   Make sure that anything you have noticed is reported.

8   Offer the person a mouthwash.

If you are caring for service users with a very high degree of dependency then you may need to carry out regular mouth care for them.

Keys to good practice: Cleaning an individual's mouth

✓ Mouth care can be done either with a small, soft toothbrush or, more usually, with swabs which are used to clean around the teeth, gums, palate and inside of the cheeks.

✓ Use the swabs to remove any food particles and clean all the surfaces of the mouth.

✓ You can obtain liquid toothpaste, which is probably the easiest type to use.

✓ A diluted solution of sodium bicarbonate (one teaspoon in 500 ml of warm water) can be used for mouth care, particularly where the mouth is dry and crusted, but it can leave a very unpleasant aftertaste and is better followed by swabbing out with a more pleasant-tasting mouthwash.

✓ After you have finished cleaning and moistening the person's mouth, protect his or her lips with lip salve or Vaseline.

✓ Remember that all of the equipment you use should be maintained for that individual only and should be clearly labelled and kept together.

Eye care

When people are fit and well, their eyes are kept moist and clean naturally by fluid which fills the eye and drains into the nose. However, when people are ill their eyes can often become dry, irritated and sore, and you may need to bathe them to soothe them and to remove and treat any infection.

Keys to good practice: Bathing an individual's eyes

✓ Before you begin cleaning a person's eyes, make sure that you have cotton wool swabs and a suitable bag in which to dispose of them, a bowl of clean water or saline, a paper towel and eye drops, if the person uses them. To bathe someone's eyes you will need to:

1 Make him or her comfortable and explain what you are going to do.

2 Ensure that he or she is in agreement and wants you to carry this out.

Continued

Keys to good practice: Bathing an individual's eyes

3 Ideally, the person should lie flat, with you behind his or her head. However, this may not be possible and you may need to work with the person's head leaning slightly backwards with the shoulders supported.

4 Wash your hands to ensure that they are clean, and take universal precautions (see Unit HSC 22).

5 Arrange the paper towel under the person's face, usually tucked into the clothing just below the chin. Dip a swab into the water or saline, squeeze it gently and swab the eye once, working from the nose to the outside. This should be done in a single movement.

6 Throw the swab away.

7 Repeat this procedure on both eyes until the eyes are clean and clear of any crusting or infection. Dry the skin around the eyes with clean dry swabs.

✓ Remember to use each swab once only, as it is easy to cross-infect from one eye to the other or to introduce infections into the eye.

Hair washing

Washing the hair of someone who is confined to bed can be extremely difficult. If the person is able to have a bath or a shower, then washing the hair is not a problem, but for those who are restricted to bed and only have a bed bath, you need to be able wash their hair.

Keys to good practice: Washing hair for those confined to bed

✓ The most effective way to wash hair is with an inflatable hair wash tray which allows you to wash the hair and drain the water away without the individual having to move from the bed. This is very important for people who are suffering from back injuries or other forms of paralysis.

✓ The same effect can be achieved by removing the bedhead and placing a bucket on the floor at the back of the bed.

✓ Protect the bed with a plastic sheet.

✓ Use a jug to pour water gently over the individual's hair. This will either drain into the inflatable tray or over the plastic sheet into the bucket.

✓ Check with the individual that the water is a comfortable temperature.

✓ Shampoo the hair, making sure that the shampoo does not get into the person's eyes. Then rinse with clear, warm water.

✓ Dry the hair with a towel. Then comb through gently, style and dry with a hairdryer.

Inflatable hair wash tray – the side walls are formed by two separately inflatable chambers

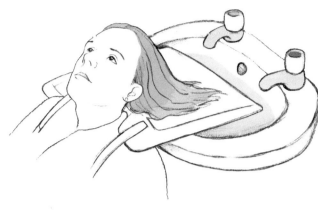

Shoulder hair wash tray – useful for wheelchair users

How to deal with problems

The commonest problem you will come across in the area of personal cleanliness is when someone refuses to be bathed or washed, or refuses to wash or bath himself or herself as often as necessary in order to keep clean. This situation can often cause problems when the person is living in a residential or hospital setting and there are other people who object to the odour that can come from someone who fails to wash regularly.

This is a case where tact and gentle persuasion are likely to be the most effective solution – an explanation of the reasons why keeping clean is important, followed by some fairly firm but friendly advice. It may be best to suggest that the individual begins slowly, rather than with a full bath. He or she should be offered the option of a wash, and then gradually encouraged over time to take a bath or a shower.

If you are faced with this type of situation, you will need to use all your communication skills. You could try this approach:

Carer: 'Would you like me to arrange some help for you to have a bath or a shower?'

Service user: 'No.'

Carer: 'That's fine. Do you think you'll manage on your own?'

Service user: 'I don't want a bath.'

Carer: 'Well, it's very important that you do have a bath or shower regularly, otherwise you could get all sorts of skin problems – and you would start to be a bit smelly.'

Service user: 'I don't smell – are you saying I smell?'

Carer: 'You will do if you don't get clean. What would you rather do – have a bath or a shower, or maybe you'd prefer a good wash?'

Service user: 'I don't mind a wash, but I'm not getting under one of those showers.'

Carer: 'Great – do you need any help with getting a wash?'

Try to find out, tactfully, if there is a reason for the person's reluctance to wash. Does he or she experience discomfort when washing, for example? You may be able to offer a solution to this problem. A person's reluctance to wash may also be a symptom of a general change in his or her condition.

You also need to be aware of people's religious views in respect of bathing and cleanliness, and take care to observe any special requirements. Make sure that you ask about religious beliefs about washing and bathing, if you are not sure.

If you experience any problems in getting someone in or out of the bath or shower you must summon help immediately. This is a potentially dangerous situation and one you should not attempt to sort out on your own. You could end up injuring either the individual or yourself quite badly. It is always better to summon help.

What and when to report

Any problems in providing people with help for their personal cleanliness must be reported to your supervisor and recorded clearly in the person's notes.

Any changes you notice in a person's body or skin could be very significant and should be immediately reported and recorded.

Getting the balance right

If you are able to get the balance right between allowing the individual independence, choice and dignity and, at the same time, offering assistance in an acceptable way, you will perform an invaluable role in promoting that person's physical and emotional well-being.

Test yourself

1 Describe three different ways of getting a person into and out of a bath or shower.

2 Why is it important to keep the skin clean?

3 Name the substances that collect on the skin if it is not regularly cleaned.

4 Is it possible to wash the hair of someone who is confined to bed? If so, how?

5 What is the key thing to remember when bathing someone's eyes?

6 How would you prepare for a bed bath?

HSC 218c Support individuals in personal grooming and dressing

Ensuring choice in grooming and dressing

To make sure that individuals really do have a choice in how they look and how they dress, you have to be sure that they are able to discuss the kind of clothes that they want, and the colours, styles and fabrics that they like to wear. It is important that people are not simply told what to wear or made to wear clothes which are convenient for the care setting. Individuals in a residential setting could be in danger of having less choice than those who are in their own homes or in a day centre.

Wherever possible you should encourage individuals to wear the style of clothes that they enjoy and find comfortable – whether the style is formal or informal, whether they like bright colours or dark colours, whether they like flowers, spots or stripes, you should try wherever possible to meet their requirements. The way people look and the clothes they choose to wear are probably the single biggest statement of their individual personality – you must never attempt to undermine their ability to be themselves.

You should also ensure that people are able to choose the kind of make-up, perfumes or aftershaves that they would like to use. Try to provide them with the kinds of product that they have always used or would like to try.

It is important, however, that people's choices should be informed choices and that you explain to them any changed factors in their lives that need to be taken into account. For example, someone who has become incontinent may need to rethink the kind of fabric that his or her clothes are made from – it may be necessary to consider buying clothes in fabrics which can be easily laundered. If someone has developed a sensitive skin condition, he or she may have to think about using particular types of make-up, perfume or aftershave.

The use of a prosthesis (an artificial breast, arm or leg, hair piece or wig) may mean that the person has to change his or her style of clothing. Someone who previously liked low-cut dresses and blouses may have to try a different style if she is wearing a prosthesis in place of a breast which has been removed. Someone with an artificial arm may want to wear clothes with long sleeves, and so on.

Helping people get dressed

There are many aids which allow people to dress themselves. Some are shown on the next page. They can make the difference between the person having to ask for help and being totally independent. Managing zips and pulling on shoes, stockings and tights can be very difficult with limited movement or weak hands or arm muscles. A well-designed dressing aid can make it perfectly possible for a person to dress himself or herself without relying on help from a carer.

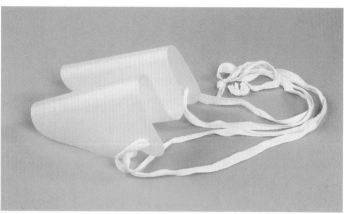

Tights aid

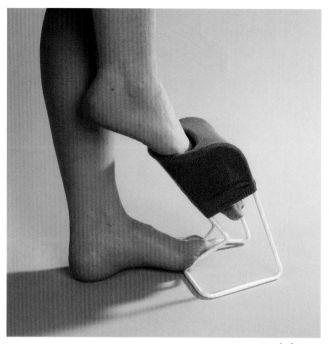

Sock frame

Similarly, specially designed combs and brushes allow individuals to continue grooming their own hair. Many will prefer this, rather than having to ask for help.

Check it out

Find out about the dressing and grooming aids used in your workplace. As well as tights aids and sock aids, they may include spring laces, shoe horns, zip aids and specially adapted combs and hairbrushes. Research the usefulness of any that are not regularly used in your workplace, but could be helpful.

How to offer support

Dressing

To offer support in dressing an individual, follow the keys to good practice outlined on the next page.

Keys to good practice: Supporting someone to dress

✓ Support individuals to communicate their wishes and preferences about personal grooming and dressing, and identify any support they need.

✓ If a person does need help in dressing and undressing, the first thing you must do is to ensure that he or she has privacy and that dignity is maintained.

✓ Ensure that you are providing active support to enable the person to dress in clothes which he or she has chosen to wear, and not clothes that you have chosen. It is demoralising and demeaning not to be able to choose the clothes you wear, and it is one of the key features of 'institutionalised' people that they lose freedom of choice over clothes.

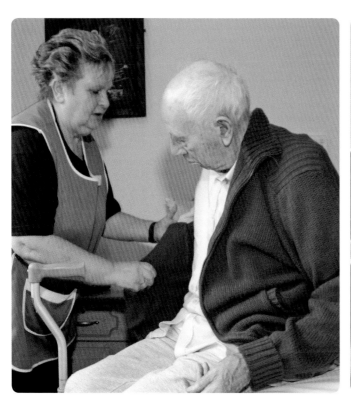

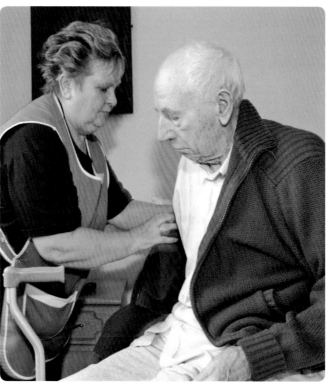

1 To put on a shirt or jacket, slip your hand through the sleeve from the cuff and hold the person's hand.

2 Pull the sleeve up around the shoulder. Remember, if the person has a 'bad side', start with that arm.

Supports, prostheses and orthoses

Once you have established with an individual which clothes he or she wishes to wear, you must also take into account any supports, prostheses or orthoses which are being used, and make sure that they are fitted comfortably.

The table below lists some of the most common aids and appliances you are likely to come across when assisting people to dress, although there are many others and you will need to be sure about the needs of individual people. They are all very significant in terms of an individual's well-being, both physical and emotional. They will have been prescribed and will be part of the plan of care.

Key terms

Prosthesis: An artificial replacement for a missing body part, such as an artificial limb or dentures.

Orthosis: An article or device applied externally to the body and designed to improve function, offer support, or prevent further injury.

Supports	Prostheses	Orthoses
Hearing aids	Artificial limbs	Surgical stockings
Glasses	Artificial breasts	Callipers
Voice synthesisers	Wigs	Surgical collars
	Dentures	Trusses/supports

It is important that you ensure that aids or appliances are used properly and that the person is wearing them correctly, that they sit well and are comfortable and that they do not rub or chafe. If you do notice that any prosthesis or orthosis is causing irritation or soreness, you must report this immediately to your supervisor and ensure arrangements are made for the necessary adjustments to be made.

Grooming

Grooming is just as important as dressing. If an individual is not able to carry out grooming for himself or herself, you will need to offer help. The main areas of grooming where you may need to assist are likely to be:

- hair care
- make-up
- manicure.

Hair care

The way that hair is styled and groomed is very individual and most people have very strong feelings about how they like their hair to be done. If you work in a residential, day-care or hospital setting, visiting hairdressers may be available on a regular basis. If you are visiting and supporting individuals in their own homes, you may be able to arrange for a mobile hairdresser to visit periodically in order to cut and perm or colour their hair.

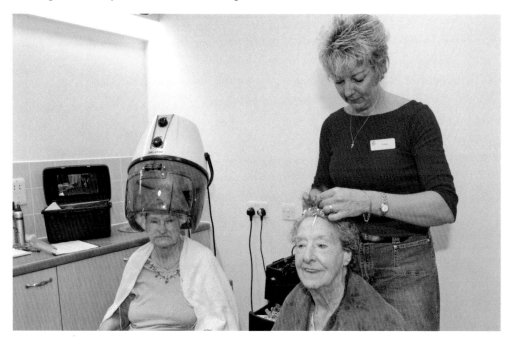

In many residential settings, a hairdresser visits on a regular basis

In between hairdressers' visits, keeping hair washed and nicely groomed and styled is extremely important in terms of a person's emotional well-being. You should ensure that you wash and dry and style the hair, as far as possible, in the way that the person wishes you to.

Make-up

You will need to discuss with the individual the type of make-up that she uses and establish what sort of help may be needed to apply it. You will need to:

- establish the type of make-up the person wishes to use, for example foundation, powder, lipstick, etc.
- check with the plan of care that there is no reason why the use of make-up could be a problem – for example, skin, mouth or eye infections
- establish whether the person has the make-up or whether she needs assistance to purchase it
- discuss colours, and try to arrange for the person to sample some different types and colours of make-up
- check with the individual which perfume or cologne he or she prefers to use – the use of perfume or cologne is a very personal matter
- ensure that each individual has her own make-up and that it is not shared – this reduces the risk of cross-infection.

Find out whether there are any arrangements for people in your workplace to try out make-up, or for a beauty therapist to visit. Check whether there are any arrangements with local beauty salons or cosmetic companies to offer their products. If there are not, you may want to discuss with your manager whether this would be possible to arrange. Makes notes on this topic for your portfolio.

Manicure

The day-to-day care of the nails will be partly undertaken during normal bathing, when you should use a nail brush to keep the nails clean. You should ensure that fingernails are regularly cut or filed to a rounded shape, to the shape of the finger. Some women may like to have a manicure and you should offer the use of nail varnish.

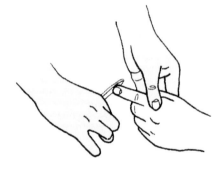

File a nail to the shape of the finger

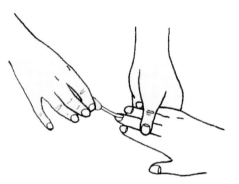

Offer nail varnish

Nail care

Toenails should only ever be cut by a trained chiropodist. This is because infection can occur via cuts to the toe and this is a particular risk for service users with diabetes.

You can be alerted to some medical conditions by the condition of a person's nails. For example, some types of anaemia can cause nails to grow into a concave shape, when they turn up at the ends, and some types of illness can cause ridging on the nails.

If you notice anything unusual, you should report it immediately and record it, as it may be an indication of a condition that needs medical attention.

Other considerations

Make sure that you always take into account people's personal beliefs and preferences in the question of hair, dress and personal grooming. These are just as important as in the area of personal cleanliness. For example, Sikhs and Rastafarians believe that hair should never be cut or shaved. Many Orthodox Jewish women wear wigs. Always ensure that you ask the individual, or seek advice from members of the family or others if it is not possible to ask the person directly.

How to deal with problems

You may be faced with an individual who refuses to use the prosthesis or orthosis which has been prescribed, because he or she thinks that it is ugly or uncomfortable or does not feel that it is providing him or her with any effective assistance. If gentle persuasion fails to convince the person of the value of it, and if you have checked that it is not because it is uncomfortable or ill-fitting, then you should report this immediately so that it can be discussed with the professional who prescribed it.

You may also be faced with a situation where a person wants to wear clothes which are unsuitable given the nature of his or her condition. For example, you may find someone who insists on wearing clothes which can only be dry cleaned, even though he or she is incontinent. The only thing you can do in this situation is to try to persuade the person by explaining the difficulties that this will present, but finally (if he or she can afford the dry cleaning bills!) it is the person's choice and you cannot impose your views.

Ultimately, the way people look, both in terms of their appearance and their clothing, is very much a matter of individual taste, preferences and beliefs – it is a very personal expression of their identities. You can only offer assistance, not direction, and you should encourage individuals to take as many of their own decisions as they can.

Test yourself

1 Name three types of dressing aid.

2 What factors would you consider when advising on suitable clothing?

3 What would you discuss with an individual when choosing make-up for her?

4 At what stage would you call in a chiropodist?

5 In what order would you dress someone who has two arms functioning well?

6 Name three types of prosthesis which you need to take into account when someone is dressing.

HSC 218 UNIT TEST

1 What do you need to consider when discussing toiletting needs with an individual?

2 What type of toiletting facility might you consider for someone who spends much of his or her time in bed and has poor mobility?

3 What are the techniques for washing or cleaning an individual after using the toilet?

4 You have to help an older woman get ready for her grandson's wedding. She has poor mobility, but can get around with a walking frame. She likes to look smart and always has her hair done. Think about what you would need to do.

   a What aspects would you need to discuss with her in advance?

   b What would she need assistance with before the day itself?

   c What would you do on the day?

   d What would you do first on the day?

   e How do you think she will want to look?

   f Why is it important for her to feel she looks good?

5 You have just admitted a service user with mental health problems to your hostel. He has been living rough for the past six weeks, and you are asked to assist him with personal hygiene.

   a What would you do first?

   b Why?

   c Why is it important to try to get him clean?

   d How do you think he may be feeling?

   e Make a list of the personal cleansing and grooming tasks which are likely to be needed.

   f How would you try to persuade him to co-operate?

Support individuals to manage continence

This unit is about supporting individuals and assisting them to manage their own continence. This is an extremely important role for any care worker, as so many people suffer from incontinence, to varying degrees. The vast majority can be helped and their condition improved. This unit should enable you to identify the contribution you can make, regardless of your work role.

What you need to learn

- What continence is

- The social and emotional effects of incontinence

- The most appropriate ways to assist individuals to maintain continence

- Ways of managing continence and improving it

- Equipment to support individuals in managing continence

- Hygiene

- Your role.

HSC 219a Support individuals to maintain continence

What continence is

Continence is the ability to hold onto or retain the body's waste products (urine and faeces) until you are in a convenient and appropriate place to dispose of them. For many people, of all ages, this is a problem – that is, they suffer from incontinence, an inability to retain the body's waste products.

It is often assumed that incontinence is a problem of old age. However, this is by no means the case, as significant numbers of younger people suffer from an inability to maintain continence, for a variety of reasons. To understand the best ways of supporting people in maintaining continence you need to understand how the process works and how the body functions in processing waste products.

How the bladder works

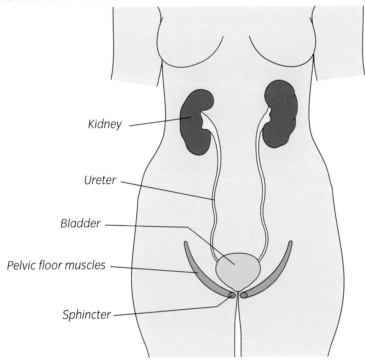

Kidney

Ureter

Bladder

Pelvic floor muscles

Sphincter

The bladder

Surplus water and waste products in the body are filtered through the kidneys, which produce urine continuously. This passes down the ureters, the tubes which run from the kidneys to the bladder, and remains in the bladder until we are able to release the urine and empty the bladder. An average human produces two to three pints of urine every day. This will vary depending on the amount eaten and drunk and how much the individual has perspired.

As the bladder fills with urine it gradually expands. It has an outlet valve known as a sphincter which holds the bladder closed and stops urine from leaking during the process of filling. The pelvic floor has strong muscles and ligaments which support the bladder and keep it in position. The same muscles also support the rectum and bowels, holding them in the correct position, and in women they also support the womb.

As the bladder begins to fill, messages are sent to the brain indicating a need to empty it. Generally, these messages begin to be sent to the brain when the bladder is about half full, so there is plenty of time to find any appropriate opportunity to empty it. The capacity of an individual's bladder will vary, largely depending on how they have been 'trained'. Those who empty their bladders frequently tend to have bladders with less capacity. Those who need to empty their bladders less frequently tend to have bladders with a larger capacity and can allow them to fill to a greater extent before emptying them.

On average, people need to empty their bladders between four and eight times each day. The process of emptying the bladder involves the relaxation of the sphincter muscles and the contraction of the muscles contained in the wall of the bladder. This then squeezes the urine out down the urethra and the bladder is emptied. The muscles in the walls of the bladder relax to allow the bladder to expand and begin the process of refilling.

How the bowel works

A Food is chewed using the teeth and the tongue. At this point the first of the digestive enzymes are added to the food, in saliva.

B Food is swallowed to the oesophagus, the tube which transfers food from the mouth to the stomach. This tube constantly expands and contracts in waves of muscular activity known as peristalsis, moving food along.

C Food arrives in the stomach, where the digestive process begins. Food is broken down through enzyme activity and the stomach's acids. Food remains in the stomach for one to three hours.

D By this stage food is completely liquidised. It travels through the small intestine for two to six hours. Throughout this process nutrients from food are absorbed into the body.

E Food then moves into the large intestine where it remains for 12 to 48 hours. By this time most of the nutrients and water content have been absorbed and the remains become solid.

F The solidified waste products which are not required by the body are stored in the rectum as stools or faeces, until they are expelled through the anus by the muscular contractions of the rectum.

The bowel

How the digestive system operates varies from person to person. The length of time food takes to move through the system from being swallowed to the waste products being expelled as faeces can vary from 20 hours to over 100 hours. Also, people open their bowels at different intervals – anything between three times a day and three times a week is considered normal. As the rectum fills with stools the messages which are sent to the brain identify whether the contents of the rectum are solid, liquid (diarrhoea) or gas (wind). The anus has two sphincter muscles which keep the anus closed and prevent leakage. People are normally able to squeeze the external sphincter to keep the rectum closed and prevent the expulsion of faeces until an appropriate time and place.

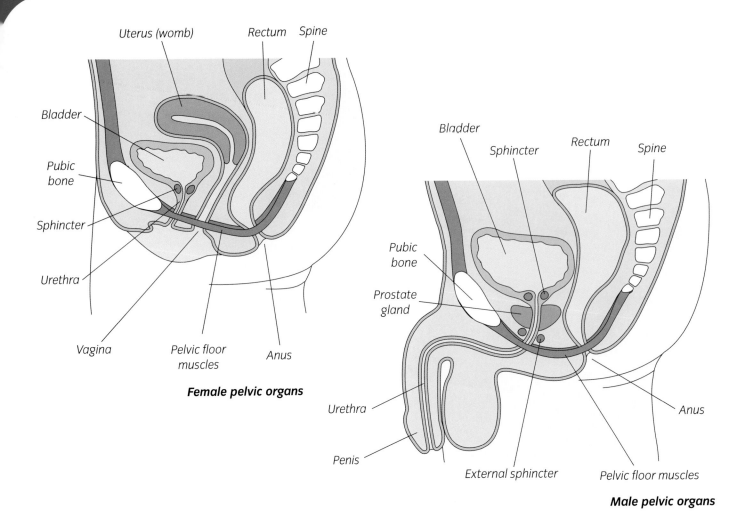

Female pelvic organs

Male pelvic organs

What can go wrong

Many things can go wrong with the system of expelling waste products. Any of these can cause incontinence. Someone who is incontinent is unable to retain their urine or faeces until they are in an appropriate place, and may leak urine or faeces involuntarily.

There are many different potential causes of urinary and faecal incontinence. Neither is a natural or normal part of the ageing process, so it is important, as a care worker, that you do not take the view that incontinence is natural or normal for older individuals. Most types of incontinence can be treated and possibly cured; they can certainly be improved. However, before you can encourage individuals to take steps to improve their condition, you need to understand what the possible causes are and their effects.

Causes of urinary incontinence

Urinary incontinence is the loss of control of the bladder in expelling urine. Some causes of urinary incontinence are temporary and can be managed with simple treatment. These are conditions such as the ones shown on the next page.

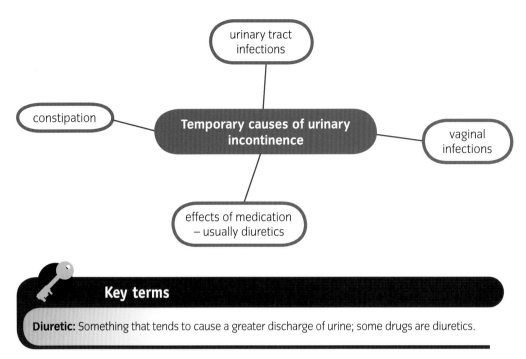

urinary tract infections

constipation

Temporary causes of urinary incontinence

vaginal infections

effects of medication – usually diuretics

Key terms

Diuretic: Something that tends to cause a greater discharge of urine; some drugs are diuretics.

All these conditions are temporary and the incontinence should improve when the conditions have cleared up. A urinary tract infection means that the infection will cause irritation to the bladder and the urethra so that urine will be expelled more frequently than otherwise. It is important to seek medical advice and obtain antibiotic medication if necessary. Also it is important to maintain a large input of bland fluid, such as water or barley water, to allow the urinary system to 'flush' itself clear.

Constipation can cause urinary incontinence. This is because an overfull rectum causes pressure on the bladder, which then expels urine.

If an individual is taking diuretic medication, this can cause excessive amounts of urine to be processed through the body, which the bladder is unable to cope with. All these conditions should improve when the causes are removed.

Other causes of urinary incontinence which are more permanent are:
- damage to or weakness of the pelvic floor muscles, which are important for maintaining the position of the bladder
- weakness of the sphincter muscles, which hold the neck of the bladder closed
- overactive or unstable bladder muscles, which cause the bladder to contract involuntarily and without warning
- a blocked urethra (this is more common in men and results from an enlarged prostate gland)
- hormone imbalance (this is more common in women)
- neurological disorders such as multiple sclerosis or a spinal cord injury
- lack of mobility.

Types of urinary incontinence

The conditions described above can cause different types of urinary incontinence. These affect people in different ways and cause different types of problems.

Urge incontinence

People with urge incontinence are unable to control urination long enough to reach the toilet in time. As soon as they feel the need to urinate they lose urine and are unable to 'hold on' until they reach a toilet.

Stress incontinence

This is the commonest type of incontinence among women. It is extremely common in women who have given birth, because the muscles of the pelvic floor are stretched during labour and childbirth. This can mean that the bladder is no longer held in its correct position by the muscles of the pelvic floor, and that the sphincter muscles which control the neck and outlet of the bladder are no longer able to hold it shut because of its change in position.

Stress incontinence means that urine is leaked when coughing, laughing, sneezing or doing any exercise or activity, such as running – sometimes even walking.

Mixed incontinence

In this case people suffer a mixture of both stress and urge incontinence. This is most commonly seen in older women.

Overflow incontinence

This results from retention of urine in the bladder, where the bladder cannot be completely emptied. This means the bladder is often full and it leads to frequent or constant dribbling. It occurs most commonly in men and is often caused by an obstruction such as an enlarged prostate gland. This can be treated by the removal of the obstruction, which is normally done by surgery.

The prostate gland in men is wrapped around the neck of the bladder like a collar. Its function is to squeeze fluid from the prostate gland into semen when a man has an orgasm. The prostate is small in boys and young men but it becomes larger as men age. It is a process which can cause problems for some men because it becomes so enlarged that it restricts the outlet from the bladder until it interrupts the flow of urine through the urethra. This can mean the flow of urine may be slow and the bladder may not empty completely as a result. It's also possible for the urethra to become blocked completely, and this needs emergency treatment.

Functional incontinence

This occurs when someone with normal bladder control is unable to reach toilet facilities in time because of poor mobility.

Remember

Everyone with incontinence can be helped to a greater or lesser extent. No one has to simply 'put up with it'.

Tests for diagnosis of types and causes of urinary incontinence	
Test	**Purpose of test**
Cytoscopy	Explores the possibility of abnormalities in the bladder and urinary tract. A fibre optic tube is inserted into the bladder for an exploration.
PVR measurement (post-void residual)	This measures how much urine is remaining in the bladder after it has been emptied. It can be done by placing a tube in the bladder or, more commonly today, through an ultrasound scan.
Urinanalyis	This test examines the urine for signs of infection or any other abnormal content.
Urodynamic testing	This examines the function of the bladder and urethra. This may involve x-rays and the insertion of equipment to measure the strength of the sphincter and bladder muscles.
Blood tests	This examines levels of chemicals and hormones in the blood.
Stress tests	These examine how the bladder functions under stress such as when coughing, lifting or exercising.

These tests may be carried out at a specialist urodynamics department at a hospital, in the department of urogenitary medicine, and some of them may be carried out by the individual's own general practitioner. It is important that tests are carried out in order to establish the causes of the incontinence and to ensure that it is not a symptom of a more serious underlying condition. The tests will help to identify the causes of the condition and this will indicate the treatments which are available in order to improve or cure it.

Causes of faecal incontinence

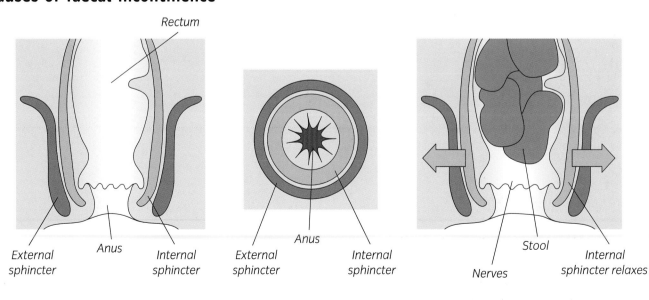

Side view

View from below

Stool moves down

Faecal incontinence is the loss of bowel control. Like urinary incontinence, faecal incontinence has many different causes. It affects fewer people than urinary incontinence but is no less debilitating and embarrassing. Faecal incontinence can also be improved and cured by a range of treatments available for different types of incontinence. The most common causes of loss of bowel control are as follows.

- Damage to the anal sphincter muscles around the back passage. This can be caused by childbirth, where a significant tear across the perineum (the area of skin between the vagina and the anus) can cause damage to the sphincter muscles. Some types of surgery may also result in damage to these muscles.

- An injury or a rectal prolapse where the pelvic floor muscles have been stretched or weakened to the extent that they no longer hold the rectum in the correct position, with the result that the anal sphincter muscles are unable to hold the rectum closed.
  If either or both of these muscles are weakened or injured, then they will be unable to tighten sufficiently to hold faeces in the rectum until a toilet can be reached. This means that an individual may leak liquid or even solid faeces.

- Diarrhoea can be caused by infection or bowel disease or any other inflammation of the bowel. This means that the bowel experiences very high rates of contraction creating pressure waves, which can be so great that it is impossible to reach a toilet in time before the diarrhoea is expelled.

- Immobility or illness can cause constipation. Some medications and some types of neurological disease, such as Parkinson's disease, are also likely to cause constipation. Constipation can lead to incontinence if the bowel becomes very overloaded, so that small lumps of faeces break off and come away. The wall of the bowel can then be irritated by the hard and compacted constipated stools and produce additional fluid and mucus which leak out through the anus.

- Nerve injury or disease. Bowel control involves the co-ordination of neurological and muscular functions, so any damage or disease of the nerve can affect ability to control the evacuation of the bowels. This can affect people who have had a spinal injury or those with multiple sclerosis. Nerve damage is likely to mean that the brain does not receive the correct messages to say that the rectum is full and needs to be emptied, or it may be that the rectum will simply empty without any feeling.

The social and emotional effects of incontinence

The effect on people of an inability to get rid of body waste in the normal way can be devastating. People often avoid getting help or treatment for their incontinence because they are too embarrassed to discuss it, even with their own doctor.

Incontinence can severely restrict people's social life and contact with others. Having had the embarrassing, humiliating experience of an 'accident' in public, whether involving loss of control of the bladder or the bowel, they live in constant fear of it happening again. Many people simply stop going out because of this fear. It is also one of the reasons why many come into residential forms of care, because either they or their carers are unable to cope with their incontinence.

How many suffer from incontinence?

Most people who suffer from incontinence are unaware of the very large numbers of fellow sufferers. In fact, as many as one in three adults have problems of bladder or bowel control at some point in their lives.

At least three million adults in this country have problems with urinary incontinence or bladder control. Only half this many people suffer from diabetes, and yet people with diabetes have no problem discussing their condition with others; neither do people who suffer from arthritis or other common conditions. However, the taboos around body waste are such that many of the three million suffer in silence.

About half a million people suffer from faecal incontinence or bowel control problems. Only a quarter of this number suffer from Parkinson's disease, but this disease is researched, publicised and commonly discussed, whereas the problem of bowel incontinence is seen as embarrassing. A survey carried out in 1995 by the Royal College of Physicians established the numbers of those with urinary and faecal incontinence and categorised them by gender and by living circumstances – whether they were at home, in residential or nursing homes or long-stay hospitals (see the tables below). These results are estimates based on a wide range of studies and surveys but only record the numbers of sufferers known. There could be many more who suffer without seeking assistance.

Percentage of adults with urinary incontinence	Age	%	Percentage of adults with faecal incontinence	Age	%
Women living at home	15–44	5–7	Men and women living at home	15–44	0.4
	45–64	8–15		45–64	3–5
	65+	10–20		65+	15
Men living at home	15–44	3	Men and women in: residential homes		10
	45–64	3	nursing homes		30
	65+	7–10	long-stay hospitals		60
Men and women in: residential homes		25			
nursing homes		40			
long-stay hospitals		50–70			

Incontinence is not simply a problem for older people. Large numbers of middle-aged women experience difficulties in bladder control, as do significant numbers of young women following childbirth.

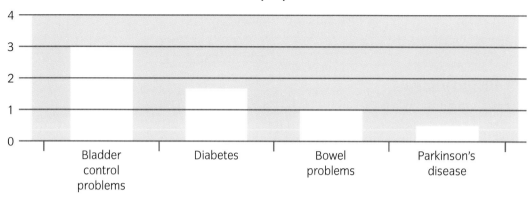

Millions of people affected

The most appropriate ways to assist individuals to maintain continence

You have a vital role as a care worker with an individual suffering from incontinence. You need to support the person in establishing the cause of his or her incontinence and in identifying ways it can be improved. Always adopt the positive attitude that incontinence is not inevitable and that there are a great many options available for improving the condition. Preventing incontinence is always the preferable option, so you should do as much as possible to support individuals and make it possible for them to remain continent despite any difficulties they may have.

Many factors will affect the level of assistance required; an individual's age, medical condition, personal beliefs and preferences all have to be taken into account. If you have concerns about any individual, such as whether the support offered is appropriate and acceptable to that individual, you should report these concerns at once to your supervisor. You may also have to deal with situations where an individual's choices and practices in connection with continence and hygiene are different from your own. See Unit HSC 218 for the ways in which different values and beliefs may need to be accommodated.

Maintaining liquid and food intake

People afraid of becoming incontinent may be inclined to reduce their intake of liquids, and even food. This is one of the worst things they can do as it results in a concentration of urine, which is more inclined to irritate the bladder and cause a greater sense of urgency, and possibly even an infection or inflammation. A reduction in the intake of liquids is also likely to contribute to constipation, which can in itself cause problems of faecal incontinence and will certainly contribute to weakening the pelvic floor muscles if the individual is straining to pass a constipated stool.

Individuals should be advised to drink at least six cups or glasses of fluid each day. This is a minimum amount and some individuals may choose to drink much more than this. Drinks which contain large amounts of caffeine, such as tea or coffee, should not be drunk in large quantities, neither should fizzy, sweet drinks. These can irritate the bladder and actually make the problem worse. Plain water, fruit juice, and fruit or herbal teas are all beneficial and will assist in maintaining the correct balance of fluid in the body.

Check it out

Find out how incontinence is dealt with in your workplace. Is there an incontinence specialist? If so, ask about his or her role. What sort of incontinence aids are used? Is expert help called upon when necessary? If so, ask if you can talk to the expert on his or her next visit.

Diet

A healthy diet should include foods which are high in fibre, as these will greatly assist any bowel problems. Fruit, vegetables, wholemeal bread and wholemeal pasta are all high in fibre. All individuals should be encouraged to east fresh fruit and vegetables daily. More details about healthy diets can be found in Unit HSC 214.

Exercise

Exercise is important for maintaining good digestive functions and will greatly assist people who suffer from constipation. Exercise is also good for improving general muscle tone and any form of exercise which improves the pelvic and anal muscles is likely to maintain continence. Exercise must be appropriate to the individual; however, for many people swimming is ideal. More information about maintaining mobility is in Unit HSC 215.

Regular toiletting

It is important that you discuss with the individual the kind of toilet facilities which he or she is able to manage and feels most comfortable with. People need to feel they can easily access the toilet facilities and that if they need assistance to reach them, this is readily available. No one should have to be incontinent because they are unable to obtain the assistance they need. People should also be given a means of calling for help when using toilet facilities or any continence aid.

Keys to good practice: Managing continence

✓ Make sure you know the type of incontinence you are dealing with.

✓ Seek expert advice about the help that can be given.

✓ Make sure the individual is drinking enough fluids.

✓ Encourage a programme of exercise where possible.

✓ Provide support to access toilet facilities regularly.

✓ Be sensitive to the embarrassment and distress that incontinence causes.

It will be helpful if you can discuss with individuals their regular pattern of elimination of body waste. For example, how often they need to empty their bladder and bowels and at what times of the day. It is useful to know if they have a regular pattern because you can then arrange to make sure that everything they need is available at the times they need it. Assistance to reach a toilet may be all that is needed for some, whereas for other individuals you may need to make sure that commode facilities or a urine bottle are available close to them, so they can maintain their own continence.

After discussing and noting down an individual's regular pattern of elimination you should always ensure that any changes in the pattern are noted and reported. More details on this will be found in Unit HSC 218. Any changes to the normal pattern of elimination can indicate potential problems or some underlying disease or infection. The volume, frequency and condition of waste products are useful indicators of overall health. A fluid balance chart may need to be kept, showing the intake and output of fluids each day for an individual. This is an important way of checking that a positive fluid balance is being maintained.

Disposal of waste products

Many individuals who use a commode or urine bottle will want to be able, wherever possible, to dispose of their own waste. This may be difficult for those who have reduced mobility, but wherever possible they should be assisted to do this. You should ensure that correct hygiene procedures are followed when disposing of waste products.

Check it out

Try making a chart for your own pattern of elimination. If you record this for a week you should have a fairly clear pattern of how often you empty your bladder and your bowels and at what times of the day.

Evidence indicator

Keep a fluid balance chart for 24 hours, to check that you are maintaining a positive fluid balance. Make notes on your findings for your portfolio.

Keys to good practice: Hygiene considerations

✓ Wash your hands, wear gloves and an apron.

✓ If the waste in a commode, bed pan or urine bottle is for disposal, it should be covered and taken to the sluice or toilet where it should be flushed away in accordance with the procedures of your workplace. You should then remove your gloves and apron, dispose of them properly and wash your hands.

✓ If the waste is required for examination, it should be covered and left in an appropriate place, such as the sluice, until the examination is carried out, and then it can be disposed of. You must ensure that disposal of any body waste complies with the procedures for your workplace.

Test yourself

1 What is continence?

2 Name three conditions which can cause urinary incontinence.

3 Name three conditions which can cause faecal incontinence.

4 What are the different types of urinary incontinence?

5 Draw an outline diagram showing the positions of the bowel and bladder in the body.

HSC 219b Support individuals to use equipment to manage continence

Ways of managing continence and improving it

Individuals who suffer any kind of incontinence should be encouraged and supported in finding the best way of managing and improving their condition. Pads, sheaths and bags to absorb waste products resulting from incontinence should only be used after all other attempts at improving or curing the condition have been tried. Always work alongside the individual and encourage him or her to look for positive ways of managing incontinence.

Simply providing the kind of atmosphere in which the individual can talk freely and openly about any difficulties will be of enormous help. Dealing openly and without embarrassment with incontinence issues makes it far more likely that the individual will be willing to discuss options and explore alternative methods of treatment. People who feel embarrassed and humiliated by their condition are less likely to be willing to consider different treatments.

Many GP surgeries and all hospitals provide specialist incontinence advisers. Many departments of genito-urinary medicine run special clinics, so you should encourage individuals to ask to be referred to such a clinic for evaluation and advice. There are a range of ways in which incontinence can be improved, depending on its cause and its severity. Broadly, these fall into the following categories:

- behavioural
- devices
- medication
- surgery.

Behavioural options for urinary incontinence

Bladder training

The major behavioural technique used to deal with urge incontinence is bladder training. This involves encouraging the individual to gradually extend the period between visits to the toilet to empty the bladder. Over a period of time it gradually reduces the urgency for visiting the toilet.

The first stage of bladder training is to establish with the individual the pattern of how often he or she needs to empty the bladder. For example, for someone who empties the bladder every hour, the first aim could be to extend this period to an hour and five minutes. Every time they have the

urge to rush to the toilet, they should attempt to 'hang on' for an extra five minutes. This may seem a very daunting prospect for people who suffer from urge incontinence. However, if they are also taught to use distraction techniques, such as counting backwards from 100 or counting backwards in groups of 3 from 100, or any activity which will distract them, they will be surprised to find that the urge which seemed so imperative has reduced considerably.

Another useful exercise is to sit on the edge of a hard chair or over the arm of a chair or on a rolled up towel. This will support the pelvic floor muscles in holding the bladder sphincter closed.

Bladder retraining is a long-term exercise and may take months before any benefit is gained. However, it has a very high degree of success in helping people with urge incontinence. The aim of bladder retraining should be to reach the normal number of times a day the bladder is emptied, that is between four and eight, and to extend the period between emptying the bladder to three to four hours. This should also assist those who wake frequently in the night in order to urinate.

Change in diet
Cranberry juice is known to help prevent urinary tract infections and is clearly of benefit to those who already suffer from incontinence. It is known that some foods and drinks are likely to increase levels of incontinence, such as coffee, tea and any other caffeinated beverages, fizzy drinks, alcohol, citrus juices, tomato-based juices and tomato-based foods, spicy foods, chocolate, sugar, honey, artificial sweeteners, milk and milk products. Some practitioners have suggested that eliminating one of the above items for a day each over a period of time should help to establish whether there is any noticeable improvement in the incontinence.

People who are incontinent during the night are recommended to stop drinking any beverages two to four hours before going to bed.

Constipation can make urinary incontinence worse, so diets should be high in fibre, fruit and vegetables.

Prompted voiding
This is a form of bladder training widely practised in residential and nursing homes. Individuals are reminded to urinate and assisted to do so at regular intervals, usually starting every hour. Once this regular emptying of the bladder results in dryness, the interval between emptying the bladder increases. This is used primarily for individuals who may be unable to remember the timing for themselves and need a reminder to use the toilet.

Exercises

Stress incontinence is particularly common among women and results in many cases from pelvic floor muscles stretched and strained during childbirth. The techniques for improving stress incontinence largely concentrate on exercise rather than behavioural changes.

Kegel exercises (pelvic floor exercises) were named after Dr Kegel, who developed them to assist women to prepare for and deal with the after-effects of childbirth. They are extremely useful for both men and women to improve stress incontinence. They work by strengthening the pelvic floor muscles which hold the bladder sphincter firmly in place. The exercises can also be useful for people who suffer from urge incontinence.

The pelvic floor is a large sling of muscles stretching across the floor of the pelvis. It reaches from the pubic bone at the front and attaches to the coccyx, which is the base of the spine, behind. The openings from the bladder, bowels and vagina all pass through the pelvic floor. Its function is to support the pelvic organs and abdominal contents and hold them in place to prevent any leakage of waste products. It is possible to exercise the pelvic floor muscles and to strengthen them by carrying out the exercises described below.

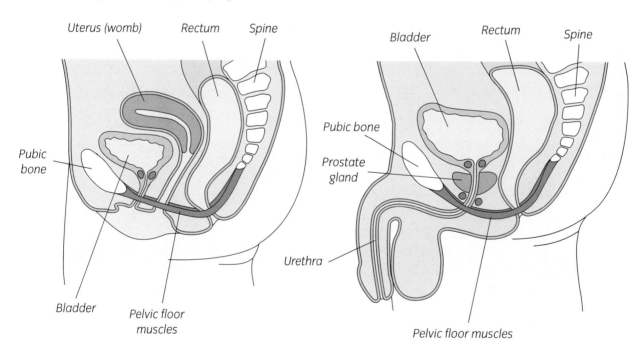

Female pelvic floor muscles

Male pelvic floor muscles

Men also experience weakness of the pelvic floor muscles. This can lead to urinary incontinence, particularly following prostate surgery, when men often experience dribbling following urination. The male pelvic floor muscles are similar to those in women and stretch from the pubic bone to the coccyx. The urethra and rectum also pass through the pelvic floor muscles, which support

the bladder and the bowel in the same way as in the female anatomy. In men the commonest reasons for weakness of the pelvic floor muscles are:

- surgery for enlarged or diseased prostates
- continual straining to pass stools following constipation
- a chronic lung condition such as bronchitis, asthma or a smoker's cough
- being overweight
- neurological damage such as a stroke or spinal injury. However, people who suffer from this type of neurological damage would need specialist treatment for incontinence.

Crossing the legs exercise for women

This very simple but effective movement has been shown to help 73 per cent of women with stress incontinence. Women cross their legs whenever they feel a cough or sneeze coming on. It prevents urine leakage almost completely in the women it helps.

Pelvic floor exercises for women

Exercise 1

Tighten the pelvic floor muscles around the back passage, vagina and urethra and pull them up inside as if you were trying to stop the flow of urine in mid-stream. Hold the pelvic floor muscles tightly for up to ten seconds, then rest for four or five seconds, and then repeat. This should gradually build up to a period of ten contractions. The exercises should be done about six times a day working up to ten contractions each time.

Note: It is important to only use the pelvic floor muscles. Most of the effort should work from the pelvic floor. The individual should not:

- pull in her tummy
- squeeze her legs together
- tighten her buttocks
- hold her breath.

Exercise 2

This exercise helps the muscles of the pelvic floor respond quickly to sudden stresses from coughing, laughing or exercise.

Practise quick contractions which draw up the pelvic floor. Hold for one second before releasing the muscles. This should be done in a controlled and steady way with strong muscle tightening for each contraction.

Repeat up to ten times.

Add to the exercise above in the six times daily routine.

Note: Individuals should see significant results within three to six months, but they should be prepared to continue the pelvic floor exercises indefinitely.

Pelvic floor exercises for men

1   Tighten the ring of muscles around the anus (back passage) as if trying to control diarrhoea or wind. Then relax. Repeat this tightening and relaxing several times until sure the correct muscles have been identified.

    Note: Do not tighten the buttocks, thighs or tummy muscles at this stage.

    To help identify the correct muscles, imagine passing urine and trying to stop the flow in mid-stream. This can be tried out in the toilet. However, this should not be encouraged as a regular practice as it can interfere with normal bladder emptying. Having identified the correct muscles, tighten the pelvic floor. The base of the penis should move towards the abdomen and this should stop or slow down the flow of urine.

2   Tighten and draw in the muscles around the anus and urethra, and lift them up inside. Hold this contraction strongly, count to five and release slowly.

    Repeat: squeeze and lift, then relax.

    It is important to leave four or five seconds between each contraction. Build up the length of time the contractions are held until it is up to 10 seconds. Repeat this up to a maximum of eight to ten squeezes. Do five or ten short and fast (1–2 second) contractions.

    Put the two parts of this routine together and carry out the whole routine four to six times every day.

    Remember to advise the individual that while doing the exercises he should not hold his breath and should not tighten his tummy, buttocks or thighs.

    As with women, it takes some months to reach the maximum effect and the exercises should be continued in order to maintain any improvement.

An individual who has problems identifying the correct muscles could practise trying to stop a flow of urine while sitting on the toilet. However, this should not be done regularly once the individual has learned the correct muscles as it can cause further bladder problems.

It is important that the exercises are continued regularly as it is only by constant repetition that the condition will improve. If they are stopped the previous level of incontinence is likely to return. Exercises should not be done more than five or six times a day; more than this can tire the muscles and cause more leakage than before.

Generally, Kegel exercises have been very effective in improving stress incontinence. They may not cure incontinence, but up to 75 per cent of individuals have reported significant improvement in their stress incontinence after using the exercises.

Check it out

Ask your supervisor about the procedures in place for supporting people who might benefit from exercises to improve continence. Is there a member of staff or a visiting professional who has expertise in this area?

CASE STUDY: Effects of incontinence

H is 73 and has lived alone since the death of her mother ten years ago. She has found it increasingly difficult to 'hold on' when she needs to go to the toilet, but apart from that she is fit and well, and until recently was very active in her local community. She was an active member of the Women's Institute, very involved in activities for the church and helped out at the local hospital's League of Friends. However, after having an 'accident' while out one day, H stopped going out and stayed at home so she could be close to a toilet. She told everyone that she found all the activities too much for her and had simply decided to give them up. Finally, the co-ordinator of the League of Friends managed to get H to confide in her about the problem. Immediately, she persuaded H to arrange a GP appointment. H was sent for tests and referred to an incontinence advisor. She was able to benefit from the advisor's help and her confidence improved; soon she was back to being involved in all her activities again.

1   *How common do you think H's first reaction to her problem is?*

2   *What could have happened if she had not told anyone about the problem?*

3   *What would you have done if she had told you?*

4   *What types of help would you have suggested?*

Devices for urinary incontinence

Biofeedback

Pelvic floor exercises are often more effective if used with biofeedback. This uses a vaginal or rectal probe to relay information to monitoring equipment. The equipment gives auditory or visual signals to show how strongly the individual is contracting the pelvic floor. This is a useful guide for individuals in showing them how well they are carrying out their exercises.

This technique can be used for men, though there is no current evidence to show it is effective.

Vaginal weighted cones

These are small weights which can be placed inside the vagina to assist pelvic floor exercises. These are sometimes useful for women who have difficulty in identifying the correct pelvic floor muscles and doing the usual exercises. The idea is to place the weighted cones in the vagina for 15 to 20 minutes while walking around and moving as usual. The pelvic floor muscles are exercised by holding the cones in place. Cones usually come in sets of different weights or as one cone which unscrews so that different weights can be placed inside it.

The exercises begin by using the lightest weight and gradually increasing the weight and the length of time. The cones are available from major chemists, or ask at your GP surgery for a list of suppliers.

One problem with the cone is that it can slip out of the vagina, another is that it simply lodges there without any muscle work required to keep it in place. A study carried out in 1999, and reported in the *British Medical*

Journal, concluded that vaginal cones did not add any benefit to pelvic floor exercises that were carried out correctly. However, some women have reported that the cones have been of assistance in identifying the correct muscles and helping them to carry out their exercises properly.

Electrical stimulation

Electrical stimulation is useful for stress incontinence and urge incontinence. It is a treatment normally carried out under medical supervision with a specialist continence practitioner. It uses a small battery-powered unit to produce an electric current in the muscles around the bladder. This current is passed by a small vaginal or anal probe in close contact with the pelvic floor muscles or via surface electrodes. This produces an involuntary tightening of the pelvic floor muscles. It is normally used for about 20 minutes to half an hour a day. This treatment produces a similar effect to pelvic floor exercises, and can be useful for people who find the exercises difficult.

The technique can be used with men, but, as in the case of biofeedback, there is no evidence so far that it is effective.

Tampons

Mild stress incontinence in women can sometimes be effectively managed using a tampon which compresses the urethra as it pushes on the vaginal wall. In one study 86 per cent of women with mild incontinence remained continent during exercise sessions when using tampons. This does not appear to be as effective with severe incontinence, as in the same study only 29 per cent remained dry.

Adhesive pads

Foam pads with an adhesive coating, available under a variety of brand names, are effective for women who have stress incontinence. They do not work for women with urge or other forms of incontinence and should not be used if there is a urinal tract or vaginal infection. The pad is placed over the opening of the urethra where it creates a seal to prevent leakage. It has to be removed before urinating and replaced afterwards. In one study, the average number of leaks dropped from 14 a week to 5, and women who were more severely incontinent saw a drop from an average of 34 leaks during a week to 10. When leakage occurred it was slight. The pad can be worn for up to five hours a day and during the night.

Shields

A nipple-shaped shield can be fitted over the urethral opening. It is an effective way to manage stress incontinence. In one study, it reduced urine loss by 96 per cent within a week, and 82 per cent of participants were completely dry. Shields are only available on prescription, and side-effects can include irritation and urinary tract infections.

Reliance urinary control device

This is a small tube which is inserted into the urethra using a reusable syringe. The tip of the tube has a small balloon which is inflated against the urethra and blocks the expulsion of urine. In order to urinate, a string must be pulled to deflate the balloon. The device is then thrown away and replaced with a new one.

Unfortunately, use of the device has resulted in a high incidence of women suffering urinary tract infections (44 per cent), and significant numbers reporting its use as uncomfortable and irritating (78 per cent).

Bladder neck support

A flexible ring which supports the neck of the bladder can be inserted into the vagina and the ridges then pressed against the walls to support the urethra. It is essential that the correct size is used in order for the device to be effective. It can cause infection of the vagina or urethra, and significant numbers of users report discomfort when using it.

Medication for urinary incontinence

Several drugs are available which can assist with urge incontinence, but there is very little medication can do to improve stress incontinence. Drugs such as anticholinergics, and antispasmodics such as propantheline and oxybutynin, work by relaxing the bladder muscles to stop abnormal contractions. These are often effective in reducing urge incontinence by stopping the involuntary contractions of the bladder and allowing the muscles to relax so the bladder can fill and empty normally. However, there are side-effects with these drugs. Some people experience a very dry mouth, blurred vision and constipation.

Surgery for urinary incontinence

Stress incontinence in the case of women can be improved by different types of surgery. The commonest is Burches colposuspension. This has the highest rate of long-term success, with an 85–90 per cent success at five years after the operation. Essentially, all surgery for stress incontinence in women involves supporting or strengthening the pelvic floor muscles. Surgery is also available for men. Prostate surgery often resolves problems of incontinence which accompany an enlarged prostate gland.

Did you know?

Many more surgical interventions are now carried out by laproscopic or keyhole surgery. This involves making very small cuts and using microsurgery techniques to correct the problem. It considerably reduces post-surgical complications and the length of stay in hospital.

> **Evidence indicator**
>
> Carry out some research into devices for urinary incontinence that are, or could be, available for use in your workplace. Search for information about who might benefit from each type, any statistics as to how effective they are, and information on possible side effects. Keep your notes for your portfolio.

Behavioural options for faecal incontinence

Exercises

Sphincter exercises are particularly useful for those who experience problems of urgency. The exercises, which are similar to those for strengthening the pelvic floor muscles, will strengthen the anal sphincter and assist in holding the faeces in the back passage. A specialist continence practitioner is needed to teach the exercises, and biofeedback is often useful.

Changing bowel habits

Having a regular pattern of behaviour, such as regular meal times, and going to the toilet 20 or 30 minutes after a meal, is likely to encourage the bowel to develop a regular pattern. The pattern also helps in planning to be near a toilet at the appropriate time.

Sometimes people will feel more confident if their bowel is empty. This may best be achieved by inserting a suppository into the rectum. The individual then needs to hold onto this for as long as possible, usually about 10 to 20 minutes, before going to the toilet. This should empty the bowel almost completely. Individuals can do this at a time that suits them; they can then feel confident that for the rest of the day, or at least for several hours, they will not need to rush to empty their bowels and are unlikely to suffer leakage.

Bowel training

Bowel training involves learning to resist the urge to empty the bowels and to rush to the toilet at the first indication of a bowel movement. Many people who suffer from incontinence and who have had the humiliating experience of having an 'accident' are very afraid that this will happen again, and so they rush to the toilet the moment they are aware of anything in their back passage. This increases the problem. So, learning to break the cycle can help in training the rectum to hold onto faeces for a longer period.

Diet

Trial and error is the only way to establish whether there are any foods which contribute to bowel incontinence. Very spicy or hot food can upset some people, and food very high in fibre can cause difficulties for people who suffer from poor control and loose faeces or diarrhoea.

Devices for faecal incontinence

There are very few devices to deal with bowel incontinence, although an anal plug has been developed to assist with bowel leakage. It is designed to be worn inside the rectum and plugs the exit of the anus from the inside. It has to be removed in order for the bowel to be emptied and can provide some relief for those who suffer from leakage.

Medication for faecal incontinence

If a cause of incontinence is diarrhoea, or very soft or runny faeces, then medication such as Imodium or codeine can be used to solidify the stools or reduce the bowel contractions.

Surgery for faecal incontinence

If the cause of faecal incontinence is external anal sphincter damage, it may be possible to correct this with surgery. The results of sphincter repair operations are good – 80 per cent of people report improvement two years after surgery.

Equipment to support individuals in managing continence

If all the options for curing incontinence have been tried and been unsuccessful or only partially successful, people can turn to a wide range of products which can make the management of incontinence much easier. These include:

- hand-held urinals
- specially adapted clothing
- sheaths and body urinals
- catheters
- protection for beds and chairs
- protection for clothing.

Hand-held urinals

Hand-held urinals help both men and women with restricted mobility to be continent and independent. People who use them can go out and participate in social activities where toilet facilities may not readily be available. A hand-held urinal can be used in bed, and when seated or standing, depending on the abilities of the individual.

Hand-held urinals for men

Men who use hand-held urinals when sitting down may find that extending the fly slide on trousers until it reaches the crotch seam will make the urinal easier to use. Male urinals come in various shapes to suit the circumstances in which they are to be used.

Single-use disposable urinals, made from lightweight plastic, can be carried in a pocket or bag for use when out.

Did you know?

A sachet of absorbent gel, such as the kind you use in hanging baskets of plants, placed inside a hand-held urinal will soak up most of the fluid and reduce the risk of spills.

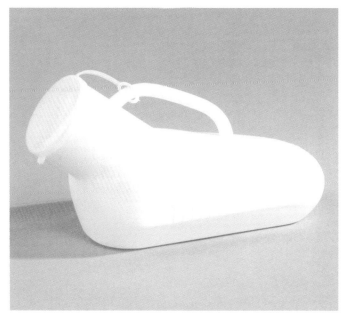

Lightweight hand-held urinal for men

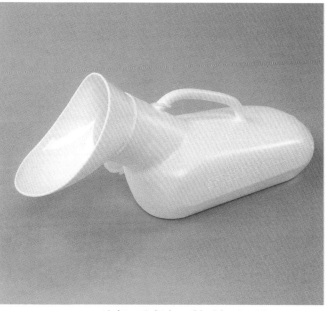

Lightweight hand-held urinal for women

Hand-held urinals for women

These are used by placing them between the legs from the front, or they can be straddled or sat on. The choice of urinal will depend on the posture the individual is able to use and her own circumstances. If you are supporting a individual who uses a wheelchair or who spends most of the day sitting in a chair, then a u-shaped cut-out in the front of the cushion may be particularly useful. This means that the urinal can be placed in the space left by the cut-out, which avoids the person having to be lifted.

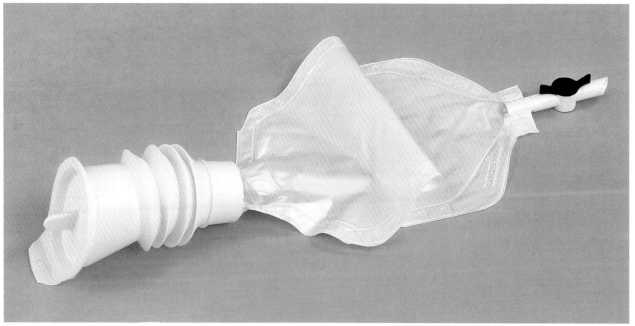

Folding unisex urine bag

Clothing

Specially adapted clothing, such as split-crotch knickers, wrap-around skirts and similar styles, may help with the use of a urinal.

Flaps can be tucked into waistband for toiletting

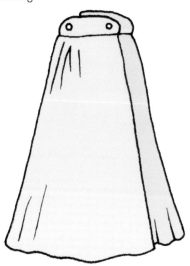

Front

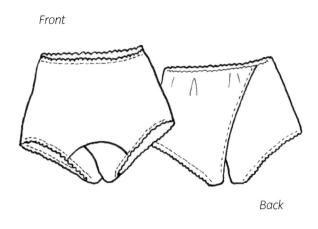

Back

Ensure generous overlap

Wrap-around skirt

Split-crotch knickers

Sheaths and body urinals

These are more commonly used by men. A sheath is fitted over the penis to collect urine and attached to a leg drainage bag. Some sheaths need to be attached with adhesive and some are self-adhesive. Sheaths must be measured and it is important that individuals understand how to apply a sheath.

Body urinals are available in several designs and can be used instead of absorbent pads or penile sheaths. They drain into a leg bag or into their own reservoir.

Pouch for penis

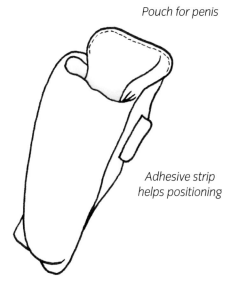

Adhesive strip helps positioning

Sheath

Catheters

Catheters should only be used on medical advice and how they are used must be carefully explained to the individual by a qualified medical practitioner.

There are two types of catheter – an intermittent catheter and an indwelling catheter. An intermittent catheter is inserted into the bladder several times each day, emptying the contents of the bladder into the toilet, a jug or other convenient container for disposal. This can be done by someone caring for an individual or it can be done by individuals themselves.

An indwelling catheter is kept in place for a longer period – a maximum of three months, by which time it will need to be changed and replaced with a new catheter.

Normally, catheters are inserted via the urethra, in the case of both men and women, placed in the bladder and held in place by a small balloon which is inflated once inside the bladder. Sometimes after surgery a suprapubic catheter can be inserted through the abdominal wall just above the pubic bone.

Most catheters empty the contents of the bladder down a tube into a drainage bag. This can be supported in a range of ways, though usually it is attached to the individual's leg. However, rather than using a bag some people prefer a catheter valve, which fits on the end of the tube and is emptied every three or four hours into a toilet or suitable receptacle.

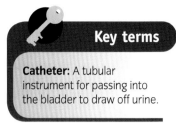

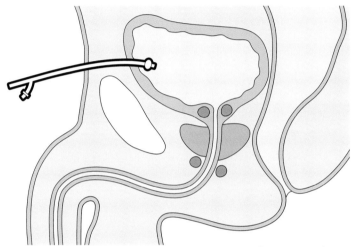

Indwelling catheter

Drainage bags

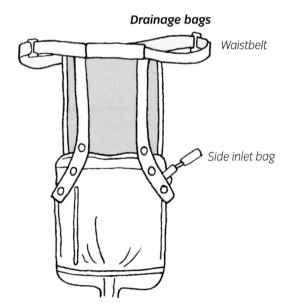

Waistbelt

Side inlet bag

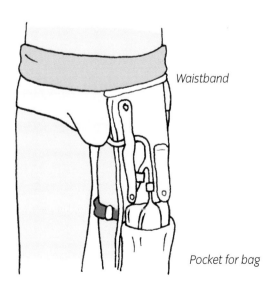

Waistband

Pocket for bag

A full drainage bag from a catheter or from a sheath is quite heavy, so it is important that an adequate support system is in place. For individuals who are not mobile this is not such a problem, but for people who are able to move around there are a range of ways of supporting a drainage bag in place under clothing. Leg straps are often the easiest way to support the drainage bag, or a waist belt can be used.

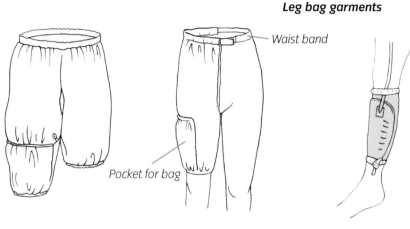

Leg bag garments

Waist band

Pocket for bag

Another option is to use leg bag garments designed to hold a catheter drainage bag and to stop it slipping. Such garments usually have an opening to empty the bag.

Protection for beds and chairs

Covers to protect mattresses, pillows, blankets and duvets are available. They can be either disposable or washable. There are different types of washable and reusable bed and chair pads. They range from basic plastic PVC covers to quilted and absorbent ones, which are much more comfortable to use.

Machine-washable bed pad

Machine-washable chair pad

If disposable pads are used, they must be disposed of in line with the procedures for the disposal of body waste in your workplace. Washable pads should be washed separately and thoroughly dried before being replaced on the bed. Many of the current washable pads are designed to absorb large quantities of urine. If these are being used it is important that the individual sleeps naked below the waist so the skin is in direct contact with the dry top surface of the pad. The urine will pass through this to a lower layer where it is held. This means that the skin does not come into contact with the urine, thus reducing the risk of skin irritation, rashes and bedsores.

Bed and chair pads are still in use but they are often not seen as good practice. When they are used, it is important to maintain the individual's dignity.

Protection for clothing

Pads are the most popular product that people use to protect themselves against leaks of urine or faeces. Like bed and chair pads they can be either disposable or washable and reusable. Several factors need to be taken into account in deciding to use these, such as the degree of incontinence, the access to washing and drying facilities, and cost.

All-in-one disposable pads are suitable for either urinary or faecal incontinence, and are particularly useful for people confined to bed.

Disposable insert pads fit into specially designed pairs of knickers and can be disposed of after use. Male pouches can be disposable or washable and can be used by men with slight or dribbling incontinence. Briefs with built-in pads can be used for moderate incontinence.

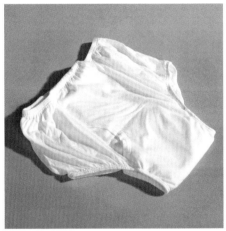 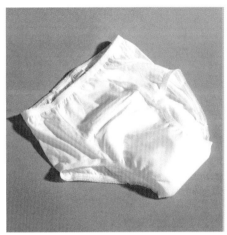

Men's brief with built-in pad   *Women's full brief with built-in pad*

Hygiene

The rules of basic personal hygiene apply to anyone who suffers from incontinence. By following these rules they should avoid the soreness and skin irritations which can accompany urinary incontinence.

- The area around the urethra needs to be kept clean and the skin should not be allowed to dry out. Incontinence cleansers are available for frequent cleansing without causing irritation. Most of them are simply applied by wiping with an impregnated cloth.
- After a bath or shower, a moisturiser and a barrier cream should be applied. Moisturisers are very important as they stop the skin becoming dry and prone to soreness and irritation. A barrier cream, such as zinc oxide, petroleum jelly or lanolin, protects the skin from the effects of urine.
- Deodorising tablets (Derisil or Nullo) can help to reduce the smell of urine. Studies have suggested that taking alfalfa several times a day reduces odour, and because it is a herbal preparation alfalfa does not react with any other medications the individual may be taking.

Your role

Your role is not that of a specialist incontinence advisor, but it is useful for you to understand the ways in which incontinence can be effectively managed. This will help you work alongside the individual to improve continence and to develop his or her confidence in dealing with it.

New products and treatments are constantly being developed and it is essential that you continually update your knowledge of what is available. One of the most useful ways of doing this is to attend exhibitions and to obtain literature on new developments from your local specialist continence advisor. The knowledge which you can pass on to the individual will be invaluable in convincing him or her that suffering incontinence is not inevitable – it can often be cured, and can always be improved.

Test yourself

1. What methods can be used to manage urinary incontinence?
2. What methods can be used to manage faecal incontinence?
3. Which muscles can be strengthened to assist with incontinence?
4. Make notes which explain how to do pelvic floor exercises.

HSC 219 UNIT TEST

1. What are the main types of incontinence?
2. What are the commonest causes of each type of incontinence?
3. List the main approaches which can be taken to improving incontinence.
4. How common is incontinence? Approximately how many people in this country suffer?
5. How would you approach someone who is too embarrassed to discuss his or her incontinence problem?
6. Plan an exercise programme for a woman suffering from stress incontinence.
7. Consider what incontinence products you would advise for an older man who has dribbling incontinence and poor mobility.

Contribute to moving and handling individuals

This unit is primarily concerned with those individuals who are most dependent upon your assistance. The level of assistance they need can vary from needing help to get out of a chair to being completely dependent on others to move them, to turn them over and to alter their position in any way, for example if they are unconscious or paralysed.

When individuals require this degree of care it is essential that they are moved and handled in the most sensitive and safe way. This is also vital for you as a worker – the commonest causes of people being unable to continue to work in health or care are that they suffer injuries, usually back injuries, from lifting and moving individuals. It is possible to minimise the risk to both you and the individuals for whom you provide care by following the correct procedures and using the right equipment.

The first element is about preparing individuals for being moved. In the second element you will need to learn about how to carry out the move and to ensure that you know the way to carry it out correctly and safely, and offer all the support people need.

What you need to learn

- What the law says
- Working with the individual to be moved
- Suitable clothing and equipment
- How to encourage independence
- Equipment for moving and handling
- Methods for manual moving and handling
- Recording and passing on information.

HSC 223a Prepare individuals, environments and equipment for moving and handling

What the law says

As you learned in Unit HSC 22, all aspects of health and safety are covered by legislation. Moving people safely is no exception. The Health and Safety Executive guidance states:

1. The Manual Handling Operations Regulations 1992, which implement the Manual Handling of Loads Directive, came into effect on 1 January 1993 and apply to all manual handling activity with a risk of injury.

2. The Regulations impose duties on employers, self-employed people and employees. Employers must avoid all hazardous manual handling activity where it is reasonably practicable to do so. If it is not, they must assess the risks in relation to the nature of the task, the load, the working environment and the capabilities of the handler and take appropriate action to reduce the risk to the lowest level reasonably practicable. Employees must follow appropriate work systems introduced by their employer to promote safety during the handling of loads.

Ensuring safety for both yourself and the person being moved is the joint responsibility of you and your employer.

The HSE provides guidelines about weights which can be safely lifted – these are very general guides and are not a substitute for a risk assessment, because many factors can affect the risks in each situation.

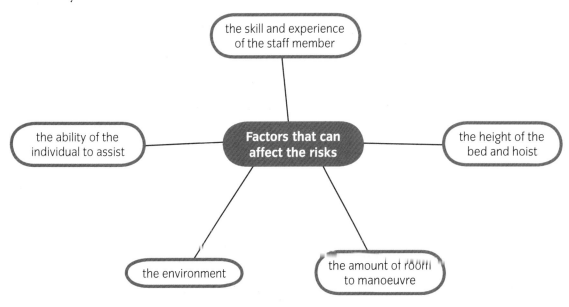

- the skill and experience of the staff member
- the ability of the individual to assist
- **Factors that can affect the risks**
- the height of the bed and hoist
- the environment
- the amount of room to manoeuvre

The HSE guidelines are based on moving inanimate objects, not people – who can move, wriggle, complain and co-operate (or not)! But these guidelines are useful in showing how little weight can be lifted safely, and serve as a useful warning to THINK RISK.

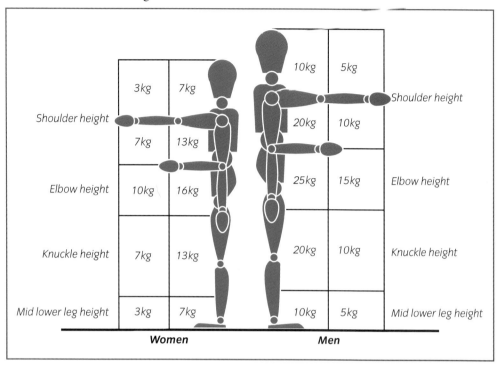

Each box in the diagram above shows guideline weights for lifting and lowering.

Observe the activity and compare to the diagram. If the lifter's hands enter more than one box during the operation, use the smallest weight. Use an inbetween weight if the hands are close to a boundary between boxes. If the operation must take place with the hands beyond the boxes, make a more detailed assessment.

The weights assume that the load is readily grasped with both hands, and the operation takes place in reasonable working conditions with the lifter in a stable body position.

Any operation involving more than twice the guideline weights should be rigorously assessed – even for very fit, well-trained individuals working under favourable conditions.

There is no such thing as a completely 'safe' manual handling operation. But working within the guidelines will cut the risk and reduce the need for a more detailed assessment.

Source: HSE 1998

How to assess risks

As you may remember from Unit HSC 22, your employer has a responsibility under health and safety legislation to examine and assess all procedures which take place in your working environment involving risk. All risks must be noted, assessed and steps taken to minimise them as far as possible. Your employer is required to provide adequate equipment for such tasks as moving and handling individuals who require assistance.

There are responsibilities on both the employer and the employee (you). The process of reducing risk is a joint responsibility – you must make your contribution in the interests of your own safety as well as that of the person you are moving.

The employer's duties are to:
- **avoid** the need for hazardous manual handling as far as is reasonably practicable
- **assess** the risk of injury from any hazardous manual handling that can't be avoided
- **reduce** the risk of injury from hazardous manual handling, as far as reasonably practicable.

Employees' duties are to:
- follow appropriate systems of work laid down for their safety
- make proper use of equipment provided to minimise the risk of injury
- co-operate with the employer on health and safety matters; a care assistant who fails to use a hoist that has been provided is putting himself or herself at risk of injury, and the employer is unlikely to be found liable
- apply the duties of employers, as appropriate, to their own manual handling activities
- take care to ensure that their activities do not put others at risk.

Look after your back

Ideally every workplace should have, or have access to, a Back Care Advisor (BCA). These are people who have training in manual handling and are able to provide expert advice to managers, manual handling supervisors and to members of staff who are involved in manual handling.

You must ensure that you follow the information provided by the BCA for your workplace, and take every opportunity to attend information and education events to make sure you are up to date on manual handling techniques and policies.

Check it out

Find out who the BCA is for your workplace, and ask him or her when the next education sessions are planned.

Checklist

1 Is individual weight-bearing? Yes ☐
   No ☐

2 Is individual unsteady? Yes ☐
   No ☐

3 What is the general level of mobility? Good ☐
   Poor ☐

4 a What is the individual's weight? _____

   b What is the individual's height? _____

   c How many people does this lift require? _____

   (Work this out on the scale devised by your workplace)

5 What lifting equipment is required? Hoist ☐
   Sling ☐
   Trapeze ☐
   Transfer board ☐

6 Is equipment available? Yes ☐
   No ☐

7 If not, is there a safe alternative? Yes ☐
   No ☐

8 Are the required number of people available? Yes ☐
   No ☐

9 What is the purpose of the move? _____

   _____

10 Can this be achieved? Yes ☐
   No ☐

A checklist for assessing risks before moving an individual

The risk assessments your employer carries out are, however, general risks for your work environment. Each time you move or lift any individual, you too must make an assessment of the risks involved in carrying out that particular manoeuvre. Even if you have moved this individual every day for the past six months, you should still assess the risks on each occasion before you put anything into practice.

No two lifts are ever the same – there are always some factors that are different. These factors could be to do with the individual and his or her mood or health on that particular day; they could be about the environment; or they could be about you and your current physical condition.

You should run through the same checklist each time before you carry out any activity which involves you in physically moving a person from one place to another. A suggested checklist is shown on the previous page. You may need to adapt it to fit your own place of work and the circumstances in which you work.

This system is best remembered as TILE – Task, Individual, Load, Environment. You should carry out a TILE assessment each time you move a service user.

You need to consider the environment carefully when you are assessing risk. You should take into account all of the following factors.

- Is the floor surface safe? Are there wet or slippery patches?
- Are you wearing appropriate clothing – low-heeled shoes, tunic or dress which has enough room to stretch and reach?
- Is the immediate area clear of items that may cause a trip or a fall, or items which could cause injury following a fall?
- Is all the equipment, both to carry out the lift and in the place to which the individual is to be moved, ready?
- Does the individual have privacy and can his or her dignity be maintained during the move?
- Is there anyone you could ask for help, for example a porter or member of the ambulance service?

Working with the individual to be moved

Make sure you wash your hands and ensure your own hygiene before and after moving individuals.

The individual who is going to be moved is the key person to be actively involved, as far as possible, in decisions about the best way to carry out the move. Unless the person concerned is unconscious or semi-conscious or so confused as to be unable to contribute to any discussion about the best way to proceed, then it is essential that you discuss with the person the way that he or she would feel most comfortable with.

Many people who have a long-standing disability will be very experienced in how to deal with it. They are the best people to ask for advice as they know the most effective ways for them to be moved, avoiding pain and discomfort as far as possible.

Discuss with the person concerned the way that he or she would prefer to be moved

ASSESSMENT FORM FOR PATIENTS WHO REQUIRE MANUAL HANDLING

Patient's name………………………………….. District nurse…….. ………………………

Body build   Obese ☐   Above average ☐   Average ☐   Below average ☐   Tall ☐   Medium ☐   Short ☐

Weight (if known)………………………….   Risk of falls   High ☐   Low ☐

Problems with comprehension, behaviour, cooperation (identify)……………………………..
………………………………………………………………………………………………………

Handling constraints e.g. disability, weakness, pain, skin lesions, infusions (identify)
………………………………………………………………………………………………………

Tasks (see examples)…………………………………………………………………………
………………………………………………………………………………………………………

Methods to be used (see examples)…………………………………………………………..
………………………………………………………………………………………………………

Describe any remaining problems, list any other measures needed (see examples)
………………………………………………………………………………………………………
………………………………………………………………………………………………………

Date(s) assessed   …………………..   …………………...   ……………………   ……………….

Assessor's signature   ………………….   …………………..   …………………...   ……………….

Proposed review dates   ………………….   …………………..   ……………………   …………….....

                                          Finishing date   ……………….

Examples

Tasks:

✓ Sitting/standing
✓ Toileting
✓ Bathing
✓ Transfer to/from bed

Methods/control measures:
Organisation
✓ Number of staff needed?
✓ Patient stays in bed
Equipment
✓ Variable height bed
✓ Hoists
✓ Slings/belts
✓ Bath aids
✓ Turntable
✓ Sliding aids
Furniture
✓ Reposition/remove

Problems/risk factors:
Task
✓ Is it necessary? Can it be avoided?
✓ Rest/recovery time?
Patient
✓ Weight, disability, ailments?
Environment
✓ Space to manoeuvre?
✓ Access to bed, bath, WC?
✓ Steps/stairs?
✓ Flooring uneven? OK for hoist?
Carers
✓ Fitness for the task, freshness or fatigue?
✓ Experience with patient?
✓ Skill (handling, equipment)?

A risk assessment form for manual handling

Once you have carried out all the necessary assessments, you should explain carefully to the individual exactly what you intend to do and what his or her role is in contributing to the effectiveness and safety of the move. This will vary according to the person's ability, but nonetheless most individuals will be able to participate to some extent.

Even where individuals are unconscious or appear to have no understanding of what is going on, you should still explain exactly what you are doing and why you are doing it and what the effects will be. We have a limited understanding of what a state of unconsciousness means to the person experiencing it. Every individual has the same right to be treated with dignity and respect and to have procedures explained rather than simply having things done to him or her by care workers who believe that 'they know best'.

Check it out

Your workplace probably uses an assessment form similar to the one shown here. Find the one your workplace uses and make sure you know how to fill it in. It may be similar to the checklist on page 333.

Each stage of the proposed move should be explained in detail before it is carried out, and it is essential to obtain the individual's consent before you move or handle him or her in any way. If you move an individual without his or her consent this could be considered as an assault. So you should always be sure that you are carrying out the individual's wishes before you commence any move.

Keys to good practice: Preparing for moving and handling

✓ Wash your hands and ensure you are wearing suitable clothing and footwear.

✓ Check the care plan and assess risks to the individual and to yourself before starting any move.

✓ Remove potential hazards and prepare the immediate environment.

✓ Ask the individual about the best way of moving, or assisting, him or her.

✓ Explain the procedure at each stage, even where it may not be obvious that you are understood.

✓ Explain how the equipment operates.

✓ Check that you have the agreement of the person you are moving.

✓ Stop immediately if the individual does not wish you to continue – you may not move a person without his or her consent.

Never be tempted to drag an individual up the bed or chair, instead of ensuring that he or she is properly lifted. Dragging someone can promote the development of pressure sores, especially on the sacrum (the bottom of the back) and heels.

Suitable clothing and equipment

Your clothing

The type of clothing you wear when you are moving individuals is very important. It can make the difference between carrying out a procedure safely and doing it with difficulty and possible risk of injury. Footwear should be supportive and flat, with soles that grip firmly.

Recommendations in respect of uniforms are that dresses should have a pleat in the skirt and a similar pleat in the sleeves. These are to allow space so that you do not find that your own movements are restricted by your clothing, possibly forcing you to move in an awkward way. It may be necessary, for example, to place one knee on a bed. This is impossible if you are wearing a straight skirt, or at least very difficult to manage at the same time as maintaining dignity – yours, not the service user's!

If you are in a situation where you do a great deal of moving and handling, it is a good idea to wear trousers, with a tunic top which has plenty of room in the sleeves and shoulders to allow free movement. Your employer should have carried out a risk assessment and ensured that the clothing that is provided for you to wear is appropriate and complies with current best practice and requirements in terms of moving and handling.

Work clothing should allow for free movement when handling individuals

Equipment

The use of equipment is covered by the Lifting Operations and Lifting Equipment Regulations (LOLER).

LOLER came into force in 1998 and covers risks to health and safety from lifting equipment provided for use at work. LOLER requires that equipment is:

- strong and stable enough for the intended load
- marked to indicate safe working load
- used safely: the equipment's use should be organised, planned and executed by competent people
- subject to ongoing examination and inspection by competent people.

Hoists, slings and bath hoists are covered by the regulations. The regulations state that lifting equipment should be thoroughly examined by competent people at least every six months in the case of equipment used to lift people, and at least annually in the case of other equipment.

In your work you may use many different types of equipment, including several types of lifting and moving equipment. It is important that you check every time you use a piece of equipment that it is safe and that it is fit for use for that particular individual.

If you do find equipment has become worn, damaged or appears to be unsafe in any way, you should immediately stop using it, take it out of service and report it to your supervisor. You must do this even if it means having to change your handling assessment for the individual you were about to move.

Under no circumstances is it acceptable to take a risk with equipment which may be faulty. It is better that the individual waits a little longer for a move or is moved in an alternative way rather than being exposed to risks from potentially unsafe equipment.

Make sure that you have read the instruction manual for each piece of equipment you use. It should give you a safety checklist – make sure you follow it.

Evidence indicator

Find out the procedure in your workplace for reporting faulty equipment. Check whether there is a file or a book where you need to record the fault. You may only need to make a verbal report, or you may have to enter the details of the fault into a computer. Make sure that you know what the correct procedure is, and make notes on it for your portfolio.

How to encourage independence

There are many ways in which an individual can assist and co-operate with care workers who are handling or moving him or her. It is important that this is encouraged and that individuals are not made to feel as though they are simply being transported from place to place 'like a piece of meat'. Co-operation from the individual is invaluable, both for maintaining his or her own independence and for assisting those who have to carry out the move. For example, you may be transferring an individual from a bed to a wheelchair. The first part of the process – getting to the edge of the bed and sitting on it – may well be possible for the individual to accomplish if he or she follows a correct set of instructions, rather than having to be moved by carers.

Any independence that can be achieved is vitally important in terms of the individual's self esteem and sense of well-being. A person may be able to transfer himself or herself from a wheelchair to a chair, to a car seat or into bed, either by the use of transfer boards or by simply being able to use sufficient upper body strength to slide across from chair to wheelchair, and vice versa, once the wheelchair arm is removed.

You may be able to use self-help techniques when an individual needs a bed pan. Rather than having to be lifted manually, he or she can be encouraged, with some simple instructions, to bend the knees and raise the bottom to allow the bed pan to be slid underneath him or her.

Techniques like this involve the active co-operation of the individual. Obviously they are not suitable for use where individuals are unable to co-operate, either because of their state of consciousness or because they have almost total paralysis. Some individuals may not be able to co-operate for emotional reasons – they may lack the confidence to make any moves for themselves because of fear of falling or fear of pain or discomfort. Where the plan of care has identified that the individual is capable of co-operation in moving and handling, this should be gently encouraged and the reasons for his or her reluctance to co-operate should be discussed with the individual.

Good preparation is the key to a successful move or transfer. Where the individual and the worker are working together, there is likely to be the maximum safety and minimum risk, pain and discomfort.

 CASE STUDY: Planning a move

Shireen is the carer for Mrs G, who is 80. Shireen needs to move Mrs G from a bed into a chair. Mrs G is only able to assist a little as she has very painful joints and is unable to bear weight. She weighs 16 stones (101 kg).

1   *What would you expect to see in Mrs G's care plan in respect of moving procedure? Give reasons.*

2   *What factors should Shireen take into account before starting to move Mrs G?*

3   *What should Shireen say to her?*

Test yourself

1   Name three factors you would take into account when assessing the risk of carrying out a move.

2   In what sort of circumstances would you consider asking an individual to move himself or herself across the bed?

3   What type of clothing is most suitable for carrying out lifting?

4   What steps should you take if you have concerns about the safety of equipment?

HSC 223b Assist individuals to move from one position to another

Equipment for moving and handling

A wide range of equipment is available, and technological advances are being made continuously in the field of medical equipment. But regardless of the individual products and improvements which may be made to them, lifting and handling equipment broadly falls into the following categories:

- hoists, slings and other equipment, which move the full weight of an individual
- equipment designed to assist in a move and to take some of the weight of an individual, such as transfer boards
- equipment designed to assist the individual to help himself or herself, such as lifting handles positioned above a bed to allow individuals to pull themselves up. This category also includes grab handles, raised toilet seats, and lifting-seat chairs.

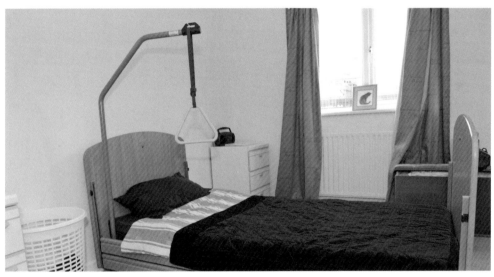

Lifting handles above a bed can help an individual to move himself or herself

Depending on the setting in which you work, you may have to use some or all of the different types of equipment. If you work with individuals in their own homes, your access to equipment may be more limited, although there is now an extensive range of equipment that can be used very effectively within an individual's own home, often removing the need for residential care.

Using equipment

Each piece of equipment will have an instruction manual. You must read this and be sure that you follow the instructions for its use. There are some general points about how to use particular types of equipment, but you must know how to use the particular equipment in your workplace.

Hoists

- Make sure that you use the correct sling for the hoist and for the weight of the service user.
- Most slings are colour-coded. Check that you have the right one for the weight of the service user.
- Ensure that the seams on the hoist are facing outwards, away from the service user, as they can be rough and can easily damage the skin.
- Only attempt to manoeuvre a hoist using the steering handles – do not try to move it with the jib, as it can overbalance.
- Place the sling around or under the service user. Lower the bed to its lowest position. Then lift the service user. It is only necessary to have a small clearance from the bed or chair – there is no need to raise the service user a great distance.

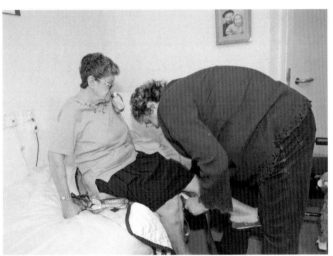

1 *Place the sling around or under the service user*

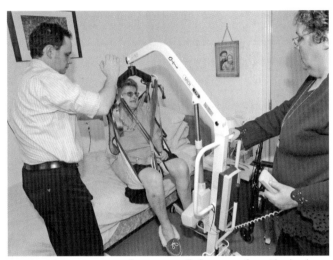

2 *It is only necessary to have a small clearance from the bed or chair*

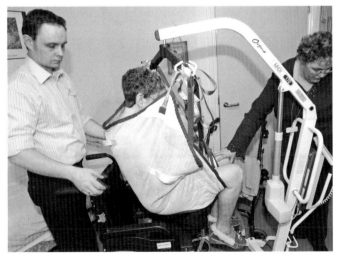

3 *Place the wheelchair in position and make sure it is steady*

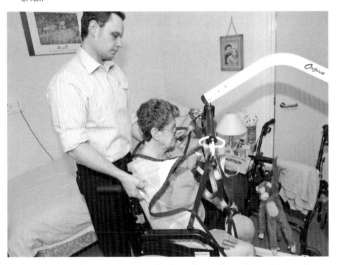

4 *Make sure the service user feels safe and comfortable at the end of the move*

You cannot learn to use a hoist safely by reading a book – you must familiarise yourself with the hoists in your workplace and ask to be shown how to operate them.

Transfer boards/sheets

These require at least two people standing on opposite sides of the bed. They allow people to be moved from bed to trolley and vice versa. They can be used regardless of the level of consciousness of the individual.

They all work on the same principles. They are made of friction-free material which is placed half under the person and half under the sheet he or she is lying on. One worker then pulls and the other pushes. The sheet, complete with person, then slides easily from one to the other. There are several types available: 'Pat-slide', 'Easy-glide' and 'Easy-slide' are among the most common.

Slideboards

The slideboard is a small board placed between a bed and a chair or wheelchair. It is designed for use by service users who are able to be quite active in the transfer and only require assistance. The board allows the service user to slide from bed to chair, and vice versa, with some assistance in steadying and some encouragement.

Turn discs

These are used to swivel service users, in either a sitting or standing position, and can be useful for service users who are able to stand. They are particularly useful for getting in and out of vehicles.

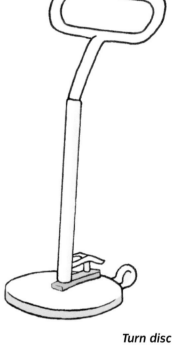

Turn disc

Monkey pole or lifting handle

This is a handle which is fixed above a bed, and swings from a metal frame (see the photograph on page 340). It is designed to allow people to assist themselves. They have to pull on the bar to lift the upper part of the body off the bed. This can enable people to help themselves to sit up, turn over and change position without having to call for assistance.

Handling belts

These enable you to assist a service user to rise from a chair, or provide a steadying hand, by holding onto the handles on the belt. It gives you a firm grip without risking bruising the service user or slipping and causing an injury to either of you.

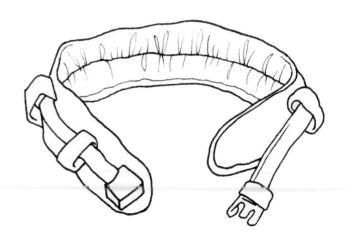

Handling belt

Assessing equipment

When you are assessing how to assist a person to move and which equipment to use, you need to consider:

- the potential risks
- what the person can do to help himself or herself to move, and what he or she cannot do – remember that it is important to encourage as much independence as possible
- what the person knows from experience to be the best method, or the method he or she prefers.

If the person's preference conflicts with safe practice, you should tactfully explain this, pointing out the potential risks and suggesting the best method. Reassure the person, if necessary. If there is still a problem, you will need to tell your supervisor immediately.

Remember

You should never move anyone without his or her agreement.

Evidence indicator

Investigate the equipment available in your workplace for moving and handling. Make sure you know where different items are kept and how they work. Make notes to refer to when necessary.

Methods for manual moving and handling

There are very few situations in which manual lifting should be carried out. Unless it is an emergency or a life-threatening situation, there should be no need to move anyone without the correct equipment. It is important that service users are encouraged to assist in their own transfers and movements.

This means that even shoulder lifts (like the Australian lift) are no longer considered to be safe. There is no safe weight limit for lifting, so the only workplaces where manual lifting should now take place are units caring for babies and small children. Even there, it is important to ensure that risk assessments are carried out to avoid the likelihood of injury, as height differences between the carer and the child, or the surface involved, present other safety issues.

Care workers in a hospital or residential setting should never have to lift or move service users without the necessary equipment. This is sometimes more of a problem in community settings, where it may not be easy to use equipment in the service user's home, or the equipment may not be available.

The Disability Rights Commission has highlighted the issues in relation to the human rights of people with disabilities. They argue that if disabled people are unable to live in the way they wish because of a 'no lifting' policy – for example, some people have had to remain in bed because no equipment was available to move them, or they did not wish to be moved using equipment – then the agency refusing to provide the care is in breach of both the Human Rights Act and the Disability Discrimination Act.

Guidance from the Health and Safety Executive – 'Handling Home Care', 2002 – states that while all risk assessments must be undertaken and equipment used wherever possible, 'no lifting' policies are likely to be incompatible with service users' rights.

The NHS 'Back to Work' guidance also states that 'no lifting' is a misleading term as it is often used to mean that lifting most, or all, of a service user's weight should not be undertaken. In no circumstances, however, should the service user or carer be put at risk.

Evidence indicator

Find copies of the Health and Safety Executive and NHS guidelines in your workplace. Check out what they say about moving service users. Find out if your workplace has its own policy, and see how it compares. Does your workplace have copies of information from the Disability Rights Commission? If not, you could obtain it. It may raise some useful points for discussion with your supervisor and colleagues. Make notes on your findings for your portfolio.

If you need to move someone manually in order to change his or her position or to provide assistance, you should follow the principles of effective manual moving and handling.

- Risks must be assessed *every time*.
- The procedures should be well-planned and assessed in advance. Technique rather than strength is what is important.
- The procedure should be comfortable and safe for the individual – creating confidence that being moved is not something to be anxious about and that he or she can relax and co-operate with the procedure.
- The procedure should be safe for the workers carrying it out. A worker who is injured during a badly planned or executed transfer or move is likely in turn to injure the individual he or she is attempting to move. Similarly, an individual who is injured during a move is likely to cause an injury to those who are moving him or her.

Remember

The interests and safety of the individual and the workers are so closely linked that you must consider them both together.

Team work

Most moving and transfer procedures, whether manual or assisted, are carried out by more than one person. If you are to work successfully as part of a team, you need to follow some simple rules:

- Carry out a risk assessment.
- Decide who is going to 'shout', or lead the manoeuvre.
- That person will check that everyone is ready.
- He or she will say '1-2-3 lift' or '1-2-3 move'.
- Everyone must follow the count of the person who shouts.

Transfer

If you are assisting an individual to transfer from a bed or chair to a wheelchair, this can be done with one person providing assistance to steady the person as he or she uses the transfer board, provided that there are no complicating factors such as an individual who is particularly heavy or tall, or who has serious disabilities. In that case, the person should be moved using a hoist or a turntable.

Rolling or turning

If you need to roll or turn someone who is unable to assist, either because of paralysis, unconsciousness, serious illness or confusion, you should:

- follow the care plan and risk assessment
- carry out the procedure with at least two workers
- roll the person using a transfer sheet or board, or use the bottom sheet to roll the person onto his or her side (make sure the sheet is dry and intact!)
- support the person with pillows or packing.

When the person needs to be turned again, remove the pillows, lower him or her onto the back and repeat the other way.

Overcoming 'pyjama-induced paralysis'

One of the key factors in a safe handling policy is to encourage people to help themselves. There is a great temptation for people to believe that they can do far less than they are capable of. This is often encouraged by staff who find it quicker and easier to do things rather than wait for people to help themselves.

If you encourage individuals to make their own way out of bed, for example, they need to follow the simple set of instructions shown below.

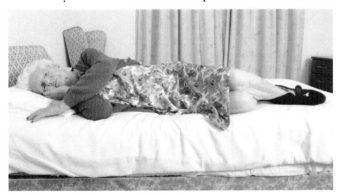

1 Roll towards the edge of the bed

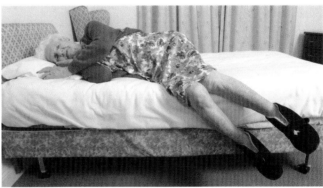

2 Swing your legs over the side of the bed while continuing to lie the top half of your body on the bed

3 Push with your hands to sit upright

You may wish to encourage an individual to roll over in the bed, rather than having to be manually rolled by a care worker. This could be necessary to allow for a change of bedding, a bed bath or to change clothes. The instructions for achieving this are quite simple, and can be carried out by all but the most severely ill or disabled individuals, as shown below.

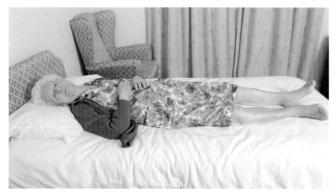

1   Turn to face the direction in which you are rolling

2   Bend the leg on the other side and keep your foot flat on the bed

3   Reach across your body with the opposite arm. This uses the counterweight of moving the arm across the upper body to assist with achieving a roll

If you need to get someone to raise his or her bottom from the bed in order to give a bed pan, or to prepare for rolling or turning, then you should ask the person to follow the instructions below.

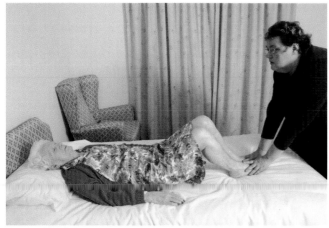

1   Bend both knees

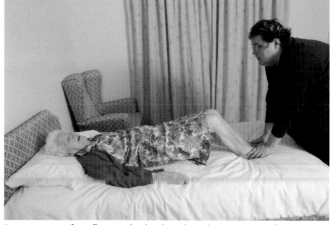

2   Keep your feet flat on the bed and push up on your feet and hands, so that your bottom is raised

Recording and passing on information

Information about the most effective ways of moving someone, or techniques which have proved effective in encouraging a person to assist himself or herself, should be recorded in the plan of care.

The plan of care should contain information on the moving needs of each individual, and it is vital that these are followed. However, you may notice a change in behaviour or response. This could be:

- a person finding movement more painful
- a loss of confidence in a particular technique
- an improvement in how much assistance a person can give
- a changed reaction following being moved.

Any of these changes, or anything else you notice, are significant and must be reported to your supervisor. Any changes may be indications of overall changes in the person's condition and should never be ignored.

The information you record should be:

- clear
- easily understood
- a good description of the person's needs.

Date	No.	PATIENT'S NURSING NEEDS/PROBLEMS AND CAUSES OF PROBLEMS (NB Physiological, Psychological, Social and Family Problems)	Objectives	Nursing Instructions	Review On/By	Date Resolved
1.5.05	8	Mobility:			8.5.05	
		Due to suffering from a congenital foot deformity, Mr K is unable to bear weight and needs the hoist to be used when moving and handling	To prevent complications of immobility and maintain Mr. K's safety as far as is reasonably practicable	a) Encourage Mr K to be as independent as possible.	15.5.05	
					22.5.05	
				b) Always give clear, consise instructions when moving and handling to gain full co-operation.	29.5.05	
					5.6.05	
					12.6.05	
					19.6.05	
				c) The hoist must be used at all times with either the Quickfit deluxe sling or the toiletting sling – depending on circumstances.	26.6.05	
					3.7.05	
					10.7.05	
					17.7.05	
					24.7.05	
				d) Ensure safe practice maintained when moving and handling.	31.7.05	
					7.8.05	
				e) Observe for any problems and reassess appropriately.		
				f) Review problem weekly		

An example of notes on an individual's mobility in the plan of care

When you are carrying out a moving procedure, it may be necessary to move items of furniture so that you can work safely. Remember that this also requires assessment: How heavy is the furniture? Is it on wheels? How many times will you need to move it? Whether you are working in a care setting or in an individual's own home, it is important that furniture is returned to its original position afterwards, so the individual can easily locate personal items in their usual places and feel reassured by the familiar surroundings.

CASE STUDY: Encouraging independence

Mr K had hip replacement surgery over two months ago. Since his discharge from hospital he has been reluctant to move as much as he should. He still insists that he needs help to move out of bed and from his chair. He has been seen again by the orthopaedic surgeon who confirms that the surgery was a complete success and that Mr K's refusal to move himself is not due to any physical problem.

1 *What do you think could be the reason why Mr K wants help?*

2 *What should the plan of care be in order to support him?*

3 *How would you approach the issue with Mr K?*

Test yourself

1 What are the three categories of lifting and handling equipment?

2 Describe how the following are used.

   a a hoist

   b a transfer board or sheet

   c a slideboard

   d a monkey pole.

3 What are the three principles of effective manual handling?

4 Describe the procedures for:

   a rolling or turning

   b transfer.

5 Why should information and changes regarding mobility be recorded and passed on?

HSC 223 UNIT TEST

1 True or false?

   a It is safe to lift people manually provided they are not very heavy.

   b People should be encouraged to move themselves whenever possible.

   c Workplaces can choose not to have lifting equipment.

   d Services provided in service users' homes do not have to have lifting equipment.

2 How can you contribute to increasing the independence of an individual by the way you assist him or her with moving and handling?

Support individuals to undertake and monitor their own health care

Individuals who are undertaking their own health care, or who are having their health care administered by a carer rather than a health care professional, are taking control of a key aspect of being independent. Being able to retain or regain control over health care makes a huge contribution to empowering individuals and giving them control over their own lives.

Providing support, advice and guidance to those who are undertaking their own health care or to carers who are providing health care for friends or relatives is an important and key role for workers in health and social care. There are many situations in which the ability to deliver health care in the community contributes to enabling individuals to remain in their own homes. The additional support provided by a health or care worker to an individual or his or her carer can ensure that a plan of care can be developed and undertaken successfully.

What you need to learn

- Ways to ensure individuals have all they need for their health care
- Regulations and procedures for administering medicines
- The correct methods of administering medicines
- How to ensure safe practice
- The range of procedures individuals may need to undertake
- Ensuring that individuals understand how to obtain specimens
- Taking physical measurements.

HSC 225a Support individuals when undertaking procedures, treatments and dressings

Ways to ensure individuals have all they need for their health care

You need to establish with people the level of support they are happy for you to provide. This may involve you in directly supporting a carer rather than the individual, so you may need to discuss with both of them the level of support they need. The support you could be asked to provide includes:

- assisting in the ordering or collection of the supplies and equipment needed
- providing explanations and guidance on carrying out the health care procedures
- demonstrating the correct techniques and procedures to be followed
- observing and offering advice
- being present in order to offer emotional support and reassurance
- providing advice, information or assistance in the disposal of waste.

Level of support

You need to discuss carefully with the individual and the carers, if any, the level of support they need you to provide, taking into account the degree of independence the individual wants in managing his or her own health care. If you have been working with a person for some time, you will be aware of the degree of independence desired and the level of support needed. However, if you have a new relationship or a job in which your role involves short periods of support to individuals, then you need to discuss the type and level of support required. You need to remember that the individual may not be aware of the types of help available and the supplies and equipment which could be provided to improve and extend his or her level of independence. So you must take a proactive role in providing this information and making sure that the person has the maximum possible information about what is available, so he or she can make an informed decision about how much to undertake personally.

Equipment and supplies

Once you have agreed the level of support you will provide, the next stage is to make sure individuals have all the equipment and supplies they need to carry out their treatments. Individuals may have a list of the supplies they need. This may have been given to them by a GP, community nurse, hospital doctor or nurse, or by a specialist health care professional. If they do not have a list of supplies, then check with the care team responsible for health care

Check it out

Take two individuals you work with as examples, and think about the type of support they need from you with regard to their health-care needs. How is your level of support decided upon in the first instance? How is it monitored?

exactly what supplies will be required and check the quantities needed at any one time to ensure that storage recommendations are complied with.

The supplies are likely to be obtained through a pharmacy or possibly from the health centre or specialist hospital clinic, depending on the treatments to be undertaken. However, it is unlikely that large quantities would be supplied from a hospital, as NHS prescribing is usually only available for in-patients receiving care or treatment. All prescribing, including supplies, is normally undertaken by the GP in the community and supplied through a local pharmacy. It can be useful to check the following list to make sure the individual has all of the necessary equipment and supplies:

1   **Source of supply.** This needs to be checked with the local GP for any medications or supplies subject to a prescription. You need to check or ask the individual to check that there is a facility for a regular repeat prescription when needed. If the supplies do not require a prescription, you should ensure that the local pharmacy always has an adequate supply and work out with the individual how often the supplies will need to be renewed.

2   **Storage facilities.** Many items needed for health care require special storage. All items need to be stored in a place not subject to extreme temperatures. Damp or excessively hot or cold places can contaminate or spoil medical supplies, equipment and medication. All medications and sterilised items will have an expiry date. Individuals should be encouraged to set up a regular system of reviewing their supplies and returning any which are outdated to the pharmacy for proper disposal. Never use outdated medications or medical supplies. If special storage requirements are needed – for example, insulin has to be kept in a refrigerator – it is essential to follow the instructions. Failing to do this could result in medication becoming ineffective or even dangerous.

3   **Ability to understand and comply with instructions.** You must stress to individuals the need to store medications correctly, and you must satisfy yourself they have understood this. If you are concerned an individual has not understood or is not able or willing to comply with storage requirements for medical supplies, then you should refer the matter immediately to the care team and your line manager. Alternative arrangements for administering medication will need to be considered.

Regulations and procedures for administering medicines

The handling and use of medicines, drugs and poisons is governed by a series of Acts and Regulations of Parliament. The main ones are:

- the Misuse of Drugs Act 1971 – which controls the availability of drugs which could be misused

- the Medicines Act 1968 – which regulates the manufacture, distribution, import, export, sale and supply of medicinal products and medications
- the Misuse of Drugs Regulations 1985 – which enables specified health care professionals to possess, supply, prescribe and/or administer controlled drugs in their practice.

Misuse of Drugs Act 1971

The Misuse of Drugs Act is designed to check and reduce the unlawful use of the kinds of drugs which could produce dependence if they are misused. These drugs are referred to as **controlled drugs** and they include cocaine, diamorphine (heroin), methadone, levorphanol, morphine, opium, pethidine, amphetamine, dexamphetamine, dihydrocodeine injection, mephentermine and methylphenidate.

Controlled drugs may be prescribed by medical practitioners and registered dentists.

Every GP or dentist is required to keep a record of all the controlled drugs which are issued. Hospital pharmacies also have responsibilities over the supply of controlled drugs and they are administered under strict control in a hospital setting. The regulations which govern the administration of controlled drugs are as follows.

- A special cupboard must be used for storing controlled drugs and it should be clearly marked 'Controlled Drugs Cupboard'.
- The cupboard should be locked and the key must be held by a state registered nurse or midwife who is in charge of the setting in which the drugs cupboard is kept.
- Supplies of controlled drugs should only be obtained on the signature of a medical practitioner and the drugs only administered to patients if there are written instructions from a medical practitioner.
- Each dose of controlled drugs that is administered must be entered into the special register with the date, the patient's name and the time the dose was given.
- The practitioner who gives the drugs and the person who checks the drugs must sign the entry.
- In most hospitals the doses must be checked by two people, one of whom should be a state registered nurse or midwife.
- The person checking should see the bottle from which the drug is taken and check the dose against the written prescription.
- All bottles or packages containing controlled drugs must be clearly labelled.
- The nurse or midwife in charge of the ward should check the controlled drugs and the accompanying records every seven days.

Your role may include supporting an individual in managing his or her medication

In your job role, you will not be involved in administering controlled drugs, although you may be providing support to an individual who has controlled drugs as part of his or her treatment.

Medicines Act 1968

The Medicines Act covers all substances used as medical products or ingredients in medicinal products. This Act divides medicines into three categories:

1   **Prescription-only medicine (POM).** This includes controlled drugs, although they are subject to the additional regulations discussed above. These may be prescribed for a patient and subsequently supplied by a pharmacist.

2   **Pharmacy medicine (P).** This is supplied by a pharmacist but can be dispensed without a prescription.

3   **General sale list (GSL).** These medicines need not be obtained through a pharmacist.

The prescription-only medicines are those which can only be obtained from a GP or a dentist. They include the majority of medicines which are used to control or relieve the symptoms of a wide range of diseases. They also include controlled drugs, but these are subject to the special regulations described above.

The pharmacy medicines include items such as very strong painkillers, some forms of cold or flu remedies and a wide range of specialist preparations which are designed to alleviate the symptoms of common illnesses.

The general sale list includes mild painkillers and preparations designed to bring temporary alleviation of symptoms of some mild common illnesses, such as throat lozenges and medicines designed to clear congestion.

In hospital or nursing home settings all drugs are kept in lockable cupboards, freezers or fridges; and even portable drugs trolleys need to be lockable. Normally, in a home setting drugs do not need to be kept in locked containers or cupboards, but they should wherever possible be kept in a secure cupboard, and must be kept out of the reach of children.

Doctors and dentists may administer or supply prescription-only medicines directly to the patient. Nurses and other health care workers can only supply medicines under the direction of the doctor, but midwives may administer specified controlled drugs under certain conditions.

When prescription drugs are supplied by a pharmacist they must be labelled and the label must show the name of the patient, the date of the prescription, the name of the drug, the quantity in the container, the dosage to be taken, any specific instructions about how to take the medication, and the name of the pharmacist supplying the medication. If the drugs are supplied for someone who is in hospital the label is also likely to show his or her unit number, date of birth and the name of the consultant.

The correct methods of administering medicines

Medicines on prescription will be accompanied by instructions for how they are to be taken. This could be a short instruction on the label or there may be more detailed instructions contained within the packaging. Instructions should be carefully read and followed.

The label on the medication will also show the dosage. It is absolutely essential that the correct dose of a medicine is always taken. If an individual is unwilling to take the required dose or wishes to stop taking the medicine prescribed because of unwanted side-effects, you should refer the matter to the appropriate member of the care team. Discourage people from stopping their medication until they have discussed the problems they are experiencing with their medical practitioner. It is likely that an alternative medication or a different dosage can be prescribed.

It is useful to keep a check on the levels of medication remaining in bottles or packages, particularly where individuals are vulnerable or maintain their medication without the support of a carer. If you have reason to suspect that an individual has exceeded the prescribed dose you must take immediate action to seek medical assistance.

Dosage instructions will be on the label of the medication. Instructions are written in English, although some doctors and other health care professionals still write in abbreviations taken from instructions in Latin. The abbreviations you may occasionally see and should be aware of are as follows.

Abbreviation	Latin	English
a.c.	Ante cibum	Before food
Ad lib.	Ad libitum	To the desired amount
b.d. or b.i.d.	Bis in die	Twice a day
c.	Cum	With
o.m.	Omni mane	Every morning
o.n.	Omni nocte	Every night
p.c.	Post cibum	After food
p.r.n.	Pro re nata	Whenever necessary
q.d.	Quaque die	Every day
q.d.s.	Quarter die sumendum	Four times a day
q.i.d.	Quarter in die	Four times a day
q.q.h.	Quarter quaque hora	Every four hours
R	Recipe	Take
s.o.s.	Si opus sit	If necessary
Stat.	Statim	At once
t.d.s.	Ter die sumendum	Three times a day
t.i.d.	Ter in die	Three times a day

Types of medication

All medications have specific requirements for the way they are taken or administered. These will be detailed in instructions with the medication, but they are likely to follow a general pattern as shown below.

Oral medicines

Tablets or capsules are one of the commonest ways of taking medicines. Not only is the content of the tablet or capsule important, but very often the structure and the materials used for the tablet or capsule will react only in certain environments. This often means that the coating on a capsule will dissolve or react in a particular way at a particular point in the digestive system, depending on the environment in that particular part of the system. This is why instructions are often given to take before food, take after food, or take with a hot or cold drink. These instructions are important to ensure that medicines are absorbed into the metabolism in the correct way.

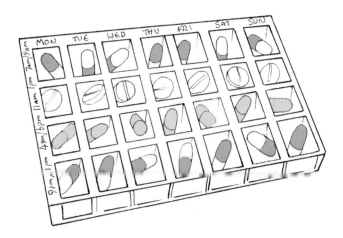

Medication box

Failure to follow instructions and take medicine in the prescribed way can result in it being less effective or having different effects from those intended. If there are no specific instructions about taking tablets or capsules, then they should be taken at specific times each day to comply with the dosage requirements and are usually better swallowed with liquid, such as water, which is unlikely to interfere with their effectiveness.

For individuals who are managing their medication without the support of a carer, the pharmacist can supply boxes designed for keeping the required doses of medication, with each compartment labelled for a specific day and number of doses. This makes it easier for an individual to keep track of which dose of their medication has been taken, and it reduces the risk of an accidental overdose. Most pharmacists will supply these boxes ready filled with the individual's medication in the compartments for the correct times of each day.

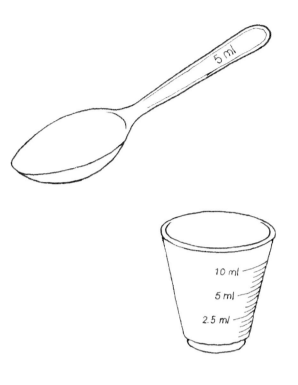

Medication cup and spoon

Liquid is the other common form of oral medication. Many liquid medicines are in suspension and will need to be shaken before being taken. All oral liquid medicines come with a 5 ml plastic spoon, or with a small medicine cup which is marked at different dose levels, usually 2.5 ml, 5 ml and 10 ml. Having the correct dose of medicine is important and the correct spoon must be used for administering medicines. A teaspoon from the kitchen drawer is not appropriate as they differ in size and can result in either too small a quantity of medicine being taken or an overdose. You should encourage the individual to wash the spoon after each dose of medicine so that it is ready to be used for the next dose.

Inhaled medicines

Those who have chronic respiratory conditions, such as asthma and chronic bronchitis, are likely to be prescribed inhalant medicines. These are usually in the form of an aerosol puff inhaler, though they can be in the form of a 'spinhaler', which works on the inhalation of breath. The principles of all of these inhaled medications is the same. The individual need to breathe out and then insert the inhaler in the mouth, take a puff and breathe inwards deeply for th required dosage. The dosage for all inhaled medicine is measured in the number of puffs.

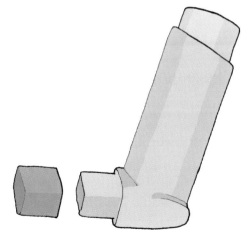

Asthmatic inhaler

A range of inhaled medicines are available, which serve different purposes. An individual may be prescribed several different inhalers, some of which will be used to relieve symptoms and some for long-term daily use as preventive medication. It is important that the individual understands that inhalers serve different purposes and that they must comply with the instructions for the number of times they need to be used.

Individuals with severe respiratory conditions may also require a nebuliser. This is a machine which pumps air through a chamber containing the drug. A fine must of the drug then passes into the face mask worn by the individual, who inhales the drug. This needs to be used when symptoms are severe.

Eye preparations

Individuals are most likely to be prescribed drops or ointment for eye problems. The method of administration is largely the same. The lower eyelid should be pulled downwards and the correct number of drops inserted in the eye 'pocket'. Some individuals find it easier to tip the head back slightly to achieve this, but it should not be necessary to tip the head right back. Eye ointment should be applied in a similar way. As with the administration of all medications, you should encourage the individual to wash his or her hands both before and after administering eye drops or ointment.

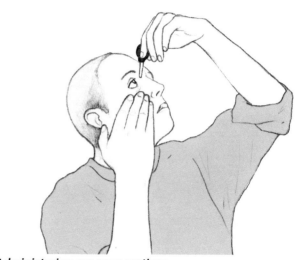

Administering eye preparations

Nasal preparations

Nasal medication is likely to be prescribed either as drops or as spray. Nasal sprays should be applied by placing the spray bottle into the end of one nostril while holding the other nostril closed. The individual should be encouraged to breathe deeply through the nose while spraying. This process should then be repeated for the other nostril.

Nasal drops, in order to be effective, should be taken with the head tipped as far forward as possible. Ideally, the individual should kneel on the floor and bend over until resting the top of the head on the floor, and then apply the nasal drops. This helps the drops have the most effect on the nasal passages. Alternatively, the same angle can be achieved by lying on a bed or across a stool with the head hanging over the edge.

Administering nasal preparations

Unless otherwise advised, nasal drops should not be applied by tipping the head backwards. In this position the drops will run down the back of the throat and so will be less effective in the nasal area for which they are intended. If an individual is unable to achieve the optimum position for applying nasal drops because of lack of flexibility or mobility, you may need to discuss this with the prescribing doctor. The type of preparation prescribed may be reconsidered.

Ear drops

Ear drops are likely to be supplied in an applicator bottle, so there is no requirement to use a separate applicator for them. The required number of drops should be dropped into the ear, being careful not to insert the applicator inside the ear and risk causing damage. It may be helpful to keep the head tipped over slightly while inserting the drops and for a few seconds afterwards, to ensure they run inside the ear as intended. Unless directed otherwise by the prescribing doctor, it is not generally necessary or advisable to insert cotton wool into the ear after administering eardrops.

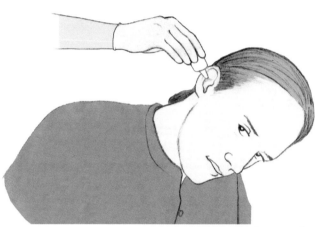

Administering ear drops

Vaginal and rectal preparations

Individuals may wish to administer these themselves and their ability to achieve this will depend on their degree of mobility and flexibility. If vaginal and rectal preparations are being self-administered by someone who has the required level of mobility, the simplest method is to place one foot on a chair or low stool and insert the preparation. This is likely to be in pessary form, or it may be a cream, ointment or spray.

It is more likely, however, that vaginal and rectal preparations will be administered by a carer, in which case the optimum positions for achieving this are likely to be as follows:

- For vaginal preparations, the individual should lie on her back on a bed with her legs bent at the knees and slightly apart. Individuals should be encouraged to relax while the preparation is inserted.
- For rectal preparations, the individual should lie on one side with knees drawn up towards the chest. This allows the most straightforward access for inserting preparations into the rectal passage.

It is essential that proper hand washing is undertaken by the individual or the carer administering these preparations both before and after administration. If these are being administered by a carer then gloves should be worn. Surgical gloves for carers' use at home can be obtained from the pharmacy.

Topical preparations

Where individuals have been prescribed specific ointments or creams for particular areas of skin, these should be applied in the dosage and with the frequency prescribed. They should be applied with clean, gloved hands and gently spread over the affected area. They should not be rubbed in unless specifically instructed. Most ointments or creams are designed to be gradually absorbed and rubbing may cause damage or infection.

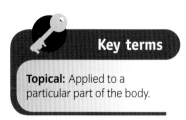
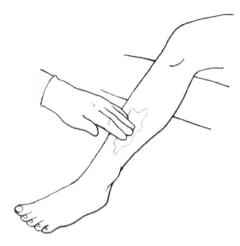

Applying topical preparations

How to ensure safe practice

Adverse reactions and side-effects

Many drugs have side-effects, so the prescribing doctor should explain the possible effects on an individual of taking the medication. Also, a leaflet identifying the potential side-effects is likely to accompany the medication. The individual may find the side-effects acceptable if they are counterbalanced by the benefits of taking the medication, and some of the milder side-effects that medication can cause, for example a dry mouth or drowsiness, may be easily tolerated. However, if side-effects cause serious disruption to an individual's daily life or make him or her feel worse than before taking the medication, then the prescribing doctor must be contacted to discuss these difficulties. Individuals should be discouraged from simply stopping the medication, however.

It is important to recognise the difference between side-effects and adverse reactions. Side-effects are often of an expected kind. They are relatively minor and do not interfere seriously with an individual's general state of health. An adverse reaction to a medication, on the other hand, can indicate an allergy or other serious side-effect. This could take the form of swelling of the hands or face, blotchiness of the skin, reddening of the skin in any part of the body, sweating or clamminess, shivering or feeling faint. If any of these conditions occur you must immediately summon medical assistance, as adverse or allergic reactions to medication can be extremely rapid and extremely serious, even fatal in some cases.

One other thing you should consider when you observe an individual showing serious symptoms is that the reaction could be to medication equipment, particularly that which includes latex or rubber, for example gloves and some clinical tubing. The effects of an allergic reaction to latex can be extremely serious and require immediate medical attention.

Your role

Your support can be a key factor in ensuring that individuals are able to manage their medical conditions safely and effectively in the community. It may also make it possible for carers to feel more confident and able to continue caring for a friend or relative knowing that support and advice are readily available to them. A central part of your role will be to ensure that there is regular liaison and contact with other members of the care team, particularly those responsible for prescribing and those who are responsible for maintaining health services to individuals in the community, such as district nurses and other members of the primary care team.

You may find that your own values and opinions in relation to an individual's health and hygiene needs differ from those of the individual himself or herself. Conflicts may arise as you try to balance the promotion of good hygiene practices, and the need to follow the individual's plan of care, with your obligation to respect an individual's right to make choices. If at any time you are unable to follow the plan of care or have concerns about hygiene, you should report the matter to your supervisor and/or other members of the care team.

Evidence indicator

Check the procedures in your workplace for the administration of medication.

Make sure that you know:

- who are the people who have access to controlled drugs
- who is allowed to check drugs
- how many people have to check controlled drugs
- where drugs are kept.

Keep notes on what you have learned for your portfolio.

Keys to good practice: Giving safe and effective support

✓ Confirm the level of support the individual needs.

✓ Make sure the person has all the necessary equipment and supplies.

✓ Check that there is a supplier for all the necessary equipment and medication.

✓ Make sure medicines and equipment are correctly stored.

✓ Use correct procedures to administer medications.

✓ Take immediate action in the case of an adverse reaction to medication.

The range of procedures individuals may need to undertake

Many individuals can undertake their own health care in their home setting. Some may require the support of their carer, if they have one, to carry out health-care procedures at home. Whether you are supporting an individual or a carer or both, you could be involved in making sure they are able to undertake any health procedures, including dealing with dressings for lesions such as ulcers or pressure sores, or other wounds which have been stitched.

Dressing a wound or lesion

If an individual is doing this in a home setting, he or she will need supplies of sterile dressing packs, which contain gauze packs, cotton wool and sterile cotton wool balls, tweezers and a dish. Small packs of saline solution (Normasol) will also be needed.

The type of dressing used will vary depending on the individual and his or her particular condition. This could be a standard gauze dressing, an artificial skin (Tagaderm) or other specialist dressing which may be impregnated with particular substances. There has been a great deal of research into the most effective dressings for various types of wounds, and wound care has become an area of clinical specialism for nurses, known as tissue viability nurses.

The length of time between changing dressings will vary, depending on the nature of the wound or lesion, and it is important that you follow instructions or seek advice about how frequently dressings should be changed. For example, for some surgical wounds which have been sutured the dressing will not be changed until the sutures are removed. It has been found that a lower incidence of post-operative wound infection occurs if dressings are left untouched in most cases.

Following a clean procedure

Dressing and cleaning an area will need to follow a clean procedure. You need to make sure the individual understands the importance of thoroughly washing his or her hands before dealing with any dressing. Although the risk of cross-infection is obviously less if the individual concerned is carrying out his or her own personal health care, it is still essential for hands to be washed before and after completing the procedure. The steps that should be taken are:

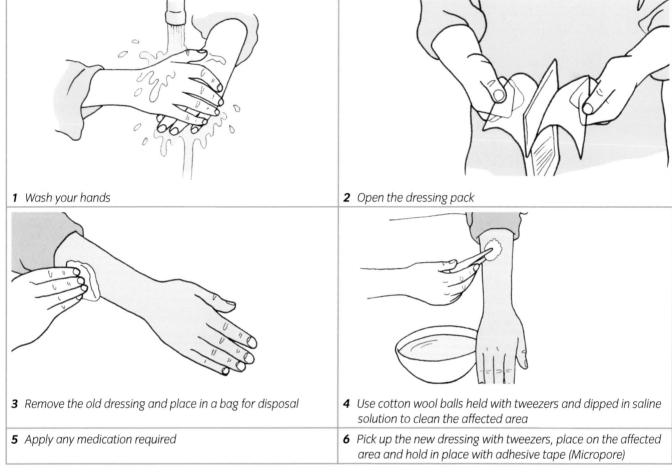

1 *Wash your hands*

2 *Open the dressing pack*

3 *Remove the old dressing and place in a bag for disposal*

4 *Use cotton wool balls held with tweezers and dipped in saline solution to clean the affected area*

5 *Apply any medication required*

6 *Pick up the new dressing with tweezers, place on the affected area and hold in place with adhesive tape (Micropore)*

This is a general guide only and specific procedures may need to be followed for a particular individual. It is essential that you and/or the individual check with the community nursing team or the hospital about the exact procedure which will be necessary.

Pressure sores

Pressure sore treatments are constantly being developed and improved, so you should seek advice from a qualified medical or nursing practitioner about the latest developments. Current practice is to use dressings which will allow moist healing of the sore. At one time it was believed that pressure sores should be dried and were best allowed to heal in their dry state. There is now little argument that all wounds including pressure sores heal far better in a warm, moist environment.

There are various dressings available which adhere very closely to the skin and will allow oxygen through but no moisture, enabling the wound to retain any moisture to assist healing. As long as a wound is not infected, these types of dressings, such as Op-site, appear to achieve quite good results.

Did you know?

The benefits of moist wound healing were first demonstrated 30 years ago. However, in a recent study carried out in a large hospital, less than 50 per cent of the people questioned knew about the procedure.

An individual's care plan will identify the treatment regime which needs to be used for his or her particular pressure sores, and the treatment will be supervised by a qualified practitioner. Treatments today will not include practices such as massaging the area or washing with soap and water, which were common some years ago. There is no evidence to support the theory that massaging the area will play any part in healing the sore and, in fact, it is likely to aggravate the situation.

The key to effective treatment of pressure sores is to attempt, where possible, to increase the general health of the individual – people who are malnourished or debilitated because of an illness or long periods of neglect are unlikely to heal pressure sores effectively until their general state of health has been considerably improved. The care plan should include arrangements for the individual to receive, if possible, a high protein, high carbohydrate diet.

Pressure sores are extremely unpleasant, but they are avoidable. Good practice and good levels of care can prevent pressure sores from occurring and can speed the healing of any which existed before the individual received care.

Did you know?

When the Egyptian pyramids were investigated, evidence was found that some of the people mummified within the tombs had suffered from pressure sores. This makes it very clear that the problem of pressure sores has always existed.

Stoma care

Stoma care is necessary in the care of individuals who have had surgery to provide an additional means of eliminating waste from their bodies. An additional surgical opening is necessary for people who are unable, either on a temporary or permanent basis, to use their bowel in the normal way. This can be the result of colon cancer, ulcerative colitis or a series of other diseases.

The most usual reason for stoma care is in individuals who have had a colostomy. Following a colostomy faeces are collected in a special stoma bag which needs to be changed regularly. Many individuals are able to do this for themselves, but it may be necessary to provide stoma care for a person who is ill or becoming frail.

The processes for changing stoma appliances are the same whether they are being changed by a carer or by the individual. The same level of hygienic practice carried out by a health care worker must be observed by the individual. Many people who need stoma care prefer to do it themselves if possible, as they find it embarrassing having someone else do it. However, if you do need to do it, or to demonstrate it to a carer or support someone else doing it, you are likely to follow a procedure similar to the one below. You must always check with the health professional responsible for the care of the individual, however, as everyone has different health care needs.

It is likely you would only be asked to provide stoma care for someone who has an established colostomy and is therefore familiar with the procedure. However, you should still check that individuals agree you can change their appliance and that they understand the procedure you are about to undertake. This is what you must do to carry out the procedure.

1   Wash your hands.

2   Ensure the individual understands the procedure and that you have provided for privacy.

3   Expose the appliance, the stoma bag. Place a towel over the individual's abdomen and a protector on the bed to keep the bed clean.

4   Make sure you have all the necessary equipment and put on gloves.

5   Gently remove the old pouch and the wafer, which is the thin layer that provides the seal between the pouch or bag and the individual.

6   Measure the contents of the bag, note any changes from normal in the contents and then dispose of it in accordance with the policy of your work setting.

7   Wipe the skin around the stoma using a warm cloth to ensure that any faeces are removed. Dry the area with a towel.

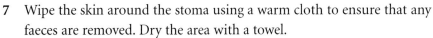

8   Prepare the new wafer by cutting it to fit over the stoma. There should not be any visible skin between the stoma and the wafer.

9   Apply the new wafer to the skin, make sure there are no air pockets under the wafer, and hold it in place for 30 seconds to help the adhesive to work.

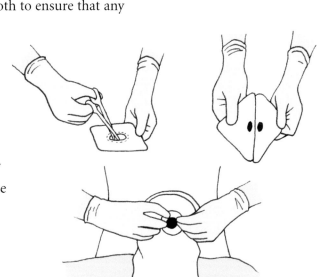

10 Apply the stoma pouch or bag to the flange on the wafer, and make sure that the bag is sealed.

11 Remove the protectors and clean the area.

12 Wash your hands.

13 Record the procedure in the individual's care plan or case notes.

Catheter care

Individuals who have an indwelling catheter to deal with urine, which is likely to be a Foley's catheter, may need support in ensuring that the risk of infection is reduced as far as possible. Many people may be used to managing catheter care for themselves and you must always check to make sure that you are not reducing the level of a person's independence by offering care they are well able to provide for themselves. For those people who need support, you are likely to follow the general procedures described below, but always check with the plan of care and the relevant health professional as each person's needs are different.

Individuals with catheters are prone to infections, and hygiene and sterile techniques must be observed to minimise the risk. In order to maintain hygiene, the site at which the catheter enters the individual's body should be cleaned regularly.

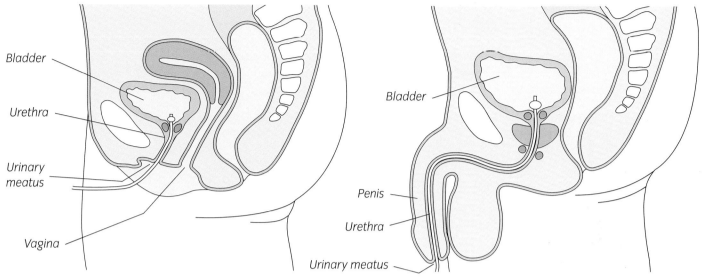

Indwelling urinary catheter in place in female   **Indwelling urinary catheter in place in male**

People who are managing their own catheters will have their own way of dealing with them, but you may need to check that they are following an adequate procedure in order to minimise the risks of infection. Follow procedures laid down for your workplace, which may vary slightly but are generally likely to be as follows:

1   Wash your hands.

2   Take universal precautions.

3   Ensure that the individual understands the procedure and that you have provided for privacy.

4   Using a sterile technique, prepare a tray with either saline or Savlon or any other medium identified in your workplace procedures.

5   Using swabs, dip one swab into the solution and wipe in one direction around one side of the entry site.

6   In a female you should ensure that you wipe away from the rectal opening in one direction only.

7   Discard the swab after one wipe and take a fresh swab to wipe the other side of the entry site.

8   Discard that swab.

9   Continue using fresh swabs for each wipe until the area is clean.

10 Do not wipe the area excessively as this can lead to irritation and introduce infection. One wipe each side of the entry site should be sufficient.

11 Dispose of the used swabs and tray in accordance with the procedures for your workplace for disposal of contaminated waste (see Unit HSC 22 page 51).

12 Remove your gloves.

13 Wash your hands.

14 Record the procedure in the individual's care plan or case notes.

You are unlikely to be involved in the insertion or removal of catheters as this is undertaken by a qualified clinical practitioner, although you may be asked to assist under direction, on occasions.

Diabetes

Individuals and carers could undertake treatments and health care at home for the control of diabetes, depending on the type of diabetes.

The treatment may consist of insulin injections which the individual needs to take on a regular, prescribed basis. Insulin needs to be stored in a refrigerator and a supply of insulin syringes must be kept. It is essential to regularly check the supply to ensure the individual does not run short.

Diabetics have close contact with a specialist diabetic nurse at the local hospital, and most diabetics are well-informed about the care they must provide to control their illness, and the consequences of failure to do this. If you become aware that an individual with diabetes is failing to follow the prescribed treatment, you must contact an appropriate member of the care team, as the consequences can be extremely serious.

Not all diabetes is controlled by the injection of insulin. Type II diabetes, which has its onset later in life, is controlled through diet rather than medication. This will be indicated in the plan of care for the individual.

Drainage or feeding tubes

Individuals having ongoing treatment for a chronic condition may have drainage or feeding tubes or shunts in place. The sites of these will need to be maintained. Any individual with an implanted appliance receives a comprehensive set of instructions about how to maintain it. This needs to be included in the care plan for the individual and you must ensure that care is undertaken as identified in the instructions. If there is anything you are unclear about, you must refer to the appropriate specialist member of the care team.

Monitoring

One of your key roles is to be aware of the potential for adverse reactions to particular treatments or procedures, and to report these without delay to the appropriate care team member. Where lesions, sores or wounds are being dressed, check for any signs of potential infection such as reddening, swelling or excessive heat in the area. You also need to report any pain, discomfort, nausea or clamminess, sweating or fever experienced by individuals who are undertaking any health care procedures or taking any prescribed medication at home.

Safe disposal of waste

Most health care procedures leave some element of waste. This could be used dressings or empty syringes or emptied catheter bags. All waste of this nature must be disposed of appropriately. Waste should not simply be placed in a dustbin; it should be carefully bagged and ideally incinerated. If incineration is not possible then it must be placed in a sealed bag before disposal.

Used syringes or other glass containers must never be placed in a dustbin. They should be put into a special sharps box, which you can get from your health centre, pharmacy or hospital. A sharps box is a rigid container which ensures that syringes do not put anyone at risk of a needle stick injury. Sharps boxes can be collected from the individual or collection can be arranged through the local health centre. For detailed guidance about safe disposal of waste and the relevant regulations and legislation, see Unit HSC 22 page 51.

Used syringes and other sharp implements must be disposed of in a sharps box

Evidence indicator

Identify an individual for whom you provide support in undertaking health care. If you do not currently work in this way, use a relative or friend as your example.

Make a detailed list of:

- the medical/pharmaceutical supplies needed
- where they can be obtained
- where they would be stored
- how any waste will need to be disposed of.

Make notes on your findings for your portfolio.

Test yourself

1   Name three types of medications you may have to administer. Describe the steps you would take for each.

2   Which Act governs the administration of drugs?

3   Who may prescribe drugs?

4   What is the key information which should be on a medication label?

5   List the key steps in changing a stoma bag.

HSC 225b Support individuals when obtaining specimens and taking physical measurements

Ensuring that individuals understand how to obtain specimens

Individuals managing their own medical conditions while remaining at home may need to take a variety of different measurements and to obtain specimens on a regular basis to monitor their current state of health.

Measurements for health purposes can include the following.

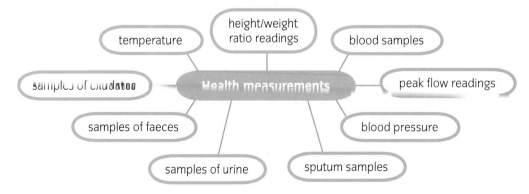

Some of these will be obtained by taking physical measurements, and others through the analysis of specimens.

Taking specimens

Any individual who needs to take specimens as part of a monitoring process will also receive very specific instructions from the appropriate member of the care team about how the specimen should be obtained and how, if appropriate, it should be analysed. You will need to discuss and agree the level of support that is appropriate.

The commonest condition requiring an analysis of specimens at home is diabetes. However, there are many other conditions where individuals may need to test their urine or blood on a regular basis to ensure that their body systems are functioning correctly.

People may also be asked to provide other specimens to aid diagnosis or plan treatment, such as sputum or exudates. It is important that you know how to carry out these activities, even if the person you are working with currently undertakes them for himself or herself.

You will need to understand how to obtain specimens of a range of bodily fluids, each of which can provide health practitioners with significant information about the state of health of the individual. There are specific methods for obtaining correct, uncontaminated specimens and for storing them in appropriate containers and in appropriate ways to ensure they are in the right condition to provide the best possible information when tested.

Specimen containers are *never* pre-labelled. You should only label a container with the individual's name after you have collected the specimen. This reduces the risk of a container being picked up by someone else and mistakenly used to put someone else's specimen in. Obviously, this is less likely to happen if you are obtaining the specimen in a person's own home, but it is good practice and therefore a habit you should adopt.

Containers are generally sterile regardless of the type of specimen which is being collected. This is important so that the laboratories carrying out the tests are not dealing with specimens contaminated by micro-organisms from a source other than the individual. You should make sure you always use the correct container for the type of specimen you are collecting.

Equipment for obtaining mid-stream sample of urine

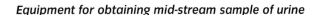

Urine

It is easiest to take a sterile urine specimen from an individual who has a catheter and to obtain it from the catheter line. To collect this you should:

1   Wash your hands.

2   Explain to the individual what you are going to do and answer any questions he or she may have.

3   Make sure you have collected all the equipment you need and put on your gloves.

4   Clamp the catheter line below the port by folding the tubing in half and applying the clamp.

5   Wait for a small amount of urine to collect in the tubing above the port.

6   Insert a sterile syringe gently into the port. Make sure you do not pierce the tubing itself.

7   Withdraw approximately 10 cc of urine into the syringe.

8   Empty the syringe into the sterile specimen container.

9   Make sure you do not contaminate the insides or the lid of the container.

10 Unclamp the catheter tubing and make sure the urine is freely flowing.

11 Label the container, complete the documentation for your workplace and send it to the laboratory following the procedures for your own work setting.

12 Wash your hands.

13 Record in the case notes or care plan the fact that you have taken the specimen.

Individuals who do not have a catheter should be supplied with the appropriate equipment to provide a **mid-stream sample of urine** (MSSU). The equipment consists of a funnel and a sterile urine container. The funnel and container should come in a sterile pack and the individual should be asked to pass urine into the funnel and fill the pot.

Testing urine

The condition of an individual's urine can provide a great deal of information about his or her state of health. There are simple tests which can be carried out on urine and many individuals undertake these for themselves. You may need to provide support for people to undertake some of these. However, it is important before carrying out any tests that you follow some basic observations which will provide you with an initial indication of any problems.

Healthy urine should be clear, pale yellow and not have an offensive smell. If urine smells offensive, is cloudy, has particles in it, has blood in it, is a bright

orange colour, or any other colour apart from clear pale yellow, these are matters for concern.

You should also check with individuals whether they have experienced any pain or burning when they pass urine, as this could be an indicator of more serious underlying conditions.

These simple observations are indicators of problems but are insufficient on their own. It is necessary to carry out further tests on the individual's urine in order to find out more detailed information about the state of his or her health.

Urine tests

There are two methods of testing urine. It can be sent to a laboratory, which would normally be a specialist uro-genital bacteriology section, where extensive testing and the growing of cultures can be carried out. However, if an initial indication of any possible underlying problems is required, the most normal method is to use **urine-analysis sticks**. These are short, flexible sticks a few inches long, containing sensitive material which changes colour depending on the substances it comes into contact with in the urine. It is possible to test for a range of factors in urine by using urine-analysis sticks. The following table shows some examples.

Test for	Indications
1 Leucocytes (white blood cells, an indicator of infection)	Change of colour – sticks range from white through to dark purple
2 Protein (another indicator of infection)	Colour changes from light green through to dark green
3 Blood	Colour changes from white to dark blue
4 Glucose (high blood sugar)	Colour changes from light blue to yellow

Urine storage

If you need to store urine prior to testing, it is important that it should be in a tightly sealed sterile container. It should be kept in a separate specimen fridge, *never* in a fridge which is used for storing foodstuffs. It must also be clearly labelled with:

- the individual's name
- the type of specimen
- the date the specimen was collected.

Faeces

To collect a specimen of faeces for testing, first collect the faeces from the individual in a bed pan or commode. Then transfer the specimen from this into a sterile universal container. A sterile container for faeces contains an implement attached to the inside of the lid which allows you to collect a small amount of the faeces and place them inside the container.

A faecal collection container

Testing faeces

All testing of stool samples will be carried out in a laboratory, so you should ensure that you clearly label the container with:

- the individual's name
- the type of sample
- the date the sample was collected.

It should then be sent to the laboratory with the required documentation which will have been supplied by the health professional requesting the specimen. If a specimen has to be stored you must ensure that it is stored in a separate specimen fridge and *never* in a fridge used for foodstuffs.

Many individuals may be embarrassed about providing a sample of faeces, so you will need to obtain the sample at a time when the individual has a normal bowel movement, rather than expecting him or her to provide a sample at a time which is convenient for you. You should explain the reason for needing the sample and explain why it is necessary to provide a sample into a bed pan or other suitable receptacle rather than use the toilet in the normal way.

Sputum

Sputum specimens are important indicators of possible respiratory infections or respiratory diseases such as tuberculosis, pneumonia or bronchitis. Sputum specimens are often better collected in the morning as individuals often have more secretions in their lungs and bronchial tubes after lying down and sleeping during the night.

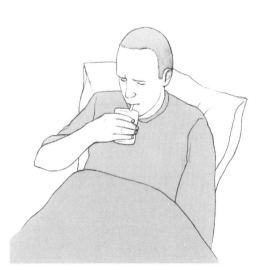

Patient giving sputum specimen

Key terms

Sputum: Saliva or spittle mixed with mucus or other matter from the lungs, chest or throat.

In order to obtain a specimen you must first explain to the individual what you need the specimen for and what you want him or her to do, and then take the following steps:

1 Wash your hands and put on gloves.

2 Make sure you have the correct supplies, which will be a sterile sputum container, similar to a normal sterile container except that it will have an inverted funnel in the top to assist the collection of the sputum.

3 You should explain to the individual that you wish him or her to cough up sputum from the lungs and then spit it out into the container. This is called 'to expectorate'.

4 After individuals have expectorated the sample, make sure you give them tissues to wipe their mouth and a drink if they need one.

5 Note that if individuals have recently eaten you should ask them to rinse their mouth before providing a sample, to lessen the risk of contamination with particles of food.

6 Cover the specimen and seal the container, ensuring that you do not touch the inside of the container.

7 Label the specimen correctly with:
   - the individual's name
   - the type of specimen
   - the date collected.

8 Remove your gloves and wash your hands.

9 Record in the care plan or case notes that this specimen has been obtained and whether it has been stored or sent to the laboratory.

Exudates

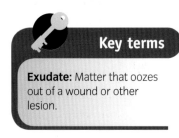

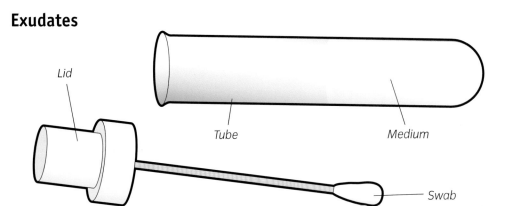

Lid

Tube

Medium

Swab

Equipment for taking exudate specimens

You may occasionally be asked to obtain a sample of exudates from a wound or other lesion. This requires a sterile technique. You should do the following:

1 Wash your hands.

2 Ensure that you have all the materials and equipment you will need.

3   Put on gloves and take universal precautions.

4   Take a swab and wipe on the surface of the wound or lesion once, ensuring that you collect some of the exudates onto the swab.

5   Unscrew the top of the specimen tube.

6   Insert the swab into the tube and screw the end firmly.

7   The swab should reach into the medium contained in the tube.

8   Label the specimen clearly.

9   Clear away and dispose of all of the equipment and materials in accordance with disposal procedures for contaminated waste.

10 Remove your gloves and wash your hands.

11 Record the activity in the individual's case notes or care plan.

Blood

There are two ways of obtaining blood samples. One is through a finger prick using a small lancet blade, and the other is through **venipuncture**, which involves using a needle and syringe to take blood from an individual's vein.

Blood which is obtained from a finger prick is obtained from capillary vessels, which are the tiny blood vessels near the surface of the skin. The blood from there is squeezed onto the testing apparatus. It is most commonly used with testing strips for testing blood sugar levels. Another such test is the **phenylketonuria (PKU) test**, which is done by pricking the heels of babies during the first few days of life.

Where larger amounts of blood are required for more extensive tests, it is necessary to take it from the relevant veins in the arm and hand. You need to be specially trained to take blood from an individual's veins. This is not something you will be undertaking as part of your job role, but you may support people in testing their blood through finger-prick techniques, and you need to understand how this is done.

Obtaining blood samples by finger prick

Blood sugar levels are tested on a regular basis (often daily) for individuals who are diabetic. The most usual method is to prick the side of the finger using a small lancet and then read the results with a blood glucose meter. There are many different types of meters so you should make sure you are familiar with the one which is used in your work setting. In order to test an individual's blood sugar level, you should do the following:

1   Wash your hands.

2   Explain to the individual if necessary what the process involves. However, if the individual has been a diabetic for some time he or she is likely to be very familiar with the procedure and may carry it out for himself

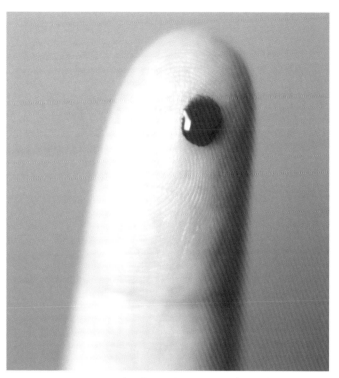

*A lancet or needle is used to prick
the side of the finger*

*The finger is squeezed gently to obtain
a large drop of blood*

or herself. If you do need to undertake the procedure for someone you should ensure that you have his or her consent.

3 Assemble the equipment you will need, which is:
   - meter
   - test strips
   - lancet.

4 Check that the test strips are the appropriate ones for the meter, remove a test strip from the container, then close the container. Do not touch the white area on the strip.

5 Place the end of the lancet firmly on the side of the individual's finger, and press the button on the top of the lancet in order to pierce the skin.

6 Squeeze the finger gently to obtain a large drop of blood.

7 Apply the blood sample to the test strip.

8 Wait the indicated amount of time for the result to appear on the meter.

9 Clean the meter and dispose of the strips in accordance with procedures in your workplace.

10 Wash your hands.

11 Document and record results in the individual's care plan or case notes.

Taking physical measurements

Physical measurements, such as temperature, blood pressure and peak flow, may be an important part of ongoing health care for a great many individuals. High or low blood pressure are symptomatic of many medical conditions and can give an early warning about an individual's health. Similarly, regular peak flow readings enable people with respiratory diseases, such as asthma, bronchitis or emphysema, to monitor lung function and identify any cause for concern about their health. It can also be useful in identifying any potential change or adaptation in the use of medication.

It is essential you are aware of the normal range of measurements expected from the individual and his or her condition. This information should be included in the plan of care and you will need to become familiar with it so that you can report any changes to the appropriate member of the care team.

How to identify the level of support individuals need

Many individuals become familiar and comfortable with the routines involved in monitoring a long-term health condition. They often know in detail about their own condition and the factors likely to cause improvement or deterioration, and they can identify very quickly alterations in measurements and the steps which need to be taken. In such cases your role will be restricted to offering any support they feel will be useful to them.

On the other hand, an individual who is concerned or anxious about his or her condition, possibly because it is newly diagnosed or a new development, may not feel confident enough to recognise the implications of the measurements taken. So you may need to have a more proactive role in monitoring the results of measurements and specimens in order to identify early indications of potential problems.

Through discussion and agreement with the individual, you need to establish the level of intervention and activity you should undertake, and precisely the nature of your role. All the key principles concerning your level of involvement are the same if the health care procedures are being undertaken for the individual by a carer. In this case you would take into account, when deciding on your role, the carer's level of familiarity with the procedures and confidence in undertaking them. Many people who spend a long time caring for someone with a chronic medical condition develop a high level of expertise in obtaining the necessary specimens and measurements, and interpreting them accurately. This should be recognised and acknowledged, and your role should be limited to those areas the carer has identified as requiring support.

Many carers, however, may feel concerned or have little confidence in their ability to maintain an extensive monitoring regime, or they may be under stress and find the level of care too much. In this case more extensive support

Remember

Caring for someone is one of the hardest jobs in the world – there is no pay, few perks and often little thanks. People who care may never make use of any support you offer, but they need to know that they can – don't stop offering the help.

may be welcomed and it may be appropriate for you to extend your role to provide some relief for the carer.

Temperature

Temperature is a useful indicator of health or illness. Temperature rises when an individual has an infection, or possibly following injury or trauma, whereas a low temperature indicates a serious condition such as hypothermia.

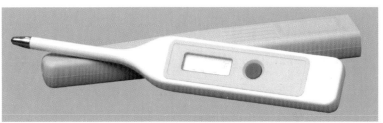

A thermometer with a liquid crystal display

Temperature can be taken with a traditional thermometer containing mercury. The mercury rises up the glass tube of the thermometer and indicates the individual's temperature on the gauge printed on the tube. This type of thermometer has increasingly been replaced by a thermometer which operates with a battery and has a liquid crystal display showing the individual's body temperature. Many health and care settings now use a disposable thermometer which records the individual's temperature on a series of dots which will change colour to indicate temperature.

The normal temperature of the human body is 37° Centigrade, 98.4° Fahrenheit. Any significant variation from this must be reported immediately to the health professional responsible for the individual's health care.

Pulse

Taking a pulse is a way of establishing an individual's heart rate by measuring the beats of the heart through a main artery, usually in the wrist. It is possible to take an individual's pulse at various other points in the body.

To take a pulse manually, place your first two fingers lightly on the individual's wrist directly below the heel of the thumb. You cannot feel someone's pulse through your thumb because you have your own pulse in your thumb.

Through your fingers you will feel the individual's pulse in the brachial artery. When you can feel a pulse you should then count the

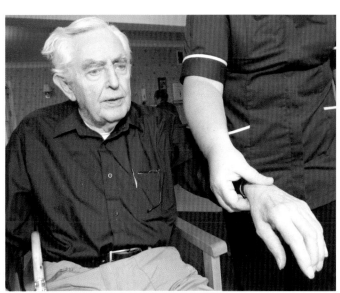

Taking a pulse from the wrist

number of beats you can feel for a period of 30 seconds. You will need to look at your watch while you count the pulse. You then multiply the number of beats by two, which will give you a pulse rate of beats per minute.

A pulse can also be taken by a **pulseoximeter**, which fits onto the individual's finger and records the pulse electronically. If you take any exercise in a gym or use an exercise bike you may well have seen a pulseoximeter.

A combined reading of pulse and blood pressure can be taken on an instrument called a **dynomap**. Normal pulse rate is around 70 beats per minute, although this can be raised by illness, anxiety or exercise. People who are extremely fit will have a lower resting pulse rate; some athletes have pulse rates as low as 50. You will need to know if an individual takes regular exercise, as this could explain a low pulse rate.

Respiration

An individual's respiration is measured in breaths per minute. You will need to observe the number of times that the chest rises and falls per minute. A rise and fall constitutes one respiration. You will need to time your observations for 30 seconds and then multiply by two to obtain the number of respirations per minute. A sudden increase or decrease in an individual's respiration rate can indicate a deterioration or change in condition and should immediately be reported to a qualified clinical practitioner as giving cause for concern.

Blood pressure

Blood pressure indicates the pressure at which blood is being pumped around the body from the heart. It is important that blood pressure remains within a defined area of measurement. Excessively high or low blood pressure can indicate illness or disease and can directly cause a health problem. Blood pressure can be measured with a sphygmomanometer and a stethoscope, although it is more ususally taken in a health setting such as a hospital or health centre using a dynomap machine. If you do need to take blood pressure using a sphygmomanometer and a stethoscope, the process is as follows:

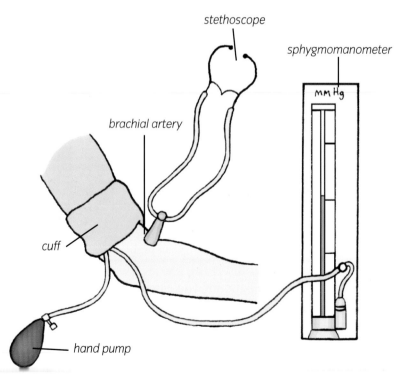

Taking blood pressure with a sphygmomanometer and stethoscope

1 Attach the blood pressure cuff to the individual's upper arm.

2 Ensure that you can feel the individual's brachial pulse at the inner elbow.

3 Put a stethoscope at the point of the inner elbow where you feel the brachial pulse.

4 Pump up the cuff until the pulse disappears (this is approximately at a measurement of 180–200 on the sphygmomanometer).

5 Decrease the air in the cuff slowly, letting it out using the valve on the sphygmomanometer until you can hear the pulse through the stethoscope.

6 Note the reading on the sphygmomanometer at this point.

7 This will provide you with your **systolic** (upper) reading. This is normally around 120.

8 Continue letting the air out of the cuff and listen until the pulse disappears. Note the reading at this point.

9 This will give you your **diastolic** (lower) reading, which should be around 80.

There can be many reasons for blood pressure being higher or lower than 120/80 and there is a fairly wide acceptable range, which can alter with age. However, you should ensure that all measurements of blood pressure are recorded and any significant variations are reported.

Blood pressure can be measured using a dynomap machine

Height and weight

A person's weight in relation to height can indicate the extent to which health is being put at risk by being excessively underweight or overweight.

There are ideal weights for heights which have been calculated to present the least risk to health. These can be identified in a height/weight chart.

Weight and health

Underweight: The health of individuals who are severely underweight could be adversely affected. This could be as a result of illness or as a result of deliberate over-dieting, which is also dangerous to health. Excessive dieting can lead to eating disorders, such as anorexia nervosa or bulimia, which result in individuals not consuming sufficient nutrients to remain healthy. However, most individuals who are underweight are likely to be suffering from an illness.

Overweight, very overweight and obese: The risk to health associated with being overweight or obese grows with the increase in weight. Excess weight can increase the risk of cardiovascular disease, diabetes, arthritis and other weight-associated complications.

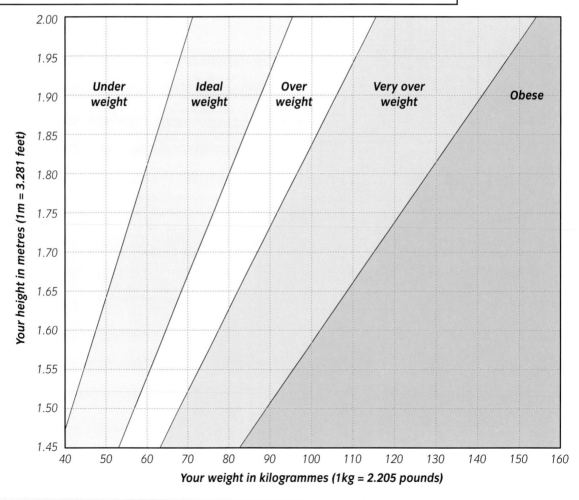

Note: There is quite a wide range of accepted weights for height which will not represent any threat to the individual's health.

Measuring weight

Where possible individuals should be able to stand on a set of scales for the measurement to be taken. Heavy items of clothing such as shoes and outdoor coats should be removed. Individuals should stand on the scales and the weight should be adjusted until the scales balance. An individual's weight should be read in kilograms and recorded in the case notes or care plan.

Where individuals are unable to stand safely on a set of weighing scales, a scale which provides a seat should be used and the weight recorded in the same way.

Measuring height

Height should be measured using a fixed-height ruler which should be attached to the wall of an examination room, or a portable fixed-height rule could be used. The individual should be asked to stand as straight as possible with his or her heels against the wall. The height-measuring bar should be lowered until it rests gently on the top of the head, and the resulting height should be read from the upright ruler. The height, which is likely to be measured in metres and centimetres, should be recorded in the individual's case notes or care plan.

Measuring girth

This should be done around the middle of the individual's torso in approximately the waist area. A tape measure should be placed around the waist area and read at the point where both ends meet comfortably without over tightening. The measurement in centimetres should be recorded in the individual's case notes or care plan.

Body mass index

Another way to assess a person is to measure and calculate his or her body mass index (BMI). BMI is weight in kilograms divided by the square of the height in metres:

$$\frac{\text{Weight (kg)}}{\text{Height (m}^2)}$$

The result obtained from this calculation indicates whether a person is underweight, at normal weight, overweight or obese:

BMI < 20	underweight
BMI 20–25	normal
BMI 25–30	overweight
BMI > 30kg	obese
BMI > 40kg	severely obese

How to calculate BMI

You will notice that metric measurements are used for this calculation. If you are able to measure weight in kilograms and height in metres, this will save doing any conversions. But for the sake of this example we will use imperial measurements   our subject is16 stone and 5 ft 6 ins tall. What is his or her BMI?

- For the top line of the equation (weight):

  Convert 16 stones to kilograms

  There are 2.2 lbs to 1 kg, so first convert 16 stones to pounds

  16 stone is 16 x 14 lb = 224 lbs

  224 lbs divided by 2.2 = 102 kg

- For the bottom line (height squared, that is, multiplied by itself):

  Convert 5 ft 6 ins to metres

  There are 39.5 inches to 1 metre, so first convert 5 ft 6 ins to inches

  5 ft = 5 x 12 ins = 60 + 6 ins = 66 ins

  66 ins divided by 39.5 = 1.67 m

  The height squared is 1.67 x 1.67 = 2.79 m

  Therefore

$$BMI = \frac{102 \text{ kg}}{2.79 \text{ m}} = 36.6$$

This result indicates that the person's health is at risk and that he or she would benefit from losing weight. We should all aim to be in the 20–25 BMI range as this presents least risk to health.

Did you know?

In 2001 a fifth of the population aged over 16 was classified as obese (with a BMI over 30). A further half of men and third of women were classified as overweight. Obesity levels tend to rise with age, peaking at 55–64 years of age.

The table shows the percentages of males and females in England (aged over 16) in each classification, according to their BMI.

	Males	Females
Underweight	4	6
Desirable weight	28	38
Overweight	47	33
Obese	21	23

Source: Health Survey for England, Dept of Health

Peak flow

Peak flow measures lung capacity. This is a useful indicator of illness or lung damage. A reduced peak flow is evident in people who are asthmatic or have any chronic respiratory disease. A peak flow meter, a hollow plastic tube about eight inches long, is used to measure peak flow. It has a small gauge on the top and a disposable cardboard blowpipe is inserted into one end. The individual should be asked to blow a short, sharp breath into the tube and this will then register on the gauge. The normal rate of lung capacity should be about 500. In asthmatics or people with chronic lung disease, such as emphysema, peak flow can be as low as 150 or 200.

A peak flow meter

Fluid balance

The fluid balance is the amount of fluid taken in and excreted from the body. It is a very important indicator of health. If a lot more fluid is excreted than is taken in, an individual can become dehydrated. Conversely, retaining too much fluid in the body can result in swelling, oedema and ultimately heart failure.

Intake and output are measured by keeping a record of the volume of fluids in and out. This is recorded on a fluid balance chart.

Input

In order to keep an accurate record of input of fluid, all fluid which the individual takes into his or her body, either through the mouth or through an intravenous drip, must be measured. If drinks are left for individuals to pour for themselves, you should measure the drinks in the jug and constantly check how much has been used. Explain to the individual that he or she should not take drinks from anywhere unless they are recorded on the chart.

Output

All fluid output should be measured. The urine in a catheter bag or in a bed pan or commode should be measured before disposal. All vomit should also be measured and its volume recorded.

Maintaining a fluid balance chart

Maintaining a fluid balance chart is not difficult, provided you do the basic calculations correctly! You will need to be sure you have done the addition and subtraction so that the balance of fluid for your individual is clearly recorded. Each individual is different as to the amount of fluid taken in and excreted from the body but, broadly speaking, everyone should have a positive fluid balance, that is they should put out slightly more fluid than they take in.

Evidence indicator

1 Take your own height and weight and, using the calculations on page 381, work out your body mass index. Practise doing this for two or three friends or family members until you are confident with the calculations.

2 Work out the fluid balance for the following figures and calculate whether this individual is maintaining a positive fluid balance.

Intake
0800:   IV Therapy – Hartman's 1000 ml
1200:   Hartman's discontinued
1300:   T 250 ml
1400:   Juice 250 ml
1630:   T 250 ml

Output
1230:   300 ml urine
1600:   500 ml urine; 100 ml vomit
1830:   600 ml urine

Keep your calculations and notes for your portfolio.

Test yourself

1   List three types of samples you may have to support people to provide.

2   Describe the steps you would take for each.

3   List three measurements you may need to take or support an individual to take.

4   Outline the steps you would take for each.

1 What are the main Acts which govern drug administration?

2 What essential preparations must be made before administering any drugs or medication?

3 Why is it important to follow the instructions on how drugs should be taken?

4 What are the essentials of safe and effective drug storage in the home?

5 How does this differ from drug storage in a hospital or nursing home?

6 How should blood samples be obtained?

7 How should urine samples be obtained?

8 What are the likely testing methods which individuals at home would use?

9 Why is it important to regularly check the levels of medication remaining in bottles or packaging?

10 Who are the key members of the care team in respect of maintaining a drug regime for individuals at home?

Glossary of key terms

Abuse   Causing physical, emotional, sexual and/or financial harm to an individual and/or failing or neglecting to protect him or her from harm.

Accidents   Unforeseen major and minor incidents where an individual is injured.

Active support   Support that encourages individuals to do as much for themselves as possible to maintain their independence and physical ability and encourages people with disabilities to maximise their own potential and independence.

Communication and language needs and preferences   The individual's needs and preferences in terms of communicating with you, and the way you communicate with and respond to him or her.

Danger   The possibility that harm may occur.

Dietary requirements   Food and drink that will provide a balanced diet that meets the nutritional needs of individuals and supports their health and well-being.

Dressings   Different types of coverings to protect wounds and other types of conditions.

Emergencies   Immediate and threatening danger to individuals and/or others.

Facilities   Goods and environments that can be provided to an individual to promote his or her health and social well-being; they can be offered at a distance or taken to the place where the individual lives.

Harm   The effects of an individual being physically, emotionally or sexually injured or abused.

Hazard   Something with the potential to cause harm.

Individuals   The people requiring health and care services. Where individuals use advocates and interpreters to enable them to express their views, wishes or feelings and to speak on their behalf, the term covers the individual and his or her advocate or interpreter.

Key people   Those people who are key to an individual's health and social well-being; the people in the individual's life who can make a difference to his or her health and well-being.

Moving and handling   Techniques which enable the worker to assist individuals to move from one position to another. Moving and handling must be consistent with current legislation.

Physical measurements   Measurements taken of the physical attributes of the individual.

Plan of care   A plan including all aspects of the individual's care needs which need to be adhered to within any setting in which the individual is placed. It address the holistic needs of the individual.

Rights   The rights that individuals have to:
- be respected
- be treated equally and not be discriminated against
- be treated as an individual
- be treated in a dignified way
- privacy
- be protected from danger and harm
- be cared for in the way that meets their needs, takes account of their choices and also protects them
- access information about themselves
- communicate using their preferred methods of communication and language.

Risks   The likelihood of a hazard being realised. Risks can be to individuals in the form of danger, harm and abuse, and/or to the environment in danger of damage and destruction.

Services   Personal and other amenities provided in the individual's home or in other places that promote the individual's health and social well-being.

Specific plan of care activities   The activities within the plan of care that you are responsible for carrying out.

Specimens   Samples of bodily fluids that need to be or can be monitored by individuals.

Treatments   Actions and activities that have to be or can be undertaken by individuals to promote their health.

Knowledge specification

In the unit specifications, the required knowledge points are detailed under the headings 'Values', 'Legislation and organisational policy and procedures' and 'Theory and practice'.

The following grid shows how to pinpoint material relating to these knowledge points in the text. The points are addressed on and following the page numbers shown. (Values point 1 is not included in the grid, since its content is fundamental to the information given in the whole unit.)

HSC 21
Values
2	2, 12, 27
3	20, 24

Legislation and organisational policy and procedures
4	28, 29, 32, 35
5	10, 32, 35, 37

Theory and practice
6	9
7	3, 27
8	2, 13
9	13, 15, 17
10	10, 29, 36
11	32, 37
12	29, 36
13	30, 37
14	32, 37
17	53
18	61, 64, 67

HSC 22
Values
2	46, 60, 79

Legislation and organisational policy and procedures
3	42, 45, 51, 64
4	42, 44, 46, 48

Theory and practice
5	49, 79
6	67
7	43, 46
8	43, 46
9	51, 55
10	46, 51, 57
11	43, 46
12	59
13	55, 56, 57
14	54, 56, 57
15	54, 57
16	53

HSC 23
Legislation and organisational policy and procedures
2	89, 93
3	93
4	89, 93

Theory and practice
5	93
6	98, 100
7	98
8	93
9	86, 87, 91
10	96
11	82, 86
12	89

HSC 24
Values
2	104, 112, 123
3	109, 135
4	116, 119
5	107, 109, 113
6	107, 108, 118, 119
7	109, 119, 121, 131

Legislation and organisational policy and procedures
8	106, 123, 145
9	123, 145
10	145

Theory and practice
11	119
12	107
13	112
14	104, 107
15	117, 141
16	117, 132

17	137
18	117, 144
19	147
20	115
21	144

HSC 25
Values
2	150, 154, 155

Legislation and organisational policy and procedures
3	153
4	159, 171

Theory and practice
5	161, 168
6	151, 155
7	160
8	171
9	154, 161, 168

HSC 26
Values
2	175, 183
3	184, 188, 192

Legislation and organisational policy and procedures
4	183
5	181

Theory and practice
6	183
7	177, 178
8	192
9	184
10	184
11	178
12	192, 192

HSC 214
Values
2	206
3	201
4	200, 207, 211

Legislation and organisational policy and procedures
5	203
6	196, 203

Theory and practice
7	202, 209

8	196
9	203
10	202
11	203
12	211
13	207, 208, 210
14	209
15	213
16	214
17	214

HSC 215
Values
2	225

Legislation and organisational policy and procedures
3	225
4	235

Theory and practice
5	234
6	218
7	222
8	218, 227, 235
9	222
10	234, 235
11	218, 222
12	235
13	235
14	227, 236
15	224
16	235
17	225, 229, 231
18	227

HSC 216
Values
2	240
3	240
4	241, 242, 255

Legislation and organisational policy and procedures
5	242, 257
6	244, 249
7	255

Theory and practice
8	241
9	250
10	256

11	241
12	244
13	243
14	256
15	256
16	245

HSC 218
Values
2	275, 291
3	275, 291
4	260, 266, 274, 276
5	260, 261
6	260, 263, 293

Legislation and organisational policy and procedures
7	273, 279
8	273, 279

Theory and practice
9	268, 281
10	270, 279
11	277, 279, 281
12	260, 266, 274
13	278
14	265
15	261
16	269, 291, 292, 299
17	270, 273, 279
18	268, 271

HSC 219
Values
2	310
3	310
4	310
5	308, 310, 313

Legislation and organisational policy and procedures
6	310, 312
7	312

Theory and practice
8	312
9	304
10	310
11	310, 313
12	308, 313
13	311
14	310
15	310

16	313
17	312, 327

HSC 223
Values
2	334
3	334
4	343
5	335, 338

Legislation and organisational policy and procedures
6	330, 343
7	330, 337, 343
8	331

Theory and practice
9	347
10	337, 340
11	337, 340
12	333, 347
13	332, 344
14	332, 344
15	332
16	329, 345
17	344
18	336
19	347
20	334

HSC 225
Values
2	360
3	360
4	350, 377

Legislation and organisational policy and procedures
5	351
6	351

Theory and practice
7	350
8	359
9	359
10	361
11	369
12	370
13	361
14	367
15	369
16	369, 385

Index

A

abuse 132–148
  and carer behaviour 140
  effects of 144–145
  emotional 134
  financial 134
  forms of 133–136
  institutional 134–135
  and the law 145–147
  physical 133
  protection from 63, 132, 143,
    147–148
  reporting and recording 144
  self-harm 141
  sexual 133–134
  signs of 137–140
accidents, reporting 48–50
active listening 17–18
active support 113–115
acupuncture 248
advice, giving 27
advocacy 120
aggressive behaviour, dealing
  with 117
allergies 202
anti-discriminatory and anti-
  oppressive practice 122–123
appraisal 90
aromatherapy 247

B

back care 332
balanced diet 196–200
bathing and showering 279–282
bed baths 283–286
bed pans 261, 264, 267
beds
  getting out of 345
  rolling over in 345–346
behaviour
  aggressive and abusive 117
  challenging 116–117

bidets 267
bladder 302–303
  training 313–314
bleeding, severe 68–69
blood loss, recording 271–272
blood pressure 378–379
blood samples 374–375
body fluids and waste
  checking 268–269
  collecting and disposing of
    272–274, 312
  recording 271–272
body language 13–16
body mass index (BMI) 381–382
body temperature 377
bowel 303
  training 331
breathing difficulties 73–74
burns and scalds 75

C

carbohydrates 196
cardiac arrest 69–70
cardiovascular system 218, 220,
  222
care planning 150–153, 155–160
care plans
  implementing 153–155
  monitoring and feedback on
    161–167
  review processes 168–172
Care Standards Act (2000) 145
catheter care 364–366
challenging behaviour, dealing
  with 116–117
child abuse 143, 145–147
  signs of 137–138, 139–140
Children Act (1989) 145, 147,
  159
choice, promoting 104–111,
  118–119
  in care planning155–158

in eating and drinking 200–
  201
in hygiene matters 274–276
in toilet facilities 260
choking 73–74
Chronically Sick and Disabled
  Persons Act (1986) 145, 147
Citizens Advice Bureaux 177, 178
commodes 261, 265, 267
communication 1–34
  and cultural differences 2–3
  and dementia 8–9
  differences in 9–11
  encouraging 18–19
  and hearing loss 5
  and language differences 3–4,
    9
  and learning disabilities 7–8
  and listening 12–18
  non-verbal 4
  and physical disabilities 6–7
  and visual impairment 56
  written 29–30
confidentiality 30–34, 37–39
conflicts, dealing with 115–116
consciousness, loss of 71–72
continence *see* incontinence
Control of Substances Hazardous
  to Health (COSHH) 44,
  46–47

D

Data Protection Act (1998) 35,
  159, 181
dementia, communication and
  8–9
diabetes 366
diet
  balanced 196–200
  incontinence and 310–311,
    314
Disability Discrimination Act
  (1995) 126, 129, 145, 147, 159

suitable clothing and
equipment 336–338,
340–343
listening 12–18

M

make-up 297–298
manicure 298
Manual Handling Operations
Regulations (1992) 44, 59, 330
Medicines Act (1968) 353
medicines/medications *see* drugs
and medicines
menstruation 266
Mental Health Act (1983), draft
Mental Health Bill 145, 147,
159
minerals, dietary 200
Misuse of Drugs Act (1971)
351–352
mixed incontinence 306
mobility 217–237
appliances 227–234, 236–237
monkey poles/lifting handles
340, 342
mouth care 288–289
moving service users *see* lifting
and handling
muscular system 218, 219, 222

N

National Assistance Act (1948)
145, 147
needles 51, 367
needs, assessing service users'
175–178
neglect 135–136
NHS and Community Care Act
(1990) 145, 147
nutrients 196–200

O

oppression 123
orthoses 296

P

pain and discomfort
expressing 241–242
measuring 249–250
responding to 242–249
theories of 240–241, 245
peak flow meters 383
pelvic floor exercises 315–317
personal care needs 259–300
personal development 81–97
personal hygiene 274–292
personal safety 57–58
physical comfort needs 239–258
physical measurements 376–384
blood pressure 378–379
fluid balance 383–384
girth 381
height 380–381
peak flow 383
pulse 377–378
respiration 378
temperature 377
weight 380–382
physical methods of pain relief
246
poisoning 76
prejudices 24–26, 121–22
pressure sores 362–363
privacy 265
professional development 81–97
planning 95
and training 93–97
prostheses 293, 296
protective clothing 56
protein 198
pulse rate 377–378
'pyjama-induced paralysis' 345

Q

quadrupeds 230
questioning methods 27

R

Race Relations Act (1976) 126

racial discrimination 126
razors 286–287
records 35–40
of means of communication
10–11
of mobility methods 347
recovery position 72
reflexology 247
relationships 112–113
problems in 115–116
reporting
abuse 144
accidents 48–50
emergencies 78–79
Reporting of Injuries, Diseases
& Dangerous Occurrences
(RIDDOR) 44, 48–50
respiration
peak flow 383
rates 378
rest and sleep 250–258
rights 123–131
risk assessments 45–46
for moving service users
330–335

S

safety *see* health and safety
salt 199
samples *see* specimens
scooters, mobility 233
security
against intruders 61–62
evacuating buildings 67
of personal property 62–63
Sex Discrimination Act (1975)
126, 127–128
sharps, disposal 51, 367
shaving 286–287
shock 70–71
showering 279, 281–282
skeleton 221–222
sleep 250–258
slideboards 342
specimens 368–375